Landmarks and Goals

Landmarks and Goals

HISTORICAL STUDIES AND ADDRESSES

BY ABRAHAM A. NEUMAN, PRESIDENT

DROPSIE COLLEGE FOR HEBREW

AND COGNATE LEARNING

DROPSIE COLLEGE PRESS

PHILADELPHIA, 1953

PRINTED IN THE UNITED STATES OF AMERICA

PRESS OF *Maurice Jacobs* INC.

224 N. 15TH ST., PHILADELPHIA 2, PENNA.

To Elsie
Beloved Wife

Preface

Doctor Cyrus Adler, of blessed memory, gave up his cherished position with the Smithsonian Institution to become the organizer and first President of Dropsie College. His able administration of its affairs and the prestige he imparted to it made the Board of Governors fearful that whenever the time might come when he would be called to the life eternal it would be almost impossible to find a successor competent in any real measure to fill his place. And yet that fear proved groundless. For, when that fateful hour arrived, Doctor Abraham A. Neuman was providentially available — he would no doubt have been the choice of Doctor Adler himself — and the Governors, with good judgment and, as the event proved, supreme wisdom, elected him to the presidency of this great institution for higher Jewish and Semitic learning.

Ten years have passed since that happy selection was made. Under his efficient guidance Dropsie College has grown and prospered to a degree probably surpassing even the fondest hopes that the Founder himself may have entertained for its welfare and pre-eminence in its own educational field. But Doctor Neuman is far more than merely a gifted administrator. He is a profound thinker, a learned scholar, a talented lecturer, an eloquent orator, and a brilliant author. When to all this is added the charm of his engaging personality there emerges a fair appraisal of the man whose studies, writings and addresses contained in this book bear witness to the versatility of his genius.

The Governors, the Faculty, and the Alumni of Dropsie College, together with some of his many friends, are publishing this volume as a tribute to Doctor Neuman in recognition of his distinguished service to Dropsie College during this first decade of his presidency.

HORACE STERN
Vice-President and Chairman of the
Board of Governors, Dropsie College.

Contents

Foreword

IN RECOGNITION of the distinguished service which Doctor Abraham A. Neuman has rendered the Dropsie College during the first decade of his presidency, the Governors, the Faculty and the Alumni of the College celebrated Doctor Neuman's decennial as President at a convocation and public celebration on March 17, 1952. In tribute, the Governors announced on the occasion of the Decennial Celebration that the College would publish a volume of Doctor Neuman's selected writings.

An editorial and publication committee representing the Governors, the Faculty and the Alumni was formed consisting of Justice Horace Stern, Messrs. Samuel B. Finkel, Sol Satinsky, Bernard G. Segal, Doctors Solomon Zeitlin, Leo L. Honor, Mortimer J. Cohen. Doctor Solomon Zeitlin was appointed chairman of the editorial committee.

In planning this volume, the committee selected from Doctor Neuman's abundant writings those essays and addresses that best portray his broad and varied interests. The present volume falls into three divisions: History, Religion, and Addresses dealing with contemporary issues.

Doctor Neuman's primary interest lies in the field of Jewish history. The first section of this volume, therefore, contains a number of his contributions to Jewish and general historiography. Here will be found his significant articles on Josippon and Saadia Gaon; Solomon ibn Verga, historiographer of the sixteenth century; Samuel Usque, author of *Consolation for the Tribulations of Israel*; Medina, the Catholic historian of the Inquisition in the Americas. Doctor Neuman's historical understanding and imagination are revealed in his vivid portrayal of the life and times of the men about whom he writes. His keen analytical judgment is illustrated in the complicated historical problems presented by his subjects and their works.

The book of *Josippon* was universally accepted throughout the Middle Ages as the Hebrew version of the *Wars* of the great historian Josephus. Modern Jewish scholars repudiated this claim and assigned the book to the ninth or tenth century. Doctor Neuman proves that *Josippon* was actually a work of the second or third century of the present era. Thus the book becomes a valuable source for the early centuries of the current era. Furthermore, he establishes the fact that the author of *Josippon* used documents and sources no longer extant, which enhances the unique value of this volume. Indeed, many passages in *Josippon* — Doctor Neuman demonstrates in his *Josippon and the Apocrypha* — are primary sources for early Judaism.

In his essay on Saadia Gaon, Doctor Neuman evaluates the man Saadia and the struggles which took place between the leaders of Palestine and Babylonia for spiritual leadership. For Saadia Gaon was not only a philosopher, a theologian and a biblical commentator, but also one of the great leaders of Babylonian Jewry in the tenth century. The battle in which he engaged the leaders of Palestinian Jewry was fateful in its outcome. In Doctor Neuman's opinion, Saadia proved himself unimaginative in his attitude to Palestine and a man who was governed by intellect rather than by intuitive insight.

As author of a two volume study, *The Jews in Spain*, published in 1942, Doctor Neuman was exceptionally well equipped to extend his researches into the life and times of the Jews of the sixteenth century — the dark period that followed their expulsion from Spain. It was a period of suffering and tribulation. Despair engulfed the masses of the people. He graphically portrays this mood which drove many into Messianic vagaries and others to doubt and skepticism about the future.

Among the historians that arose in the sixteenth century to counteract this dangerous mood, Doctor Neuman treats of two Jewish writers. These historians were Solomon ibn Verga, principal author of the *Shebet Yehudah* and Samuel Usque, himself a Marrano, who escaped from Portugal and the clutches of the Inquisition and subsequently composed in his native Portuguese tongue the *Consolation for the Tribulations of Israel*.

Doctor Neuman makes clear the different approaches of these men to the problem of Jewish persecutions. He shows how Ibn Verga viewed Jewish suffering and survival analytically from the social, economic and historical background of the times. Usque, on the other hand, portrayed Jewish sorrows as a thread in the divine tapestry of history which would change to brighter hues of hope and happiness. For was this not the vision and the promise of Israel's prophets of old?

Doctor Neuman clarifies many passages in these historical works and presents the entire panorama of Jewish historiography in the sixteenth century. He shows how their books mirrored forces that are as valid for our times as they were when they were written. These essays are illuminating contributions to the study of historiography.

Pursuing his interest further in the works of the Inquisition, Doctor Neuman made a study of the writings of the Catholic historian Medina, especially as they concerned the Jews who made their home in the New World. The Inquisition, a product of medieval Christian civilization, had spread from Spain and Portugal to Mexico and South America when these latter became the conquered domains of the former.

Doctor Neuman presents Medina, historian par excellence of the Inquisition in America, in a stirring and eloquent essay. He creates a clear picture of this fateful Institution as portrayed by Medina in all its gruesomeness, and its terrifying effects on the lives of South Americans from the sixteenth to the beginning of the nineteenth century. In this essay is compressed a consider-

xiii

able body of knowledge relating to the history of the Americas.

Doctor Neuman, in his earlier years, was in the active rabbinate and has from time to time written on religious themes. His approach, however, is not primarily theological but historical.

His essay on Judaism deals with the nature of Judaism and explores its relation to the Jewish people, contrasting it with Christianity — all this in the framework of history. Doctor Neuman probes into the nature of Jewish theology and its problems; he analyzes fundamental Jewish concepts, such as Torah, the nature of man, the future of society, Messianism and immortality. He describes in detail the religious institutions of Judaism, touching them with the pen of poesy: the Synagogue, the Sabbath, the Festivals, the Fast Days. He interprets with scholarly objectivity the ideologies of the religious groups in American Jewry: Orthodox, Conservative and Reform, and the new emergent Reconstructionism.

This presentation of Judaism is one of the ablest discussions of the Jewish way of life to appear in recent times. It contributes new insights into the nature of Judaism, its development through the ages, and its effect upon Christianity.

Doctor Neuman's addresses at the annual Founder's Day Exercises of the Dropsie College and on other significant occasions comprise the third portion of this volume. They are eloquent, poetic and warm with the emotions of a spiritual leader who appeals not only to the facts of history but also to the spiritual values that these facts imply.

Because these addresses on contemporary issues and problems, ranging over the entire gamut of Jewish life in America and in the world in this turbulent twentieth century, speak so eloquently for themselves, there is little need to comment on them individually. Within them shines the light that comes only from the recorded and evaluated experiences of men through the ages.

In his addresses Doctor Neuman reveals not only the knowledge of the historian but also the fervor of the prophet. Against the background of Jewish history, he analyzes the present trends in Jewish life, often raising his voice to sound a warning to Jewish leaders and to point out the danger signals in contemporary Jewish life. His addresses are more than passing comments on the changing scene. They have a lasting value for history.

The Committee is indebted to Miss Sarai Zausmer, Registrar of the College, for her ever-ready co-operation and helpfulness in the selection of the essays and in the preparation of the volume. For this we express our warm appreciation. We also wish to thank Miss Dorothy G. Gerson for helping in the task of proofreading.

SOLOMON ZEITLIN
Chairman, Editorial Committee

HISTORICAL STUDIES

Josippon: History and Pietism

AT THE summit of Josephus' life, after he had already published his *Jewish War* and the monumental *Antiquities*, Josephus, in one of his final literary utterances, *Against Apion*, pointed proudly to the high place assigned to history and historians in Jewish literary annals. Hebrew historical works, he wrote with pride, were part of sacred Scriptures. Prophets and priests were assigned the role of historians. He, Josephus, was a priest.[1]

Little did Josephus realize that with his passing, the art of the Jewish historian, which he rightly extolled, would vanish from among his people for many centuries to come. Supreme egotist that he was, it would still have saddened him to know that his monumental works sealed Jewish historical literature; that his writings were to be the epilogue to national Jewish historiography for a millennium and a half.[2] For although future Jewish generations were destined to create a rich and unique literature — the Mishna and kindred tannaitic works, the Talmud in the twin versions of Palestine and Babylonia, the various Midrashim, the geonic and subsequent rabbinic literature, covering a wide variety of theme and content — there was neither prophet nor priest nor lay scribe to continue the tradition of the historian.

With the Temple reduced to ashes, the Jewish state crushed and national independence wiped out, there was no incentive to keep the historian's art alive.[3] This enigmatical turn of national psychology was not and could not have been anticipated by Josephus, the protegé of the Caesars, living in the

Published in *Alexander Marx Jubilee Volume*, New York 1950.

gilded cage of his country's conquerors. Stranger still, he who wrote so frequently of fate and destiny, and ascribed fatalistic powers to blind Fortune,[4] could not foresee that by a curious combination of obscure factors, a fantastic Hebrew version of his own writings was destined to kindle a limited historic consciousness among his people in all parts of the world. In its dim light, furthermore, his image would be viewed piously by later generations who paid him homage that was bitterly denied him by his own contemporaries.[5]

We refer, of course, to the book of *Josippon*, which was uncritically accepted throughout the Middle Ages as the Hebrew work of the Jewish historian Josephus. It was the strange destiny of this book to fill a gap in the historic consciousness of the Jewish people till the rise of historical Hebrew literature in the sixteenth century.

The book of *Josippon* presents many baffling problems. It was one of the most popular books in Hebrew literature, and its very popularity adds to the perplexity of unraveling its composition and the origin of its parts. It was a folk history book, read by scholars and populace alike. Aside from the Bible it was without rival in Hebrew literature as a narrative book unfolding a great dramatic theme in free, felicitous Hebrew, easily understood by the people.

The universal demand for the book caused it to pass through the hands of numerous scribes who were not always noted for meticulous accuracy in transcription. Scribes in ancient and medieval times were frequently more than literal copyists. They were often men endowed with knowledge and imagination and would, on occasion, embellish the text with their own comments. In copying non-sacred books, in particular, Hebrew copyists would be under no constraint to adhere faithfully to the wording of the text. Among the numerous copyists who were engaged upon the book of *Josippon*, many found the theme peculiarly inviting to additions and embellishments. Thus,

2

fragmentary layers of history, legend and folklore were added anonymously to the original book, or the Ur-text, creating a number of composite texts that vary considerably in length and in the contents of their interpolations.[6] Notwithstanding the keen critical analysis of the text by modern scholars, it is impossible to ascertain with certainty the dimensions of the original work or even to establish the termini of its beginning and end.[7]

In this essay we shall not attempt a new dissection of the text. Nor shall we follow the elusive search in pursuit of its affinities in the Latin Hegesippus and in the later Arabic rendition. Our aim is rather to portray the fictional or pseudo character of Josippon and the range of his thoughts as they appeared in final form, rooted in the imagination and the thinking of later generations. We shall treat of the composite literary product as it appeared from the tenth century onward. The *editio princeps* of Mantua, 1476–79, and the Constantinople edition, 1510, from which most of the later printings were copied — both of which are based on a careful scrutiny of numerous manuscripts[8]— will serve as the principal texts for the present study. An examination of some of the chief characteristics of *Josippon*, a comparison of the narration with the authentic Josephus and a focusing upon its own leitmotifs, should prove doubly rewarding. It will reveal the intellectual and spiritual atmosphere of the medieval Jewish community which accepted the Hebrew *Josippon* as an authentic work and derived inspiration from it. It may also shed light upon the origin of *Josippon* by mapping a chart of its ideas and spiritual concepts.

In the Constantinople edition and all its derivatives, *Josippon* is supposedly divided by the author into six books which were later subdivided by the editor into ninety-seven chapters.[9] Josippon asserts his authorship and identity early in the work: "I am Joseph ha-Kohen, son of Gorion, whom Titus and

3

Vespasian exiled from Jerusalem." He refers to a book called *Josephus*, which he wrote for the Romans. He then proceeds: "And behold this book, I, Joseph, son of Gorion the priest have written for Israel. The narratives in it I have related. I expounded there the tribes, the nations, and the countries mentioned therein. This is the first section, or Book I.

"I followed this with Book II, which I began with an account of the reign of Alexander, son of Philip of Macedonia and גביארש.[10] Thus I speak of his birth, his wisdom, his heroism and all his experiences with the kings of the earth; also all the events that happened to the people of our God during his lifetime. In Book III, I deal with the events following upon the death of Alexander when his kingdom was partitioned and Antipater, his general, ruled over Parthia as his successor. I included also all that happened to our ancestors, the holy nation, at the hands of the Roman rulers, the Greek kings and the kings of the other nations as well as the Jewish kings, from the time of the above-mentioned Antipater (and the other kings who succeeded Alexander upon the division of his kingdom) to the reign of the Hasmonean priests.

"In Book IV, I treated of the events that happened to our ancestors at the hands of the Roman and Greek kings and the rulers of other nations, from the beginning of the Hasmonean dynasty to the end of the reign of Alexandra, the wife of Alexander, son of Hyrcanus.

"In Book V, I dealt with the history of our ancestors from the death of Alexandra, through the reigns of her sons Hyrcanus and Aristobulus till the coming of my own period, when I and my associates were to fight the wars of the Lord and the end arrived, the time for the unhappy disastrous exile in the days of King Agrippa. And that which I witnessed in my time, and to which I bear testimony, I, having fought the wars of the Lord with all my power, I have put down in Book V.

"The sixth Book is called *Josippon* in Hebrew (יהודית); also

4

The Wars of the Lord. In Greek it is called *Joseppus* and in the language of the Romans, *Josephus*, for this is my name among them. Indeed this book is called by the name *Josippon* which is also the name for the entire work. What I have narrated therein I have witnessed and testified to in person. And that which I wrote in the earlier books I have drawn from reliable writers such as Nicolaus the Roman chronicler from Damascus, whom I have known, Strabo of Cyprus, Titus the Roman chronicler, Togatos of Jerusalem, Porphyrius, Polybius the Roman, and many other writers.[11] I also drew upon the traditions of many generations of my saintly fathers, high priests and scribes, teachers of the Torah.

"Verily all the six books I composed in the Hebrew language and all of them are the writing of Joseph the priest, son of Gorion, and all six are comprised under the name *Josippon.*"

The most personalized part of the long History is comprised in what is here called Book VI. In theme it corresponds roughly to Josephus' *Jewish War*, and the two accounts run parallel to each other. In both, the author plays also the stellar role of actor and commentator. A comparison of the two narratives reveals strikingly the contrast between the candid self-portrayal of Josephus and his imaginary counterpart created in the image of an early Jewish pietist. The former portrait was drawn according to Roman taste which later proved also pleasing to the Church. The latter etching, drawn on Hebrew canvas by an anonymous writer, was engraved with Jewish features that expressed more faithfully the agony of a Jewish soul that witnessed the doom of his people and the ascension in flames of God's sanctuary in the Holy City.

For the purposes of the present study our attention will be principally focused on the two parallel accounts: the so-called *Wars of the Lord* in *Josippon* and the *Jewish War* by Josephus. Josephus' narrative in Greek was, from a Jewish viewpoint, cold, detached, defeatist, frequently revealing a pro-Roman and anti-Jewish bias. The Hebrew *Josippon*, on the other hand, was intensely and proudly Jewish. Casting no blame upon the Romans and sorrowing deeply for the shortcomings and the sins of his people which provoked God's wrath upon the nation, Josippon tearfully and prayerfully looks up to God. For He who decreed the chastisement of His people will in the end lead them to redemption.[12] These contrasting viewpoints are reflected in the titles of the two books. Josephus called his history *Concerning the Jewish War*, which the Church, to suit its theological position, changed to read *Concerning the Jewish Captivity*. In the Hebrew version an anonymous author gave it the prophetic title, *The Wars of the Lord*, to inspire later generations with the belief that Israel was continually waging the wars of the Lord which could have but one ultimate end: religious triumph and moral vindication. This was actually the conviction that steeled Jewish hearts throughout the exile.[13]

The autobiographical accounts in Josephus and *Josippon* are parallel in many respects and yet also strangely divergent. Josippon is represented as being Josephus himself, the descendant of an aristocratic priestly family, the intrepid commander-in-chief in Galilee, the honored prisoner of Vespasian, the counselor of Titus, the protegé of the Caesars in the Roman palace. But throughout the book of *Josippon* he calls himself repeatedly Joseph, the son of Gorion, instead of Matthias, who was the father of Josephus. There appears to be no satisfactory explanation for this puzzle.[14] Other family references scattered in various parts of *Josippon*, which seem bizarre and contradictory, may be ascribed to confused, clumsy interpolations, for they do not occur in the earlier Mantua edition. Thus, according to the Constantinople version, Josippon was born fifty-one years before Julius Caesar (*sic*) and he was sixty-seven years old at the siege of Jerusalem![15] That both parents were alive during the siege and imprisoned by the revolutionary leaders in Jerusalem is attested in the two accounts, which run parallel;[16]

but Josippon adds that his father was then 103 years old and his mother 85.[17] Josippon was the eldest of eighteen children and was the lone survivor of them all according to his mother's pathetic account.[18] In another passage, a brother Bonin comes to life.[19] No reference to the former occurs in any of Josephus' writings, while in his *Life* mention is made in a different connection of a brother by the name of Matthias.[20]

Maritally, the accounts of Josephus and *Josippon* do not agree with each other. Josephus was at least thrice married — a fourth marriage is implied — had three children by one wife, and two sons by his last spouse.[21] Josippon speaks of but one wife, the dearly beloved wife of his youth, of noble descent, who was precious to him even though she bore him no children.[22] This "beloved wife of his youth" may indeed be the first wife of Josephus to whom an unnamed reference is made in the parallel passage in *Jewish War*. In any event, however, *Josippon* did not allude to any of the wives that dot the pages of Josephus' *Life*. Evidently the author of *Josippon* knew not the *Life* of Joseph son of Matthias, even though he was at home in the highways and byways of *Jewish War* and followed their paths in *The Wars of the Lord*.

Puzzling as these points may be, they are comparatively irrelevant and immaterial in relation to the emergence of two contrasting personalities that engage our attention. The historical Josephus basked in the favor of the Caesars. He was still a young man in the prime of life when his nation was crushed, and he lived the greater part of his life in the luxury of a Roman palace.[23] Indeed the most effective part of his life, the period of literary creativeness, was spent there in ease and comfort, thanks to the benevolence of his royal patrons, they who had amused themselves by throwing countless thousands of his countrymen to a cruel death in the gladiatorial arenas. In the case of *Josippon*, the curtain falls as he hovers over the ruins of Jerusalem, breaks forth into a heart-rending dirge and in the

7

midst of desolation and despair looks with hope to the distant horizon.

Josephus' works were honored in Rome and highly esteemed by the Church, which preserved them for posterity in the Greek original and in Latin translation. For the Synagogue they were non-existent.[24] It may be properly argued that this did not betray conscious hostility on the part of the Synagogue. For even so Jewish a work as I Maccabees, written in Hebrew with fervent patriotic spirit, was soon lost to Judaism, apparently by default. But it is significant, nevertheless, that Josephus, who was a target of Rabban Simon b. Gamaliel's suspicion and distrust,[25] and who was also a contemporary of Rabban Johanan b. Zaccai and the other rabbis who strove heroically to preserve Judaism after the shock of the destruction of the Temple, should have been so completely ignored by them as to leave no trace of his name in the writings of that period.

In this instance, however, the vacuum created by the silence of the rabbis was compensated for later by a popular rendition of the lost "Josephus" in which imagination was given free rein and the Roman-tinted facts of history were transformed into themes of Hebraic moral-religious teachings. Inevitably, the author too took on the character and personality that suited the mood of his theme. Whereas Josephus adopted Vespasian's family name Flavius, his alter ego became the son of Gorion, who was himself one of the Jewish generals in the war against the Romans and in supreme control in Jerusalem at the outbreak of the revolt!

In the opening chapter of the *Wars*, Josephus defends his feeling of grief at the calamity that befell his nation and his country — "indeed, in my opinion, the misfortunes of all nations since the world began fall short of those of the Jews." He pleads with his critics for their indulgence "for a compassion which falls outside an historian's province." He adds: "should, however, any critic be too austere for pity, let him credit the history with the facts, the historian with the lamentations." [26]

In the light of his own subsequent narrative, one may well wonder why such defense was at all necessary. But assuming that his grief was genuine and deep, he held forth no hope, no ray of light, to his stricken brethren mourning over the ruins of the Temple or dispersed as exiles throughout the Roman Empire. With studied silence he seemed to deny the future restoration of his people to nationhood and independence. In craven fear of the Romans, he suppressed the Messianic hope, and not even a prayer for the restoration of the Temple crossed his lips. [27]

As a prologue to *The Wars of the Lord*, on the other hand, Josippon or his amanuensis, a glossator, writes: "My heart trembles as I am now about to recite the destruction of our holy Temple which we have seen built and destroyed — yea, its visitation has come, its perplexity is now at hand. With my eyes, I beheld the wars of God against the adversaries who oppressed us; God having aroused their spirit in order to wreak vengeance upon us for the desecration of His Law. We have named this book *The Wars of the Lord*.

"Would that the grace of God permitted me to behold the Temple rebuilt once again! But the order of nature will not be altered. How indeed can I hope to have my days prolonged till Israel will once more through penitence be restored to happiness and prosperity in its own land? I do not merit such grace, for I am sinful. But we shall declare happy the generation that will escape and be among the remnant of Israel when the time will come for the Temple to be built for the third time. Happy he who waiteth and liveth to see the goodness of the Lord and to behold the loveliness of His grace which will be manifest in Israel in those days." [28]

Filled with faith in God's covenant with Israel through

9

eternity, he exclaims: "Therefore be ye greatly comforted who witness this day our distress. For the time will come when your sons will yet rule over this land. And they who hear of our present suffering may indeed take comfort, for this is the last affliction that will be visited upon Israel and no other sorrow will come to the people of God thereafter." [29]

Whether the Hebrew writer of *Josippon* had before him the Greek original of Josephus' *Wars* or a loose Latin translation [30] may well depend on whether his domicile was located in Palestine, the Byzantine Empire or Italy. Even an original version in Aramaic, although highly unlikely, is not altogether precluded, if we adopt a sufficiently early dating for *Josippon*. However conjectural these issues may be, certain facts stand out clearly. Josippon's narrative follows the account in Josephus closely, page after page, sentence after sentence. [31] Major events and minor incidents, obscure geographical names and unfamiliar Graeco-Roman names are repeated in *Josippon* in identical sequence, though the spelling of strange nomenclature frequently appears obviously corrupted in the Hebrew. [32] But what is equally clear and at times more significant are the lapses between the two accounts, the omission of highly pertinent details in *Josippon*. Thus all references to Josephus' claims to prophecy are studiously avoided in *Josippon*. We do not hear of his nightly dreams in which God spoke to him of the impending fate of the Jews and of the destinies of the Roman sovereigns. Josippon does not represent himself as "an interpreter of dreams and skilled in divining the meaning of ambiguous utterances of the Deity." To *Josippon* it would no doubt have appeared blasphemous to make such claims and with such pretensions to address God in the words of Josephus: "Since it pleases Thee who didst create the Jewish nation, to break Thy work, since fortune has wholly passed to the Romans, and since Thou hast made choice of my spirit to announce the things that are to come, I willingly surrender to the Romans and consent to live;

but I take Thee to witness that I go, not as a traitor but as Thy minister."[33]

At this critical passage in the life-story of Josephus, he is summoned by his Jewish companions in the cave to take his own life in preference to surrender to the Romans. By means of a desperate stratagem he succeeds in saving his life by proposing a pact of self-immolation to be determined by the casting of lots, but the Hebrew writer frankly calls it a ruse (מרמה, תחבולה) and does not hypocritically ascribe the outcome to the intervention of Fortune or the providence of God.[34]

Josephus dramatized his interview with Vespasian as he appeared ostensibly as a captive, till he revealed himself the messenger of God. "You imagine, Vespasian, that in the person of Josephus you have taken a mere captive; but I come to you as a messenger of greater destinies. Had I not been sent on this errand by God, I knew the law of the Jews and how it becomes a general to die. To Nero do you send me? . . . . You will be Caesar, Vespasian, you will be Emperor, you and your son here. . . . . . . You, Caesar, are master not of me only, but of land and sea and the whole human race." The skeptical doubts of the Romans, he continued, were dissipated when upon investigation, it was found that he had proved "a truthful prophet in other matters." This phase is completely eliminated in the Hebrew version of *Josippon*, which in all other respects reproduces the setting fully and faithfully.[35]

It may seem inconsistent for a "prophet" to boast of his military prowess and worldly self-esteem; but Josephus had no such misgivings. Vespasian, he tells us, "considered that the issue of the war depended largely on his (Josephus') capture."[36] His Jewish companions in the cave, threatening him with death, still held the general in reverence. "Sweeter to them than life was the thought of death with Josephus."[37]

In the Hebrew version, Josippon, though no prophet, is also accorded exalted rank, but this is treated with spiritual sensi-

11

tivity in harmony with Jewish feeling and tradition. In the same setting as in Josephus, Josippon's companions in the cave upbraid him for his willingness to surrender: "We are astonished at thee, O Prince Joseph! For thou wast chosen from the multitude of thy people for priesthood and kingship before the Holy One, the Lord, God of Israel, and thou hast been appointed a supreme commander at the head of thy nation. And now that thine eyes behold the reproach of thy people and the ruin of thy flock dost thou still desire to cling to life? What hath life to offer? Better is death than life now . . . . .

"The Sacred Torah is enshrined in thy heart. Thou art annointed. Thou art a priest. Thou hast taught and expounded the holy Torah so that we may know how to love the Lord our God with all our heart and all our soul and all our might. And if this doth not mean that we serve Him and love that which He loveth and that we die for His covenant, His Torah and His Sanctuary, what can it mean?"[38]

Although Josephus and his shadow Josippon are thus sharply contrasted, their narratives agree not only in fact but in the historic and moral interpretation of the events they record. The rebels are held up not as heroes but villains. That they were patriots to whom tyranny was hateful beyond endurance and liberty more precious than life, that they were religious visionaries and fanatics who set the kingdom of God above the powers of almighty Rome is indicated grudgingly and held up to scorn as arrogance and foolhardiness by Josephus;[39] and *Josippon* too follows in the same vein, deploring the unfortunate militant intransigence, although, it must be said, with a sorrow greater than bitterness. The ringleaders are made to bear sole responsibility for the war and its terrible consequences. The Romans acted in defense of their legitimate sovereign rights. Time and again Vespasian and later Titus offered the leaders of the rebellion honorable terms. They did not seek to destroy the land or the people. They had deep reverence for the Sanctuary of the God of Israel. The Jewish nation, its responsible heads, the elders and the priests, the Pharisees and the nation at large desired peace with honor. They were content to live under Roman rule as long as their religious beliefs and practices were not interfered with. They did not provoke the war initially and were ready to negotiate peace terms with the Romans during the course of the rebellion. It was the wicked malcontents who were the incendiaries. They inflamed the youth, instigated the revolt and ruthlessly suppressed and crushed any and all attempts to bring about peace. [40] Thus we read in *Josippon*: "When I fought against the Romans in Galilee, I knew that in the end I would yield to them. But I was helpless to take action for the brigands at my side were denouncing me, and I feared lest they attack and kill me if I considered surrender and submission to the Romans." [41]

Political freedom, national sovereignty, had no lure or glamor for *Josippon*. He professed alternately, sorrow, pity and indignation at those who were inspired by the hope and dream of liberty to give their lives in its cause and to place in jeopardy all they held dear, their beloved ones, their nation, and most precious of all, the national shrine, the Sanctuary of the God of Israel. Jewish history, he convinced himself, set no high value on national independence. "Brethren and friends," he declaimed before the fighters on the ramparts of Jerusalem, at a discreet distance: "You declare we would all rather die as one than serve foreign kings; that death is more to be desired than life to escape this evil and the sight of our Sanctuary in ruins. Inquire then of your fathers of old, when were you free and sovereign without overlords and the yoke of other nations?" Reviewing their history from this slant, Josippon recalled that the Jews served many nations for long periods, to wit, Egypt, Assyria, Persia, Chaldea; and they fought in the wars of other nations. At times they met with defeat; at times they also gained victories. In the light of this historic record, wherein lies the shame or humiliation in submitting now to the Romans, the great world conquerors? [42]

And yet both Josephus' and *Josippon's* accounts allow that despite the overwhelming power of Rome and the enormous superiority of Roman armies, the revolt might have succeeded if not for the fatal dissension within the Jewish ranks of the warriors. The deficiency of the Jews in military equipment and experience was overbalanced by their tenacity, passion and fanatical courage. Roman military science and strategy were outmatched by Jewish daring, intrepidity and resourcefulness. The battle-scarred veterans of many hard-fought campaigns retreated before the impetuous, reckless fury of the fighters of Israel. The Romans fought for honor; the Jews battled for country, for God and liberty. But all their bravery, sacrifices and bloodshed were for naught because of factionalism and fratricide within the ranks of the defenders of Jerusalem. Lust for power and jealousy blinded the fierce leaders of the revolt. [43]

The charges against the "men of violence" are identical in the accounts of Josephus and *Josippon*, but the latter's indictment appears if anything blacker and gloomier because of the more emotional tone of his recital. All the enormities of fiendish crime and violence were perpetrated by the brigand chieftains who wrested the control of Jerusalem. The streets of the holy city flowed with innocent blood. First in the line of victims were the nobles and the priests, men of holiness and apostles of peace. But a reign of general terror followed. Suspicion and jealousy were rife among the insurrectionists. Fierce warfare broke out among them. Jerusalem was converted into a series of bristling camps of hostile forces. The sacred precincts of the Temple were trampled upon and violated by men of violence. The altar of God was defiled by the slain bodies of the priests and the corpses of other victims heaped upon it. All the evils of bitter civil war were visited upon the inhabitants: murder, rapine, loot, famine. [44]

Blind was the faith of those who put their trust in the inviolability of the City of God and its Sanctuary. For God had turned His face from the city of pollution. Jerusalem was doomed. God was on the side of the Roman legions. Rome was the instrument of God's will. [45]

To Josephus this represented the turn of the wheel of Fortune. For God "went the rounds of the nations bringing to each in turn the rod of empire and this now rested over Italy." [46] Josippon raised this thought to a higher level. He assumed that the Jews might well believe that though God had given dominion over the world to the Romans, He had reserved one people as His peculiar treasure and nation, the people of Israel. But he cried out to the men of Jerusalem: "Are you not covered with shame? You are indeed children of the people of God and His peculiar treasure, but alas, your iniquities have separated you from your God." [47]

Josippon cried out against leaving the arbitrament of the Jews' cause to force of arms. There is a greater ring of sincerity in the Hebrew version than in the parallel wording of Josephus — "Ye rebellious sons, declare now: have your fathers ever prevailed over their enemies by the sword, the spear, and warfare? Was it not through prayer, penitence, and the good and upright heart in the service of the Lord that God came to their aid? . . . . Who does not know that prayer is more effective than weapons of war for prayer hastens the help of God and His salvation?" [48]

Citing the heroes of the Bible — the patriarchs, judges, kings and prophets — he illustrated through their vicissitudes that it was by means of prayer that "our fathers have always prevailed . . . . Whatever evil has come upon us in our long history has been our own doing. Our enemies never injured us as much as we hurt ourselves." [49]

These reflections were in harmony with the prophetic tradition of Israel and with the depressed condition of the Jews in the centuries of exile after the calamitous war. But what is particularly striking and revealing is the portrayal of Titus in *Josippon*, so similar to, even though also different from that of Josephus.

In the *Wars* of Josephus, Titus is the heroic figure who fills the center of the stage. Josephus glories in Titus' exploits and deeds of valor as if Titus were fighting the cause of the Jewish people.[50] The adulation of Titus extends to his associates, including the renegade Jew, Tiberius Alexander.[51] When Titus sanctioned the crucifixion of countless hopeless victims, driven by famine out of the besieged city — "so great was their number that space could not be found for the crosses nor crosses for the bodies"— Josephus condoned the act as a war measure.[52] He rationalized his unnatural sympathies by asserting that the destroyers of Jerusalem were the foes within, "doing all that their besiegers could have desired . . ." "For I maintain that it was the sedition that subdued the city, and the Romans the sedition, a foe far more stubborn than her walls; and that all the tragedy of it may properly be ascribed to her own people, all the justice to the Romans."[53]

Titus appears throughout as the would-be savior of Jerusalem, the Temple and the Jewish people.[54] He is filled with compassion for the suffering population.[55] He stands in awe and reverence of the holiness of the Temple.[56] In turn, he lives under the special protection of the Deity.[57] He owes much to the favors of Fortune.[58] The very springs around Jerusalem which had dried up flowed copiously for Titus.[59] In the midst of the holocaust, as the Temple was burning in flames, Titus, peering into the Holy of Holies and desperately striving to save the Temple from the doom of fire, still dominates the scene.[60] And when the tragedy is over and a ghastly silence settles over the ashes of the Temple and the ruins of Jerusalem, the Jewish historian does not drop his pen or raise his voice in lamentation. He marches on with his idol through lavish feasts and banquets at which the chief entertainment was furnished by Jewish captives thrown to the wild beasts or compelled in opposing masses to fight each other to death.[61] Thus he continues to plot the progress of the conquering hero on his triumphal march to Rome. The significance of the spectacle presented by the triumphal procession in Rome, the colorful pageants re-enacting the devastating war scenes, the flaunting exhibition of a captured scroll of the Law and the sacred vessels taken from the Temple in Jerusalem, the public execution of the last surviving rebel leader, all these are paeans of glory to the illustrious career of Flavius Titus.[62]

The portrayal of Titus in *Josippon* seems like a faithful replica of Josephus' original, but the effect is different. Without reducing the stature of Titus or altering the character features as they are depicted in Josephus, the Hebrew writer changed the perspective and thus created a subtly different mood. Not Titus and his exploits but the relentless tragedy of Israel is the focusing point around which the theme of *Josippon* is centered. That the Siloam and other springs around Jerusalem started to flow, benefiting the enemy, is recorded as an unhappy fact, not a Titus miracle. The Hebrew writer believing solely in the providence of God allows no play for the whims and caprices of Fortune. Thus Titus loses the charm which Fortune cast over his life in Josephus' portrayal.

At a critical moment, when Titus barely saved himself by cutting through the cordon of Jewish soldiers who surrounded him, Josippon accounts for this narrow escape not by assuming a charmed existence for Titus but by the prosaic explanation that the assailants desired above all to capture him alive.[63] With the moral faith of a Hebrew, he believed that God helped to preserve Titus in order to surrender Jerusalem to him in expiation of the sins of the Jews. It was Titus the pagan who then perceived that "the hearts of kings are in the hands of God."[64]

These changes in perspective and viewpoint reflect the outlook of the Hebrew author of *Josippon*; but they did not alter in any essential degree his character portrayal of Titus from its prototype in Josephus. For Josippon too viewed Titus as one who did not seek the destruction of his Jewish subjects. "For he had compassion on Jerusalem, the Temple of God and the people of God" . . . . . "When he saw that the Jews were ready to sacrifice their lives and to die as one man in combat, for they preferred to die rather than live, he pleaded with them and entreated them to make peace."[65] He was distressed because the rebels were obdurate and had no regard or pity for their own lives or the lives of their wives, sons and daughters. When Titus saw the terrible and gruesome casualties resulting from the famine that he had imposed upon the inhabitants of the besieged city, "when he beheld the corpses of those who died of hunger thrown into the Kedron valley as dung upon the field, he trembled exceedingly and raising his hands to heaven exclaimed: 'O God of heaven and earth, Thou in whom the people of Israel believe, render me innocent of this guilt, for I did not desire to bring this about. I cried unto them for peace but they would not have it, and they brought on this evil.' "[66]

With Josippon acting as interpreter, Titus challenges John the rebel chief to leave the precincts of the Temple and to fight the battle in the open. "Wherefore do you make war from the sacred altar and profane the Lord your God and His Sanctuary? We do not mean to wage war against the Temple, for it is the house of the great God. Our battle is with you and not with the Temple." But John replied: "We have no better sacrifice to offer upon the altar than our own flesh and blood, for we shall battle and die for our God and we shall be acceptable unto Him as a continual burnt-offering. As free men we shall give up our lives in the Sanctuary."[67]

As the siege was nearing its climax, Titus, with Josippon at his side, again and again with mounting intensity pleads with the rebels to come to terms. He offers them a covenant "in the presence of the God of this sanctuary." With God as his witness he swears that he will not break his covenant, that he will not requite them evil, that he will not take loot or lead them into captivity, but he will set a king over them from one of their own notables. If they willed it — according to one version — he would appoint Joseph the priest (Josippon) over them as king. He would set free the men of faith who were with him and they would return to their land and every man would freely eat of the fruit of his vine and drink of the water of his own well. "And ye will live and not die, and the service of the Sanctuary of your God will not be interrupted." [68]

Josippon giving free rein to his imagination excels Josephus in interpreting Titus sympathetically to his Hebrew readers. The Roman general is well versed in biblical history which his fathers taught him and which he learned from Jewish scholars, especially Josippon. [69] The prayers put in the mouth of Titus echo the ancient voice of Jewish prayer: "O Lord of the Universe, before whom secret things are revealed, Thou knowest the mysteries of my heart that I did not come to this city to wage war but to proclaim peace unto her" . . . . . [70]

As in Josephus, so in *Josippon*, Titus is absolved of responsibility for the burning of the Temple. With greater intensity, the Hebrew author describes the general's frantic efforts to stamp out the flames which the soldiers had started against his strict orders. He shouted to his soldiers to desist but in their frenzied condition and in the general tumult, they paid no heed. Drawing his sword, he shouted, upbraided and cursed his officers to stop the stampede but it was of no avail. Hoarse, weary and fatigued, he dropped to the ground in a faint. When he came to, he arose and approached the Holy of Holies which at that time had not yet been burned out. There he saw the glory and the beauty of the Sanctuary and he beheld that this was indeed the house of God and the dwelling place of the God of heaven, more glorious than the Roman or any other temples that he had ever seen.[71]

The tenor of the description in *Josippon* is highly significant. That Josephus should paint his patron and protector in flattering colors was to be expected; but not so in the case of the independent Hebrew writer of *Josippon* who did not hesitate to deviate from his model when his sentiments or convictions were in conflict with Josephus' views. In the eyes of the early rabbis and later generations, Titus was the enemy of God, the ruthless conqueror who laid waste the sacred land, brought low the holy city, destroyed the Temple and set into motion the long, bitter exile of their people. From the third and fourth centuries onward, Titus was pictured in the Talmud as the wicked archenemy of the Jewish people. His name was coupled with the epithet הרשע, "the wicked." There were indeed lingering memories of Titus at the burning of the Temple but these associations were bitter and filled with hate toward Titus. Legend attributes to him vile and obscene conduct in the Holy of Holies, defilement of the Torah and the blaspheming of God. As a fitting punishment for his arrogance, God caused a tiny creature, a gnat, to enter his brain and to bring about his death.[72]

Not a trace of these legends or the attitude reflected in them is to be found in *Josippon*. On the contrary, in the final chapter — probably an interpolation — there is the following summation of Titus' character: "And the Emperor Titus was a great rhetorician in Greek and in Latin and he composed many learned works in these languages. And Titus was a righteous and upright man and all his judgments were just. Against his will he was compelled to bring desolation and destruction upon Jerusalem. For this great evil which was visited upon Jerusalem came about wholly because of the men of violence among the Jews and on account of their wickedness as we have related."

In another connection, various scholars have similarly

20

pointed to the omission in *Josippon* of the talmudic legend concerning the miracle of the cruse of oil on account of which Hanukkah is celebrated eight days. It is hardly to be assumed that the author of *Josippon* knowingly set himself in opposition to the talmudic tradition. We must conclude therefore that this Hebrew work basically was composed before the completion of the Talmud at the end of the sixth century and probably earlier, before the contents of the Talmud and the Midrash were orally disseminated from the centers of rabbinic study in Palestine and Babylon.

This conclusion is borne out by the religious ideas to be found in *Josippon*, which show no specific characteristics of talmudic thinking, even though they are closer to the general trend of Jewish thought than the corresponding passages in Josephus' *Jewish War*. The life of the soul in the hereafter is a recurrent theme in *Josippon* and also in Josephus and thus affords interesting multiple comparisons.

The Roman, pagan view of life after death is voiced eloquently by Josephus in the speech he ascribed to Titus. [73] Immortality is reserved for those who die in battle. Their souls are received into the ether and placed among the stars. They are turned into genii and heroes that reveal themselves benevolently to later generations. But they who die of disease, however pure their lives may have been, "are obliterated in subterranean night and pass into profound oblivion, their lives, their bodies, aye and their memories are brought simultaneously to a close."

Immortality along military lines found no echo in the soul of a Jew. Josephus made no distinction between the fate of a warrior and a non-combatant in the hereafter. The human being, he states, possesses a soul which is "a portion of the Deity housed in our bodies." [74] The bodies are composed of perishable matter but the souls are immortal and live forever. Man derives his being from God and when he dies a natural death — in contradistinction to suicide — he repays the loan which he received from God and wins "eternal renown." [75] The soul which remained spotless, obeying the divine laws, is allotted a holy place in heaven. In partial reward for its virtue on earth, the security of the house and family is assured. Its celestial sojourn, however, is only temporary. Its ties with an earthly existence are not altogether severed. For the soul repeatedly returns to earth to take lodgment in another human being. The transmigration of the soul is a process of progressive purification. In the revolution of the ages, the soul is granted renewed existence in a more desirable human body. [76]

The wicked soul has its abode in the dark regions of the nether world. These regions receive those who treated God's gift of life with scorn, namely, those who took their own lives and thus cast out of their bodies the deposit which God had placed there. [77]

Josippon's views are expressed in the parallel chapter in language more characteristically Jewish. God, in whose power is the soul of every living creature, breathes the soul, the living spirit into the human body, causing us to live before Him. He deposits within us the living spirit and it is locked therein until in His gracious will He chooses to break the lock and release the soul. A natural death is therefore to be welcomed, for the soul then returns in peace to the heavenly sphere where it abides in the saintly company of Abraham our patriarch, and the other righteous and pious souls of our ancestors. He who dies, even prematurely, in fighting the battle of the Lord — for His covenant, His sanctuary and the Law — is covered with glory. His death is an atonement for the soul and he ascends to the Great Light and is illumined with the light of eternal life. But he who takes his own life, for whatever cause, breaks faith with the Creator. He has broken the lock which God had sealed. He has violated the trust which God reposed in him when He placed the soul of life in his bodily frame. Such a person is doomed to perdition and to the nether regions of She'ol. [78]

Thus far the views of Josippon, although set in a different framework, are fairly analogous to the views of Josephus with one striking difference: the concept of the transmigration of the soul, which is stressed by Josephus and ascribed by him to the Pharisees, is completely disregarded in *Josippon*. [79]

It would appear that the Hebrew author is more concerned with the fate of the soul after death than was Josephus. He reverts to the subject more frequently and his descriptions of its heavenly abode are more graphic — at times, even spatial — and therefore cruder. [80] But in none of these aspects is there any distinctive trace of talmudic influence.

As death stalks amidst the bloody scenes of murder and violence within the beleaguered city of Jerusalem, so luridly described in *Josippon*, the victims are given to long discourses on the fate of the soul. Death causes the separation of the soul from the body. It releases the soul from the bondage of the flesh. The severance of the spirit normally comes about at the natural termination of life in the divinely appointed time; the older the person, the more facile the exit of the soul. Hence the heavenly passage of the souls of the aged is accomplished in quicker time than is the case with young persons whose winged flight is slowed down by the weight of the body which is not yet prepared for severance from the soul. [81]

No allusion is made to the resurrection of the dead, a dogma that was already prominently featured in the Mishna early in the third century. [82] The spirit is completely free of bodily entanglement. It does not return earthward to another human frame through transmigration nor is it reincorporated in bodily resurrection. Josippon's heroes look to eternal life in heaven as the end goal and the reward of the pure soul. This heaven, reserved for the righteous, is referred to under the biblical name,

Gan Eden, the Garden of Eden, but it is used only as a literary allusion denoting a state of peace. Heaven is not described by any attributes save that of light. Repeatedly the characters in *Josippon* speak of heaven as a world illumined by eternal light, the illumination emanating by implication from the supreme Source of Light. To ascend to heaven is "to walk to the Great Light and to be illumined in the light of eternal life." [83]

The soul retains its individual existence and character in the celestial regions. Parents are united with their children in heaven if their earthly lives are equally meritorious. The priest Amitai or Amatthus, facing death together with his three sons at the hands of the executioner exclaimed defiantly: "The murderous tyrant Simon may separate our dead bodies but he is powerless to part our souls." [84]

The numerous spirits dwelling in heaven are conceived of as a community of saints. They rank according to the holiness of their lives on earth. They who ascended to heaven by way of martyrdom are especially favored. This apparently means that they are admitted closer to the circle of Israel's elect and nearer to the divine source of light and life. [85]

More concrete but strangely out of harmony with this vague picture of the heavenly state is the vision of Amitai, or Amatthus, the priest, in an elaborate recital. Addressing his sons who were about to be executed before his eyes, he comforts them with the assurance that as he too would be killed after them he would soon overtake them in the flight to heaven, for the souls of the aged ascend more speedily to the world of light and life than the souls of young men whose flight is impeded by their steeper entanglement in corporeal matter.

"Hasten now my sons," he implored, "and seek out a lodging for us and prepare it for length of days. Would that I could precede you and make these preparations for myself and for you . . . . But now, my sons, being that you go before me, as you approach the eternal lodging-place, they who dwell there will make room for you and assign a more desirable place for you than they would for me; for while I have sinned grievously [in admitting Simon to Jerusalem] you are blameless and righteous."

Amitai reminds his sons of the fate of Hannah who in the Maccabean revolt against the Syrians yielded her seven sons to die in martyrdom for the people of God, His covenant and His Torah. They too preceded their mother in death and they prepared for themselves and their mother "a dwelling-place of light and of life with the Lord our God."

"My sons, would that you and I could share with them their lodging-place, for theirs is an honored place, as they, mother and sons, died in righteousness and saintliness. However, if we cannot rise to their height and dwell with them, we do not fall far below them and we may be their neighbors. For we too are dying in innocence for our sins and for the sake of God's Law and His covenant."[86]

Amitai concluded his address to his sons by telling them that in their heavenly journey they would very likely meet Jonathan, son of King Saul, who too was killed before his father, and he instructed them to relate to Jonathan all the terrible deeds of the tyrants in Jerusalem. He, Amitai, would report similarly to King Saul and to all the saintly company of martyrs who were gathered in heaven.[87]

Even with this peroration of Amitai, which is included in all the versions of *Josippon* (but not in Josephus), with or without this fantasy — the picture of the soul in the heavenly state as portrayed in *Josippon* is bare and shows no trace of the poetic imagery and the ethical overtones of talmudic theology. There is no glimpse of the seven heavens, the radiance of the divine presence, the ministering angels, the crowns which adorn the heads of the righteous, the ecstasy of the soul feeding upon the splendor of the divine majesty or any of the countless images in the treasure-house of rabbinic literature. Josippon's celestial conceptions are not colored by the warm poetic imagination of the *aggadic* rabbis nor are they affected by the halakic views of the rabbis in their theological aspects. Viewed from any standpoint, it is clear that *Josippon* is a non-rabbinic composition. Its range of thought and conception is indeed closer to some of the apocryphal works than either to the Talmud or the literature of the later medieval period.[88]

The non-rabbinic character of *Josippon* is furthermore illustrated in its occasional references to Jewish law. Thus, the question whether an oath is valid and binding if its fulfillment involves a breach of the divine law is discussed in terms that do not reflect any contact with the rabbinic mode of thought or expression.[89] In regard to the laws governing a suicide, a strange dissimilarity is to be noted in which Josephus and Josippon differ from the talmudic law as well as from each other. According to Josephus, it is a Jewish law that the body of a suicide is exposed until sunset; and, alluding to an Athenian custom, he adds that among other nations the law requires that the suicide's right hand be cut off.[90] Josippon, without referring to the first clause, asserted it was a Jewish law that if a slave committed suicide, his right hand was cut off and his body was denied burial.[91]

While the book of *Josippon* is non-talmudic and its theological views and occasional references of a legal nature are not altogether in accord with rabbinic opinion, it does not contain such legal or doctrinal matter as would arouse the ire of a strict Talmudist. Essentially, *Josippon* is history fused with pietism. The relentless historic tragedy of the fall of Jerusalem, with which the work reaches a peak and climax, its somber, brooding, emotional coloring, lighted with occasional flashes of hope and faith in the ultimate redemption, blended readily with the mood of medieval Jewry.[92] It became singularly popular in later generations, from the tenth century onward, when it appeared or reappeared in versions of varying length and content. Its wealth of historic and legendary matter in the earlier part of the work, touching on the biblical period and also the Hasmonean era, was also useful to the learned scholars engaged in Bible and Talmud exegesis. Rabbinical and biblical celebrities such as Rashi, Abraham ibn Ezra, David Kimhi, and Isaac Abravenel refer to *Josippon* as a classic authority.[93] A unique work, it exerted fascination upon the learned and unlearned alike.

Thus, a strange metamorphosis came about. The historic Josephus was displaced by an unknown Hebrew author under the guise of Josippon, who readily found his way into the hearts of his people. Whereas Josephus, neglected or rejected by the Jews, was welcomed into the bosom of the Church, the pseudo-Josephus received the adulation of his people as patriot and hero, as a sage and a man of God. Fantastic as it must seem to the modern reader, the eulogy of an early editor of the fourteenth century faithfully expressed the appraisal of many generations: "Joseph b. Gorion, man of God; mighty warrior; anointed for battle; priest to the Supreme God."

NOTES

References to *Josippon*, indicated by chapter, apply to all the editions following the Constantinople, 1510, edition, excepting the Gotha printing of 1710, edited by Breithaupt, who pursued an arbitrary division of his own design. A numeral preceded by "M" refers to the Günzburg reprint of the Mantua *editio princeps* of 1476–1479, the number referring to the column as in the original edition.

References to Josephus' works are to the Loeb Classics series.

[1] *Against Apion* I, 29.

[2] "The Shebet Yehudah and Sixteenth Century Historiography," below, pp. 83 ff.

[3] Cf. TB Shab. 13b.

[4] Cf. *Jewish War* III, 396; V, 367, 465; VI, 63, 84, 109–10, 249–50, 267–68; VII, 515 *et passim*.

[5] See p. 27.

[6] Cf. Introd. to the Günzburg edition of *Josippon* by Abraham Kahana, Berdichev, 1896–1913.

[7] See Neubauer, *JQR* (O. S.) XI, 335 ff.; cf. S. Zeitlin, *Josephus on Jesus*, Philadelphia, 1931.

[8] See Note 6. The Constantinople version is considerably larger than the *editio princeps*. It is amplified partly with obvious interpolations which do not occur in the earlier Mantua edition. These additions, in some cases, are fanciful or incongruous passages that mar the credibility of what appears otherwise as authentic history, and were deliberately omitted by the earlier editor. But in many instances the amplifications are genuine and are of an emotional, dramatic and poetic nature which appealed strongly to the imagination and the emotionalism of its Hebrew readers. Textually, therefore, the Mantua edition is more restrained and may be closer to the original text; but, as a mirror of the feelings of the medieval Jewish community, the later edition is decidedly to be preferred. Virtually all subsequent republications of *Josippon* followed the text of the Constantinople edition, with the exception of the Basel edition of 1541, which has a Latin translation and preface by Sebastian Münster. Only one reprinting of the Mantua edition was published in recent years: ed. Günzburg, Berditschev, 1896–1913.

[9] *Josip.*, Ch. 3; cf. Ch. 82.

[10] In the Alexander Romance narrative in *Josip.*, Ch. 6, the mother of Alexander (Olympies) is called גבּיראשׁ.

[11] Cf. *ibid.*, Ch. 6 (beginning).

[12] See Ch. 65, end: רק נאמר אשרי הדור אשר ימלט ויהיה לפליטה ולשארית מישראל עד הגיע זמן בנין הבית פעם ג' ואשרי המחכה ויגיע לראות בטוב ה' ולחזות בנועם חסדו אשר יהיה לישראל בימים ההם. ועתה אנחנו בהיותנו כואבים בצרותינו זאת נרפא מחץ כאבנו ושבר לבנו כי נזכור גדולות התשועה ההיא ונשמח ונשיש כי נחשוב בה מה שעשו הרואים את כבודה אשר עין בעין יראו בשוב ה' את שיבת ציון וירושלים ונשכחו הצרות הראשונות העוברות ואלה לא יזכרו ולא יפקדו ולא יעלו על לב.

[13] Cf. Tam b. David ibn Yahya's Introduction to *Josippon*.

[14] Abraham Zacuto who made use of *Josephus* as well as *Josippon* (see note 88 below) tried to solve the puzzle of Joseph's paternity by suggesting that the name of the father of Joseph b. Gorion was Mattathias. He must have assumed that Gorion was a patronymic.

[15] *Ibid.*, Ch. 15: ובשנת קל"ד לאימפראוס נולדתי אני יוסף הכהן בן גוריון הכהן ואני הוא יוסף הנקרא יוסיפוס היהודי אשר הסיפור עליו בעולם כי כתב ספר מלחמות ה' והוא החלק הששי מזה הספר ובחלק ההוא והוא הספר הששי תראה עוד עדותי על זה נאמנה. See Ch. 85.

[16] Cf. *Jewish War* V, 533, 544: *Josip.*, Chs. 85, 90.

[17] *Josip.*, Ch. 90.

[18] *Ibid.*

[19] *Ibid.*, Ch. 95.

[20] *Life*, §8, 75.

[21] *Ibid.*, § 1, 75, 76; *Jewish War* V, 419.

[22] *Josip.*, Ch. 85.

[23] *Life*, § 76. Cf. Eusebius, *Eccles. Hist.* 3, 10.

[24] The hypothetical identification of Josephus with Joseph ha-Kohen, mentioned in *Hallah* IV, 11 and *Moed Katan* 23a, cannot be taken seriously. The biographical data in these passages preclude such identification.

[25] *Life*, 38–39, 60.

[26] *Jewish War* I, 12.

[27] Cf. F. J. Foakes Jackson, *Josephus and the Jews*, pp. 72–3, 83–5, 90.

[28] *Josip.*, Ch. 65 end.

[29] *Idem.*

[30] Cf. Zunz, *Die Gottesdienstliche Vorträge der Juden*, pp. 154 ff.

[31] *Josippon's* occasional departures from the original *Josephus* are striking and unexplainable. Thus, according to the Hebrew version in the Constantinople edition, Vespasian, upon the advice of his counselors, brought Josippon, chained as a prisoner, under protective custody with him to Rome, where he witnessed the coronation. Also Agrippa and his son Monobaz were in Vespasian's retinue. Subsequently, Agrippa and his son were executed for treason (*sic*) while Josippon, who enjoyed the favor and confidence of Vespasian, was set free and sent back to Titus to serve him as trusted adviser and fatherly counselor. In this story is interwoven the description of Vespasian's coronation ceremony, which is generally conceded to be an anachronism and a late interpolation dating from the tenth century.

The Mantua edition entirely omits this chapter and faithfully follows the historic account in *Josephus*.

[32] A curious geographical transformation in *Josippon* is Goshen, Egypt, for Gophna, a small town near Jerusalem. Cf. *Jewish War* VI, 115 with *Josip.*, Ch. 92, M 510. The confusion of Menahem b. Saruk for Mannaeus son of Lazarus, a gatekeeper in Jerusalem, who gave an account of the corpses carried out of his gate from May 1 to July 20, in 70 CE, is peculiar to the Constantinople edition and its derivatives. The Mantua edition does not name the keeper but calls the gate, "the gate of Menahem." On the other hand, the figures cited (M 498 = 115,000, Const. ed. Ch. 91 = 115,808; *Jewish War* V, 567 = 115,880) reveal the interdependence of the various texts.

[33] *Jewish War* III, 351–54; cf. *ibid.*, 399–408.

[34] *Josip.*, Ch. 72, end: ועוד אמר ריע יוסף כדברים האלה ליוסף כי ירא ממנו
פן ימיתהו בחרבו כי יוסף היה גבור ממנו וגם הוא בחרו אליו לבן זוג בלתי בעל
גבורה בתחבולה ובמרמה למען יהיה מתגבר הוא עליו ובזה רב שכל יוסף מדעתו
כי נמלט מחרב הפתאים הרשעים ההם ונמלט מחרב רעהו ולא נשחתה נפשו; M. 414.

[35] *Jewish War* III, 399–408.

[36] *Ibid.*, III, 340.

[37] *Ibid.*, III, 390.

[38] *Josip.*, Ch. 71, M 406–9.

[39] Cf. *Jewish War* II, 539; III, 120, 256–57; V, 343, 365, 401 ff., 458–59;
VI, 99–102, 566, *et passim*.

[40] Cf. *Josip.*, Chs. 75, 82, 84, 85, M 457–58, 464, 471–72.

[41] *Josip.*, Ch. 84; Cf. M 471.

[42] *Ibid.*, M 459 ff.

[43] Cf. *Jewish War* III, 472–84; V, 257; VI, 34–35; *Josip.*, Chs. 68, 69,
70, 74, 82, etc.; M 447, 470: כל הרעה אשר באתנו מימי עולם מידינו היתה בנו.

[44] *Josip.*, Chs. 75, 77, 79, 80, etc.

[45] Cf. *Jewish War* IV, 318; V, 19, 559; VI, 99, 110, 411; *Josip.*, Ch. 84:
הנה סר צל ד' מעליכם כי חטאתם לו ומעלתם בהיכלו ובכהניו

[46] *Jewish War* V, 367.

[47] *Josip.*, Ch. 84: ...הלא תבושו ותכלמו באמרכם זה ותחפרו בקלון וחרפה
ואף כי אתם בני עם ה' וסגולתו... ועונותיכם מבדילים ביניכם לבין אלהיכם

[48] *Ibid.*, Ch. 85, M 464–64, 466–67.

[49] *Ibid.*, M 470, Ch. 85: ומי לא ידע אשר התפלה נכבדת מכל כלי המלחמה
כי התפלה תחיש עזרת ה' וישועתו... וכל הרעה אשר באה אלינו מימינו מעולם
ומראש מידינו באה אלינו כי צדיק הוא ה' אלהינו על כל מעשיו אשר עשה עמנו.
ולא הרעו אויבים לנו כאשר הרענו אנחנו לנפשותינו

[50] *Jewish War* I, 27–29, III, 324–485 ff., IV, 70 ff., V, 54–66, 81–97,
VI, 486 ff., etc.

[51] *Jewish War* V, 45–46. Cf. V, 97, 310 ff.

[52] *Ibid.*, V, 449 ff.

[53] *Ibid.*, V, 257.

[54] *Ibid.*, VI, 128, 236 ff., 249, 251, 254–66.

[55] *Ibid.*, 214–9.

[56] *Ibid.*, V, 241; VI, 94 ff.

[57] *Ibid.*, V, 60–61; VI, 411.

[58] *Ibid.*, V, 88, 409; VI, 57, 413.

[59] *Ibid.*, V, 409.

[60] *Ibid.*, V, 254–80.

[61] *Ibid.*, VII, 24, 37–40.

[62] *Ibid.*, VII, 132–157.

[63] *Josip.*, Ch. 81, M 439.

[64] *Ibid.*

[65] *Ibid.*, Ch. 84, M 455–56.

[66] *Ibid.*, Ch. 88, M 482. Cf. *ibid.*, Ch. 91.

[67] *Ibid.*, Ch. 92, M 507–8: ויאמר אל יוחנן הפריץ מה חטא לך ההיכל הזה
אשר תגרה עליו את הרעה הגדולה להורסנו אם בכח ובגבורה תתהלל צא עם גדודיך
וגבוריך אל השדה ונלחמה שם ועתה הלא היום הזה יום חגכם מדוע אתם נלחמים
במקום הזבח והעולה ואתם מחללים את י"י אלהיכם ואת קדשיו ואין אנחנו נלחמים

עם ההיכל כי בית האלהים הגדול הוא אך מלחמותינו עמכם ולא עם ההיכל ואם
תאמרו כי לא נוכל להלחם הכניעו לנו עורף ונשאתם עלינו ואם תאמרו הבה
ונלחמה הלוך ונצא השדה ושם נערוך את מלחמותינו ולמה זה תשבתון זבח עבודת
אלהיכם . . . אז ענהו יוחנן שר הפריצים ויאמר אין לנו לזבוח זבח בקרב ההיכל
טוב מבשרינו ודמינו כי על אלהינו נמות ונלחמנו ונחשב לפניו כעולת התמיד
לרצון ונמות חפשים בתוך הקדש.

68 *Ibid.*, Ch. 92, M 510.
69 *Ibid.*, Ch. 93, cf. Ch. 88 end, M 482.
70 *Ibid.*, Ch. 93.
71 *Ibid.*, Ch. 94, M 525–26.
72 Genesis Rabba X: Gittin 56b.
73 *Jewish War* VI, 46–48.
74 *Ibid.*, III, 372.
75 *Ibid.*, III, 374.
76 *Idem.*

These views on immortality and transmigration of the soul which Josephus expounds to his comrades in arms follow what he had previously interpreted to be the theories of the Pharisees. "Every soul, they [the Pharisees] maintain, is imperishable, but the soul of the good alone passes into another body, while the souls of the wicked suffer eternal punishment." *Jewish War* II, 163.

They are only partially in accord with the teachings of the Essenes as Josephus understood them. They agree about the dual composition of the human being: the body being corruptible and transitory, the soul, immortal and imperishable. The Essene views are expressed more graphically and picturesquely. Thus we are told that the soul emanates from the finest ether. Prior to its descent into the human body it existed in an ethereal state. It was dragged down, as it were, by a sort of natural spell and became entangled in the prison-house of the body. Death sets the soul free. "Sharing the belief of the sons of Greece," writes Josephus for the benefit of his Graeco-Roman readers, "they [the Essenes] maintain that for virtuous souls there is reserved an abode beyond the ocean, a place which is not oppressed by rain or snow or heat, but is refreshed by the ever gentle breath of the west wind coming in from the ocean; while they relegate base souls to a murky and tempestuous dungeon big with never-ending punishments." *Jewish War* II, 154–58. But, it is to be noted that the theory of the transmigration of the soul was not part of the Essene theology.

77 *Ibid.*, III, 375.
78 *Josip.*, Ch. 71, M 409–13.
79 See Note 76 above.
80 This is especially true of the Constantinople edition and its derivatives. As usual, the Mantua version is more restrained and chaste and less picturesque.
81 *Josip.*, Chs. 71, 89, 90, 93, *et passim*, M 409–10, 487–90, 498, 502.
82 Sanh. X, 1. A single exception may be noted in the Venice edition, Ch. 90. But the passage does not occur in any of the other editions and is obviously a unique and late interpolation.
83 See Note 81 above.
84 *Josip.*, Ch. 89, M 487: ואם ירצה שמעון הרוצח להפריד את פגרינו לא

יוכל להפריד את נשמותינו כי אחרי אשר אקבל משפטי זה על ידי שמעון האבזר
זה הנה אבטח ולא אפחד כי תשועת ה' תהיה לנשמתי בעולם אור החיים
בעולמי.

[85] *Idem.* Cf. Ch. 71, M 409–10.

[86] *Ibid.*, Ch. 89, M 487–90: ואם אנחנו לא נוכל להגיע למעלתם לבוא אליהם
אל מלונם הנה לא נהיה שפלים מהם כי נהיה שכנים להם אשר גם אנחנו בתומתינו
ובעונותינו נמות ועל תורת ה' ובריתו.

[87] *Idem.*

[88] The book of *Josippon* ends with the fall of Masada (ועד הנה מלחמות
בית שני), followed by an elegy in which Josippon mourns the destruction of
Jerusalem, the burning of the Temple, the exile of the Jewish people from its
land and patrimony, and concludes with the prophetic hope for the restoration of the glory of Zion, the rebuilding of the Temple, and the gathering-in
of the exiles.

This moving passage is then followed by what appears as an appendix,
having no connection with what preceded it. The addendum reads as follows:
"Titus left a Jewish remnant in the land of Israel in Jabne, Betar and Usha
and their surrounding territories with Rabban Yohanan ben Zaccai as head
and prince. He also appointed Bonin, the younger brother of Joseph the
Priest [Josippon] as ruler over the remaining Jews in Jerusalem as a tribute
to his brother, Joseph the Priest. At that time, Rabban Simon, son of Gamaliel,
Prince of Israel and High Priest, and Rabbi Ishmael, son of Elisha, were
executed. Titus wanted to kill also Rabban Gamaliel, the father of Rabban
Simon, but Rabban Yohanan ben Zaccai prevailed upon him not to do so.
Rabban Yohanan ben Zaccai is he who left Jerusalem at the time when
Vespasian, father of Titus, rose up against Jerusalem. The Emperor Vespasian
showed him great honor and when he left for Rome, as we narrated, he com-
mended Rabban Yohanan ben Zaccai to his son Titus requesting him to
extend him high honor and station for he recognized that he was a great
sage." The addendum concludes with a tribute to the character and the
wisdom of Titus.

This is the only section in the book in which Rabban Yohanan ben Zaccai
is mentioned. The passage is inserted out of sequence. Furthermore, the
talmudic story that Rabban Yohanan forecast the elevation of Vespasian as
Caesar is not mentioned. On the other hand, Josippon's statement that Titus
executed Rabban Simon ben Gamaliel and Rabbi Ishmael ben Elisha is not
recorded anywhere in the Talmud. The execution of these sages — an apocryphal tale — is mentioned in *Semahot*, Chapter 8, but not in connection with
Titus. It is interesting to note, however, that this entire passage is incorporated in toto by Abraham ibn Daud in his abbreviated version of *Josippon*
entitled, *History of the Second Temple* (דברי מלכות בית שני), and is also embodied
in his historical chronicle, *Seder ha-Kabbalah*.

It is quite clear that this entire passage does not belong to the original
text. Not only is it missing in the Mantua edition, but even in the Constantinople edition it appears out of context as a loose appendix added by a
later scribe. It is quite possible that Abraham ibn Daud may indeed be the
source of this addition. This may be inferred from the final concluding para-
graph which follows immediately after the above passage. It is a midrashic

commentary on Zechariah, Chapter 11, which is also repeated in its entirety in Ibn Daud's abbreviated version. In *Josippon*, this passage again has no connection with the preceding section and is an appendix to an appendix. On the other hand, in Ibn Daud's text it follows logically and coherently after an independent section which he inserted concerning *The Ten Captivities of the Jews*. The interpretation of Zechariah's prophecy is an appropriate sequel to this chapter, and as Ibn Daud states expressly, it rounds out the theme and vindicates the underlying thesis of his *Seder ha-Kabbalah*. אמר אברהם הלוי בן רבי דוד זכרונו לברכה כבר זכרתי למעלה בתחלת ספר סדר הקבלה הזה שהיתה כוונתנו בחבורו להודיע לתלמידי איך נמשכה קבלת תורתנו הקדושה ממשה רבינו עליו השלום ... וכן מצאנו שכל הנזכר לעיל בענין מלכי בית שני כבר נבא עליו זכריה בן עדוא הנביא עליו השלום ורמזו קודם לכן בנבואתו כמו שנבאר לפנינו. וזו היא תחילת נבואתו כה אמר ה' אלהים רעה את צאן ההרגה ... זה בית שני.

It is comprehensible, therefore, that the late editor of the Constantinople edition, who certainly had before him Ibn Daud's abbreviated version, in this instance borrowed an extraneous passage and inserted it in *Josippon* because its sentiment harmonized with the theme of *Josippon*. By the same process, he may also have incorporated the immediately preceding passage concerning Rabban Yohanan b. Zaccai and the apocryphal story concerning Rabban Simon ben Gamaliel and Rabbi Ishmael ben Elisha.

[89] *Ibid.*, Ch. 72: וכי תאמר מה נעשה על השבועה אשר נשבענו ועל הברית אשר קיימנו הלא לך לדעת כי השבועה לחטוא אשר יפירנה לא יחטא כי לא יקפוץ האדם להשבע ברצון האלהים כי אם לקיים דת ומצוה וחק. ודוד אמר על ככה נשבעתי ואקיימה. ואמנם הנדר והאסר והשבועה לחלל דת ולהפר חק מצות לא יכונו לפני ה' אלהינו: This discussion is not to be found in the Mantua edition nor in the parallel chapter in Josephus.

[90] *Jewish War* III, 377–78 (note b).

[91] *Josip.*, Ch. 71: והלא ידעתם אשר כי יהיה לאיש עבד בער ואיש זדון ורשע והוא סורר ומורה וקשה עורף כאשר תביאהו עת צרה עת חסר דעת וירא כי צר לו ולא יקום לו לתשועה ילך ויתלה באילן או בזולתו ויחנק או ידקר בכלי וימת משפט הנבל ההוא אז הוא להכרית יד ימינו אשר המיתהו וגם משפטו לנזר עליו לבלתי יקבר בקבר כי את נפשו השחית. This passage is omitted in the Mantua edition.

[92] See Preface to *Josippon* by Tam b. David ibn Yahya.

[93] Zunz *G. V. d. J.* cites the following references to *Josippon* by Rashi: II Kings 20.13; Ezek. 27.17; Dan. 5.1; 6.29; 7.6; 8.11; 21.22; 11.2, 17; Berak. 43a; Yoma 23a; Baba Batra 3b. Zunz also cites single references by R. Gershom, in the *Aruk* of R. Nathan, Ibn Ezra's Commentary (Ps. 120.5), Judah Hadassi's Commentary (I Chron. 11.17) and R. Isaac b. Samuel (*Tosafot, Aboda Zara* 10b). To these may be added David Kimhi, *Sefer ha-Sharashim* s. v. משך; and Isaac Abravanel who quotes *Josippon* frequently. The following references, drawn from his Commentary on Genesis alone, indicates his customary usage of *Josippon*: Part I, 20a, 24a, 25a, 26d, 27a; Part II, 29a, 29b, 30b; Ed. Warsaw, 1862. He refers to Joseph b. Gorion's writings in general (I, 20a, II, 29a, and also under specific titles: *Book of Antiquities* הקדמוניות ס' or הקדמונים ס' (I, 24a, 25a); *Book of the Wars of the Second Temple* מלחמות בית שני ס' (II, 30b) and in one instance (I, 26d–27a) to Book II wherein he evidently followed the classification of the Constantinople

33

edition. The passage alluded to is to be found in Book II, Ch. 11. Cf. above pp. 3 ff. See also *Mashmia Yeshua* (Offenbach, 1767) 23c, 94d. Abraham Zacuto frequently referred to *Josippon* in his *Sefer Yuhasin*: (ed. Filipowski, 8[a], 13[a], 24[a], 83[b], 202[b], 231[b], 244[b], *et passim*). He regarded *Josippon* as an authoritative source. Note especially 244[b]; but at times he was also sharply critical, 231[b].

Zacuto used Josephus' *Antiquities* as well as *Josippon* but referred to both under the latter name. Thus on p. 8[a], Zacuto cited a talmudic statement that Saul and Samuel died in the same year, which, said Zacuto, contradicted the statement of Joseph b. Gorion, who said that Saul reigned for twenty years, eighteen years during Samuel's lifetime and two years thereafter. Zacuto's reference in this instance is not to *Josippon*, which does not treat of the life of Saul, but to *Ant.* VI, 378. Zacuto had before him the Latin translation which has the correct reading, eighteen years during the lifetime of Samuel and two years after the latter's death. The Greek version, which reads twenty-two years after Samuel's death, thus raising the reign of Saul to forty years, is obviously a doctored emendation by a pious Christian scribe so as to reconcile Josephus with Acts 13.21, where Saul's reign is given as forty years. See Marcus' note f to *Ant.* VI, 378. See also *Ant.* X, 143.

It is surprising that Zacuto attributed the *Antiquities* and *Josippon* to the same author. See above, n. 14.

Josippon and the Apocrypha

A CRITICAL edition of *Josippon* is still a desideratum in Hebrew literature. For a thousand years this book was accepted as the Hebrew version of Josephus and served as the classic Jewish history for the learned scholar and the common folk alike. Rashi, Abraham ibn Ezra, Isaac Abravanel are typical of the scholarly class that drew their historic knowledge from Josippon's narrative, and regarded the book and the author with a degree of reverence due to an ancient religious authority.[1] The high esteem which *Josippon* enjoyed all through the Middle Ages was more than offset by the disparagement cast upon the book in modern times.

The elements contributing to its depreciation are readily understandable. Even a superficial examination of the various versions of *Josippon* in print and in manuscript reveals the composite overlapping and confusing nature of the book. A search for the Ur-text seems hopeless. The apocryphal identification of the author of *Josippon* with Josephus, stressed so frequently in the Constantinople edition and in all its derivatives, is all too transparent and flimsy. The numerous interpolations, the grotesque nature of many passages which thus crept into the narrative tended to discredit the authenticity of the book in its entirety.[2] Finally, the late date of the ninth or tenth century ascribed to *Josippon* by Zunz, which was generally accepted, made the book, at best, historically of dubious value.[3]

However, no reliable judgment of the book either as to its genesis or its historic relevancy is possible without a critical edition; and this in turn calls for a series of preliminary detailed studies, preferably comparative studies in those areas where it

Published in *The Jewish Quarterly Review*, Vol. XLIII, 1952. Written for the Jubilee volume in honor of Professor S. Assaf, where it will appear shortly in Hebrew.

is possible to trace a relationship with the more firmly authenticated documents.

Trieber's critique of *Josippon* marked the first radical departure from the generally accepted theories as to the date, scope and authentic purpose of the author. [4] Adolph Büchler in a critical evaluation of I Esdras utilized the text of *Josippon* in a manner which vindicated its essential authenticity, although Büchler failed to draw the natural consequences of an early dating. [5] More recently, Professor Solomon Zeitlin, in a number of valuable studies cited proofs to substantiate an early date for *Josippon* and correspondingly to enhance its value as a source document. [6]

The present writer has already dealt with some general aspects of *Josippon* in relation to Josephus; [7] and also with the question of the authenticity of specific passages dealing with John the Baptist and Jesus of Nazareth. [8] It is now proposed in this paper to examine some of the accounts in *Josippon* in which parallels are to be found in the Apocrypha, and by a comparative study to ascertain the degree of historic credibility to be attached to these sections of *Josippon*.

A complete survey of all the parallels of *Josippon* and the Apocrypha including the First and the Second Book of Maccabees, The Letter of Aristeas and others, would be beyond the limitations set for this paper. Here we shall limit ourselves to a consideration of the narratives centering around the personalities of Daniel and Zerubbabel. These occupy a prominent place in *Josippon*. They also form the theme of I Esdras and the Additions to Daniel, i. e., Prayer of Azariah and Song of the Three Children, Susanna, and Bel and the Dragon. A comparison of these sections of the Apocrypha with the *Josippon* narrative will reveal omissions, parallels and divergences from which pertinent deductions may be made.

It will be noted first that the Additions to Daniel form part of the Septuagint version of the Book of Daniel; yet no account whatsoever is to be found in *Josippon* to correspond either with the Prayer of Azariah and Song of the Three Children or with Susanna. On the other hand, unmistakable parallels, with significant divergences, of the theme of Bel and the Dragon occur in *Josippon*, and this is likewise true of the Zerubbabel narrative in I Esdras and *Josippon*.

That the author of *Josippon* made use of the historical books of the Apocrypha is certain. It is also axiomatic that he drew heavily upon the writings of Josephus. Some of the narrative works in the Apocrypha such as Tobit or Judith did not belong within the historic framework of *Josippon* and their omission from the latter was but natural. This may likewise explain the absence of the story of Susanna from *Josippon*. For its theme hardly had any bearing upon the historic Daniel and his time. Indeed, the allusion to Daniel in Susanna is doubly questionable; first as to whether the name Daniel was specific or, in a sense, generic; and secondly whether the name was not altogether an interpolation.

The omission of the Prayer of Azariah and the Song of the Three Children is more puzzling, especially in view of the author's marked predilection for oratorical declamations. Perhaps the explanation is to be found in the fact that *Josippon* unlike Josephus did not aim merely to retell the Bible story. He was selective in the use of biblical material choosing only the episodes which legend enriched with midrashic motifs. In the Septuagint, the Prayer of Azariah and the Song of the Three Children are part of the Book of Daniel, following naturally upon chapter III verse 23. The masoretic text too by its abruptness between verses 23 and 24 seems to indicate an earlier version which must have contained the Septuagint addition or its equivalent. If an argument *ex silentio* be acceptable in this instance it would evidently point to a pre-masoretic date for the Ur-*Josippon*. For otherwise *Josippon* would certainly have incorporated the theme of Azariah's Prayer and the Song of the Three Children.

A position midway between the Bible and the Apocrypha is presented in the *Josippon* version of the story of Daniel in the lions' den. Unlike the Apocrypha narrative, Daniel's being thrown into the lions' den according to *Josippon* was not connected with Daniel's destruction of the Babylonian idols. As in the Bible and also in Josephus' *Antiquities*, so in *Josippon*, Daniel was cast among the lions because he prayed to the God of Israel in defiance of Darius' command to pray to none other than the king himself for a period of thirty days. [9] But in this latter narrative there is interwoven the legend contained in Bel and the Dragon that the prophet Habakkuk while carrying the evening meal for the reapers in the field of Judaea is lifted by an angel by the hair of his head and transported to Babylon into the den of Daniel and the lions where, unharmed, he hands the food to Daniel. Habakkuk is then returned to his home by the angel; while Daniel, found safe by the king, was lifted out of the den, and his accusers were thrown among the lions and immediately devoured. Thus the power of God was made manifest to Darius who issued a proclamation glorifying and magnifying the God who delivered Daniel from death. [10]

In *Josippon* as in Scripture the entire episode takes place in one day; in the Apocrypha it is seven days. The Habakkuk story evidently required the longer period, so as to account for the need of having food miraculously brought to Daniel on the sixth day. This motive escaped the writer of *Josippon* and he did not alter the biblical account. In Bel and the Dragon, the king is not identified in the Septuagint version while in Theodosian the implication points to Cyrus; [11] in *Josippon* the king is Darius the Mede as in the Bible and also in Josephus. The statement of Darius' age at this time — sixty-two years in Scripture — harmonizes with the description in *Josippon* "in his

old age," ודריוש המדי קבל את מלכות כשדים לעת זקנתו. The motivation of the conspirators is likewise the same in both accounts.
On the other hand, a number of minor motifs, such as the
number of lions, the itemized food that they were fed daily
and the strange web of the Habakkuk story reveal the closest
affinity between *Josippon* and the Apocrypha. Either *Josippon*
borrowed directly from Bel and the Dragon, departing at will
from his source in many respects and then arbitrarily combined
his material with the biblical narrative, thus creating a fantasy
of his own, or he in common with the Apocrypha writer of this
legend drew upon other early writings that are no longer
extant.

The problem is sketched more sharply when we consider
the more definite parallels between the main narrative of Bel
and the Dragon and the corresponding parts in *Josippon*. The
story proper is identical in the two accounts. The Babylonians
have a god whose name is Bel (ביל אלהי בבל). His image is in
a temple erected for his worship, with numerous priests in
attendance. On a votive table, enormous quantities of food are
daily placed as sacrifices to Bel who supposedly consumes the
offerings during the night. The consumption of the food is
regarded by the Babylonian king and people as the act of their
living deity Bel. Daniel mocks at this belief when the king calls
upon him to do homage to Bel. He derides the notion that it
is the image that consumes the food. He offers to put the
matter to a test, and his challenge is accepted by the king. At
the close of the day, with the sacred table laden heavily with
food for the deity, the doors of the temple are sealed with the
seal of the king after the departure of the priests. With the
knowledge of the king but unbeknown to the priests, Daniel
had the floor of the temple strewn with light ashes before the
temple doors were closed. Early in the morning, the king and
Daniel repaired to the temple, broke the seal and lo, the food
had vanished. The ecstasy of the king, however, was quickly

39

dispelled when Daniel pointed to the footsteps that had left traces on the ash-strewn floor, proof that the priests had stealthily entered the temple through secret passages and had removed the food to their own living quarters. The king thereupon ordered the destruction of the Bel image, while the priests were confounded and variously treated according to the different accounts.

The story of the Dragon follows as a natural sequel, alike in *Josippon* and in the Apocrypha. The dragon, *Tanin* in Hebrew, was not an image but a live serpent worshiped as a deity, devouring great quantities of food which the worshipers devoted to it. In *Josippon*, the deity is described as a huge monster, a serpent, dwelling in a cave.[12] Every night he came forth to be fed and swallowed the food which the worshipers threw into his mouth. With a touch of satire or naïveté, the king challenges Daniel: in the Septuagint version, "Thou wilt not, wilt thou, say of this also that it is bronze? Lo, he liveth, eateth, and drinketh: do homage to him"; in *Josippon*, "Hear now, O Daniel, and hearken to me and I shall speak to thee. Wouldst thou craftily deny this deity, the dragon, as thou didst with Bel that had no breath in it? Behold this is a living, mighty and powerful god and who can stand up against him and do him harm?"[13] Daniel's reply is in its essential part verbally identical in all the texts: "Give me leave and I shall slay also this dragon without sword or staff (or spear)."[14] This permission is granted and Daniel makes a fatal mixture (cakes made of pitch, fat and hair, in the Greek versions; in *Josippon*, iron nails joined as combs with sharp points covered over with fatty substances) which the dragon swallows, with death resulting immediately in dramatic fashion.[15]

The populace is infuriated and with threats pointed at the king, demands the death of Daniel. At this point the Hebrew version and the Greek part company. In the former, the king suppresses the mob with violence; and in the latter Daniel is thrown to the lions to appease the mob.[16]

While in the main, the plot and the denouement in the Apocrypha versions and in *Josippon* bear such close resemblance as to preclude their independence of each other, there are distinctive features in each account which bear analysis. In the Apocrypha, the story of Bel and the Dragon forms a supplement to the Book of Daniel, and this is also true of the Vulgate in which Bel and the Dragon comes at the end of the Book as Chapter XIV. In *Josippon*, the story of Daniel as a whole does not fall in line with the order followed in Scripture. But here too the story of Bel and the Dragon seems detached from its immediate context and appears as an extraneous interpolation. After Daniel's delivery from the lions, the Babylonian king Darius issues the proclamation (which is later repeated in the name of Cyrus as in the Bible) authorizing the Jews to go up to Jerusalem and to rebuild the Temple, and calling upon the officials of the empire to render generous aid to the Jews in the fulfillment of the plan. The passage following abounds in difficulties to which we shall revert later; but the intent is clear. Forty thousand Jews go up to Jerusalem under the leadership of "Ezra the scribe, Eliakim the high priest, Jeshua and Mordecai and the other chiefs of the houses of Judah and Benjamin."[17] The building of the Temple is begun. But the adversaries of Judah and Benjamin, Sanballat the Horonite, Tobiah the Ammonite, Geshem the Arabian and other enemies sent accusations against the Jews to the king and the work was stopped till the second year of Darius' reign.[18]

It is at this point that without any transition the Daniel narrative is resumed, leading to the story of Bel and the Dragon. Abruptly, without any link to the preceding narrative the story commences: "And it came to pass as Darius, the king, was sitting upon the throne that he called for Daniel the man greatly beloved." Daniel's wisdom greatly delighted the king who loved him exceedingly and appointed him Councillor and Viceroy "as in former days," whereupon there follows the story of Bel and the Dragon which is introduced in biblical style: "And it came to pass one day as King Darius was celebrating the feast of Bel, the god of Babylon" etc.[19]

It is clear that the story of Bel and the Dragon was loosely incorporated into *Josippon* from an extraneous source precisely as the Septuagint drew upon an extra-biblical source and appended it to the biblical Daniel without any integral connection. This similarity in construction, added to the essential identity of the narrative itself in the Apocrypha and in *Josippon*, raises the important question about their mutual relationship. Did the author of *Josippon* lift the story bodily out of the present Apocrypha version? If so, how is one to explain the wide gap in the conclusion of the narrative? In the Apocrypha, the story of Daniel's triumph over the Babylonian idols reaches its climax in the sequel when, to appease the fury of the enraged idol-worshipers, the king casts the hero to the lions; whereas in *Josippon*, the end appears anti-climactic; the threatening mob is dispersed by the king's forces and Daniel seeks retirement from his burdens and official honors.

Another alternative is to assume that *Josippon* as well as the Septuagint drew upon an earlier, more elaborate Daniel literature, which is no longer extant, from which each author selected the material of his own preference.[20] This would account for the common as well as the divergent elements in the different versions. It is to such a source that Josephus presumably refers: "For the books which he (Daniel) wrote and left behind are still read by us even now."[21] If this assumption proves acceptable, it offers startling corroboration of an early date for the composition of *Josippon*, earlier than any date that has been thus far advanced. This conclusion is reinforced by a closer examination of the two texts.

A careful analysis of the detailed features of the two versions indicates that the two accounts are interdependent; that they are supplemental; that there are missing features in each account, which can best be explained on the assumption of earlier sources, some common to both, and others drawn upon by each writer individually. The Septuagint begins the story of Bel with the prologue: "From the prophecy of Habakkuk the son of Jesus of the tribe of Levi. There was a certain man a priest, by name Daniel, son of Abal, a companion of the king of Babylon." The Theodosian version substitutes another opening: "And King Astyages was gathered to his fathers, and Cyrus the Persian received his kingdom. And Daniel lived with the king, and was honored above all his friends." The historical and factual inaccuracies of the superscriptions do not concern us in this discussion. The significant element is the fact that neither superscription is introduced in the *Josippon* narrative. The Greek rendition, Septuagint and Theodosian alike, combined the story of Daniel in the lions' den and the Habakkuk episode with Bel and the Dragon as indicated above. In *Josippon*, the two parts are separated, and the former narrative (with the addition of the Habakkuk element) is recorded as in the Bible. In view of the radical differences, it is difficult to assume that the writer of *Josippon* followed as his model the present version of the Apocrypha.

On the other hand, the interdependence of the two versions is illustrated in the course and sequence of the narrative proper: in the colloquy between the king and Daniel; the manner in which food was ceremoniously offered to Bel; the ruse of the priests who deceived the worshipers; the artful device by which Daniel exposed the deceit of the priests. But there are also divergences in which one account supplements the other. In the Greek versions, Daniel agrees to the king's challenge that either he or the priests be put to death in accordance with the outcome of the test. In *Josippon*, no penalty is provided for in

43

advance except the request of Daniel that "the priests be surrendered to him." But when Daniel is finally vindicated, the
surrender of the priests is not mentioned in *Josippon* but is
featured as their penalty in the Septuagint recension, where
one would have expected a verdict of death. Likewise, in
Josippon only the priests are originally charged by Daniel with
consuming the food offered to Bel, without reference to their
wives and children, whereas in the Greek versions the priests
are from the beginning bracketed with these dependents.
However, in the denouement when those who consumed the
food are traced by their footsteps, the *Josippon* narrative, too,
alludes to the footprints of "men, women, youths and little
ones."

The Dragon story, which in the main reveals the same
relationship between the Hebrew version in *Josippon* and the
Greek rendition in the Apocrypha as in Bel, yields a striking
clue which may even help us to trace the provenance of the
two respective versions. In the Greek recital, which is brief and
comparatively colorless, the people who are wrought up by
Daniel's mockery and destruction of their idol gods complain:
"The king has become a Jew."[22] There is no echo of their
outcry in the Hebrew version which in other respects is dramatic and eloquent. It is hardly plausible that the emotional
writer of *Josippon* would have glossed over a striking phrase of
this character if this Greek text were the primary source of his
narration. The natural conclusion seems to be that the Septuagint version reflects the Hellenistic anti-Jewish milieu of Egypt
while *Josippon*'s source was of Palestinian provenance and may
have belonged to "the books," quoting Josephus, "which he
(Daniel) wrote and left behind (and which) are still read by
us even now." This assumption will furthermore explain the
religious ethical motivation in the *Josippon* portrayal of the
Dragon narrative which is totally absent in the Greek. To
the king's plea to Daniel, "Do homage to the dragon," he

bluntly replied according to the Greek version, "Give me the power and I will destroy the dragon without sword or staff." Contrast this with the Hebrew reading: "Pray let not the king err also in this for it is only a beast to be subdued by the hand of man. The spirit of God is not in it. And now if my lord the king will allow me, I shall also smite and slay this dragon without sword, spear or weapon, for it is but a crawling reptile and the Lord put the fear of man into the being of every beast that crawls or creeps upon the face of the earth for in the image of God was man created and his fear is upon all." In the light of the foregoing considerations this religious embellishment which might otherwise be ascribed wholly to the individuality of the author is more likely to be equally at least a reflection of the religious character of the early Daniel literature upon which this section of *Josippon* is based.

Most illuminating for the present discussion is the story of The Three Pages, with Zerubbabel the central figure, as related in I Esdras, *Josippon* and also in Josephus.[23] The story is introduced most naturally in *Josippon*, where a link is forged between Daniel and Zerubbabel, a link which is wholly original with *Josippon*, and is unknown to the Bible or the Apocrypha. For in the canon, the chronicler (the writer of Chronicles, Ezra and Nehemiah) who speaks of Zerubbabel knows not Daniel; and the Book of Daniel makes no mention of Zerubbabel. Nor do these personages meet anywhere in the pages of the Apocrypha. *Josippon* brings them together ingeniously by having Daniel introduce Zerubbabel to King Darius as his successor.[24]

The story is skillfully woven together. The scene is set in the twilight of Daniel's earthly career. He had grown old in the service of the king. He wearied of the attacks directed at him by the jealous courtiers and the fanatical idol-worshipers. He therefore pleaded with the king to permit him to retire to his native home and there in peace to worship the God of his fathers. Reluctantly the king offered to grant his wish if he would find him another Jewish counsellor equally endowed with wisdom and the spirit of God. Such a man was Zerubbabel, scion of the house of David. Daniel found him among "the Congregation of the Exile" and forthwith led him to the king, who was greatly pleased with him. Daniel then retires to the city of Shushan in the land of Elam, and Zerubbabel takes his place in the court of King Darius.

Thus the ground is laid for the story of The Three Pages at the Court of King Darius — Zerubbabel and two other princes — who stood guard at the bedside of the king when he slept. One day while waiting for the king to awake, the pages enter into a test of wits and he who would win the contest, such was the covenant, was to be made viceroy. He was to sit on the throne, ride in the royal chariot and enjoy many other privileges pertaining to royalty. The contestants wrote down, each in his turn according to lots, an aphorism which was to reveal his understanding and wisdom. These were recorded in a book which was placed under the king's pillow. The king overheard their conversation although he pretended sleep. When he presumably awoke, he agreed to carry out the terms of their covenant. Before a public assembly, each of the contestants was called upon to read his aphorism. The first page read: "In all the earth there is none so powerful as a king." The second said: "In all the earth nothing is so powerful as wine." The third page, Zerubbabel, proclaimed: "In all the earth nothing is so powerful as woman." Each of the contestants, in turn, defends his oracular statement with a rhetorical declamation. Most dramatic of all is Zerubbabel's brief on woman's power which is singularly lacking in the ethical virtues lauded in the Book of Proverbs. His oration had hardly taken full effect, when Zerubbabel startled his hearers with the now famous Praise of Truth. "For let it be known to the king and all assembled," he exclaimed, "that all is but vanity: the king who rules the earth; the wine that rules the king; and the woman with her iniquity who rules all three. But truth reigns over all things in heaven and on earth. In the seas and in the depths truth prevails before God and man, for where truth dwelleth falsehood cannot abide. Verily, heaven and earth are founded upon truth, and the Lord our God is eternally true." The sentiment is applauded by the king, the princes and all the people who conclude with one voice: "True is the God of Zerubbabel who hath filled him with the spirit of truth to praise and to glorify truth before God, king and man."

Zerubbabel's triumph leads up to the main theme, which is the ascension of the exiles from Babylon to Jerusalem. For eager to reward Zerubbabel beyond the honors written into the scroll by the pages, Darius said to Zerubbabel: "Ask, in addition, something that your soul desires, even unto half the kingdom, and I shall grant it." To this Zerubbabel replied: "O my lord the king, I pray thee, remember the vow which thou and King Cyrus made unto the God of heaven to rebuild His house, to restore the vessels of His Sanctuary, to turn back in peace the exiles of the God of heaven to worship Him in the Temple that is called by His name and where His presence dwells, so that they may pray to the great heavenly God for thee and thy kingdom. For it is not meet to delay a vow made to the God of heaven."[25] Thus Darius the Mede, king of Babylon is linked to Cyrus in a promise to restore the exiles and to rebuild the Temple. This association of the two kings is a unique feature in the *Josippon* narrative. It is the key to many riddles and problems that beset the other accounts of the return of the exiles from Babylon, as we shall see.

To continue with the narrative: Darius ordering Zerubbabel's request to be officially recorded sends a message to Cyrus King of Persia to join him in fulfilling their vow to rebuild the ruins of Jerusalem. Cyrus complies by issuing a brief proclamation in his own name throughout his own kingdom

47

and by joining with Darius King of Media in an elaborate joint proclamation "to the princes, governors, and rulers on the other side of the river, to the Idumeans, Tyrians, Sidonians, Samaritans and to Asaph, governor of the forest of Lebanon." The proclamation declared it to be the will of the two kings to send back the exiled people who chose to return to Jerusalem; to restore the holy vessels of the Sanctuary; to rebuild the Temple, the altar, and the holy of holies as well as the palace and the walls of Jerusalem. The loyal subjects, officials and governors of the various provinces were requested to assist the Jews by supplying them with all their needs which are carefully and meticulously enumerated. The decree sealed and signed is handed over to Zerubbabel son of Shealtiel and (sic) to Nehemiah son of Hachaliah.[26]

It is significant that no allusion is made in this narrative to the previous proclamation of King Darius after Daniel's deliverance from the lions' den. This omission is particularly striking inasmuch as the wording of the two proclamations is almost identical. We have already noted above that the earlier proclamation interrupted the continuity of the story of Daniel's experiences in the court of Darius. It would seem therefore that the previous passage was inserted inadvertently out of context or was an outright interpolation. Once the assumption is accepted, the *Josippon* narrative is internally consistent and logically cohesive which cannot be said for the Apocrypha version, as we shall see. As to the historical facts, which it is difficult to reconcile with *Josippon*, they are equally out of joint with the biblical narrative, with Josephus' history and the Apocrypha version.

Although the *Josippon* narratives, as a rule, freely depart from the order of the Bible, the climax of the story in this instance approaches the biblical model in which Cyrus is the king in whose reign the exiles march out of Babylon to the heights of Jerusalem. For, so the story continues in *Josippon*,

Darius approaching death turned over his kingdom to Cyrus who was his son-in-law. Thus Media and Persia were now united under Cyrus, as Darius was gathered to his people. In this manner, the story which wandered far from the biblical course is blended with the biblical narrative in content and style, to wit: "And in the first year of his reign, the Lord stirred up the spirit of Cyrus King of Persia and he remembered the vow which he had made to return the exiles and holy vessels from Babylon to Jerusalem."[27] The Jewish elders were summoned before Cyrus and he said to them: "Whosoever there is among you of all the people of the God of heaven whose heart prompts him to go up to Jerusalem to the footstool of the great God to build this temple, let him go up and build and may his God be with him. And I, Cyrus servant of your God by whose will I became king shall provide from my riches and treasures for the reconstruction of the house of the great God who caused me to reign over the kingdom of Media and Persia and who helped me destroy the kingdom of the Chaldeans."

For our purpose, we need not follow the story beyond the statement following that "all the elders of the exiles, Ezra the scribe, Nehemiah son of Hachaliah, Mordecai and Jeshua, with Zerubbabel son of Shealthiel at their head, and the other chiefs of the captivity went up to Jerusalem and built the temple of God."[28]

We may now compare the narrative of Zerubbabel as told in *Josippon* with that of I Esdras. For purposes of clarification, we shall first analyze the story of The Three Pages — to which there is a further parallel in Josephus — and then proceed to a comparison of the historical context which serves as a frame for this picturesque story in each version.

Set side by side, the two versions of the contest among the three pages show the same relationship between *Josippon* and the Apocrypha indicated above: an identical theme, with motifs and features essentially alike, but with important divergences sufficient to preclude the likelihood that one is either an improvement or an imperfect copy of the other. An earlier source common to both — a cycle of Zerubbabel stories similar to a Daniel saga — is clearly to be assumed.

As in *Josippon,* so in I Esdras the three pages are King Darius' bodyguards who watch over him as he lies on his couch heavy with sleep after much wine and feasting. In I Esdras the three guards agree in advance that the theme of the contest is to be "what one thing is the strongest of all." This supplements *Josippon* where the agreement upon a theme is implied but not mentioned. The terms of the award to the victor and other related details are substantially the same. However the order in which the three contestants make known their answers varies significantly. In I Esdras, the first proponent upholds that wine is strongest; the second puts forth this claim for the king; and Zerubbabel, who is third, proclaims "that women are strongest; but above all things Truth beareth away the victory." In *Josippon* the order is the king, wine and woman. The paean in honor of truth is introduced by Zerubbabel at the end of his declamation as a climax and surprise.

The heightened effect of the manner in which truth is climactically introduced in *Josippon* is not merely the result of a literary device. For the construction of the whole narrative indicates a superiority which is not one of style but of internal genuineness, attributable to a better source. This is illustrated, for instance, by the order in which the first two orations are arranged. Obviously the proper sequence is the ascending order in which the speakers are marshaled in *Josippon:* first, he who upheld the power of the king and then he who spoke for the greater power of wine, which can overcome the king, and finally Zerubbabel pleading for woman whose seduction weakens kings and whose blandishments are more potent than wine. In I Esdras, however, where the power of wine precedes that of the king, the ascending intensity is lost, for whereas strong drink can overpower the king, the reverse is meaningless.

Moreover a closer examination of Zerubbabel's peroration in I Esdras reveals that the original order was that of *Josippon*. For thus speaks Zerubbabel: "O sirs, is not the king great . . . and wine is strong? Who is it then that ruleth over them? Are they not women? Women have borne the king and all the people that bear rule by sea and land . . . and they nourished them up that planted the vineyards, from whence the wine cometh." Thus it will be noted from this summation that the king's power and not wine was placed first in order of sequence. On the other hand, it is also interesting to observe that the significant reference to woman as the mother who bears the planters of the vine is supplemental to the oration in *Josippon* which does not contain this important allusion. The two versions are clearly supplemental, interdependent, yet sufficiently different to exclude the likelihood of a direct borrowing of one from the other.

We are thus led to the conclusion that the author of *Josippon* in its earliest form lived at a time when sources older than or different from the extant Apocrypha versions were still available for use as source material. This viewpoint is strongly corroborated as we now turn to consider the historical context of the data which we have hitherto examined.

The circumstances under which Zerubbabel came to leadership during the return of the exiles from Babylon to Jerusalem are left strangely vague in the meager records of the canonical Ezra. To fill this vacuum in the biblical narrative is the motive for the insertion of the story of The Three Pages in the apocryphal I Esdras which in all other respects follows closely the canonical record. This romantic tale is introduced not as a belletristic embellishment but to fill a gap in the history of the Return and in the life-story of Zerubbabel. From it, we learn that Zerubbabel gained the favor of King Darius through a brilliant exposition of the cosmic and divine nature of truth. It was through his prodding that Darius was led to decree the return of the exiles and the restoration of the holy vessels. For, we are told, Darius had previously vowed to rebuild Jerusalem when he gained the throne and also to build up the Temple and to send back the sacred vessels. These vessels, we are strangely informed, had been set apart by Cyrus "when he vowed to destroy Babylon and vowed to send them (the Temple vessels) again thither." No further information about this complicating statement is offered. As it was Zerubbabel who reminded Darius of the vow it was but natural for the grateful monarch to appoint him as his emissary and chief of the returning colony. This, therefore, is the "explanation" of the rise of Zerubbabel to leadership as told in I Esdras, chapters III to V, 6.

In the context of I Esdras, the story is hopelessly out of consonance not only with the canonical Ezra but with its own version of the Return, which otherwise follows closely the biblical record. The passage bristles with problems that are well-nigh insoluble judging by the unsatisfactory solutions attempted by many of the commentators. The great emancipator according to this story was Darius who carries out what presumably Cyrus had planned but not fulfilled. Indeed Darius' proclamation for the Return makes no allusion to a prior proclamation on the part of Cyrus. And yet according to the context, the return of the exiles had already taken place under Cyrus, the rebuilding of Jerusalem had been suspended under Artaxerxes, and the story is presumably set in the reign of "Darius King of the Persians." Not only is the historical orientation thoroughly confused; it is difficult to render intelligible the summation: "He (Darius) sent away all the vessels from Babylon, that Cyrus had set apart; and all that Cyrus had given in commandment, the same charged he also to be done, and sent unto Jerusalem," this enigmatical statement evidently referring to the vow previously alluded to. [29]

The key to the mystifying problems presented by the whole narrative and its context is to be found in the person of King

Darius. Once his identity is established, we are able at least to fix the story in its proper setting. Who then is this Darius who is linked so mysteriously with Cyrus by vow and in the accomplishment of the return of the exiles and the restoration of the holy vessels? No allusion to a vow previously taken either by Darius or Cyrus is to be found anywhere in the Bible or in any part of the Apocrypha. The vow therefore affords no clue. Two kings after Cyrus, known by that name, come under consideration: Darius I (Hystaspes) 521–485 and Darius II (Nothus) 424–405. The identification of our King Darius with either one of these Persian monarchs leads to hopeless confusion and certainly renders any contact with Cyrus absurd.

There is, however, another Darius King of the Medes, conqueror of Babylon, who is prominently featured as such in the Book of Daniel and who appears in the book as an older contemporary of Cyrus. Like the other figures associated with Daniel, legends gathered around him. He is the King Darius of the book of *Josippon* who loved Daniel, who sorrowed when he was cast into the lions' den and rejoiced at his deliverance; he is the monarch associated with the Bel and the Dragon episodes. He is the king at whose court Zerubbabel and the other two pages held their famed debate. Undoubtedly it is the same Darius concerning whom the account in I Esdras has been found so puzzling. But what is most significant, all the clouds of doubt and confusion which obscure the latter version vanish completely in the light of the fuller account to be found in *Josippon*.

Here we learn that Darius King of Media and Cyrus King of Persia had been vassals of Belshazzar, King of Babylon, and rebelled against him. Cyrus married Darius' daughter and became his son-in-law. Belshazzar's ill-fated banquet was in celebration of a victory over the rebel kings. But he provoked God's wrath when he ordered wine to be served in the holy vessels taken from the Temple in Jerusalem. The ominous

53

vision, Daniel's interpretation, his admonition of Belshazzar for desecrating the sacred vessels are reported to the rebel kings by a eunuch, Belshazzar's chamberlain, who severed his king's head and brought it to Darius and Cyrus. The kings were overawed. Cyrus then vowed — Darius too by implication — "to build the Temple of the Lord our God in Jerusalem and to send back the exiles from Babylon to Jerusalem and to restore the holy vessels to the Temple in Jerusalem."[30] Together the two monarchs ravaged the land of the Chaldeans and conquered the capital, Babylon. The conquerors divided the land between them. Darius occupied Babylon and sat upon the throne of Belshazzar; to Cyrus fell the rest of the land of the Chaldeans. Cyrus was thus presumably subordinate to Darius in the kingdom of Babylon.[31]

On this background, the story in I Esdras becomes clearly intelligible without further complications. The king before whom Zerubbabel displayed his wisdom was none other than Darius the Mede, king of Babylon and father-in-law of Cyrus. Cyrus' vow to destroy Babylon and to return the sacred vessels to the Temple in Jerusalem was already anticipated. As long as Darius lived and "sat upon the throne of Belshazzar," Cyrus his son-in-law and future successor to the throne might set apart the Temple vessels for ultimate restoration, but he was not empowered to send them back and thus make good the vow which he had taken. The monarch who had the authority to do so was Darius who was equally involved in the vow. Hence it is the latter king who issues the decree for the return of the exiles and the sacred vessels.

But here again the passage in I Esdras is truncated at the conclusion as it was at the beginning. For the original story as it is told in the amplified version of *Josippon* does not end with Darius usurping, as it were, the role which the Bible assigns to Cyrus. As we have seen above, Darius at first called upon Cyrus to join him in fulfilling their vow; they issue a joint proclamation but before the edict could be implemented, Darius died and Cyrus in his new role as the sole monarch of their joint kingdoms issued the proclamation in the first year of his reign as told in the Bible, and the Return takes place thereafter.

The conclusion to which this analysis leads is quite obvious. The passage in I Esdras is a segment of a larger section torn out of its context. It has many gaps. It was inserted without much thought in its present place by the editor who confused Darius the Mede with Darius the Persian king. With the aid of *Josippon* we are enabled to reconstruct the story in its original form. In other words, the author of *Josippon* drew upon a source identical with or similar to the one which the editor of I Esdras utilized in reproducing the distorted story of the three pages and the rise of Zerubbabel. This is indeed striking testimony to the early age of *Josippon*, the pseudo-Josephus of Hebrew historiography.

As indicated above, Josephus too relates a parallel story concerning the three pages in the court of Darius, which may now engage our attention.[32] Josephus places the story definitely in the reign of Darius Hystaspes who succeeded Cambyses the son and successor of Cyrus.[33] The inclusion of the story which is not to be found in the Bible is not surprising. For in his treatment of this period. I Esdras was his primary source, not the canonical Ezra. In characteristic fashion, though he sensed some of the difficulties inherent in the story, he did not proceed critically to solve them by tracing the text to its original source but sought to smooth them out of existence with imaginative additions and alterations which superficially at least seemed to remove some of the complications. He modified, for instance, the beginning of the story and departed from his model in I Esdras which in this instance agrees with *Josippon*. Thus whereas in the two latter versions the idea of arranging a debate to test their wits originates in the minds of the three guards who seek to while away their boredom while the king is asleep, in Josephus it is the king who assigns to each of the pages the subject which he is to propound, viz., the power of wine, the king, or woman and truth. [34] Thereby, Josephus deliberately destroyed the artistic effect of surprise and suspense in order to avoid a very obvious commonplace question, namely, how could the guards presume to fix such a glamorous royal award to the victor without the previous consent of the king. In like manner, the question of Zerubbabel's recalling the vow of Darius — a vow for which there is no record in I Esdras but which is nevertheless the crux of the narrative is met by Josephus through the bland insertion in an earlier passage that "while still a private citizen he (Darius son of Hystaspes) had vowed to God that if he became king, he would send all the vessels of God which were still in Babylon to the Temple in Jerusalem." [35] As to the crucial problem concerning the central figure, Zerubbabel — how to reconcile his early beginnings under Darius Hystaspes when he already appeared as the leader of the returning Jews under Cyrus — Josephus glossed over the difficulty by drawing upon his imagination and creating an otherwise unknown old friendship that existed between Zerubbabel and Darius when the latter was still "a private citizen." His role as a page in the court of Darius is therefore introduced in this manner: "Now at that time (when Darius son of Hystaspes became king) there happened to come to Darius from Jerusalem, Zorobabelos, who had been appointed governor of the Jewish captives, for there was an old friendship between him and the king, and having been on that account judged worthy of a place in the king's bodyguard together with two others, he was enjoying an honor for which he had hoped." [36] This is but another illustration of the manner in which Josephus characteristically 'reconciles' contradictory sources.

Aside from these and other minor variations which are readily explained, Josephus' narrative is a faithful replica of I Esdras. Setting the three parallel stories side by side, we see that Josephus' narrative is a doctored version of I Esdras. The latter, in turn, is a fragmentary sketch torn out of another narrative and misplaced out of context, thus interrupting the continuity of I Esdras with resultant confusion. For the original story and for the reconstruction of I Esdras as well as Josephus we must turn to the version in *Josippon*. This analysis may not yield a precise date for the origin of *Josippon* but it definitely points to the early centuries of the common era when Jewish sources different from and, in some instances, older than the Apocrypha and Josephus were still available and could be freely used by an independent author such as the talented, pious and patriotic writer of the original book of *Josippon*.

NOTES

[1] See above p. 27.

[2] *Supra*, pp. 6 ff.

[3] Zunz, L., *Gottesdienstliche Vorträge der Juden*, pp. 154–62; in contrast, cf. Gaster, M., *The Chronicles of Jerahmeel*, Introd., pp. XIV ff.

[4] Trieber, K., "Zur Kritik des Gurionides," in *Nachrichten der k. Gesellschaft der Wissenschaften Zu Göttingen* (1895), pp. 381–409.

[5] Büchler, A., "Das Apokryphische Esrabuch," *MGWJ*, vol. 41 (1897), pp. 1–16, 49–66, 97–103.

[6] Zeitlin, S., *Josephus on Jesus*, pp. 52–60; The First Book of Maccabees (Dropsie College Edition) ed. S. Zeitlin, pp. 58–60.

[7] *Supra*, n. 1.

[8] "A Note on John the Baptist and Jesus in *Josippon*," in *The Hebrew Union College Annual*, vol. 23, part 2, pp. 136–49.

[9] Cf. Dan. 6.8–25; *Antiq.* X, 250–62. According to Josephus, the command was not to pray to or petition even the king himself, *Ant.* X.253.

[10] *Josippon* ed. Günzburg, D., pp. 13–16.

[11] See Charles, R. H., *The Apocrypha and Pseudepigrapha*, I, 658; Rabbi Moses ha-Darshan (eleventh century Bible commentator), in citing this narrative follows closely the Theodosian version, naming Cyrus as the king who threw Daniel into the lions' den. He follows the Apocrypha, departing from *Josippon*, in the explanation that Daniel was thrown to the lions to appease the mob. Ginzberg, L., *The Legends of the Jews*, VI, 432, n. 6.

[12] היה לכשדים אלוה והוא תנין גדול יושב במערה, p. 18.

[13] הגם על התנין האלוה הזה תערים מחשבותיך להכחידו כאשר עשית לביל אשר אין רוח בו הלא זה אל חי גבור וחזק ומי יתיצב לפניו להרע לו, *ibid.*

[14] גם התנין הזה אני אכנו ואמיתנו בלי חרב וחנית ולא מלחמה כי שרץ חיה הוא השורץ על הארץ, *ibid.*

[15] For a rabbinic parallel, see *Bereshit Rabba* 68, 13. Here the story is referred to briefly and utilized for illustrative purposes. The king in this version was Nebuchadnezzar.

[16] Cf. n. 9 above.

[17] P. 16.

[18] Pp. 16–17.

[19] As will be seen below, the entire passage concerning Darius' proclamation for the return of the Jews to Jerusalem was misplaced and did not belong in this context.

[20] This view would seem to be corroborated by the Dragon story in Ber. Rab., 68, 13 (see above n. 15), where the king is named Nebuchadnezzar. This version therefore stems neither from the Apocrypha nor *Josippon*. Linguistically, too, the midrashic text cannot be related to either source. But the manner in which it is utilized in the Midrash and its connection with R. Joshua ben Levi would indicate that the story was well-known among the Jews in Palestine in the third century.

[21] *Ant.* X, 267.

[22] Ἰουδαῖς γέγονεν ὁ βασιλεύς.

[23] Cf. Büchler, "Das apokryphische Esrabuch," *MGWJ* (1897), pp. 1 ff., who reached conclusions similar to ours although his study was focused primarily upon I Esdras.

[24] *Josippon*, pp. 19 ff.

[25] P. 24.

[26] This was evidently a confusion of the Nehemiah named in Ezra 2.2, a contemporary of Zerubbabel, with the later famous Nehemiah son of Hachaliah, the associate of Ezra.

[27] *Ibid.*, pp. 25–6.

[28] For *Josippon*, the three periods connected with Zerubbabel, Ezra and Nehemiah are catapulted into one. Büchler's attempt to reconcile the *Josippon* reading with Ezra 2.2, through forced emendations (*op. cit.*, pp. 52, 55) was not only far-fetched, it failed to take into account the essential difference of the timing in the two narratives.

[29] Cf. Charles, R. H., *op. cit.*, pp. 16 ff.

[30] אז נדר המלך כורש לבנות את היכל י"י אלהינו אשר בירושלם ולשלח את
Josippon. הגולה מבבל לירושלם ולהשיב את כלי הקדש אל ההיכל אשר בירושלם
ed. Günzburg, p. 11.

[31] *Ibid.*, pp. 9–12.

[32] *Ant.* XI, 31–74.

[33] *Ibid.*, 31.

[34] *Ibid.*, 36.

[35] *Ibid.*, 31.

[36] *Ibid.*, 32.

Saadia and His Relation to Palestine

IN 1892, the thousandth anniversary of the birth of Saadia was celebrated through a project which was to have resulted in the publication in nine volumes of Saadia's collected Hebrew and Arabic writings but of which only five volumes appeared.[1] The alleged date of his birth was ten years in error as was learned subsequently through a Genizah fragment discovered by the late Jacob Mann and published in an early number of *The Jewish Quarterly Review*.[2] But needless to say, the literary monument, incomplete as it was, lost none of its timeliness and it is an enduring testimony of the devotion and reverence felt by the past generation of scholars toward the memory of the greatest genius of the geonic epoch.

This year marks the millennial year of his death. There can be no doubt as to the date when Saadia died. His death occurred Monday morning at two o'clock on the twenty-sixth day of Iyar, or May 15, 942, according to the unimpeachable testimony of his own sons, She'erit and Dosa.[3] This certainty is itself but one of a horde of new facts that has come to light in recent years concerning Saadia's life and works. Indeed, the half century that elapsed since 1892 may be characterized in the annals of Jewish scholarship as the Genizah period, when the knowledge of the entire geonic era was completely revolutionized through the discovery of the Genizah, the hidden store of Hebrew and Arabic manuscripts in the old Cairo synagogue. The late Henry Malter, utilizing the Genizah material, was able for the first time to attempt a narrative and descriptive biography of Saadia. So unpredictable are the new finds that before his

Published in *The Jewish Quarterly Review*, Vol. XXXIII, 1942.

biography was off the press an important part of the narrative portion upon which much ingenuity and erudition were expended was rendered obsolete through the discovery of a tattered, mutilated Genizah fragment.[4] Nevertheless, no attempt has been made on the occasion of this anniversary to collect the widely scattered Saadiana documents to supplement Derenbourg's enterprise when the *Oeuvres complètes de R. Saadia ben Joseph Al-Fayyoûmî* was produced.

If the will and the means could be harnessed, it would be most fitting and desirable to publish this year Malter's posthumous edition of Saadia's philosophic classic, the *Emunot ve-De'ot*.[5] Otherwise, it is to be feared that this *opus magnum* may be buried in the debris of a modern Genizah, created not by reverence for the Hebrew page as in the days of old, but by wanton neglect and indifference. Undoubtedly, the outstanding work that will be worthily associated with this anniversary as a landmark in Saadia studies will be the learned and impressive edition of the *Siddur*, or Order of Prayers, of Rab Saadia Gaon, in which the late Professor Israel Davidson and S. Assaf and B. I. Joel collaborated so admirably.[6] The editors of *The Jewish Quarterly Review* in dedicating this number to Saadiana studies in memory of the great Gaon have been moved by a feeling of reverence to attempt through this collection of articles to make a modest contribution to a better understanding of Saadia's life and works.

Saadia, son of Joseph, born in 882 of obscure parentage in the village of Dilaz, in the district of Fayyum, Upper Egypt,[7] and ending his days in Babylon one thousand years ago as the renowned Gaon of the Academy of Sura, vindicated in his day the inherent democracy of Jewish spiritual leadership. In the tenth century, the gaonate was a sacrosanct institution. During the Arabic rule and under the influence of the Caliphate, the headship of the academy in Sura and later also in Pumbeditha, which formerly had been a purely scholastic office, developed into the gaonate, an authoritarian institution with powers rivaling the exilarchate itself. [8] The greater the power and the more lucrative the office, the more determined was the tendency to restrict the gaonate to a small scholarly group, preferably to those that could lay claim to noble Davidic or priestly descent. Saadia did not belong to this charmed circle. He was a stranger, a "foreigner," a man of humble, obscure family. [9] When late in Saadia's career the Exilarch David b. Zaccai broke off relations with him and appointed Joseph b. Jacob Bar-Satia in his place as Gaon, his spokesman was able to appeal to popular prejudice by contrasting Saadia's questionable antecedents with the aristocratic geonic ancestry of the new incumbent. [10] It is true that when the diatribe turned into a malicious attack upon his family origin, he retorted that he, too, was of Davidic descent, but this vague boast made under attack hardly carried conviction. [11] Certainly it was no factor in his election to the gaonate or his later restoration. His elevation was a personal triumph over an oligarchical tradition. It was the fruit of repeated victories that he had scored in the defense of rabbinic tradition against the Karaites and, even more so, of his victorious vindication of Babylonian Judaism against the claims of Palestine leadership. These victories had been achieved through brilliant strategy on the religious battlefield, through force of character and unmatched control over the whole range of Jewish lore. These qualities endeared him to the people and gained for him initially the confidence and support of the Exilarch. The hold of the aristocracy for the time being was broken. A man of the people, with the genius of a born leader, was crowned with the title of Gaon.

Of his physical appearance, his stature or physiognomy, there is not a trace or a descriptive phrase in the contemporary writings to aid the imagination in reconstructing this noble, historic figure. A late legend describes Saadia as tall, handsome and awe-inspiring, but it is entirely untrustworthy.[12] In his own works, however, there stands revealed a tumultuous personality with giant mental powers that broke through new paths of thought and learning, an exquisite personality that was sensitive to beauty of language and nobility of diction, a prophetic figure, zealous for righteousness and grappling with the eternal problems of the human spirit and, withal, an essentially earthy character, bold, aggressive and hard-hitting in the many battles he fought in defense of his ideas and in protection of his personal honor against foul attack.

In some of his attitudes and in much of his thinking, he strikes a modern chord, notwithstanding the passing of a millennium since his death. His writings from the *Agron*, one of his earliest compositions on language and diction, to the *Emunot ve-De'ot*, the great philosophic classic which crowned the end of his literary career, are distinctive and personalized. Thus he is the first authentic author in rabbinic literature. His compositions are not a string of unrelated homiletic comments or a loose collection of halakic opinions. Nor were they issued as anonymous writings or ascribed mythically to an ancient biblical or talmudic character. Whatever the problem which Saadia attacked, he dealt with it systematically as a disciplined thinker. Whether the subject was language or commentary, poetry or calendar, halaka or philosophy, the theme was clearly and broadly defined, the subject matter was submitted to keen, rigorous analysis and the treatment was logical, so logical, at times, as to aim artificially at arithmetical precision.[13] Saadia was too clearly conscious of his own powers and purposes to resort to the subterfuge of anonymity or pseudo-authorship. Not only do his books bear his name and the indelible stamp of his personality and genius but they are almost invariably preceded by formal introductions, a literary feature virtually unknown in rabbinic literature prior to Saadia.[14] In this he may have been outwardly influenced by Arabic style and standards;[15] but undoubtedly he was psychologically impelled by the force which led him to undertake his work, by a strong pride of authorship, and a keen consciousness of the beneficent role which the scholars of every generation play in the destiny of their people.[16]

In the introduction to the *Sefer ha-Galui*, his *apologia*, he wrote with evident pride that his own life experiences and the achievements which he wrought for his people by the grace of God led him to the conviction that "God does not abandon His nation at any time without a scholar whom He teaches and inspires so that he in turn may instruct and guide it to the end that through him its well-being shall be secured."[17] In the same vein, he wrote: "As the prophets led the nation in their time, so shall the righteous lead it in their generation."[18] More eloquent and personal is his introduction to the *Emunot ve-De'ot*:

"My heart grieved for mankind and my soul was moved on account of our own people Israel, as I saw in our times many of those who adhere to their faith entertain impure beliefs and unclear ideas; while those who deny the faith boast of their unbelief and triumphantly deride the men of truth, albeit they are themselves in error. I saw men sunk, as it were, in a sea of doubt and overwhelmed by the waves of confusion, and there was no diver to bring them up from the depths and no swimmer to come to their rescue. But as God has granted unto me some knowledge by which I can be useful to them, and endowed me with some ability which I might employ for their benefit, I felt that to help them was my duty and guiding them aright a moral obligation upon me."[19]

Thus spake Saadia the philosopher, the man who felt the burden of destiny, who was inspired to fashion a philosophy of Judaism and to create a new epoch in the history of his people which strongly influenced the world of human thought. Such language had not been uttered in Jewish literature since the days of Philo, another philosophic son of Egyptian Jewry. No Babylonian Jew in a thousand years had given utterance to

such clarity of speech and sustained thought as Saadia's philosophic work reveals. Although as Gaon of Sura, Saadia was the
official head of Babylonian Judaism, his entire range of thought
was uncharacteristic of the country which thus honored him.
Indeed his opponents charged him with secretly holding Babylonian scholars in contempt.[20] From what we know of the
deplorable state of Babylonian Judaism prior to Saadia's
ascendancy to the gaonate, it is only too likely that the charge
contained a grain of truth, even if it was exaggerated for
trouble-making purposes. Outside the range of halaka,
Saadia had no literary predecessor in the Babylonian gaonate,
and even his halakic writings display an originality of form,
style and symmetry of thought which clearly distinguishes them
from the products of the typical geonic literature as if he had
stamped them with his own official seal.[21] As for the philosophic
approach to Judaism, even Hai Gaon, who otherwise held
Saadia in high esteem, showed scant respect for it.[22] Saadia's
range of thought is not to be explained in terms of Babylonian
Judaism. He may have become its official head but his own
roots are to be found in his native country, which was under
strong Palestine influence.

The Jews of Egypt had a long, proud history. They shared
the fortunes of their country as it changed political masters and
one culture was superimposed upon another. They were
populous, wealthy and influential. On the eve of the Arabian
conquest of Egypt (639–41), Alexandria alone is reported to
have had a Jewish population in excess of 100,000 souls. When
this city surrendered to 'Amr ibn al-'Asi in 641, the Jewish
rights of residence were guaranteed in the terms of capitula-
tion.[23] It is hardly to be assumed that the status of the Jews
deteriorated as a result of Arabic rule. Shortly after the Arabic
conqueror founded the city of Fustat and made it the capital of
Egypt, an important Jewish community was settled there.[24]
Notwithstanding local and temporary persecutions which were

directed against Jews and Christians alike, the Jews prospered in the land and some of them attained high political office. Jewish influence and affluence waxed still higher under Fatimide rule from the tenth century onward, so that a contemporary Egyptian poet exclaimed derisively: "The Jews of our time reached the goal of their desire and came to rule. Theirs is the dignity, theirs the money! Councillors of state and princes are made from them. O people of Egypt! I give you advice: Turn Jews, for Heaven has become Jewish."[25]

Culturally, Egypt was fertile soil. It had ancient traditions of learning, and the influence of the Alexandrian schools of philosophy was felt in the time of Saadia. Thus his older contemporary, Isaac Israeli, who was hardly touched by the theories and discussions of the Mutakallimūn, the dominant school of Moslem philosophic thought, showed himself to be at home in Aristotelian and Neo-Platonic ideas.[26] The practice of medicine, in which Israeli was not the only Jew of his country to gain fame,[27] was always associated with general culture as well as Hebrew learning. While it is regrettable then that we have no concrete factual information about Saadia's cultural background, we are safe in assuming that his strong philosophic propensities were awakened in him natively in his own country.

In the sphere of Jewish learning, Egypt was tributary both to Babylon and Palestine. Early under Arabic rule, Babylonian Jews settled in Egypt and together with some native Jews established Babylonian synagogues, or communities, which maintained close relations with the academies of Sura and Pumbeditha.[28] Simultaneously there grew up Palestine synagogues and congregations in the country whose ties were linked with the Holy Land and the academy in Jerusalem.[29] The loyalties of these 'denominational' groups were not necessarily exclusive, but, undoubtedly, rivalry existed between them as both spiritual centers made their appeals to them for primacy and allegiance.[30] The question naturally arises: which center exerted the greater influence upon Egypt's educated classes? More intriguing still, did Saadia in his youth belong to the "Palestinians" or the "Babylonians"? And if in his community there was no such demarcation, the question still remains: did Babylon or Palestine wield the greater influence upon his intellectual and spiritual development?

These questions hardly admit of a categorical reply, but we cannot stray far in following clues suggested by various pertinent considerations. While Egypt was the nearest country in North Africa en route from Babylon to the Occident, it was, of course, much closer to Palestine, with consequent greater facility in travel and communication between the two countries. Moreover, in 878, four years before Saadia was born, the whole of Syria including Palestine was invested by the militant Egyptian viceroy, Ibn Tulun, who annexed the conquered territory and made it a dependency of Egypt.[31] As a result, the geographical proximity between Palestine and the land of the Nile was reinforced by political bonds, whereas the relations with Babylon were correspondingly strained. It is difficult to believe that this situation did not have intellectual and spiritual repercussions.

As the heavy mist that covered Palestinian Jewry during the geonic centuries is lifted, it becomes increasingly evident that during that entire period, Palestine radiated with intellectual and spiritual activity. Unlike the one-sided halakic activity of the Babylonian academies, Palestine was the scene of manifold literary creativeness.[32] In Tiberias was the school of Masorites.[33] In Jerusalem and Ramleh,[34] alternately, was the seat of the academy, also styled the Sanhedrin, the supreme religious authority of the Holy Land, with a Gaon as the titular head, followed in rank by the *Ab Bet-Din* and lower members of the judicial and religious hierarchy.[35] This institution, furthermore, was not created *ad hoc* by an ambitious leader who was determined to wrest Jewish religious supremacy from

67

Babylon and to transfer it to the beloved Holy Land. On the contrary, the Palestine academy was hoary with age and co-existent with the Babylonian gaonate.[36] Nor did the Sanhedrin, like its sister institutions in the East, thwart literary expression in homily and poetry. In Palestine, the muse stirred the *payyetanim* to sing hymns and compose prayers and songs of praise.[37] Others, imbued with deep religious sentiment, composed or collected midrashic homilies which may be described as the poetry of religion in prose. In contrast to Babylonian Judaism, which was dominantly intellectual, Palestine Judaism was suffused with deep emotion.

The allegiance given to the heads of the Babylonian academies was chiefly authoritarian in nature. The power wielded by Palestinian leadership was derived partly from the mystic nature of the Holy Land itself. The heads of the Babylonian schools were convinced — and they succeeded in making this conviction general — that they alone possessed the traditions of the talmudic teachers in unbroken continuity. Palestine, it was claimed, suffered a fatal lapse during the Byzantine persecutions and its chain of tradition was irreparably broken.[38] Nevertheless, even the Babylonian scholars conceded that the Palestinian authorities by virtue of their association with the Holy Land had legal prerogatives which they themselves did not possess. Palestinian judges, for instance, had the right to put into practice the laws governing *kenas*, or fines, (דיני קנסות), but not so the Geonim of Babylon.[39] The right to proclaim the new moon — a cardinal function in Judaism, as the entire religious calendar was determined by it — was the sole prerogative of Palestine till the appearance of Saadia on the Babylonian scene.[40] As late as 835, a proud exilarch declared in clear, unmistakable terms, that in order to preserve unity in Israel, it was the invariable custom of the Babylonian authorities to accept the calendar as it was ordained in Palestine. "It must be so," he declared, "in order that the ranks of Israel shall not be disrupted," and so likewise in that year, he concluded: "I, the heads of the academies, the scholars, and all Israel rely on the calendar which has been dispatched (from) before the scholars of Palestine."[41]

Waving aside formal considerations, the hearts of the Jews in the Diaspora were drawn to Palestine with mystic chords of love and reverence, and they could not but be deeply affected by the spiritual currents that flowed from that land. No sooner were the gates of Jerusalem thrown open to the Jews by the ruling Arabs, when pilgrims and visitors from the East and the West flocked to the Holy City to worship and to pay divine homage within the sacred precincts from which they had been shut out by the pagan Romans and their Christian successors.[42] Many visitors remained as permanent settlers. Among them were ascetics, "Mourners of Zion," who spent their days in fasting and lamenting over the destruction of the Temple and in praying for the coming of the Messiah and the promised salvation.[43] This was not the temper of the majority, who regarded them as idle dreamers.[44] But the love of Zion and the hope of its full restoration were a common bond that united all Jewish hearts within the land and outside its borders.

Throngs of Jewish pilgrims from all over the world, including, of course, the populous communities of Babylon and Egypt gathered in Jerusalem during the Succot festival for the solemn procession to the Mount of Olives on Hoshanah Rabbah.[45] These processions attracted the attention of the Arabs[46] and were viewed enviously by the Karaites.[47] There on Mount Olive under the presidency of the Gaon, solemn assemblies were held. The Gaon, surrounded by his official retinue, addressed the assemblage. He used these opportunities to exhort distant communities and to communicate to them points of law and religious guidance. Public proclamations of wide concern were broadcast on these occasions. During these sessions, the religious calendar was announced, usually by the Gaon himself.[48] The

Babylonian Geonim, too, were granted the courtesy of having their messages relayed to the assembled hosts. Bans of excommunication emanating from the authorities in Babylon were publicly proclaimed on the Mount in Jerusalem.[49] The Mount of Olives was the sounding-board of world Jewry.

When Jews in far-off lands, sore of heart and deeply troubled about their fate, turned to the supreme heads of world Jewry for light in their perplexity, the Gaon in Jerusalem appeared at times to take precedence over the heads of Babylonian Judaism. Thus, in the tenth century, the people in the Rhine country, it seems, were agitated by a rumor concerning the coming advent of the Messiah.[50] On this burning question it was to the scholars of Palestine to whom an inquiry was sent by "the people of the Rhine" (אנשי רינוס).[51] In the fascinating Khazar correspondence, when the Khagan Joseph wrote earnestly to Hasdai ibn Shaprut about the time of the coming of the Messiah, Jerusalem preceded Babylon as he wrote: "Our eyes are directed to the Lord our God and to the sages of Israel in the academy of Jerusalem and to the academy in Babylon, while we are far from Zion."[52]

We must bear this general picture in mind if we are to understand the influence of Palestine upon Egypt and, particularly, upon Saadia's development. Without concrete data as posts to guide us, we cannot help but feel the strong tide of Palestine events in the Nile country. Communication between the two adjacent countries, which were also politically linked together, was naturally carried on frequently and with great facility. To the Egyptian capital at Fustat, emissaries from Palestine would come to plead the cause of their people before the central authorities.[53] Between these representatives and the leaders of Egyptian Jewry who sponsored and supported them at the court were forged many spiritual links. We can well picture the warm reception these Palestine personages received on their visits to the synagogues and the schools of the

country, and whenever they lectured, how rapturously their
audiences listened to the men who carried tidings of the beloved
and holy land. In addition, we must picture the pilgrims to
and from Zion as they could be seen on the ancient highway
from the land of the Pharaohs to the city of Jerusalem. They
were indeed spiritual intermediators, as they returned to their
homes laden with religious treasures of Palestine: newly composed prayers and poems; interesting parchments of Hebrew
writing drawn with vowel-points by a scribe in Tiberias;
Massorah charts and Bible scrolls in which the rules of the
Massorah were meticulously observed; warm picturesque homilies that comforted and soothed the troubled heart, and sections
of the Mishna and the Talmud in the Jerusalem rendition.[54]
With these gifts, they also brought a novel appreciation of the
Hebrew language, its diction, its grammar and the classic
beauty of its style.

The Palestine synagogues founded in Egypt nurtured these
spiritual values, and Saadia's broad program of studies reflected
the intensive Palestinian influence upon him.[55] His pioneer
work in the science of the Hebrew language, the early interest
he manifested in the art of versification, his lifelong occupation
with the liturgy which he enriched with so many of his own
compositions, his profound studies as translator and commentator of the Bible, all these activities place him in the ranks of
Palestinian scholarship. That he was master of the Babylonian
Talmud and its related subjects does not affect this character-
ization. It may be accepted as axiomatic that the Babylonian
Talmud had primacy in Egypt even among the so-called
Palestinian communities. In the period under consideration,
the importance of the study of the Babylonian Talmud was
recognized in Palestine itself. But it is significant that Saadia
was the first Gaon of Babylon who also knew and quoted the
Jerusalem Talmud.[56]

All the more enigmatical becomes the role of Saadia in the

crucial controversy between the authorities of Babylon and Palestine when Ben Meir, Gaon of the academy in Jerusalem, startled the Jewish world by a vigorous, militant reassertion of the right of the Palestine leadership to announce the new moon days and to arrange the dates of the religious holidays, thereby determining the religious calendar of the Jewish people. [57] We are not concerned here with the calendrical minutiae upon which the controversy hinged. The simple historical fact is that in the summer of 921 CE, Ben Meir announced a three year calendar which was at variance with the calculation of the Babylonian authorities. He took this position on the ground that the Babylonian scholars erred in their calculation by failing to take into consideration a differential of thirty-five seconds [58] and, most important of all, that the sole authority to declare the new moon and to fix the calendar was vested in the spiritual leadership of the Land of Israel. [59]

In deliberate defiance of the Exilarch and the Geonim of Sura and Pumbeditha, he maintained this stand and appealed to all the Jewish communities of the Diaspora, including those in Babylonia, to support the authority of the Holy Land on this sacred issue. A sorely perplexing situation confronted the Jewish people. Were they to begin the observance of Passover in the spring of 922 on Sunday or Tuesday? Were they to usher in the New Year in the autumn on a Tuesday or Thursday? And again in the spring of 923 was Passover to commence on Thursday or Saturday? And was the New Year following to fall on Saturday or Monday? Of course, all the other holidays were thrown into similar confusion.

These questions deeply stirred the religious conscience of the people. Whichever side erred would be guilty in the course of time of eating leavened bread on Passover, and eating, drinking and working on the Day of Atonement. Dissension was rife and communities were torn asunder. Ben Meir made a profound impression everywhere, even in Babylon. Undeterred by the

storm he had aroused, Ben Meir followed up his informal
announcement by an official proclamation, probably on the
Mount of Olives at the annual pilgrimage on Hoshanah Rabbah,
in the year 921. The danger of a serious rift was grave. It
would appear that for a year or more communities actually
split on this issue, and days which were observed as solemn and
holy by one party were spurned as mere working days by
members of the opposition. The unity of Israel was seriously
disrupted.[60]

In 835, when a similar situation threatened, we have seen
that the leaders of Babylonian Judaism — the Exilarch, the
Geonim and the official members of the two academies — fore-
stalled the danger by acknowledging the unquestioned supremacy of Palestine in the vital function of fixing the calendar.[61]
But the temper of the Babylonian authorities had changed
drastically. They now refused to regard themselves as sub-
servient to Palestine, and considering themselves more expert
in the rules of the calendar than Ben Meir, they rejected his
novel calculations. Had these leaders been left to their own
resources, it is doubtful what the outcome might have been.
David ben Zaccai, the Exilarch, was a man of vigorous spirit
but altogether too quarrelsome and too frequently at logger-
heads with his own spiritual leaders to inspire a large religious
following. The Sura academy was at a low ebb, while the rival
school at Pumbeditha had been weakened by a protracted feud
with the Exilarch.[62] No one in official position in Babylon was
a match for Ben Meir of noble lineage, redoubtable in fighting
skill, possessed of ancient Palestinian traditions and determined
to restore the Holy City as the spiritual capital of Judaism.
There was only one man that could meet the challenge of the
hour and he was Saadia of Fayyum of the land of Egypt.

Saadia was a wandering scholar in the West when the
rumor of Ben Meir's agitation reached him at Aleppo, in Syria.
He was then without official position or responsibility. It is

73

not even clear by what means he supported himself during his long journeys. But he was already a man of fame, whose name and reputation were known in every important Jewish center, and his word carried great weight everywhere. The news of Ben Meir's proposal struck him violently and he reacted at once and with characteristic vigor. On his own initiative, he dispatched one letter after another to Ben Meir defending the correctness of the established calendar and warning him of the consequences of his attempted innovations. Ben Meir's reply was the official promulgation of the new calendar, presumably on the Mount of Olives. By that time, Saadia returned or was recalled to Bagdad, the official seat of the exilarchate, where he associated himself with the Exilarch and the Geonim of Babylon in the campaign to defeat Ben Meir and to thwart his far-reaching designs. Saadia bore the brunt of the fight which was bitter and by no means one-sided. As happens all too often in religious controversies when intellect and passion are mixed, the discussions frequently dropped to the level of personal recriminations. But the details of the controversy do not concern us here. In the end, Saadia defeated his opponent overwhelmingly. Unity of religion was restored, but with it vanished for the time being the dream of Palestine ascendancy. For this triumph, Saadia was rewarded by election to the gaonate several years later, in 928.

One may well wonder in view of Saadia's strong sensitivity to Palestinian spiritual influences, what impelled him to act as the protagonist of Babylon against Palestine. Was his attitude dictated solely by legal considerations? His predecessors in the gaonate being unfamiliar with the Jerusalem Talmud and the Palestinian traditions were only too prone to denounce the religious practices that prevailed in the Holy Land whenever these differed from Babylonian custom. Their disapproval was couched at times in harsh language or was based more temperately on the assumption that the persecutions which were

74

visited upon Palestinian Jewry during the Byzantine rule had created religious confusion and bred erroneous laws and practices.[63] But with his more intimate knowledge of the Palestinian Talmud and his deeper understanding of the sources of Palestine halaka, Saadia could not in fairness have identified himself with the sweeping deprecating attitude toward matters Palestinian.

In the last analysis, the question at issue — the time limit for the appearance of the new moon if that day was to be declared *Rosh Hodesh* — rested not so much on law as on tradition. It is hardly to be credited that Ben Meir invented the basis on which he founded his calculation. Rather is it to be assumed that he was acting according to an old Palestine tradition.[64] If that be so, would one not expect Saadia — if not the official heads of Babylonian Judaism — to respect a Palestine tradition at least in that one phase of Judaism which from time immemorial was peculiarly the domain of the Holy Land?

Saadia's enigmatical attitude toward the Palestine of his day is also curiously illustrated in a liturgical ruling excising the passage אור חדש — "Oh cause a new light to shine upon Zion and may we all soon be worthy of its brightness" — from the end of the first benediction preceding the *Shema*.[65] This beautiful passage and the prayer for the future redemption, which was inserted in the *Geulah* prayer before the *Amidah*,[66] were interpolated in Palestine by poets whose prayers were prompted by emotion rather than logic.[67] Needless to say, Saadia's attitude had nothing in common with the opposition of present-day Reform Judaism to the inclusion of prayers for Zion in the prayer book. Saadia omitted only these specific passages, and solely on the ground that they did not fit the context of the benedictions of which they were a part; for they were prayers for the future whereas the theme of the benedictions was praise unto God for past and existent blessings. With regard to the אור חדש prayer, in particular, he felt that it injected a foreign theme into the benediction, the one speaking of light in a figurative sense and the other referring to the light of the sun. Nevertheless, it does give one pause for thought that Saadia should have been so insistent on the omission of this prayer as actually to agitate for its excision when he was Gaon in Sura. [68] His efforts were in vain as his "logic" carried no conviction in Sura nor even later in the rival academy under Sherira and Hai, who were legalists par excellence. [69] It may also be pointed out that in his didactic poem on the 613 precepts of the Law he indicates cryptically that the commandment, "And ye shall reverence my sanctuary" (Lev. 19.30), applies only to the Temple of the future restoration, not to the ruined site of the present. [70]

All these circumstances point in one direction. Saadia lacked warmth and poetic sentiment in his attitude to the Palestine of his day. His liturgical compositions in some instances have as their theme the vanished glory of the ancient land and the Messianic hope of Israel's restoration to the ancestral home, but they are singularly devoid of the glow and fervor of a true lover of Zion. What was the genesis of this apparent spiritual detachment and when did it take place?

Early in life, he was drawn to Palestine. He made his home there for a number of years after he left or fled from his native country. He was a mature, brilliant scholar even then and his reputation must have preceded him on his arrival in Palestine. No doubt, he met the leaders of the community and took a deep interest in the schools of Tiberias, Ramleh and Jerusalem. He had excellent opportunity to judge the caliber of the spiritual and intellectual leaders of the country. Did his close contact with them create disillusionment or was he perhaps rebuffed in the official academic circles? Ben Meir and he were much of the same temperament, proud, independent and fearless. Did they meet and clash in Palestine years before they locked in combat on the major issue of their time?

In the absence of documentary evidence, these inferences must remain in the nebulous realm of surmise. However we interpret the subconscious motives, this much is clear: Saadia was convinced that supreme religious authority belonged to the academies in Babylon; that the very fate of Judaism was linked with their traditions and leadership, and that Ben Meir's grandiose challenge had to be resisted as a threat to the unity of Israel. To one who fought all his life against the inroads of Karaism, the depredations of which were most evident in Egypt and in Palestine, the prevention of a new rift in Judaism must have appeared more urgent and primary than any romantic claims set up in the name of the Holy Land.

Was this realistic policy or was it the unimaginative attitude of a philosopher who was governed by his head rather than his heart? History cannot be appealed to as an oracle. Within a century the glory definitely departed from Babylonian Judaism. Another half century later, Jewish life in Palestine, too, came to an abrupt and cruel end with the advent of the first Crusade. The destiny of Judaism for a thousand years to come lay no longer in the East but in the West, in the European settlements which were to Asia what America is to the world today. But whereas Babylon never witnessed the miracle of resurrection, Palestine has experienced more than one revival. After the throes of the Spanish expulsion in 1492, the mother country awoke to new life; a great spiritual center arose on the ancient sites; and the mystic spirit of Israel found reincarnation in the souls of Cordovero, Luria and Hayyim Vital. And now, too, a thousand years after the death of Saadia, amidst the greatest ruin that has been visited upon the Jews since the destruction of the Temple, Palestine is again the scene of a wondrous spiritual and intellectual awakening — a living symbol of the indestructible soul of the Jewish people.

NOTES

[1] The project was planned and inaugurated under the direction of J. Derenbourg and was continued after his death by Hartwig Derenbourg and M. Lambert. The following volumes were published: Vol. I, *Version Arabe du Pentateuque* . . . par J. Derenbourg; Vol. III, *Version Arabe d'Isaïe* . . . par J. Derenbourg et H. Derenbourg; Vol. V, *Version Arabe du Livre de Job* . . . par W. Bacher; Vol. VI, *Version Arabe des Proverbes* . . . par J. Derenbourg et Mayer Lambert; Vol. IX, *Traité des Successions* . . . par Joël Müller.

[2] XI, 423–25.

[3] *Ibid.* See H. Malter, *Life and Works of Saadia Gaon*, Phila., 1921, 421 ff.

[4] *Ibid.*

[5] See below, pp. 294 ff.

[6] *Siddur R. Saadja Gaon, Kitāb 'Gāmi as-salawāt Wat-Tasābīh*, edited by I. Davidson, S. Assaf, B. I. Joel, Jerusalem, 1941.

[7] For the literature on the birthplace and the form of the name of Saadia, see Malter, *op. cit.*, notes 1–4.

[8] Cf. L. Ginzberg, *Geonica*, I, 1–71.

[9] Thus Sherira wrote of Saadia: ולא מבני רבותינו של הישיבה היה אלא ממצרים וידעי בפיומי, Neubauer, *MJC*, I, 40.

[10] Harkavy, *Zikron*, V, 228–30; cf. Bornstein, מחלקת רב סעדיה גאון ובן מאיר, Warsaw, 1904, 90, n. 5; Schechter, *Saadyana*, 20, n. 3.

[11] Harkavy, *Zikron*, V, 229. On Saadia's ancestry, see Schechter, *Saadyana*, 65, 66, 68, 73; *JQR*, N. S., IX, 153–60; Malter, 28, n. 11.

[12] Berliner, פליטת סופרים, Mayence, 1872, 30, n. 8; Malter, 297–98.

[13] Saadia's predilection for arithmetical formulae is well-known; cf. Malter, 202, n. 473.

[14] J. Müller, *Oeuvres complètes*, IX, Introduction, viii–ix; Malter, 164, n. 374.

[15] *Ibid.*

[16] Harkavy, *Zikron*, V, 158; Ginzberg, *Geonica*, I, 6, n. 1.

[17] Harkavy, *op. cit.*, 158, ll. 7–9: ותוסיף האומה תודה לאדוניה [לה'] על [לה'] אשר לא יעזבנה ריקם בכל דור דור מאיש שבו חכמה להאיר לה.

[18] *Ibid.*, ll. 12–13: וכמו שהיו הנביאים בזמנם מנהיגים אותה כן יוליכוה הצדיקים בדורותיהם.

[19] David Slucki, ed., *Emunot ve-De'ot*, 3. The translation follows Malter, 200.

[20] Harkavy, *Zikron*, V, 232.

[21] Cf. Müller, *Oeuvres complètes*, IX, Introduction, *passim*; Ginzberg, *Geonica*, I, 162–67; Malter, 157–67.

[22] תשובות הגאונים, ed. Musafia, Lyck, 1864, no. 99; Ginzberg, *Geonica*, I, 201.

[23] Lane-Poole, *History of Egypt in the Middle Ages*, second edition, 11; Jacob Mann, *The Jews in Egypt and in Palestine under the Fatimids*, I, 13.

[24] Cf. *JQR*, XVII, 426–30, where Abû 'Ali Ḥasan appears as the Head of the Congregation of Fustat in a document dated 750 CE.

[25] Cited by Mann, *op. cit.*, I, 16–17, from Kremer, *Culturgeschichte des Orients*, I, 188; cf. *Heb. Bibliog.*, XVII, 68–69.

[26] Cf. I. Husik, *A History of Mediaeval Jewish Philosophy*, 1–16.

[27] Mann, I, 14, 15, 18.

[28] Cf. *JQR*, XVII, 426–30; XVIII, 11, 564; XIX, 460; also *JQR*, N. S., VII, 477 ff.; VIII, 343 ff.

[29] Cf. Schechter, *Saadyana*, 113; *JQR*, XVIII, 1–39, 564; XIX, 460; *JQR*, N. S., VII, 477; *REJ*, XLVIII, 157–60, LV, 58; cf. Mann, I, 94 ff.; II, 97 ff.; Ginzberg, *Geonica*, I, 122, n. 1.

[30] See Schechter, *Saadyana*, 113: כאשר המקום הזה על שמי יהיה המקום האחר על שמו . . . בשם בני בבל וזה בשם בני ארץ יש' האמנם יבקש לעקור שם ישיבת ארץ יש' מארץ מצרים לבלתי היות לה שם . . .

[31] Lane-Poole, *op. cit.*, 158 ff.; Mann, I, 16.

[32] Cf. Ginzberg, *Geonica*, I, 72–73, 93, 121–22; A. Z. Rabinowitz, תולדות היהודים בא"י, Jaffa, 1921, 13–20.

[33] Cf. Mann, II, 43 ff.

[34] Mann suggested that Ramleh was chosen as the seat of the academy in place of Jerusalem because of the dominance of the Karaites in the Holy City. As the more flourishing commercial city, Ramleh also possessed greater advantages than Jerusalem: Mann, I, 65; cf. *ibid.*, 42.

[35] Bornstein, *op. cit.*, 62–63; *REJ*, LVII, 50; Mann, I, 54, n. 2, 65.

[36] See Marx, *JQR*, N. S., I, 68–69; Bacher, *MGWJ*, XLIII, 345–60; Mann, I, 54, n. 2, 55, n. 1, 57–59. Poznanski's earlier views regarding the origin of the gaonate in Palestine (*Babyl. Geonim im nachgäonischen Zeitalter*, 82) is no longer tenable. Nor is it to be assumed with Klein (תולדות הישוב היהודי בא"י, 88) that the Palestinian gaonate dates from the middle of the ninth century when the academy was transferred from Tiberias to Jerusalem.

[37] Cf. Elbogen, *Der jüdische Gottesdienst*, 281–82; Eppenstein, *MGWJ*, LII, 465–66. The contrasting attitudes toward *piyyut* in Palestine and Babylon and, within Babylon, between the academies of Sura and Pumbeditha, is a frequently recurrent theme in Professor Ginzberg's brilliant geonic studies. See especially *Ginze Schechter*, II, 508–27.

[38] Cf. the letter of Sherira Gaon in Neubauer, *MJC*, I, 23: ונפיש שמדא בא"י ואימעיטא הוראה תמן טובא; also S. Assaf, תשובות הגאונים מהגניזה, no. 211. Highly important is the text of פרקוי בן בבוי, *Ginze Schechter*, II, 551–52; *Tarbiz*, II, 383 f., 397–98; *Pardes*, ed. Constantinople, 56b; Ginzberg, *Geonica*, II, 50–51; *JQR*, N. S., VII, 437; see Ginzberg, *A Commentary on the Palestinian Talmud*, I, Hebrew Introduction, 89 ff.; A. Aptowitzer, מחקרים בספרות הגאונים, Jerusalem, 1941, 13 ff.

[39] Cf. *Pardes*, 24d: והכי אמר רב כהן צדק ז"ל אם טוען ואמר כיון שאין דנין דיני קנסות בחוץ לארץ שלח עמי בעל דיני לארץ ישראל שם דנין דיני קנסות משלחין אותו עמו. See also שערי צדק nos. 7, 13; Mann, *JQR*, N. S., X, 357–58.

[40] Bornstein, מחלקת רב סעדיה גאון ובן מאיר, 8 f.; cf. *JQR*, XIV, 249, 472; *ibid.*, N. S., V, 553; Schechter, *Saadyana*, 131; Poznanski, *JQR*, X, 152–60; Epstein, *REJ*, XLII, 173–210; XLIV, 230–36; *Ha-Goren*, V, 118–42.

[41] Mann, I, 52–54; II, 41–42.

[42] *Ibid.*, I, 45–49; cf. Klein, *op. cit.*, 72 ff.

[43] See Chronicle of Ahimaaz in Neubauer, *MJC*, II, 113, 128; *Pesikta*, ed. Friedmann, 158b; Mann, I, 47–49; Klein, *op. cit.*, 91 ff.

[44] To be inferred from the passage in *Pesikta, l. c.*: אלו אבילי ציון שהשפילו את רוחם ושמעו את חרפתם ולא החזיקו טובה לעצמם.

[45] Cf. Neubauer, *MJC*, I, 79; Epstein, *REJ*, XLII, 18; Büchler, *REJ*, XLIV, 241 f.; Poznanski, *REJ*, XLVIII, 153, n. 2; Krauss, *Jahrbuch für jüdische Geschichte u. Literatur*, 1919, 38 ff.; Mann, *Texts and Studies*, I, 310–11, 315–16. The Jerusalem community was dependent economically on the revenue from Jewish pilgrims in the same manner that Paris in recent times looked to the tourist trade as an essential aid to prosperity. Cf. the Genizah letter published by Cowley, *JQR*, XIX, 107–08: ולא נכחד ממך יקירנו כי בשנה הזאת היו החוגגים מעט במספר ואשר קבצוהו לא היה בו כדי העונש אשר עלינו בכל שנה והוצרכנו ללוות מה שנשאר ולא די לנו העונש אשר אנו שוקלים בכל שנה עד אשר היכנו צורנו במכת הרעב לא נמצא דבר בכל ארץ פלשתים והעניים רבים ואנו פוחדים מן המס.

[46] The Arab historian, Albiruni (c. 1000), mentions these processions in his *Chronology of Ancient Nations*, translated by Sachau, London, 1879, 270; cited by Marx, *JQR*, N. S., I, 67, n. 14.

[47] See Abraham ibn Daud, in Neubauer, *MJC*, I, 79: וכשהיו ישראל חוגגים את חג הסכות בהר הזיתים היו חונים בהר מחנות מחנות אוהבים אלו את אלו ומברכין אלו את אלו. והמינים חונים נגדם כשני חשיפי עזים ...

[48] Cf. Harkavy, V, 215; Mann, *Texts and Studies*, I, 316; see *ibid.*, n. 12; see Marx, *JQR*, N. S., I, 63 ff.

[49] Cf. Harkavy, V, 215.

[50] D. Kaufmann, *Gesam. Schrift.*, II, 201.

[51] Perles in *Graetz Jubelschrift*, 31 f.; הצפירה, XXIV, 543–49: Büchler, *REJ*, XLIV, 237 ff.; Marx, *JQR*, N. S., I, 75 ff.; S. Klein, *op. cit.*, 89 f.; Mann, I, 64; cf. *Pardes*, ed. Ehrenreich, 216 f.: ר' משולם בר' משה שאל את פי אריות יושבי ירושלים עיר הקדש.

[52] ואנחנו עינינו אל ה' אלהינו ואל חכמי ישראל הישיבה שבירושלים ואל הישיבה שבבבל ואנו רחוקים מציון: end of letter. The correspondence between Hasdai ibn Shaprut and the Khagan Joseph was originally published by Isaac Akrish, קול מבשר, Constantinople, 1577, and has been frequently republished independently or as an introduction to the *Kuzari*.

[53] Mann, I, 16.

[54] All these literary gifts of Palestine to Egyptian Jewry are richly illustrated in the remains of the Cairo Genizah.

[55] Ginzberg, *A Commentary on the Palestinian Talmud*, I, Hebrew Introduction, 100 f.; Malter, 43 ff.

[56] Ginzberg, *loc. cit.*, 99 f. On the moot question whether the earlier Babylonian Geonim — Rab Amram Gaon, in particular — used the Palestinian Talmud, see Poznanski's monograph, הגאונים והירושלמי, in his ענינים שונים הנוגעים לתקופת הגאונים, Warsaw, 1909; also Ginzberg, *Geonica*, I, 77, n. 2; Aptowitzer, *op. cit.*, 10 ff.

[57] Bornstein, מחלקת רב סעדיה גאון ובן מאיר, Warsaw, 1904; Malter, 69–88, 351–53, 409–19; *JQR*, N. S., III, 500–09.

[58] Cf. A. Epstein, *Ha-Goren*, V, 125 ff.

[59] The usurpation of this right by the Babylonian authorities during the Amoraic period against the protest of Palestinian Jewry is traced by Bornstein, *op. cit.*, 10; also Poznanski, *JQR*, X, 158; Epstein, *Ha-Goren*, V, 120 f.

[60] For the narrative account, see Malter, 69–88, who cites the literature; see also the appendix, 409–19, where he analyzes the documents bearing on the Ben Meir controversy; see Bornstein, *op. cit.*, 7 f.

[61] See above, p. 68.

[62] See Letter of Sherira Gaon, Neubauer, *MJC*, I, 40. As to the conflict between Sherira's version and the account of Nathan ha-Babli, see Graetz, *Geschichte*, V, 391–94; Ginzberg, *Geonica*, I, 62–66.

[63] See above, n. 38.

[64] Epstein, *Ha-Goren*, V, 133.

[65] *Siddur R. Saadja Gaon*, Jerusalem, 1941, 37, note to line 6; Lewin, *Ginze Kedem*, I, 5–6.

[66] Cf. Ginzberg, *Geonica*, II, 91; Lewin, *Ginze Kedem*, I, 6.

[67] Elbogen, *Der jüdische Gottesdienst*, 18–20.

[68] *Seder Rab Amram ha-Shalem*, Jerusalem, 1912, I, 96b: והכי אמר רב הלכך מאן דמדכיר ליה שפיר ,also ;סעדיה גאון ז"ל מי שחותם אור חדש הוא תועה דמי לשתוקיה. See also note following.

[69] Lewin, *Ginze Kedem*, I, 6: ומינהאנא בי מדראשי קביעי דנהרדעא ודסורא עדיין למימר ואור חדש ואע"פ דרב סעדיה ז"ל הוה ליה ראש מתיבתא בסורא לא קבילו מניה אפילו בחייה ולא סליקו למימר ואור חדש ועדיין הוו אמרין ליה.

[70] *Siddur R. Saadja Gaon*, 157, l. 5, note; cf. J. F. Perl, לרס"ג ספר המצוות. I, 220.

The *Shebet Yehudah* and Sixteenth Century Historiography

THE *Shebet Yehudah* is an historical classic with many facets. In composition it is a kind of historical anthology, written in clear, lucid, felicitous Hebrew, occasionally sharpened by rapier-like insight and wit. Its contents consist of a series of unrelated narratives drawn allegedly from many varied sources — Hebrew, Arabic, Spanish and Latin.[1] A fair proportion of the narratives are stories of living contemporaries and of the author's personal experiences, he himself having lived through the terrors of the Expulsion and the Inquisition.[2] The character of the stories related in the book varies greatly. Some of the items consist of a few obscure lines; others are well-rounded narratives constructed with consummate literary skill. Some of the stories are clearly historical records of authentic validity; others appear in confused order or are otherwise derived uncritically from sources which blend history with legend; still others are patently historical fiction, the original creations of the chief author, Solomon ibn Verga.

A critical study of the work obviously poses many problems. What sources did the author command? Were they the well-known Hebrew works of Josippon, Abraham ibn Daud's chronicle, Abravanel's historical chapters and the like; or did they also include unknown Hebrew writings and, in addition, a wide range of non-Jewish chronicles as claimed by the author without direct citation of names? These and many other questions relating to sources and methodology can be answered only by a detailed examination of individual chapters or parts comprising the work.

Published in *Louis Ginzberg Jubilee Volume*, New York 1945.

Such studies have appeared from time to time. Wiener who translated the *Shebet Yehudah* into German promised in vain a supplementary volume dealing with these problems, which never appeared. Fragmentary studies were made by Graetz in various excursuses.[3] More light was shed by Isidore Loeb in a series of brilliant studies.[4] The latest and most comprehensive study is that of Yitzhak (Fritz) Baer, who with characteristic thoroughness subjected the *Shebet Yehudah* to microscopic examination with very interesting and useful results.[5] He has laid the foundation for all future studies of this fascinating historical work.

These basically important studies illuminate many passages which otherwise would remain obscure. They trace many individual narratives to the original sources. They throw light on the author's control and range of historic data. But they leave other fundamental questions unanswered. What was the author's principle of selectivity? Within the known range of his historic material why were so many comparatively irrelevant and insignificant selections included and others far more important omitted? What was the thread of continuity followed by this admittedly skillful writer inasmuch as he clearly did not pursue chronological sequence in these narratives? Furthermore, if his aim was primarily to write a purely historical work, it is difficult to see why an historian so gifted and critical as he often shows himself to be should also include material totally unworthy of his critical insight. These difficulties can be resolved only by an over-all consideration of the motive which prompted the writing of the *Shebet Yehudah* and in general inspired the genesis of Jewish historiography in the sixteenth century. The present paper is intended to elucidate this aspect of the *Shebet Yehudah* as part of a new historical manifestation in Jewish life during the sixteenth century.

For Jewish historiography presents a startling lacuna. The art of historic writing among the Jews came to a sudden and abrupt end with the destruction of the Jewish state in Palestine.

In the annals of history it is difficult to find a parallel phenomenon. The Jews had been one of the earliest peoples to develop
historic consciousness and with it the art of historic composition.
The historical books of the Bible antedate the earliest writings
of the classic Greek historians. The biblical books furthermore
represent an advanced state in the evolution of historiography,
for they aim to present not merely a record of past events but
to construct a philosophy of history which in turn is based on
records of earlier chronicles which are alluded to by title. This
historic art was maintained on a high level throughout the
prophetic period and was continued through the Second Commonwealth in the writings of the Apocrypha, notably in the
books of the Maccabees, and reached the final climax in the
monumental works of Josephus.

Thereafter, coinciding with the destruction of the national
state, all interest in history was abandoned. In the national
shipwreck, every secular literary interest was submerged. Even
the comparatively recent records of Maccabean heroism and
the tragic glory of the fatal war against the Romans were
deliberately cast overboard. Only the historical record of the
Bible was preserved for purely religious ends as part of the
religious consciousness. The living historic motivation was gone
from the national consciousness. So sudden was the transformation that it would appear figuratively as if a surgeon had cut
the historic nerve in the national brain.

During the succeeding millennium and a half, such few
writings as may even remotely be described as historical are
compositions without claim to style or literary merit and are
completely devoid of historical motivation. With the sole
exception of *Josippon*, all the medieval Hebrew chronicles were
written for purposes other than that of the annalist of history.
The earliest Hebrew chronicle, the *Seder Olam*, dating back to
the second century, aimed to establish chronological order in the
biblical record. It is a tannaitic composition applying arbitrary

exegetical principles to chronology. It obviously represents an attempt to establish a semblance of order even by forced logic in the only world which still had meaning for the dispossessed people, the vanished world of the Bible. Occasionally a family chronicle appears such as the obscure *Seder Olam Zuta*, whose motive was partisan and dynastic, to bolster the claim of one branch of the exilarchate family; or it is a work like the more literary *Chronicle of Ahimaaz*, a fanciful tale of the wonder-working powers of some family ancestors. More serious and fertile are the literary chronicles that trace the order of rabbinic succession. They were obviously written to serve specific religious ends. It was necessary for halakic reasons to determine the proper sequence of the rabbinic teachers, as the earlier authorities took precedence over the subsequent successors. Moreover, as rabbinic Judaism staked its validity on the existence of a continuous, unbroken oral tradition, it was essential to substantiate this difficult claim through annals tracing the order of spiritual succession. The *Seder Tannaim ve-Amoraim* (ninth century) served both these ends. Stronger defensive literature, however, became critically necessary whenever Judaism was threatened by anti-rabbinical movements which arose periodically and gathered dangerous momentum in Karaism. For the leaders of Karaism especially were learned and aggressive, and concentrated their attack upon the very foundation of rabbinism, the Oral Law, by seeking to demolish its fundamental claim to a continuous, unbroken oral tradition.

To meet this challenge, Sherira composed his famous Letter, *Iggeret Rab Sherira Gaon*, at the end of the tenth century, and Abraham ibn Daud followed in a more militant vein with his *Sefer ha-Kabbalah*. A pattern was thus set, and some of the later rabbis, especially in the Provence, conventionally prefaced their halakic works with a listing of rabbinic authors to bring the record down to their own time. None of these works betrays any objective historic interest. The very element of

85

causal connection which is the beginning of the narrator's art and around which history is constructed is totally absent. Intellectual interest was centered almost exclusively in halakah, exegesis and philosophy, no branch of which was hospitable to history. Even the famed astronomer and mathematician, the Spaniard Abraham ibn Zacuto, writing at the end of the fifteenth and at the beginning of the sixteenth century was moved to apologize for his truly remarkable and erudite chronicle, *Sefer Yuhasin*, prefacing his work with the curious explanation that it was the loss of his library during the Expulsion that led him to undertake what by implication was unworthy of a serious man's efforts. Not content with this explanation alone, he offers as a secondary apology that the righteous who constitute his theme are comparable to the stars, hence the analogy with astronomy, which is a worthy science. Furthermore, he hoped that his work would find merit because of the numerous halakic and exegetical excursuses with which he embroidered his book, which would otherwise have been a mere chronicle![6]

It is against this background that one must view the sudden rise of Jewish historiography in the sixteenth century and find the underlying motif of the *Shebet Yehudah*. Within a period of two decades, about the middle of the century, three books of a truly historical nature made their appearace: two in Hebrew, the *Shebet Yehudah* and Joseph ha-Kohen's *Emek ha-Bakah*; and one in Portuguese, *Consolaçam as tribulaçoens de Israel*, by Samuel Usque. To these may be added a series of other Hebrew works extant in full or in part dealing with Jewish history on the broader background of general history: Elijah Capsali's histories of Venice and of the Turkish Empire, written during the first quarter of the sixteenth century; Joseph ha-Kohen's *History of the Kings of France and Turkey* which followed within a decade; also his curious writings on the discoveries in the New World; and at the end of the century, David Gans' *Zemah David*. In a distinct and far superior category one may also cite Azariah dei Rossi's unique contribution, *Me'or 'Enayim.*

With the exception of the latter work and, in a different sense, the *Shebet Yehudah*, the histories enumerated above do not rate as historical classics; but they signalize at least an awareness on the authors' part of the value of historic knowledge, an appreciation of its importance in the life of a people, and an earnest attempt to apply the lessons of history to the problems of their time.[7] Considering the dearth of historic interest in the preceding centuries, these writings mark a veritable renaissance in the long dormant consciousness of the historic people. They reveal a profound psychological mood which stirred the Jewish world throughout the sixteenth century due to the prolonged agony following upon the Spanish expulsion of 1492.

The mood which overwhelmed the exiles from Spain and the victims of the Inquisition is mirrored in the *Shebet Yehudah*. It was not merely a mood of suffering and pain, but one far more difficult to bear, a blend of personal despair and national futility. Why were the Jews singled out for such cruel torment, the people lamented. If this was divine retribution, wherein lay their grievous guilt? Their own inner fears were echoed openly in the taunts of their enemies. The most cruel thought of all was that their suffering might be purposeless and that the Jewish people as a whole was doomed to extinction.

This mood expressed itself in many forms and had various repercussions. The aged and venerable Isaac Abravanel was impelled to preach the imminent coming of the Messiah and he boldly set the date for his appearance, as if thus dramatically to rally the faltering hopes of his people.[8] Empirical Messianism failed, but it was replaced by the more imaginative redemptive Messianic Cabala which idealized the suffering of the exiled people as the travail of the Messianic era and the imminent redemption of mankind.[9] There were those, however, who could find no refuge in mystic flights and Messianic dreams. They probed for the key to the riddle of Jewish existence in the inner recesses of Jewish historic experience. Anxiously they scanned the dim outlines of the past, the better to understand the course of the future. Thus it was deep concern with Jewish fate that led to the revival of interest in Jewish history.

Their hearts seared by the same burning flame, three contemporary writers turned historians: Samuel Usque, the Portuguese Marrano who had found temporary shelter in Ferrara, Italy; Joseph ha-Kohen, the son of a Spanish exile, who then lived in Votaggio; and Solomon ibn Verga, the principal author of *Shebet Yehudah* who also found refuge in Italy. Differing widely in temperament and in mode of expression, their works form an interrelated trilogy. Each author turning to the historic past seeks through his own medium to interpret the contemporary Jewish tragedy in a manner to instill hope and courage in the hearts of the surviving remnant. Usque, the poet, chooses as his medium a symbolic pastoral dialogue with three shepherds as the *dramatis personae*: Ycabo — the patriarch Jacob — lamenting the fate of Israel; Numeo, or Nahum, acting as the comforter; and Zicareo, or Zechariah, recalling the past, with its promise of healing redemption. Through this poetic device, Usque marshals the facts of Jewish history in the Socratic conviction — to use his own words — "that when people find themselves in trouble, they should compare the evils of the past with those of the present and they would readily find solace"; also, "as I hope and pray, this storm which till now has persecuted us and is still upon us is beginning to abate, and the longed-for dawn is about to break after this tempestuous winter night." [10]

Under the impact of Usque's *Consolaçam*, the physician Joseph ha-Kohen was inspired to write a more comprehensive history of the Jews, which as the title indicates — *Emek ha-Bakah*, The Valley of Tears — is a tearful account of Jewish suffering and persecution from the days of the destruction of the

Temple to his own time. Less naïve than the poet, he is also not so sanguine about the breaking of the dawn; but he too shared Usque's conviction that his people would be greatly strengthened in the struggle for survival by a knowledge of what Israel had successfully endured in the past.

In contrast to these contemporaries and to a surprising degree, Solomon ibn Verga viewed the problem of Jewish suffering and survival analytically and dispassionately. He too was filled with wonder and anguish at the pitiful plight of his people. He was incensed by the senseless blood libels and the varied assortment of false accusations which resulted in such bloody consequences to the helpless Jewish victims. One of his own forebears who died under the tortures of the Inquisition, Judah ibn Verga,[11] had compiled a melancholy collection of martyrs' tales and stories of mass persecutions.[12] This collection was to be the nucleus of his own work, which he supplemented with the results of his wide reading in other Hebrew and non-Hebrew sources. But his purpose was not merely to recount tales of woe, which he could have heaped mountain high. Nor did he expose the wounds of his people to arouse sympathy, or even to plead for divine compassion. He collated these stories as a scientist collects data for analytical study and cumulative evidence, by means of which it might be possible to reach rational conclusions, or at least to attain to clearer insight into the nature of the social problem.

This is the keynote to an understanding of the *Shebet Yehudah* and its author. This historical anthology is the earliest sociological study of the Jewish question. The anecdotes which are historically authentic were copied by the writer from previous sources. They provide the true historic background. But interspersed are the original stories created in the fertile imagination of Solomon ibn Verga, not as factual narratives, but as a mirror which reflects the truth under the artist's lights and shadows. Within the limits of this paper, it is impossible adequately to

89

delineate the entire train of thought of the author. What we may attempt here is to suggest the general trend of his ideas, which will be supplemented in further studies later.

With artistic effect the author blended his literary material of fact and fancy. He followed no set pattern of time or place. The artistic or emotional effect was an important element in the literary construction. Opening his book with several bleak tales of persecutions, massacres and mass conversions, which he selected from a variety of historical sources, both Jewish and non-Jewish, Ibn Verga dispels the dark atmosphere with a long narrative of a symposium on the Jewish question, in which two illustrious but fictitious characters participated: King Alfonso and his courtier and philosopher Thomas.[13] This type of literary construction is characteristic of the entire book. The theme of the symposium in all its nuances is repeated like a refrain throughout the historical collection. Thus early in the book the author lays the foundation of his literary composition. An analysis of the symposium therefore affords an insight into the nature of the *Shebet Yehudah*.

The staging of the symposium reveals Ibn Verga's conception of the political forces which determined the fate of the Spanish Jews. On the one hand the priests — not the pope who, on the contrary, appears as friend and protector[14]— play upon the cupidity and the credulity of the masses and incite them against the Jews.[15] At the other end there stands the king, wise and benevolent, who out of self-interest and a sense of justice opposes their evil machinations.[16] The philosophers and royal counselors are more vacillating; they are alternately friendly and hostile.[17] This array of conflicting political and social forces is Ibn Verga's simplified formula of the Jewish position in Europe: "As a rule the kings of Spain and France, the princes, the educated classes and the men of prominence are friendly to the Jews. Hatred of the Jews exists only in the populace who are aroused by jealousy."[18]

Thus the dialogue opens. The wise and lovable monarch consults with his sage counselors as to how best to protect his Jewish subjects from the wrath of the masses who are instigated by their bishop and threateningly demand royal action against the Jews. The immediate subject of discussion is the blood libel with which the bishop enraged his ignorant followers. The king realizes the utter stupidity of the charge. Time and again the blood libel has been proved false and baseless. Nevertheless the pressure of the priest-incited masses is well-nigh irresistible; the monarch is in danger of losing the confidence of his people. Tossed between conscience and political self-interest, he seeks the opinion of the philosopher, who by reputation is well versed in the Talmud as well as the Hebrew Scriptures. Against his own conviction, the king raises the question whether there could possibly be any basis in the Jewish religion or literature for a belief in the use of human blood in the Passover ceremonies. If so, he would order their expulsion from the country; otherwise he would stake his life to protect them, "for they are my serfs."[19]

Without waiting for the reply of the philosopher who, he rightly anticipates, would scoff at the charge, he broaches the deeper question: how to account for the continuous decline of the Jewish people since ancient times, a phenomenon which, in his opinion, cannot be explained either on rational grounds or supernaturally as divine punishment. For, argues the monarch, the Jews have certainly sinned far less grievously than other nations which prospered greatly. Moreover, the "holy site which is in Jerusalem" should not have suffered for the sins of the Jews as it is equally sacred to Jews, Mohammedans and Christians. Surely history affords ample proof that the Jews were not lacking in the four qualities necessary for the victorious life of a nation: clever resourcefulness, heroism in combat, riches, and numbers. As to resourcefulness, it is universally conceded that the Jews "are the most clever and astute of all nations."[20]

Thus the basic problem of Jewish weakness is propounded. The problem is elaborated as Thomas, the philosopher, engages the king in the dialogue, and the discussion is enlivened with the clash of the two personalities and the exchange of sallies of wit and sarcasm. Skillfully, Ibn Verga leads the discussion into bypaths with numerous digressions, anecdotes and flashes of wit, after which the chief problem emerges again and again in bolder relief: Why then have the Jews fallen so low?

Answering the question through the medium of the Christian philosopher, Ibn Verga is unsparing in the criticism of his own people as he is frank in baring the unsavory motives of their enemies. "I have never seen a man of sense hate the Jew," said Thomas. "Only the common masses hate them, one reason being that the Jew is arrogant and domineering... Acting as lords and princes, they arouse the envy of the masses, and there is no cure for hatred which springs from envy. When they first settled in this country and for many years remained poor, dressing modestly and displaying no pride of power, the blood libel was unheard of. When they gave no cause for envy, they were met with love. But now the Jew plays the aristocrat. If he has two hundred gold sueldos he decks himself and his family in silk dress which even the princes with a yearly income of many thousands would not do."

From this Thomas proceeds to the economic motive. The Jews amassed the riches of the country. Through usury and clever manipulations, they succeeded in acquiring three quarters of all the farms and estates in Castile. This issue of usury evidently displeased the king, who profited from the interest transactions, and he retorted: "True enough, but who compelled the Christian to borrow from the Jew?"

Alfonso then continued the symposium by touching off another cause for the popular antipathy, the social estrangement and resentment caused by the Jewish dietary laws, especially the refusal of Jews to drink from wine touched by gentile hands.

Here the philosopher intervened, exonerating the Jews from the charge of being antisocial and blaming the Talmudists who forced such measures upon them. A clever anecdote concerning a Jewish physician in the court of Alfonso's father puts the king in good humor and he turns to his counselor: "What then is your advice concerning the Jews, and the manner in which they can be saved from destruction among my people?"

By thus pointing the question, Ibn Verga paved the way for the rationalization of the harsh, restrictive decrees which the Spanish kings issued against the Jews. It is Thomas the philosopher who counsels the king: "My advice is that you decree that all the estates which Jews have appropriated in consequence of usury should be restored to the original owners as the judges of the land see fit; and that no Jew be allowed to wear silk garments; and that they all be required to wear a red badge in order that they may be recognized as Jews." Alfonso's expressed approval is punctuated by an incident which is skillfully introduced to illustrate the king's benevolent intentions in sanctioning those anti-Jewish measures. For a delegation appears upon the scene charging that they found a murdered body in the home of a Jew, who committed the crime for ritual reasons. The king is so outraged at the libel that he cannot trust himself and requests Thomas to address the people. As Thomas finds that logic and reproaches are unavailing, he concludes his remarks as follows: "The king is well aware what really ails you, and your grievance is justified. For these accursed Jews took your wealth and your lands. The king has already commanded that your lands and money taken from you through usury be returned to you and that Jews shall not be permitted to wear silks and your customary clothing. Be therefore content with these measures for your relief and do not disgrace yourselves by chasing after falsehoods in which you yourselves will be ensnared." Gratefully, the people bow before the king and laud his wisdom, imploring him "to drive the Jews out of his kingdom." The climax is reached when with the promise of immunity they confess that they found the corpse on the open highway and threw it into the house of the Jew to start the hue and cry of ritual murder.

It would exceed the bounds of this essay to elucidate all the issues and the sparkling witty generalizations with which the symposium abounds. Only a few significant comments will suffice. The lineal aristocracy of Spanish Jewry is freely acknowledged. The Davidic descent of the Abravanel family is defended by the philosopher and finally conceded by the king. No nation has so clear a title to noble origin as the Jews, the king admitted — neither the Romans nor Greeks, Spaniards, French nor Germans. "And how is this to be wondered at," he continued, "inasmuch as in our faith, our Savior's family is not clearly established. For Matthew attributes his paternity to Joseph, Mary's husband, and states that Joseph was of the seed of David, while according to Luke, Joseph was not of royal descent.[21] And as we believe that Joseph knew not Mary either before or after the birth of Jesus, but only the Holy Spirit, how can we ascribe his ancestry to David and say Obed begat Jesse and Jesse begat David and David begat Jesus?" Rebuked by Thomas who explained that only Mary's origin is ascribed to David,[22] while Jesus had no relationship to man but only to God and His Spirit, the king demurs: "Thus I believe and in Him I repose my soul. I merely meant to say that there exists no clear family lineage excepting among these poor Jews."

The criticism leveled against the Jewish dietary laws was answered in a manner that revealed the Jews' proud religious consciousness. This was illustrated in the course of a debate which Thomas once had with a member of the Abravanel family, the substance of which he now related to the king. Said Abravanel: "The coral stands between the mineral and the plant; the sponge is midway between the plant and the animal; and the ape is between the animal and man; man is midway between the animal and the Jew; the Jew stands between heaven and earth; and the heavens are midway between the angels and the Jews. Therefore the food upon which the Jew feeds is different."[23]

On the other hand, Ibn Verga slantingly describes the inner dissension which marred Jewish life. Thus Thomas relates an episode which took place in the time of the king's father, who intended to destroy the Jews of the kingdom, but who was restrained by this cynical advice of one of his counselors: "Beware, O lord, for no king succeeded in such an endeavor. If you wish to avenge yourself, command that they all be settled in one city with no stranger among them. Let them elect their own heads and you will see that they will never reach any agreement and will kill off one another and you will have no hand in it."

The political and religious views voiced by Ibn Verga through the ingenious medium of the dialogue seem at times strikingly advanced. Thus the king to Thomas: "You answered Abravanel quite well. But you must not break friendship with him because of his opinions. For it is universally agreed that all religions are matters of imagination. The Jew thinks with all the power of his imagination that there is no other religion or faith but his, and anyone who believes otherwise is in his eyes like an animal; the Christian imagines that the Jew is but an animal in human form and his soul is consigned to the lowest region of hell; and if you inquire of the Moslem, he will say of both that hell is full of us."[24]

With true religious instinct, Ibn Verga scorns pietism that is not accompanied by ethical practices. Violations of human rights are more sinful than religious offenses against God because the order of society and the peace of the world depend upon the laws regulating the relations between man and man. Through Thomas, the Christian apologist, Ibn Verga contrasts the Christian who is honest in his business dealings and lax in

95

religious observances, praying but once a year, with the Jew who may be meticulous in prayer but derelict in business ethics. "Therefore," moralizes Ibn Verga through the unctuous Thomas, "God who hates evil doing has punished the people and prolonged their suffering without a redeeming Messiah, notwithstanding their calling for him regularly at the conclusion of the Sabbath."

The king rejects the notion of his royal predecessors who believed that they could force baptism upon the Jews but actually succeeded only in driving them to observe their faith underground.[25] "For it is said that three waters are wasted: baptismal water on a Jew, water flowing into the sea and water poured into wine."[26] This sentiment is reinforced later in the statement that Judaism cannot be uprooted from the hearts of the Jews, "For Judaism is one of the incurable diseases."[27] Striking indeed is the utterance: "In essence the nation is the king; the king is sovereign in name."[28]

Viewing the dialogue externally and as a whole, it is worth noting that it exceeds in length the previous six historical narratives in the proportion of three to one. The emphasis is thus focused not on the individual episodes, but on the central theme — the anomalous position of the Jew among the nations and the roots of the insensate hatred which caused the unending Jewish tragedy.

This theme which, as indicated, supplies the primary motif of the book is developed with heightened dramatic effect in the recital of the succeeding chapter.[29] On the eve of Passover the heinous blood libel was raised in the town of Ecija. A dead body had been stealthily hurled into the house of a Jew, who was promptly thrown into jail, charged with ritual murder. A riot broke out in the city and every Jew in sight was killed. The report spread like wildfire into other communities, and fierce attacks upon Jews followed. The danger was great and the Jewish communities united to send a representative delegation to the king's court. This is the new note introduced into the story which otherwise would be a repetition of the previous symposium, namely, the presence and the presentation of the views of the distinguished Jewish delegation.

Once again, the king — Alfonso the Great — appears in the role of a just, wise and benevolent monarch, who treats the blood libel with contempt and abhorrence. As in the previous instance, the discussion is quickly shifted from the symptom to the cause, as the king clearly recognizes that the false charges were but a mask for a deep-seated social malady. In this story, however, the king voices the nation's grievances and the Jewish delegates plead the defense. The economic motive is again stressed: "You came to our lands naked and hungry; the population received you with friendship; but you requited evil for good, for through usury you seized their lands, their herd, and their cattle." Similarly, the note of ostentation in dress is cited as a cause of envy and hatred. New grievances hitherto unmentioned are aired by the king: Jews parade the streets in crowds during festive occasions and their rich dress makes them the more conspicuous — "and you the leaders of your people are concerned only with your own prestige without giving thought to the fact that your flock is perishing."[30] Christians are deeply offended, said the king, when Jews who eat with them refuse to drink their wine. Furthermore, why do Jewish parents teach their children singing when weeping and wailing would be more proper for them according to the pattern that God has set for them? Wherefore, too, are the Jewish youths taught the art of fencing inasmuch as they do not go to war? Why is it that you adopt the vices of the populace and not their virtues, and they in turn take on your bad habits? "And do not consider my words," he concluded, "as those of an enemy, for if your God Who from the beginning knew your traits loved you, how can I despise you? My object in speaking to you thus was only to save you from your enemies." The fundamental problem is thus restated with renewed emphasis.

The delegates gratefully acknowledging the graciousness of

the king beg leave to reply, and the king responds: "Would that you have the proper answer. For I have no desire to triumph over you. You may well deem it an honor that I discuss the matter with you in such detail."

A new note is subtly introduced in the opening remarks of the Jewish spokesman, through whom Ibn Verga exposes the psychology of the high-sounding Christian apologist. "Among all our failings which our lord recounted, he forgot a very serious one from which we suffer: namely, that no one who comes to our defense is entirely free of envy or enmity, even if our innocence is crystal clear. The very speech of our lord and his anger, do they not reflect the views of our defamers?"

One by one, the counts in the king's indictment are taken up and answered briefly. The practice of lending money on interest was faithfully abandoned by Jews when the king prohibited it, till three months ago when the Government temporarily rescinded the law as an aid to the farming population who otherwise had no means of purchasing seed for cultivation.

"And as for theft" (a charge which was not mentioned) "we are like mice; one eats the cheese and all are blamed . . . Even among the Christian population, who possess all the virtues and ethical qualities, is it not a daily occurrence that individuals are hanged for theft or robbery? But power covers many faults as a woman's white powder hides many blemishes, while our exile has the opposite effect for it exposes and exaggerates minor defects so that a mustard seed looms as big as the ball of the sun."

As to the silk dress, ever since this was forbidden to Jews by royal decree, it has been faithfully observed, they claimed, as demonstrated by the inexpensive black clothing of the delegates at Court. Whereupon someone interposed: "But the women still wear silk and finery and gold jewelry." To this the delegates replied that the prohibition did not include women "and we thought that it was the custom of royalty to accord privileges and honor to women." Thereupon the king exclaimed: "If so, you walk like a blacksmith's ass and your women like the Pope's mule, and this is not right!" [31]

The habit of congregating is conceded by the Jewish spokesmen without apology. Our clinging together, they said, is a phase of the lovingkindness instilled into us by our religion and is besides a means of survival for a lowly nation like ours. But as to indulgence in song on the part of the young, they confessed that it was a frailty of youth and was induced by the environment — a doubly significant commentary on the temper of Jewish life in Spain.

At this point the discussion was interrupted and resumed on the following day with the suggestion by a high official that the suspect of the ritual murder be interrogated under torture. The protest of the Jews was supported by the king, who from past experience was convinced that evidence obtained under torture was deceiving. [32] Only the greatest power could reveal the truth, said the king. What was the greatest power, was the query. Some ventured the opinion that it was woman; others said it was wine. But the king's opinion prevailed that it was money. [33] A munificent reward was then offered for the discovery of the true culprit and it resulted in the conviction and execution of Juan de la Vera, an attendant in the king's court. [34] "The land feared and was still." [35]

The narrative is obviously an historical novelette. The king by name and personality is merely a type. The Jewish delegates on the other hand were well-known historical figures who appear in a later chapter in a true historical setting. The story itself is undoubtedly reminiscent of numerous episodes which did not always have such a happy ending. The literary form centering around a symposium or debate was ideally suited for Ibn Verga's purposes because thereby he was enabled to express diverse and daring views, through the medium of a king or courtier or even a Moslem diplomat, [36] on the one hand; and, when it seemed more suitable, through a rabbi or other Jewish notable. With true literary instinct, he avoided both pedantry and moralizing. Nor did he attempt a systematic presentation of his views in schematic form. His views are given clarity and cumulative emphasis through being skillfully interwoven in many narrative weaves which supplement one another. Other strands in the complex picture of the Jewish world as portrayed by Ibn Verga are revealed in subsequent chapters, and we shall deal with them elsewhere; but the present study is illustrative of the ensemble.

That the views expressed through the symbolic characters are fundamentally Ibn Verga's own views is clearly demonstrated in the latter part of the work when, dropping the literary artifices, the author openly gives vent to his feelings. "Said Solomon: if one allows the thoughts of these terrible afflictions to pass before his mind, he must greatly wonder why the wrath of God's fierce anger has thus come upon us. He hath not done this to any of the nations who are far more steeped in sin than the Jews. The answer to these and all similar questions is to be found in one verse alone: 'You only have I known of all the families of the earth . . . (Amos 3.2).' " But, he continued, there were additional specific causes for the misfortunes that befell the Jews. First he enumerates the theological conception of the "sins of the fathers." Secondly, unless human merits are sufficiently great to evoke divine intervention the sufferings of the exile are bound to continue indefinitely because of religious hatred and the passion of a ruler to bend everyone to his religion and faith; thirdly, the crucifixion of Jesus the Nazarene; fourthly, there are three fierce passions, or jealousies, induced respectively by religion, women and money, and all of these are evoked in Israel's relations with the nations. For in Spain Jews have come to cast their eyes upon the daughters of the land, unmindful of religious principle and law or the religious consequences when children are born. The envy of wealth is aroused through competition with their crafts and commerce. Moreover, if one Jew proves dishonest all the Jews are smeared with this taint, and God's name is thereby profaned for they say that Jews have no religion. The fifth cause is the habit of the people to take false oaths, which sin, according to Ibn Ezra, is in itself sufficient to prolong the exile. The sixth and final cause is the arrogance of some Jews who seek to dominate everyone, even the native population. In fact, this general trait of arrogance was responsible for a public scandal which broke out in the Synagogue on the eve of the Day of Atonement in the very year of the Expulsion. Such occurrences are all too frequent. "God is just," he concludes.[37]

It would seem, furthermore, that in his choice of historical data from the various sources that were accessible to him, Ibn Verga selected such stories as lent themselves to his general theme. Not the intrinsic factual value of the event but the manner in which it could be made to illustrate and illuminate the Jewish problem either in its social or political, economic or religious aspects was the determining reason for its inclusion. Thus the book opens with the story of the marriage of Anthony and Cleopatra, which led Augustus to wage war upon Anthony and then supposedly to march upon Judaea because it was rumored that the marriage had been planned with the aid of Jewish counselors.[38] Obviously, the story was selected because it was reminiscent of the troublous circumstances under which Abraham Senior had aided and abetted the courtship and marriage of Ferdinand and Isabella. It also afforded Ibn Verga the opportunity through Augustus to pay this tribute to the Jewish warriors against the Romans: "We are not fighting against men but lions and leopards."

Similarly, the confused account of Sisebut's persecutions and the measures which the Jews resorted to in vain to save themselves from compulsory baptism stirred up memories of scenes in the court of Ferdinand and Isabella. Many are the parallels, as when the Jews pour out their gold and silver as gifts to the nobles and offer all their possessions to the king to rescind his decrees, and he exclaims: "Shall I then among kings, bear the name the King of Greed? Forsooth, they will say of me that it was not the baptism for Jesus that I wanted but the extortion of money!" [39]

It is a tribute to Ibn Verga's craftmanship that despite the great diversity of his material he was enabled through the skillful weaving of these strands of history and sociology to stamp his work with unity of authorship and style.

NOTES

[1] Cf. Ibn Verga, *Shebet Yehudah*, ed. Wiener, nos. 1, 3, 6, 12, 17, 32 end; p. 35. A thorough study of the sources of the *Shebet Yehudah* was made by Yitzhak (Fritz) Baer. See below, n. 5. An annotated edition of the *Shebet Yehudah* by Azriel Shohet was published by the *Mosad Bialik*, Jerusalem 1947, with introduction by Professor Baer. Page references below refer to the Wiener edition.

[2] *Idem*, nos. 49, 50, 52, 60, 61.

[3] Graetz, *Geschichte*, VIII [4], Appendix, Notes 1, 3, 4.

[4] *REJ*, XVI, 211–35; XVII, 74–95, 269–71; XXIV, 1–29.

[5] Fritz Baer, *Untersuchungen über Quellen und Komposition des Schebet Yehuda*, Berlin 1923. See also his additional notes in *Tarbiz* VI, 152–179 and Francisco Cantera Burgos, *Ghébet Jehuda, Traducción Española*, Granada 1927.

[6] Zacuto, ס' יוחסין השלם, ed. Filipowski, Introd.

[7] Ibn Verga praises the Christians for their appreciation of the values of history and deplores the lack of it among Jews. See no. 3, end; also p. 11.

[8] Abravanel, מעיני הישועה, ed. Amsterdam, 1647, p. 80 f.

[9] See G. Scholem, *Major Trends in Jewish Mysticism*, Jerusalem, 1941, pp. 241 ff.

[10] An English translation of part III of the *Consolaçam* was prepared by Dr. G. Gelbart in connection with his doctoral thesis for the Dropsie College.

[11] Verga, no. 62.

[12] *Idem*, introductory superscription.

[13] *Idem*, no. 7. The same characters appear again, pp. 115 ff.

[14] Cf. nos. 14, 40, 41, 57. See also *REJ*, XXIV, 5–7.

[15] Cf. Verga, p. 53: nos. 13, 38, 44, 60.

[16] *Passim*. Even King Manuel of Portugal, whose treachery and cruelty, climaxed by the edict of expulsion in 1497, left a hateful impression in Jewish literature is described as מלך חסיד. Verga p. 94. See Baer, *op. cit.*, 71–72. It is not surprising that Mohammedan rulers are especially singled out for their benevolence and justice. Verga pp. 2–3: ומלך ישמעאל מלך חסד היה כמו שנמצא תמיד שכלם מלכי חסד ואוהבי היושר.

[17] Cf. dialogue in Verga no. 7 and pp. 53–55.

[18] Verga, nos. 24, 44; also p. 119.

[19] כי עבדי הם. This political concept is restated in fiscal terms by the Archbishop of Toledo in no. 10, p. 32: כי היהודים הלא הם אוצר למלך אוצר טוב.

[20] "Jewish cleverness" פקחות היהודים is a favorite notion of the *Shebet Yehudah*. This was the king's phrase when he first heard the story which has often been referred to as the original of Lessing's "Three Rings." Verga, p. 54; see also p. 35: אין פקחות כפקחות יהודי; also p. 42.

[21] This assertion is not supported by the Gospel according to Luke, ch. 1.

[22] This too is apocryphal.

[23] Baer, *op. cit.*, p. 79 traces this conception to Judah ha-Levi's *Kusari*, I, 103. See *Tarbiz* VI, 175.

[24] See also Verga, p. 64.

[25] *Idem*, p. 96: כי האנוסים יותר יעבדו את דתם הראשונה אחר האונס ממה שהיה קודם האונס.

[26] Opposition to the use of force in proselytism is pithily expressed elsewhere in the book: to resort to forced conversions is like defying the force of gravitation. Verga, p. 54. Cf. p. 3: כי הדת המוכרחת אין תועלת בה לעולם.

[27] *Idem*, pp. 96–97: כי היהדות הוא מן החולאים אשר אין להם רפואה.

[28] *Idem*, p. 21: והמלך בעצם הוא העם והמלך הוא מלך בשם.

[29] No. 8.

[30] The arrogant attitude of the lay leaders toward their own spiritual heads is alluded to in Verga, p. 84.

[31] Baer, (*Tarbiz* VI, p. 154) traces this sarcastic analogy to an earlier Spanish source, the *Vision delectable de la filosofia y artes liberales, metafisica y filosofia moral* by El Bachiller (Alfonso) de la Torre.

[32] See also p. 41.

[33] The same question is propounded in I Esdras, Josephus and *Josippon*. See above pp. 46 ff.

[34] See Baer, *op. cit.*, p. 62, n. 4.

[35] Ps. 76.9.

[36] Verga, no. 17.

[37] *Idem*, no. 63.

[38] This story is, of course, unhistorical. According to Baer, p. 52, it is based on *Josippon*, ed. Venice, 1544, fol. 30. But the motif that the alleged attack upon Judaea was caused by the supposed role of the Jews in arranging the marriage of Anthony and Cleopatra does not occur in *Josippon*. Clearly this is a case of reading history backward.

[39] Verga, no. 9. Similarly in no. 4 are to be found echoes of later Marrano experiences.

Samuel Usque: Marrano Historian
of the Sixteenth Century

IN THE annals of bibliography, the name of Usque is principally associated with the famous Ferrara Bible, *La Biblia en
Lengua Española*, produced by Abraham Usque at his printing
press in Ferrara in 1553. The subject of this essay, Samuel
Usque, probably a kinsman, was associated with Abraham in
his literary ventures at Ferrara but is known to posterity primarily as historian and the author of *Consolaçam as tribulaçoens de
Israel*, a Consolation for the Tribulations of Israel, which was
published by Abraham Usque shortly after the Ferrara Bible
on September 7, 1553.[1] The historical circumstances which
led Samuel to write this dramatic history, the bigotry and religious hatred which infested most European countries, causing
Jews in particular to take flight to distant lands in search of
freedom, and also the revival of Palestine as a center of Jewish
life and spiritual creativity with the mystic promise of political
self-rule under Joseph, Duke of Naxos — all these facts which
are portrayed in the *Consolaçam* with fervor and pathos suggest
an historical parallelism which renders a discussion of Samuel
and his work peculiarly timely.

I

The Usques of the sixteenth century were a Portuguese
Marrano family, stemming originally from Huesca, Spain, the
ancient Osca, from which the name Usque was derived. The
heads of the family migrated from Spain to Portugal in the wake

Published in the Jubilee Volume in honor of A. S. W. Rosenbach, entitled
To Doctor R., Philadelphia 1946.

of the Spanish expulsion in 1492, [2] when they like thousands of other refugees, accepted in good faith the shelter and protection offered them by King João II of Portugal for which they paid a heavy ransom. [3] Like most of their compatriots they were subsequently caught in the snare of royal treachery and painfully submitted to baptism rather than face another exile with its attendant horrors of hunger, poverty and utter helplessness. Forced at the point of death or exile to adopt an alien faith, "many," to quote Usque, "have become Christians in body, yet no stain ever touched their souls, and they always bore the seal of their ancient Law."

Vividly Usque continued: "It was not enough to have brought them into their faith by such vicious and unnatural means and to wrest them from the Law into which they had been born. For even now they did not suffer them to live in peace but hurled insults at them, hurting them with humiliation and treating them with baseness and contempt. And this also they would have borne with patience, had not calumnies and false testimonies been raised against them to destroy and annihilate them. For the preachers preached in the pulpits, the lords asserted in public places and the townspeople and villagers repeated in the squares, saying that whatsoever famine, plague or earthquake occurred in the land, it was because they (the *conversas*) were not faithful Christians but were Judaizing in secret." [4]

Into these unhappy surroundings Samuel Usque was born early in the sixteenth century — the exact date is unknown. He was reared secretly in the Jewish faith. [5] Early in life and at great risk, he was taught to recite Hebrew prayers and to read the Bible in the sacred tongue. Thus the groundwork was laid for a mastery of Hebrew Scriptures and liturgy which may well have made him a co-worker in the Bible translation of the Usque printing press and the primary translator of the Hebrew prayerbooks issued by the house of Abraham Usque in Ferrara. [6]

The danger and secrecy which surrounded the practice of the Jewish religion created an atmosphere of intense spiritual excitation which left a deep impress on Samuel and is vividly reflected in the highly charged, emotional writing of the *Consolaçam*.

Samuel Usque appears to have been a gifted, sensitive youth, if one may judge by the wide range of his literary and cultural interests. The history of nations and the fate of his own people in particular held special fascination for him. He was a keen observer of men and events and kept abreast of the political currents of his time. He was especially adept in the study of languages. In addition to Hebrew, he mastered Latin, Spanish and Italian; there is also some indication that he studied Greek. As for Portuguese, he loved it as a mother tongue, and even in exile in a foreign country, he writes of the language and in it with tenderness and love befitting an author whose work ranks among the classics of Portuguese literature. He appears to have been admitted into the inner circle of the Lisbon literati and to have enjoyed the friendship and confidence of the famous poet Bernardim Ribeiro (1482–1552) who introduced the pastoral genre into Portuguese literature. Ribeiro's classic *Menina e Moça* was published posthumously after the *Consolaçam* and yet its influence is so clearly marked in the *Consolaçam* that one is impelled to assume the existence of an intimate relationship between Usque and the elderly poet and Usque's ready access to his friend's great poem in manuscript.[7]

In later years, Usque wrote critically but with understanding pity of the secret Jews who were lulled into a false sense of security. Speaking through an imaginary character who symbolized the genius of Israel, he makes this collective confession: "And I, ignorant, hidden as I was in the guise of a Christian, it seemed to me that by this means I was saving my life, whereas the contrary holds."[8] "The New Christians had become so utterly absorbed in the acquisition of power and its delusions that they were on the verge of forgetting their ancient Law, and were losing fear of the Fountain whence flows our life, what with the great wealth which they acquired, the dignities and noble offices which they procured in the kingdom and the peace they enjoyed, for they imitated assiduously the Christian people though indeed they never forsook the secret of their hearts." [9]

It is quite possible that in this penetrating observation we may see in part a reflection of Samuel Usque's own state of mind before the terrifying alarm that heralded the coming of the Inquisition to Portugal during the reign of King João III (1522–1557). But with the introduction of this dreaded institution, all doubts vanished. There was no alternative but flight to a more hospitable country.

The fear which convulsed the hearts of its potential victims stands congealed in a terrifying picture of the Inquisition which Usque painted on the background of Spain in the reign of Ferdinand and Isabella. He conceived of the Inquisition "as a ferocious monster — brought over from Rome — of a shape and appearance so grotesque and hideous, that at the mere sound of his name all Europe trembles. His carcass is of crude iron tempered with deadly poison and covered with an impenetrable shell of thick scales made of steel. A thousand black venomous wings lift him from the earth and a thousand noxious, destructive feet carry him on the ground. His shape is partly of a fierce lion and partly in the horrible forms of the serpents of the African deserts. His fangs surpass the tusks of the elephants. The sound of his hissing slays more swiftly than the deadly basilisk. Flames of consuming fire shoot ceaselessly from his eyes and mouth. The food on which he gluts is kneaded of human bodies. He excels the eagle in speedy flight, but wherever he hovers, his black shadow spreads the gloom of darkness, however brightly the sun may shine. Wherever he sets foot, the verdure he touches, every pleasant tree on which he alights, shrivels up, withers and dies. With his poison he lays waste the land within his ken, turning it like unto the desert and sand plains of Syria, where no plant grows, no grass sprouts." [10]

Of the ravages which the Inquisition wrought in Portugal, Usque writes vividly with the freshness of one who had only recently witnessed the devastation: "Though it is only a short time since the monster arrived from Rome, he has already wrought cruel and fearful havoc among the enforced converts. His coming brought pallor to their faces, wrecking the tranquility of their spirits and filling their souls with pain and sorrow. He drove them from the comfort of their homes into dark dungeons, where they live in constant fear and moaning. For there he sets the trap which hurls them into the fire to be burnt therein. There he tortures them so that they are driven to kill their children with their own hands. He makes orphans, multiplies widows, impoverishes the rich, destroys the mighty, turns the well-born into thieves, fills the places of shame and infamy with modest and virtuous women by reason of the poverty and destitution to which they are reduced. . . . When the burning takes place a multitude of Christians gather, who glory and rejoice at the sight of those being burnt at the stake and they poke the fire and feed it with the fuel which they bring on their backs from far places." [11]

As Usque describes the constant state of fear of those who had not yet been caught in the clutches of "the monster," the overhanging dread that haunted them when they walked on the streets by day and when they slept fitfully through the night, he creates the impression of one who is reliving a reign of terror which he experienced personally. In this vein he continues: "Not even one of the thousand evils caused by this beast could I explain at length to you, brethren, for innumerable are the manners of their martyrdom. But this I can say to you, that driven by fear, many of these converts have departed, fleeing from a land trodden by so deadly a monster." [12]

Samuel Usque was among those who fled in terror. He followed the route which had been paved before him by countless Marranos: first toward a haven in Italy, where the Inquisition was not tolerated and it was still possible to live religiously in peace without fear of secretive prying and spying;[13] and then, years later perhaps, a voyage by sea to Turkey, possibly Palestine, where under the crescent one could discard the hateful mask of religious duplicity and be reunited openly with the religion of the fathers.[14]

The route which Samuel followed was circuitous, probably planned so as to ward off suspicion. From Portugal he directed his course through Spain and Flanders into Germany, then across the Alps into the canton of Grisons in Switzerland and then southward into Italy.[15] Here in close proximity to Rome it was possible for the Marranos to breathe more freely.[16] Here too Samuel Usque was reunited with two kinsmen from Lisbon who bore the name of Usque: Abraham of the printing-press fame and Solomon the poet, best known for his celebrated Spanish translation of Petrarch's Sonnets.[17]

It is not possible to trace the order in which these three personages reached their Italian destination. That Samuel preceded Abraham is a fair assumption, inasmuch as the latter published a Latin grammar in Lisbon under his Christian name Duarte Pinhel as late as 1543, so that a number of years must have elapsed since the establishment of the Inquisition in Portugal with which we associate Samuel Usque's exodus.[18] But it is clear that by 1551 both Abraham and Samuel Usque were safely sheltered in the beautiful city of Ferrara under the protection of the Duke Ercole II, that "most sublime and generous prince of a beauteous and plenteous people."[19]

A fruitful literary association united the two kinsmen. Abraham founded a publishing house with his own funds or perhaps, as has been suggested, with the financial aid of that gracious Jewess Gracia Mendesia.[20] One of the first tasks sponsored by the Usque press was a Spanish translation of the Hebrew Bible according to the Jewish tradition.[21] A Spanish Marrano Yom Tob Atias whose Christian name was Geronimo de Vargas undertook to finance its printing.[22] That Samuel Usque was one of the collaborators in the great undertaking which is said to have engaged the co-operation of a hundred scholars is a plausible suggestion.[23] In the theme of the *Consolaçam*, he manipulated biblical verses with the deftness of a musician playing upon the keys of his favorite instrument. More than the translator's skill, the primary purpose of the project — to bring the Bible close to the hearts and minds of the Marranos — carried an irresistible appeal to the romantic historian who sought to bring them consolation in their tribulations.

That the undertaking was accompanied with danger is shown by a bit of strange bibliographic evidence, which confounded the earlier bibliographers till the mystery was cleared up in the great work of Heinrich Graetz.[24] For it was discovered that the same *editio princeps* appeared in two versions, alike in every detail but for the dedication, the names of the printer and his financial aide and a slight but significant variant in the translation of only one verse: Isaiah 7.6.[25] This puzzle Graetz resolved simply but ingeniously: namely, a special printing of several copies of the translation was struck off for the benefit of the Inquisition. In these copies the names of the publisher and the Maecenas appear under their Christian appellation and the translation is dedicated to the Duke Ercole. Thus the approbation of the Inquisition was obtained. The remainder of the edition, however, intended for Jewish usage bears the Hebrew names of its sponsors with "the most Illustrious Lady Gracia Nasci," the object of the dedication. Most fittingly the dedication reads: "As it was my intention to serve our Portuguese nation with this tiny cluster of fresh fruit, it was appropriate that I should offer it to your Excellency as the heart of this body, for in the remedies you have given you felt and still do feel for their sorrows more deeply than anyone else."[26]

Samuel Usque is credited with a major role in the preparation of popular Hebrew prayerbooks with Spanish translation, which, together with the other Hebrew and Spanish publications, made the Usque press in Ferrara a Marrano publishing house.[27] The Usques were also Portuguese at heart and loved the Portuguese language despite the treachery and cruelty of the nation that drove them into exile. Thus it was in Ferrara at the press of Abraham Usque that one of the great classics of Portuguese literature, the *Menina e Moça* of Bernardim Ribeiro, was published for the first time.[28] It is another Portuguese classic, however, noted for its moral regenerative power even more than its literary quality, which had appeared earlier in 1553 also as a product of the Usque press which is of primary concern in this essay: the *Consolaçam as tribulaçoens de Israel* by Samuel Usque.

Usque's *Consolation for the Tribulations of Israel* is the creation of a poetic soul and a philosophic mind. The poet struggled with the eternal problem of his people's endless sorrow. Implicit faith in God did not resolve the problem. It only deepened the mystery surrounding Israel's destiny. To be sure, his people fell short of the divine ideal set before them. They were not always true to their prophetic calling. But what of the other nations? Who among them could lay claim to higher standards of morals, justice or the perception of religious truth? Was it the English, forsooth, their one-time persecutors who made a scapegoat of the Jews and pinned on them the responsibility for all the misfortunes that came upon the land? "O cruel Englishmen," he exclaimed, "Such righteous and saintly people you were that it was impossible to presume your misfortunes to be a punishment of your own deeds?"[29]

It was not however the application of Job's theme to national experience that made for the distinctiveness of the *Consolaçam*. The novel element in this work is the assurance that the solution to the moral perplexity of the age is to be found in the history of the past. This evaluation of history, strongly reminiscent of the ancient prophetic note, was not the accidental mood of an individual author. The *Consolaçam* is a unit in an historical trilogy which came into being in the mid-sixteenth century within the period of one or two decades. It was a new phenomenon in Jewish literature and marked a temporary awakening of an historical consciousness which had been dormant among the Jewish people for fifteen hundred years.

At the very time when Usque was pondering over the theme of the *Consolaçam* there lived in Italy two other recent arrivals, one of Spanish and the other of French origin, similarly engaged in unraveling the mysteries of Jewish destiny through the medium of history. The *Shebet Yehudah*, The Rod of Judah, by Solomon ibn Verga of the Spanish exile was being written almost simultaneously with the *Consolaçam*, both authors, unknown to each other, using a common Hebrew source as their chief Jewish authority.[30] Joseph ha-Kohen, of French descent, was immersed in writing his *Annals of the Kings of France and the House of Othman the Turk* when the *Consolaçam* appeared off the press, and he was so deeply stirred by its theme that within a few years he in turn wrote his famous *Emek ha-Bakah*, The Valley of Tears. Thus within a brief span of hardly twenty years, three historical works appeared in Italy — two in Hebrew and one in Portuguese — any one of which would rightly have been regarded as a landmark in Jewish historical writing. It is on this background as a unit in an historical trilogy, as an expression of a new school of thought, that the *Consolaçam* appears in its true light.[31]

To appreciate this phenomenon more fully, one must bear in mind that a strange deterioration of the historical faculty, sudden and complete, made itself manifest in Jewish consciousness when the Romans destroyed the Jewish State and dispersed its people in the year 70 CE. The transformation was not superficial. It was a deep-seated psychological metamorphosis. Before this critical turning point, the Jews were distinguished for their highly developed talent of historic perspective and reconstruction. The narrative books of the Bible represent an advanced stage of historic writing. They are selective and interpretative. They are based on a broad historic literature which was lost. In the Hellenistic period, the books of the Maccabees continue the historic tradition. Josephus' work — whatever may be said in critical appraisal of the author's scientific methods — stand forth as an impressive monument of historic writing. But with the close of his period, the very art of narrative composition was lost among his people, as historic instinct and vision died with the political extinction of Jewish nationhood.

The Talmud, including also the tannaitic sources, is deficient in historic conception. Such talmudic passages as may be classed under history are, in the main, so confused that often they defy the historian's best efforts to validate them. The same dearth of historic understanding and apparent loss of the narrator's art characterized the post-talmudic period. Indeed, it was solely the need of establishing the continuity of the oral tradition and defending it against challenging sects that gave rise to the few meager chronicles that belong to the first millennium of the Common Era. These bare, literary annals and a few family chronicles, plus the much discussed work *Josippon*, constitute the entire output of what may be included under the category of history in a period of over a thousand years.

As the Middle Ages, however, were heading toward the climax of the Jewish tragedy in medieval Christendom, first during the early Crusades, then following in closer succession, the expulsions from France, the persecutions attendant upon the Black Death, the massacres of 1391, the wholesale conversions of 1412, the subsequent establishment of the Spanish Inquisition and, finally, at the end of the fifteenth century, the expulsions from Spain and Portugal, a profound spiritual disturbance made itself manifest among the masses as well as among the intellectual leaders. Was their suffering to be endless? Was there any purpose, human or divine, to be discerned in their prolonged agony?

The mood of dark despair reached dangerous proportions a generation after the exile from Spain and Portugal, when the full significance of the extinction of the noblest Jewish settlements in Europe came to be understood and caused even the stoutest hearts to lose courage and hope. The peril of surrender from within was more grave than the threat of extermination from without. Many were those who sought shelter in Messianic dreams.[32] Greater still was the number that fled from the cares and sordidness of the world in mystic flights on cabalistic wings.[33] But the realm of mysticism afforded no retreat for those who viewed the world realistically and resisted the lure of fantasy. Intuitively, they were led to seek the key to the riddle of Jewish fate in a re-examination of the past experiences of their people. History was to become the guide to the perplexed. Thus the historic consciousness was awakened once more after a lapse of a millennium and a half and there arose a new understanding of history and its relation to historic destiny.

In Italy, the land of the Renaissance, the muse of history found its awakening. It inspired three votaries simultaneously: Ibn Verga the rationalist who analyzed the Jewish problem from an historical social viewpoint; Joseph ha-Kohen, the annalist who interpreted Jewish history as a divinely inspired martyrology; and Samuel Usque, the imaginative poet, author of the *Consolaçam*, to whom Jewish history was a divine drama of retribution which held forth the promise of glorious fulfillment.

II

Unlike the works of Ibn Verga and Joseph ha-Kohen, which were written in Hebrew, the *Consolaçam* belongs to two literatures, Jewish and Portuguese. In language and stylistic form it is Lusitanian; in theme and inspiration it is of the essence of the Hebraic spirit. The choice of language on the part of the author was deliberate. He was importuned to write his masterpiece in Spanish which was a universal language; but intense loyalty to his Portuguese brethren and a deep attachment to the language as his mother tongue determined the issue. The consequence was unfortunate. The book was neglected in both literatures. Catholic Portugal, Inquisition ridden, was in no mood to extol the literary graces of a work which exposed its national barbarism and religious savagery. On the other hand, to the Jews — outside the range of Portuguese Marranos — the language proved to be a barrier and a stumbling block rather than a highway of communication. As a result, the *Consolaçam* remained locked within linguistic Portuguese borders. There is no translation of the *Consolation for the Tribulations of Israel* in any language.[33a]

Usque was not unaware of the fate to which he consigned his life's work through the choice of a Portuguese medium. He defends his cause on a note of defiance born of passionate loyalty: "Some people were pleased to say, before they knew of my reason that it would have been better to have composed it in the Spanish tongue; but I believe that I was not wrong in this. For as my chief intent was to address myself to the Portuguese and to present an account of our exile in a manner which might through diverse means bring some alleviation of the pains which we have endured, it would not have been fitting to desert the language I learned at my mother's knee and to seek another borrowed one in which to address my compatriots. And even though at one time there were many of those exiled from Spain whence also my ancestors came, yet it seems to me proper that I should now consider those that are in the majority at present."[34]

It might have comforted him to know that almost four hundred years later a shamefaced Portuguese king would applaud his sentiment and embrace his spirit with somewhat mixed patriotic fervor.[35] Nevertheless he would have been all but forgotten if it were not for the Hebrew chroniclers of his own period who kept his memory alive through frequent citations of the *Consolaçam* and the revival of Jewish historiography in the nineteenth century which rescued that noble work from oblivion. But the miracle of resurrection is still reserved for the future. A complete translation of the *Consolaçam* into one of the present world languages, preferably English — and, most of all, also into the living Hebrew of today — should not be long delayed. Its faith and fervor may yet yield a measure of consolation for the still greater tribulations of modern Israel.

The problem of the *Consolaçam* is cast in the form of a pastoral idyl. A prologue in which the author explains the purpose of his work and the nature of the theme and its manner of treatment forms a general introduction. It is addressed "to the people of the Portuguese exile."

"I have seen that this our nation which is now pursued and driven from the kingdom of Portugal is wavering and submitting to the afflictions more than is necessary, allowing itself to be crushed by them, some from poverty, others from fear and most because of the scant constancy inherent in our souls. Therefore I propose to relate the tribulations and the woes that have befallen our people together with the causes that brought about every calamity. . . . And since it is not right to leave the cruel wounds gaping open, I decided to close them with the consolations offered by our Lord and to give in writing the happy conclusions which we hope ultimately to realize."

Holding up the mirror of the past to the present was an essential part of the consolation. "Socrates was wont to say that when people find themselves in trouble, they should compare the evils they have left behind them with those of the present time, and they would readily find solace. Certainly if we viewed the matter closely and did not abandon ourselves to the passions of our soul there is no suffering afflicting us now, however great, that our ancestors have not experienced and borne greater than it."

He takes strange comfort in the thought that "this people

has shrunk so considerably that the evils because of their very magnitude find no object against which to direct their forces." But in true Hebraic rhythm this melancholy thought is followed by the prayerful hope that "this storm which till now has persecuted us and still does pursue us is beginning to abate and the longed-for dawn is about to break after this tempestuous winter night."

With the conclusion of the prologue, the idyl proper opens on a pastoral landscape in a far-off lonely meadow. The *dramatis personae* are three shepherds whose names reveal their symbolic character: Ycabo, Numeo, and Zicareo. These names "slightly altered after the manner of ancient writers" represent Jacob, the ancient patriarch — in this story the living embodiment, or genius, of the Jewish people — and the prophetic characters Nahum and Zechariah whose roles are suggested by the meaning of their names: Nahum, the comforter, and Zechariah, the embodiment of memory, or he who recalls the past.

Numeo and Zicareo come upon Ycabo in this pastoral retreat whither he had gone in solitude to pour out the grief of his soul before the heart of nature, for he despaired of human sympathy. They are stricken by his appearance. "His eyes are heavy, without sparkle, his hair dishevelled, his hands cold, his fingernails dull and colorless as he lies prostrate under a tree, showing no feeling as one who lost all capacities, even the sense of fear." [36] With true understanding they plead that he seek relief of his grief by unburdening himself before them "since pains are soothed by the telling of them." Ycabo gratefully accepts their advice.

The author has now created the framework for his theme. Ycabo is the chief narrator. The history of the Jewish people from its earliest beginnings to the very year when the *Consolaçam* was completed is recited by Ycabo as a personal experience which he and his children lived through. The story is unfolded as one long continuous martyrology. But the narrative is too long for one day's recital and it is too harrowing a tale for the narrator to suffer without interruption and rest. He is therefore led to tell his story in three parts in as many days. These constitute the three Dialogues into which the book is divided.

Ycabo's theme readily lends itself to the threefold division. The first day is given over to the early history of Israel down to the destruction of the Temple and the end of the kingdom. The second day's recital comprises the story of the Second Commonwealth to the burning of the Temple and the destruction of the Jewish State by the Romans. The climax is reached on the final day with the recital of the calamities that befell his children in Europe from the early persecutions in Visigothic Spain to the shameful desecration of the synagogues in Pesaro the year when the book was written.

These "calamities," thirty-seven in number, arranged according to date in chronological sequence, frequently faulty, form thirty-seven brief chapters in Dialogue III. Ranging in date from 317 (to be corrected to 617) to 1553, they exemplify every form of medieval bigotry and persecution directed against the Jews. England, France, Germany and Bohemia are among the countries thus indicted; but Spain and Portugal, burning with the hellish fires of the Inquisition, are the torch-bearers in the unholy procession of medieval cruelty and perfidy. It is in these chapters that Usque turns historian, citing his sources, Latin, Italian and Hebrew, and making an original contribution to Jewish history, most valuable for the period from 1492 to his own day.

At the end of each day's recital, Numeo and Zicareo, like the comforters of Job, but with greater success, seek to console Ycabo. Their task is facilitated in part because, unlike Job, Ycabo confesses the sins of his children and accepts the premise that punishment follows in the wake of sin.[37] Divine justice is vindicated by Ycabo's interlocutors through the retribution which they point out was visited upon the persecutors of Israel from ancient times to the emperors of Rome. [38] The "medicine of their words" takes effect each day and he is refreshed by sleep. But when on the final day, he recalls the agonies which his children endured in Christendom for a thousand years; the false accusations raised against them, the charges of ritual murder, poisoning of wells, desecration of the host, the incitement to mass murders, expulsions, forcible conversions and the snatching of children from their mothers' arms, he raises his voice in a final loud lament: "Oh world, why didst thou create in thee that which thou wast bound to abhor and despise so utterly?" [39] Pleading in vain with man, yea, with heaven and earth, for a hearing for "the slave whose plea has not been heard," he cried out, "Peace, peace, O Lord unto this mighty strife! . . . Now that I have suffered all Thy indignations, it may be high time, O Lord, that a haven be found where this battered body should find rest from this terrible storm. Shouldst Thou, however, desire to cleanse me further, see, O Merciful One, that I am but a frail subject for the mighty fire of Thy wrath." [40]

III

The *Consolaçam* is a work of many moods. The gloom of despair is relieved by flashes of hope. Grim realism yields to mystic faith, and passion to reason. Rebellion against the injustice of man is softened by submission to the will of God. Anger gives way to pity. The wings of poetic flight at times lift one high above the revolting sight of men turned into beasts, priests into vultures, nobles and kings into brigands. It is thus impossible to trace a logical pattern in the development of the author's theme. He is alternatively the poet-prophet and the philosopher-historian. This is most pronounced in the third and concluding Dialogue in which he deals not with the abstractions of ancient history but with the baffling reality of the European world. Precisely for this reason, however, it is this Dialogue

which reveals the soul of Samuel Usque and his literary significance as historian and philosopher of Jewish history.

The Dialogue opens as follows: "The third Dialogue which
treats of all the tribulations suffered by Israel since the loss of
the Second Temple, which was destroyed by the Romans, till
this day, followed by all the prophecies that were fulfilled therein,
and lastly, by Israel's consolation, both human and divine.

Ycabo, Zicareo, Numeo—

Interlocutors

Ycabo:

Tonight I have enjoyed a somewhat better rest than usual,
so effective was the medicine of the words which Zicareo administered to this old wound of mine. Rightly they say that for
the ailing soul there is no better physician than a master reasoner.
I have great hopes of obtaining from him easement for the ills
which I am now going to relate to him.

Numeo, Zicareo:

Good morning, Ycabo.

Numeo:

We rose earlier this morning than you would believe, for
our mastiffs, having scented wolves, were giving them a brisk
chase, so that we were obliged to come to their aid. Thank God,
however, the wolves did us no harm whatever. It seems to me,
on the contrary, that one of them was much bitten up, to judge
by our long-eared dog which is all covered with blood, yet is
not injured. Now, if you wish, we will retire with our flocks to
a meadow which lies below, at the foot of the hill, a pleasant
place with an abundance of water. There, stretched under a
green poplar tree, and watching our sheep graze, we could
continue our discourse.

Ycabo:

I wish nothing better.

Numeo:

Lead the way, Zicareo.

Zicareo:

Forward, then. A step or two, and here we are. Now be seated, Ycabo, and proceed with your discourse.

Ycabo:

I will proceed, and do you listen attentively. After the passing of that Roman storm, the force of which scattered me throughout the world, I have suffered countless and diverse misfortunes."

Ycabo then proceeds to describe thirty-seven calamities, which befell his children during a period of a thousand years. These thirty-seven brief chapters constitute Usque's original historical contribution. The events, all but four of which are laid in European Christian countries, are treated as separate accounts without any connection or interrelation. They include major national catastrophes and local persecutions. The earlier accounts are drawn from literary sources but the closer events associated with the Spanish and Portuguese expulsions are described from personal observation and the accounts of eye-witnesses. [41]

His literary sources were comparatively meager. They were limited to one or two Hebrew records and a few Latin-Spanish-Italian chronicles. Among the latter, paradoxically enough, the most important single source was the venomous *Fortalitium Fidei* of Alfonso de Spina, a Franciscan monk. [42] This work, in the part devoted to Jews, is a concoction of all the poisonous tales that were invented about Jews desecrating the host, slaying Christian children for the Passover rites, their poisoning of wells, setting fire to churches and perpetrating other atrocities in their alleged unbridled hatred and thirst for revenge. The barbarous persecution of the Jews was thus attributed in these witches' tales to the wrath of the Christian population who were driven in frenzy to avenge the atrocities of their enemies.

To Usque the fatal consequences appeared true enough; the premises, however, were patently the devil's invention. In his own account, therefore, he reconstructed Spina's distorted facts by his own version of the origin of these grotesque charges. They were libels inspired by lust of loot and the hatred fed by religious fanaticism. "They chose to persecute me," said Ycabo, "with false accusations, so as to lend a semblance of justice to any execrable act that they might commit. Some said that I made sacrifices of Christian children, killing them in subterranean chambers, and that I taught the servants in my house to Judaize. Others maintained that church vessels, such as the chalice, pyxes, crucifixes and other similar objects were accepted by me in the banks as pledges from the hands of thieves and that I put them to profane uses, and drank out of them, although it is a thing strictly forbidden by my Law to use any vessel or equipment belonging to the service of other Gods, and that furthermore I threw a book of their gospel together with a crucifix into a filthy place. . . ." [43]

"Consider O princes, for a moment the reason or cause that prompts you to do me harm. See you not how manifest is the false testimony and how unjustly I was punished?" Citing the evil consequences that pursued the Philistines when they laid hold of the ark of the Lord, Ycabo pleads: "Now, how can you believe with regard to the hosts, the chalice, the crucifixes, the books of the gospel which you hold to be so holy and consecrated that they suffer themselves to be so grossly abused and insulted? Yet your priests record it and write it down in their books with the intention of inciting the people against me. Obviously there is no reason why you should believe such charges; on the contrary, there are good reasons why you should punish those ignorant people that fabricate them out of hatred, unaware that by so doing they wrong themselves." [44]

Usque is not content, however, to reduce Jewish suffering to the level of a sordid conspiracy of kings, priests and mobs. There breathes in his soul the spirit of the ancient Hebrew prophets. "These misfortunes came upon me from a much higher quarter,"

123

said Ycabo, the genius of Israel. True, his children are innocent of evil-doing toward man. But he cannot exculpate them from sin toward God. "The truth was that the Lord having granted me in that kingdom great resources of wealth . . . I used them for the enjoyment of things earthly and deemed those successes to be my purpose and my due. Daily I grew more remiss in the service of God, distorting many of the teachings of His will." Base kings are but the instruments of divine displeasure. Thus he continues: "And for these sins, the punishment in person and property not yet sufficing, the king (Philip Augustus) ordered furthermore to destroy all the synagogues in which we had made our prayers scarce, and to turn them into churches. Out of the riches which he looted he caused many noble structures to be built in France. Among them were the palaces and walls of the Bois de Vincennes, a delightful place near Paris, as well as the Champeaux, now known as the Halles, where the city's commerce is carried on." [45]

By such methods of noble simplification, Usque without troubling to refute Spina's stories created the Jewish version of the historic experiences of Israel in medieval Europe, which became the norm of later Hebrew chroniclers until the conception of Jewish history was amplified and recast with the advent of modern Jewish historiography in the nineteenth century.

IV

In the course of his narration, Usque at times touches upon contemporary European events which take on strange significance as he describes them. Addressing himself to the England of Henry VIII, he writes: "Behold within the few years of the reign of King Henry, how many acts of adultery were committed against him by his own queens? How many attempts at treason were made by the highest nobles, the king's near kinsmen? How many heads were displayed on the Bridge of London for these and other outrages? And how many queens were killed by the sword and others deposed from their royal station? The churches, where you once used to pray, you destroyed with your own hands, and others you converted into stables. Your priests you cast out and injured. The images of gold and silver, before which you once humbled yourselves, you broke up and those of wood you burned in the fire, while still others were flung on dung heaps and filthy places. You turned your Pope, your cardinals, your bishops into a byword and reproach among yourselves." [46]

It may be recalled that Usque was a contemporary of Martin Luther and witnessed the rise of the Protestant Reformation. Without revealing his personal sympathies, he viewed the Protestant revolt as divine retribution visited upon the Church for using violence in forcing religious beliefs upon those who would not freely accept them. In the hearts of the descendants of Jews who were dragged by force to the fount of baptism, there was implanted a profound religious restlessness which had a direct bearing upon the outbreak of the Lutheran revolt. Describing the forced conversions in France, which were particularly effective in Toulouse, he adds, "It is in this way that that province was populated by this seed, of which even now there must be many offshoots, restless in the faith which they accepted so much against their will. And it would not be a gross error to presume that it is of them that the Lutherans are, who have risen throughout Christendom. For seeing that everywhere the Jews have been compelled to forsake their Law, it appears to be the fact of divine justice that they should hurt the Christians with the very weapons placed in their hands, as a punishment for those who had forced them, and as a detriment to the faith which had been imposed upon them, and that they should themselves destroy its pride, and by means of these principles endeavor to enter once more upon the road which they left so long ago. You should, therefore, consider, O princes, how much damage you cause by forcing the Jews to accept your religion. For the ways of injustice, whereby mortals deem to further their designs, prove in the end to be the very means and mainspring of their own undoing." [47]

Like a parched desert traveler who comes upon an oasis, Usque responds joyfully to any haven that offers religious freedom. The "spiritual enemy" of Israel may deride those who flee to the Ottoman Empire because they will be "devoured by the wretched poverty of Turkey and the grievous captivity under the Turks and Moors." [48] But for Usque, Turkey appeared like "a vast, expansive sea, which our Lord had opened up with the rod of His compassion so that the burden of your perils might be thrown and perish therein. . . . Here the gates of liberty are wide open, and never closed, for the free observance of Judaism." [49]

The city of Salonica is highly praised. "There is a city in the kingdom (Salonica) which in former days belonged to the Greeks but which in our time is a veritable mother in Jewry, for it is built on the deep foundations of the Lord, full of superlative plants and fruitful trees such as are found nowhere in the wide world. Their fruit is divine, for it is watered by a great abundance of alms. Holy works of exalted and supreme merit constitute its walls. In it have taken refuge many of my children who were persecuted and driven out of Europe and other parts of the world, and it receives them with utmost love and affection, as though it were our ancient and exquisitely tender mother, Jerusalem." [50]

Palestine mourns her exiled children. It is desolate and barren; it denies its fruit to the strangers that inhabit it. It is indeed so poor that Jews are discouraged and "many refuse to go and live there on account of the great misery in which it surpasses all other countries." [51] Nevertheless, "from all the corners of Europe, as well as from all the other parts of the world, there is flowing thither at present a larger number of them by far than has ever been seen in the past." [52] The end of Israel's wandering may be at hand. The return to Palestine may be the beginning of the final act in the divine drama. Prophecy is being fulfilled and we "are in the midst of its realization." [53]

Throughout the book, Ycabo holds the center of the stage. In the concluding portion of the third Dialogue, however, the interlocutors play the major role. Ycabo's part was to unroll the tribulations; theirs to bring the tidings of consolation. "Now that we have sorrowed for your wounds," said they, "and, like a surgeon, allowed them to bleed freely in order to apply the medication, it is time that we endeavor to find the consoling cure; for this is the purpose of our coming, and with the mercy of God we hope to offer it to you in a number of ways." [54]

The interlocutors, Numeo and Zicareo, are allegorical figures but they are also cast in the role of divine messengers. To Ycabo's feverish imagination, their appearance at first suggested Messianic expectations. "Which of those whom we are expecting are you?" he asked. "We are not of those whom you are awaiting," was the reply. [55] But at the conclusion, they reveal that they are divine messengers from the celestial world. They have come to relate to Ycabo that his sufferings have reached the heavens, where the ancient patriarchs dwell in glory and pray daily for Israel's salvation. Through their intercession, "the prayers and laments of the Jews ascending to heaven soar ever upward in heavenly circles, now having reached the ninth, which is the Heaven of Pleiades." [56] But there was no intent on the part of the dramatic author to drift into the mists of supernaturalism or apocalyptic visions. For when Ycabo prods the messengers, Numeo replies loftily: "I had not meant to dwell on this subject, as it is not food meet for every constitution. There is yet much to be said which you would delight in were you sufficiently trained in divine contemplation for your soul to receive those sublime mysteries." [57] The tidings of which they are the messengers, the comfort and consolation which they bring to Ycabo, are "vivid and sweet reasonings," setting forth Israel's tribulations in the perspective of Jewish faith, history and divine prophecy.

For sorrow, suffering, retribution are part of the divine law of nature. Adversity is not solely an affliction but a means to moral improvement. The Inquisition itself may be regarded as a surgical instrument. It operates with steel and fire to save the Jewish body from the fatal effects of an assumed and false faith which like a cankerous disease infected the Jewish people.[58] Human perfection, as in a diamond, is processed by "the grinding wheel of many afflictions." It is a process to which Israel must be subjected if he is to qualify for the glorious blessing of the future.[59]

The reasoning of the interlocutors is skillfully dealt with as the argument shifts from one phase to another. The worldly suffering of the body must be weighed against the celestial happiness of the soul. "They that suffer for their sins in this world, while maintaining their Jewish faith, cleaving unto the Lord and His Law have a portion in the world to come."[60] The dispersion of the Jewish people throughout the world, cruel as the fate may seem, renders Israel indestructible. "For if a ruler rises up against you in Europe to inflict death upon you, a kingdom in Asia permits you to live therein; and if the Spaniards expel you and burn you in Spain, the Lord wills it that you are received and allowed to live freely in Italy."[61] Contrasted with the fate of the Ten Tribes, "this is a mysterious and sublime favor which heretofore you have deemed the reverse."[62]

The prophets are called to witness. As Ycabo had summoned Moses, Amos, Isaiah, Jeremiah and other prophets to confirm and illumine Israel's tribulations, so the interlocutors now called to mind the glorious prophecies of fulfillment "in the latter days." So glowing and overwhelming was the vision that Ycabo cried for "a new soul and new faculties."[63] With new and fervent hope he peers into the future. He pleads in vain with the divine messengers to reveal the day of the redemption. "It is at hand to come," they echoed.[64]

The story ends, as it began, on the pastoral scene. The trio retire. Zicareo asks Ycabo to sing "some sweet canticle, one of the songs that the maidens of your highlands were wont to sing of old, as they drove their flocks upon the hills of Zion." Ycabo chants the immortal Psalm of hope:

> "When the Lord brought back those that returned to Zion,
> We were like unto them that dream."

Thus the Dialogue ends; thus too the life of Usque reached its finale. For a curtain of silence descends upon the author of the *Consolaçam*. Vague rumors follow his traces to the Holy Land. But like Judah ha-Levi, the Spanish bard with whom his soul was united in the love of Zion, his soul ascended to Jerusalem on high in a mystic cloud of silence.

NOTES

[1] The title page bearing the device of Abraham Usque's printing house reads: CONSOLAÇAM AS TRIBULAÇOENS DE ISRAEL: COMPOSTO POR SAMUEL USQUE. Empresso en Ferrara en Casa de Abraham aben Usque 5313 Da criaçam a 7 de Setembro. The book was printed in Gothic characters, 292 leaves, quarto volume. Another edition printed in round characters, 272 leaves, 12 mo bears spuriously the original date and place of publication on its title page, with the curious mistaken substitution of Sept. 27 for Sept. 7. This printing is generally regarded as having originated in Amsterdam in 1599 and is known as the Amsterdam edition, sometimes erroneously referred to as the *editio princeps*. Both editions are among the rarest of books. Cf. H.M. King Manuel, *Early Portuguese Books 1489–1600 in the Library of His Majesty the King of Portugal*, vol. II, pp. 302 ff.

A faithful reprint of the *Consolaçam* was published by José Mendes dos Remedios in three parts, in volumes 8–10 of the Series, "*Subsidios para o Estudo da Historia da Litteratura Portuguesa*," Coimbra, 1906–8. In this Remedios edition, the book appears in three parts with independent pagination, and is so quoted below.

Among the basic studies on this subject in addition to Remedios' valuable Preface and Notes the following may be cited: Isidore Loeb, "Comparison d'Usque et de l'Emek habbakha," *REJ* XVI, 212–23; Fritz Baer, *Untersuchungen über Quellen und Komposition des Schebet Jehuda*, 2–37, Berlin 1923; Julius Steinschneider, "Zur Geschichte jüdischen Martyrologien. (R. Samuel Usque's "Trost Israel in seinen Trübsalen,") in *Festschrift zum X. Stiftungsfest des Akademischen Vereins für jüdische Geschichte und Literatur*, 24–77, Berlin, 1893; Graetz, *Geschichte der Juden*, IX 4, Note 7, *et passim*. M. Kayserling, *Biblioteca Española-Portugueza-Judaica s. v.* Usque, Strasbourg, 1890.

[2] *Consolaçam*, Prologue, 5a.

[3] *Idem.* Dialogue III, Ch. 26; Graetz, *Geschichte*, VIII, 348 *et passim*.

[4] Dialogue III, Ch. 29.

[5] That Samuel Usque was reared under Marrano conditions is clearly to be inferred from the tone and theme of the *Consolaçam*, even if it is not stated explicitly.

[6] See pp. 110 ff.

[7] Cf. Manuel, *op. cit.*, II, 545.

[8] Dialogue III, Ch. 30.

[9] *Ibid.*

[10] Dialogue III, Ch. 25.

[11] Dialogue III, Ch. 30.

[12] *Ibid.*

[13] The Duke of Ferrara received the exiles hospitably, so that they "regained that breath of life of which the fatigue of the long journey had robbed them." Dialogue III, 53a.

[14] Dialogue III, 53b.

[15] Dialogue III, Ch. 36.

[16] Dialogue III, 53a.

[17] Solomon Usque's translation of Petrarch's Sonnets was published in Venice, 1567. Graetz, IX, Appendix, Note 7; Kayserling, *Biblioteca Esp.-Portug.-Judaica*, 107.

[18] Graetz, IX, Note 7.

[19] Cf. Cecil Roth, *A History of the Marranos*, Phila. 1932.

[20] Graetz, IX, 310; Roth, *op. cit.*, 324.

[21] Graetz, IX, 310 f. The completion and publication of a new and revised edition of this translation together with the Hebrew text was recently announced in Buenos Aires, Argentine.

[22] Graetz, IX, 310 f.

[23] *Idem*, 310, n. 5.

[24] *Idem*. Appendix, No. 7.

[25] In the one group, הנה העלמה הרה is translated "*he la mosca concibien*," and in the other, the rendition bears a Christological slant: "*he la virgen concibien*."

[26] Manuel, II, 304.

[27] J. B. De Rossi, *De Typographia Hebraeo-Ferrariensi*, Parma, 1780, cited in Graetz, IX, n. 3.

[28] For this service, King Manuel paid a warm tribute to Abraham and Samuel Usque: "These two Jews surely had a great love for Portugal, and many regrets must have been born of this love; one can understand their desire to publish the works of Bernardim Ribeiro. . . . In publishing his works, the two learned Portuguese Jews, with their homesick love for Portugal, wished to pay a tribute of gratitude to the author of *Menina e Moça* — the *Livro de Saudades!* — and at the same time to render service to their country's literature." Manuel, II, 545.

[29] Dialogue III, Ch. 13.

[30] Fritz Baer, *Untersuchungen über Quellen und Komposition des Schebet Juhuda*, 37.

[31] Cf. above, pp. 82 ff.

[32] Cf. Abravanel, מעיני הישועה (*Fountains of Salvation*), ed. Amsterdam 1647, 80 f.

[33] See G. Scholem, *Major trends in Jewish Mysticism*, Jerusalem, 1941, 241 ff.

[33a] Subsequent to the original publication of this essay, a Yiddish translation was published by E. Lipiner זיין ,שמואל אושקי. ר' שמואל פון פארטוגאל. ביי די טייכן פון "ישראל פון ליידן די צו "טרייסט זיין און תקופה. Buenos Aires, 1949.

[34] *Consolaçam*, Prologue, IVa.

[35] Manuel, II, 545.

[36] Dialogue I, 3b.

[37] Dialogue III, Ch. 4: "As for my sin, whose outcry was demanding from the Lord a chastisement, He satisfied it with the mortal agony which I suffered."

[38] Dialogue III, 51a-b.

[39] Dialogue III, 41b.

[40] Dialogue III, 45b, 46a.

[41] Cf. Isidore Loeb, *REJ*, XVI, 212–23; Fritz Baer, *op. cit.*, 2–37.

[42] See *Catalogue of Printed Books in the British Museum s. v.* Fortalitium Fidei.

[43] Dialogue III, Ch. 10.

[44] *Ibid*.

45 *Ibid.*

46 Dialogue III, Ch. 13.

47 Dialogue III, 20. Similarly in regard to Flanders, for which Dr. Gershon Gelbart suggests the substitution of Brussels, he writes: "From their seed, nigh all that principality was populated, and although this was long ago, they still signalize their origin by adopting new Lutheran beliefs that prevail among them at the present time, for they are not yet at rest in the faith which they embraced so unwillingly." Dialogue III, 14.

48 Dialogue III, Ch. 31.

49 Dialogue III, 53b.

50 Dialogue III, Ch. 34.

51 Dialogue III, 67b.

52 Dialogue III, 57b.

53 *Ibid.*

54 Dialogue III, 47b.

55 Dialogue III, 42a.

56 Dialogue III, 59b.

57 Dialogue III, 49b.

58 Dialogue III, 51b.

59 Dialogue III, 48a.

60 Dialogue III, 49b.

61 Dialogue III, 50a.

62 Dialogue III, 50b.

63 Dialogue III, 63a.

64 Dialogue III, 68a.

Medina — Historian of the Inquisition

THE Inquisition was a creation of medieval Christian civilization but its span of life extended to the dawn of the nineteenth century, long after the institution had forfeited whatever sanction it had enjoyed within the fold of the church that had sponsored it. Its native home was on the European continent, chiefly concentrated under the aegis of Spain and Portugal. A derivative home was established for it on the American continent when Spain and Portugal extended their conquests to the new world.

The Inquisition in Mexico and South America — the subject of Medina's studies — was a replica of the older European model. The tribunals of the Holy Office in New Spain presented no new aspects of theory or of practice. They were physical transplantations of the European institution on foreign and virgin soil. Ideologically and functionally the Inquisition of the American colonies was identical with the institution in the mother country under whose direction it operated as a subsidiary branch. It is important to bear this fact in mind in evaluating Medina's contribution to the history of the Inquisition.

A thousand years of preliminary indoctrination preceded the actual formation of the Inquisition in the thirteenth century, and additional legal refinements were formulated prior to its establishment in Castile toward the end of the fifteenth century. The literature which this engendered within the framework of Catholic thought was considerable even before the outbreak of Protestantism. The very nature of the Inquisition, striking deep

Address delivered at the Centennial Celebration of the famed Chilean scholar José Toribio Medina (1852–1930) held in Washington, D. C., November 6–8, 1952, under the auspices of the Pan American Union with the co-operation of the Embassy of Chile and the Library of Congress.

into the recesses of human conscience, wielding virtually untram-
melled power over body, mind and soul was bound inevitably
to arouse passion and controversy. It is understandable that
with the rise of Protestantism, a new literature arose, which
attacked the Inquisition for the havoc it wrought in the lives
of the many thousands whom it condemned for the crime of
heresy. But this led ultimately to historic scientific literature
by Catholic and Protestant scholars analyzing the basic concepts
upon which the Inquisition was founded and by which it
operated.

These writings dealt almost wholly with the Inquisition in
Europe, its origin, its principles, its concepts of faith and salvation, heresy and treason, its manifold relations to the king or
state, the pope and the episcopacy. The outlying posts in the
colonial regions presented no new principles or radical change
in method or procedure. They were therefore not accorded a
significant place in the general literature on the Inquisition. It
was the role of José Toribio Medina to bring into sharp focus
the history, the operations, the influence, the decline and the
ultimate disappearance of this institution in the southern countries of the American continent.

As in every other branch of Medina's literary productivity,
his work on the Inquisition in Spanish America was thorough,
methodical, documented and voluminous. In chronological
sequence, we record his two volumes on the Inquisition in Lima,
1887; two volumes on Chile, 1890, now republished by the
Chilean government in honor of the Centenary; three volumes
in 1899 dealing respectively with Cartagena, the Philippines
and the Provincias del Plata; the latter was reprinted by Hermes
in 1945; one volume on Mexico, 1905, now reprinted in a handsome edition in honor of the Medina Centenary by the Ediciones
Fuente Cultural, with Doctor J. J. Rueda as editor; and finally
La primitiva inquisición americana (1493–1569); estudio histórico in
1914.

All subsequent works may amplify but cannot alter the structure erected by Medina. Thus the learned editor of the volume on Mexico, Doctor J. J. Rueda, though somewhat critical of Medina's method and viewpoint, and inclined to be more apologetic for the Inquisition and to emphasize its political economic motivation, actually strengthened Medina's structure by adding supplementary cases at the end of each of the first nine chapters in Medina's work.

These works are basic to any study of the subject. Indeed, no better authority than Henry C. Lea need be quoted. "Thanks to the unwearied researches of Don José Toribio Medina," he wrote in the preface to *The Inquisition in the Spanish Dependencies*, "a fairly complete and minute account can be given, based on the confidential correspondence of the local officials with the Supreme Council and the reports of the *visitadores* or inspectors who were occasionally sent in the vain expectation of reducing them (the tribunals) to order."

And yet it is safe to say that Medina was not an historian of the Inquisition *per se*. He was first and foremost an Americanist, enamored and proud of his country, desirous of resurrecting its past. He came upon the subject of the Inquisition almost by accident while he was exploring the Spanish archives in search of documentary material bearing on the colonial history of Chile. It was then, while he was browsing in the archives at Simanca, that he came across massive bundles of documents stored away in the basement, documents that opened up hidden vistas of the Inquisition in the Spanish-American colonies and particularly of Lima, the ancient capital of Peru, documents which cast a lurid light on early colonial history. It was this discovery that set him upon the trail of the Inquisition in the Spanish colonies and he treated the subject as part of American history rather than as a phase of Catholic Christendom whose heart and soul were in Europe.

Medina wrote his volumes on the Inquisition in Lima fresh

under the impact of his newly discovered documents. It was but a year after he returned from Europe that these volumes appeared off the press. The preface reveals Medina's pained reactions to the documented revelations. He aimed studiously to be objective in the narration. He declared that he would present the reader with the documents and the "facts." He would wherever possible let the old contemporaries tell the story in their own words. The interpretation of the facts would be left to the reader who would judge them in accordance with his own cultural background, temperament and viewpoint. Nevertheless, Medina could not repress his own feeling of revulsion as the vivid account of the trials by the tribunals of the Holy Office unfolded before his eyes.

Medina was no rebel or iconoclast. He wrote as a liberal person whose religious sensibilities were wounded by the actions of the Inquisition in the name of God and in defense of faith. As a patriot and lover of his people he deplored its baneful influence upon his countrymen which he said was still evident in some of the unpleasant traits of his contemporaries.

Medina realized that the actions of the Inquisition which he found so revolting were in part due to the spirit of the times which reveled in autos-da-fé. All the more he gloried in the "law of progress" which enabled society to shed its shame and to free itself from wrong-doing. Thus far the preface, which reveals Medina the man, the historian as well as the spirit of his work.

In the historical work proper, Medina is strictly the documentary historian. His history of the Inquisition in Lima — and this is true of his other related works — is based largely upon the mass of letters, reports, trial records and kindred documents which the American Inquisitors and other officials sent to the Supreme Council in Spain and which he found in abundance during his explorations in the Spanish archives, among which Simanca proved most fertile. Much of this material is reproduced by Medina verbatim. Owing to this literal adherence to documentary sources, his writings betray at times unevenness in literary proportion.

The story of the American Inquisition begins with King Philip II and his Inquisitor-General Espinosa, who jointly gave birth to the Holy Office in the Americas between 1569 and 1570. By order of the King and under the direction of the Inquisitor-General, two independent tribunals were set up almost simultaneously in Lima and Mexico "for the augmentation and conservation of our sacred Catholic Faith and Christian Religion." The territories placed under the jurisdiction of these tribunals were vast, comprising the entire Spanish dominion in the Americas. To meet these extensive responsibilities, the Holy Office in the two capital centers stretched a vast network over their enormous provinces through a system of officials known under various titles who worked as spies, police, jailers and experts in the art of torture as well as a staff of legal and fiscal officials to attend to sequestration and confiscation of the property of those who were caught in the net of the Inquisition.

Thus originally Chile, Argentine, New Granada, among the important provinces, came under the jurisdiction of the tribunal in Lima while the Philippine Islands, for instance, were under the aegis of the Holy Office in Mexico. As the work of heresy hunting became more arduous and the results more plentiful, another tribunal was established in Cartagena in 1610. The other provinces were placed under the control of representatives of the Holy Office known as Commissioners, who carried on the activities with the same zeal and methods as the Inquisitors themselves. Their *familiares*, or spies, were particularly active in seaports and coastal cities, on guard against the importation of heresy by persons or books.

Notwithstanding the fact that the Inquisition ran a parallel course in all these areas, Medina patiently recorded the history in each country separately with all the details that his documents afforded, thus compensating perhaps through detailed accuracy for the lack of the integration of the parts into a greater inter-related unit.

For the purposes of this paper, in which the emphasis is on Medina in relation to his subject, it will be best to begin with the author's first work which treats of the Inquisition in Lima and then relate his subsequent works to the initial treatise.

Medina's work opens with the arrival in Lima on June 9, 1570 of the Licentiate Servan Cerezuela "for the service of the Lord and of his Majesty and the growth of our Christian religion." His shadow hovers over the pages of this book and its sequel on Chile. He appears as the model inquisitor, relentless, fanatical and burning with zeal to purge the country of heresy, sorcery and immorality.

His associate Inquisitor died and Cerezuela came alone, armed with formidable powers, spiritual and temporal. All officials of the government were required to take an oath of obedience to the Inquisitor. The bishops were strictly enjoined to transfer all pending and future cases involving matters of faith to the Holy Office. The machinery of the government was placed at his command and none dared to obstruct, defy or deny the authority of the Inquisitor and his subordinate officials.

Citing original letters and documents, Medina described the ceremonious installation of the Inquisition: the summoning of the population to the Cathedral with drum and trumpet; the solemn procession of the Inquisitor to the service under the escort of the dignitaries of church and state; the reading of the royal proclamation denouncing heretical propaganda and commanding the government to give all aid to the Holy Office and to execute its sentences; the administration of the oath of obedience; the solemn pronouncing of the edict of faith which called upon the population under fearful malediction to denounce all possible offenders even if the denunciation was based on suspicion or mere hearsay. Thus was established a new power in the state which exceeded the power of the state itself. Resentment was widespread in governmental circles but was particularly keen among the bishops whose rights of jurisdiction were sharply curtailed.

Cerezuela proceeded to organize the tribunal's staff which was considerable: an assistant or junior inquisitor who was appointed in Spain; a fiscal, a secretary, a treasurer; an *alguazil*, a nuncio, a barber, a physician, and a surgeon; advocates, *consultores* and *familiares*. For distant communities, commissioners were appointed with similar but more restricted staffs of officials. It was an expensive organization, financed originally from the royal treasury with the expectation that it would soon become at least self-sustaining by reason of fines and confiscations. In time, the revenue more than met these expectations, but the Inquisitors continued their drain upon the depleted treasury causing endless friction between the Holy Office and the Crown officials. This condition effectively deterred the Spanish kings from establishing additional tribunals of the Holy Office despite the pleading of the American Inquisitors.

Operations of the Inquisition started promptly and arrests followed in quick order. Curiously enough, among the first targets were two canons of the Cathedral and two royal officials who were tried and fined for relatively minor offenses. Before long, in 1573, Cerezuela staged a dramatic auto-da-fé in Lima's public square. It was comparatively a poor affair. The staging was not yet perfected and there were only a few penitents. It was, however, sufficiently exciting and thrilling for the dignitaries to vie with each other for preferred places from which to witness the dread ceremony as sentence was pronounced: one to perpetual imprisonment, another to lifelong galley-service, a third to two hundred lashes and finally the climax: the burning at the stake of a Frenchman whose complete sanity was in question but who was nevertheless convicted as a heretic and a Protestant.

Medina casts a lurid light upon the mystic cults of the age in which women were inspired in trances with visions and revelations. This was, of course, the work of demons. But about this time a young woman, María Pizzarro, had visitations from the angel Gabriel revealing to her the mystery of the Immaculate Conception and other occult manifestations which lured a number of divines into the mire of heresy, including a learned Dominican theologian of the highest repute and two Jesuits noted for their saintliness. This is the backdrop for the staging of the second auto-da-fé held in Lima in 1578.

A period of five years intervened between the initiation and the final processing of these cases. In the interim, death visited the inquisitorial prison and mercifully removed some of the characters, including the tragic heroine María herself. The episode furnished the auto-da-fé with a strange collection of priestly penitents. Considering the gravity of the offense, the clerical penitents were dealt with moderately, with one solitary exception. This was the brilliant Dominican, Francisco de la Cruz. His visions had grown more fantastic, his claims shockingly sacrilegious as he imagined himself the son of God and the Virgin. Although to all appearances hopelessly insane, he argued too nimbly with the theologians, who sought to convert him, to be adjudged irrational. There was no other course but to burn him at the stake.

Following upon this account, Medina proceeded to describe the inquisitorial process in all its stages, leading up to its finale in the auto-da-fé. Heresy did not have to be proved. It was enough to establish a suspicion of heresy, for this in itself was a crime. Hence the ordinary rules of evidence did not come into play in heresy trials. Mere rumor, surmise, the observation of suspicious circumstance or some loose utterance was deemed sufficient ground to imprison the suspect and to impound his property. Disreputable characters and unsubstantiated evidence were acceptable in heresy trials if they tended to incriminate the suspect. Accusation and denunciation were dignified as acts in defense of the faith and were demanded of the faithful, regardless of previous vow or oath. Faltering or unwilling witnesses frequently opened up in the torture chamber. Failure to bring testimony even against father, mother, brother or sister made one an accomplice in heresy. Such testimony of relatives and servants, however, was acceptable only if it was adverse to the accused but not in defense.

The weaker the link of evidence the more important it seemed to induce the suspect to make a confession. Medina related the wiles practiced by the Inquisitors to trap the victim into confession. When this failed, the prisoner was brought into the torture chamber and was interrogated in full view of the implements of horror. If the mere threat was not effective, torture was applied with diverse instruments and increasing agony till confession was wrung out of the racked victim. If in the face of torture, the suspect denied his guilt and the evidence against him was deemed sufficient or if he admitted the heresy and remained steadfast, refusing to abjure his errors, the verdict was clear. The Inquisition "relaxed" him to the civil authorities for burning at the stake. Any attempt to retract the confession led to further torture.

Confession did not lead to forgiveness. Two hundred lashes, incarceration or the galleys and total confiscation of property were the usual prescribed punishments, varying with the degree of the crime and depending on the inquisitor's arbitrary judgment. The penitent was required formally to abjure the heresy. Thereafter, any sliding back to the previous error could be construed as a relapse and could lead to "relaxation," or burning at the stake.

Theoretically, Medina pointed out, the inquisitors were required to consult with the bishops in rendering sentence. In any event, the bishops and the chief magistrates of the civil government attended the final ceremony when sentence was publicly pronounced upon the guilty. This was the occasion of the auto-da-fé.

Medina ironically referred to this solemn celebration as a fiesta. Recurrently, he dwelt on the details of the ceremony as he recounted the identical story of the Inquisition in various lands: the brilliant array of church and state dignitaries; the festive throngs who came from far and near; the stage specially erected in the center of the church for the penitents; and finally the procession of the penitents with green candles in their hands, attired in weird costume, each bearing a hideous symbol of his dereliction; each penitent marching with two *familiares* at his side.

Medina takes his readers with him into the Cathedral, so graphic is his description of the proceedings. We behold the Viceroy and his officials, the bishops and all who were present, high and low, arise to swear the oath of obedience to the Inquisitors; the chief Inquisitor delivers a sermon; the notary of the Holy Office reads the charges against each prisoner and the verdict reached by the judges. He summons the penitents to recite with him, word by word, the declaration of abjuration. They were called in ascending order according to the degree of their offense, leaving to the end those who were doomed to be burned. The *quemadero* was already prepared in the public square, at the Plaza de Acho, in Lima, and thither the assembly repaired after the service, or more frequently the following day when the sentences were executed in gala surroundings — from the lashing of men and women stripped to the waist, to the burning at the stake of heretics, Calvinists, Lutherans, Judaizers. If at the last moment the victims repented, they were garroted first and then burned; otherwise they were committed to the flames alive. It must have appeared anticlimactic after the extinction of these human torches to burn the exhumed bodies of posthumous heretics and the effigies of those who fled beyond the reach of the Inquisition. As even these executions were accompanied by confiscations, the effect of these symbolic "executions" was felt with painful realism by the families who were rendered destitute and by the descendants who were tainted for generations to come.

It is surprising to find how few were the cases of Spanish or native Catholic heretics cited by Medina among the penitents who marched in the autos-da-fé. Propositions, or theological deviations implicated a number of priests and Jesuits but the intellectual soil of the colonies was not conducive to the growth of doctrinal heresy. Among the early victims, Jan Bernal, burned in 1581, and Miguel del Pilar similarly executed in 1587, were Flemings. English mariners and prisoners of war furnished the largest single contingent of foreigners tried by the Inquisition. Medina intimates that in these cases, economic and political considerations reinforced the fear of the inquisitors regarding the penetration of Lutheran and Calvinistic influences.

The major and most lucrative phase of the battle for the defense of the faith was that directed against Judaizers, the New Christians who were suspected of adhering secretly to the Jewish faith underneath the cloak of Catholicism. It appears to have been Medina's method — perhaps in his own defense as the objective historian — when he was about to describe a chapter of the Inquisition that was most repellent to his conscience to unroll the story in the original narration as he found it in the records of the Tribunal and the Supreme Council. The stark tragedy of the Jewish martyrs is thus unfolded in hundreds of pages culled from the inquisitorial archives.

Beginning with the auto-da-fé of December 5, 1592, Judaizers, usually identified as Portuguese, became increasingly conspicuous in the melancholy procession of penitents, some to be burned, or, if repentant in the face of death, to be "reconciled," a mocking name covering up the penalty of confiscation and the added punishment of flagellation, imprisonment for a term of years or life, or possibly service at the galleys. Of the ten Judaizers named in the trials that led to the auto-da-fé of 1592, one died in prison, five were "reconciled." Of the remaining four, one weakened in the face of death and was strangled before burning; the other three were burned alive. The numbers of Judaizers rose to fourteen in the auto-da-fé of 1600 and sixteen in 1605. The auto-da-fé of 1625 was marked by the fact that in addition to those who were burned alive two victims who had committed suicide in prison were disinterred and their corpses burned with their bones. The climax was reached in 1639, the greatest auto-da-fé staged in Spanish America. The celebrated case of Maldonado de Silva, author, surgeon, martyr, whose heroic life story is comparable to the martyrology of his ancestors in Bible times, reached its tragic culmination in the flames of that "auto" on January 23, 1639. It is recorded that when the decree was read sentencing him to "relaxation" a whirlwind blew away the awning and as he beheld the sky overhead he exclaimed "The God of Israel does this to look upon me face to face!"

Of greater public concern than the most intense individual drama was the furor created by the mass arrests which led to the famous "auto" of 1639. Among those arrested were some of the most prominent citizens, Jewish Portuguese merchants, bankers and financiers. There were not enough prisons in Lima to house the prisoners. New cells were hurriedly constructed and additional prisons improvised. An extra force of inquisitors was drafted to sift the evidence, to supervise the torture and to sequester the enormous wealth represented by the prisoners. The economic upheaval threatened the city with general bankruptcy, and the lure of wealth corrupted the officials who worked under the inquisitors. In the end, the Holy Office reaped a harvest of gold and an array of sinners that was unprecedented. Eleven paid the ultimate penalty of martyrdom for their belief. Fifty more were "reconciled." Of these, twenty-one aggregated in punishment four thousand lashes, one hundred and six years at the galleys and two condemnations for life.

In the concluding chapter of his work on the Inquisition in Lima, Medina in summary estimated that three thousand cases were tried before that tribunal. In an appendix, he listed alphabetically 1,474 persons who were processed by the tribunal and who were mentioned by name in the course of this book. These he classified significantly according to the status of class and the nature of the offense. Following are the figures under the first category: persons tried: 108 women; 101 secular clergy; 49 Franciscan monks; 34 Dominicans; 36 Mercenarians; 26 Augustinians; 12 Jesuits. The remainder of 1,126 were laymen. The second category, the nature of the offenses, fell under the following headings: propositions 140 cases; Judaizers 243; Mohammedanism 5 cases; Lutheranism 65; blasphemy 97 cases; violations of moral law 40; bigamy 207 cases; sorcery 172; solicitations in confessionals 109; miscellaneous 306. Altogether there were 34 autos-da-fé celebrated in Lima from 1573 to July 17, 1806, the last active date of the Inquisition in Peru.

As in the Preface, so toward the end of the book Medina reiterated that the final judgment of the Inquisition was left to the reader. Nevertheless, he could not refrain from pointing to the glaring inconsistencies in the punishments meted out to the convicted. Thus the most shocking offense in the list of derelictions, the abuse of the confessional for the seduction of women by priests, was treated with such tender moderation as to lift it out of the class of penalties associated with the Holy Office. For a slight deviation in an article of faith, the culprit in one instance was sentenced to thirteen years imprisonment and exile whereas a priest who defiled himself and his calling through solicitation was merely deprived of the right to confess women for a limited period. Quoting Medina: "The pen is reluctant to write the infamies" of the accused monks with whom the Inquisition deals very leniently.

Above all, Medina deplored the evil influence which the Inquisition had upon the character of the people of Peru. These are his concluding words: "If the people subject to such tyranny did not sink to a lower moral, intellectual and social level it was perhaps because there are limits to human degradation which cannot be broken down." But this phase of the national history, he concluded, will always have to be studied if one is to understand the causes and the elements that entered into the making of the social texture of the people.

Medina's abhorrence of the Inquisition and its works became pronounced in increasing progressive measure as he proceeded from area to area till he covered the history of the Inquisition in all the major regions of Spanish America. Although the story was virtually the same in all the regions and but for a change of names of persons and places one history could readily be substituted for another, he was determined to tell the full story in all its parts and to establish the record for all time. In this he succeeded. To follow Medina's pattern in each country is not feasible within the limits of this paper, nor is it particularly desirable. It is interesting, however, to trace Medina's personal reactions in the course of the volumes he devoted to the subject.

Chile was his native country which he loved with the fervor of the true patriot. It was but natural that evils visited upon his country would grieve him deeply. In the preface to the two volumes on the Inquisition in Chile, he bitterly voiced doubt whether it would not have been better "to dump the moth-eaten documents into the river that flows at the foot of the building where they were stored." But, he concluded, they were valuable because they threw light on the social life of the people.

Chile did not have an independent tribunal. It was subsidiary to the Holy Office in Lima. A commissioner represented the Lima tribunal in Santiago and he processed the cases in his territory for the Inquisition in Lima. The procedure followed the established pattern. *Familiares* were operating through the country ferreting out suspects and accumulating evidence for their arrest. Brought to Santiago, they were thrown into jail, tortured in one of the secret dungeons of the Inquisition till they confessed and implicated other suspects or accomplices. Their property sequestered, they often languished in prison for years till their turn came to be transported to Lima for trial and punishment. This was the process in the celebrated cases of Maldonada de Silva, the physician and philosopher, and the millionaire merchant, Manuel Baptista Perez, who fed the flames in the Lima *quemadero* in the famous auto-da-fé of 1639.

Chile was but a sequel to Lima and many of the characters appear and reappear in each story. The same intrigues came to light; the same type of offenders — bigamists, sorcerers, clerics, monks, Lutherans, Mohammedans and Jews, and foreigners in general. The lengthy account of the hostility between the Augustinian and Franciscan monks is far from edifying. The low moral character of those who were the guardians of faith and morality offend Medina's sense of decency and justice. As to the convents, "my pen refuses to write about them," said Medina, "or enter their grounds."

As the interlocking operations of the Inquisition in Lima with its branches in Santiago and other provinces come to light, it becomes apparent that the Inquisition was also used as an instrument of economic nationalism. English and French penetration was feared. Foreign merchants and sailors were eyed with suspicion. Among the English sailors who were arrested on the charge of Lutheranism were prisoners of war and some who were stranded in a storm. The persecution of Portuguese Judaizantes became virulent after the dissolution of the political bonds between Spain and Portugal.

The conflict between the bishops and the inquisitors which led to the *cédula de concordia* in 1610 does little honor to the Holy Office. The reader feels a sense of relief to be transported from ecclesiastical bickering to a genuine religious manifestation which was fascinating though heretical. I refer to the famous case of the Jesuit, Padre Francisco de Ulloa, a true mystic who influenced a circle of followers, many of them nuns, and led them into heights of religious experience and holy living through paths and doctrines that could not be other than heretical. It is a tragic story, filled with melodrama, heroic characters pitted against spies and conspirators, mystic souls soaring heavenward caught in the foils of pious treachery, with the inevitable sad ending. Medina gives us this picture in his characteristic manner by summoning the old documents to tell the story in their own uninhibited eloquence.

In this work on Chile he frequently casts off the restraint which was so marked in his initial work on the Inquisition in Lima and reveals his deep-seated moral indignation. He exulted "in the passing forever of the dark shadows which the hateful tribunal (odioso tribunal) had cast over the intellect of the "*colonos*," and he concluded with the following quotation from Mellet's *Voyage*: "All the horrors of the Inquisition in Spain cannot be compared to the perpetrations of the bloody tribunal in America."

For a decade, Medina abandoned the Inquisition for more pleasing subjects, when in 1899 he returned to the former theme with three publications dealing with the Inquisition in La Plata, Cartagena and the Philippine Islands. Like Chile, the territory of La Plata was ruled by the Holy Office in Lima through remote control by Inquisition-appointed commissioners. Nothing essentially new is revealed in this volume, save for more facts that lead to the same conclusions. A large section, approximately 150 pages, consists of *documentos*, documents from 1576 to 1754. In the foreword, Medina stressed the secrecy with which the tribunals conducted their trials and the veil of secrecy in which Spain enveloped her colonies to seclude and isolate them from contact with the freer European countries. The strange case of the conquistador, Francisco de Aguirre, in his valiant but futile battle against his political enemies who conspired against him with their inquisitorial allies in an unholy conspiracy, comes to the fore again in more elaborate detail. As Medina moved progressively from country to country, he cast aside whatever was left of his former veil of reticence. The pope and the king, he held, were responsible for making a supergovernment of the "Santo Officio." The people under its rule lived in terror. "Nobody was sure of himself," nor could he trust his neighbor. The people hated the institution but were cowed by it. Only the Jesuits occasionally dared to offer resistance. Medina found it "a shocking contradiction" for the inquisitors to be so severe in even trifling matters of faith and blithely to ignore among the priests and in their own lives the injunction of the sixth commandment.

Cartagena, too, began its inquisitorial career under a Commissioner as a subsidiary branch of the Holy Office in Lima. Character-wise, it had an inauspicious beginning, judging by the moral depravity of the Commissioners as reported in the records of the Supreme Council. By 1610, Cartagena acquired its own tribunal which was ceremoniously installed with pomp and solemnity, already witnessed earlier in Lima and Mexico.

Its operations need not detain us, except to point out that there were comparatively a smaller number of Jews and Protestants burned at the auto-da-fé, most of the denunciations having been for witchcraft, sorcery and blasphemy which it proved impossible to eradicate.

The volume on the Philippines was in a sense premature, as the volume on Mexico was not published till 1905, which was six years later, and the Philippine Inquisition was only a subsidiary branch of the Mexican tribunal. It may be that in 1899 Medina had not planned to write the history of the Inquisition in Mexico, for as he indicated in the Foreword of the latter volume, the history of the Mexican tribunal, was the one best known and only due to special considerations did he undertake to write that work. In any event, Medina explained that it was necessary to detach the story of the Inquisition in the Philippines from Mexico in order that the reader should not be confused and his attention distracted. Though the central problem was the same, he asserted, the "accompanying factors of place persons and events" were different. All his writings on the Inquisition were needed, he thought, to produce the panoramic picture of "the history and bibliography of Spanish America."

As indicated, the Philippine apparatus was but an extension of the Mexican Inquisition. The Philippine Islands being more exposed to attack and conquest than inland country, the Inquisition was employed against the English and the Dutch to ward off political danger as well as heresy. The power of the Jesuits to which Medina made reference in several of his earlier works came to light in a sensational case in which a member of the Jesuit Order was involved with a native woman, Luisa de los Reyes, in a dangerous heresy complicated by sexual aberration so revolting that Medina felt that to describe it would be "repugnante." Nevertheless, the Order was able to snatch him from the grasp of the Inquisition and take him under its own jurisdiction.

History gave a strange turn and climax to the Inquisition in the Philippines. On October 15, 1762, the British captured Manila. Some months later, the Commissioner, fearing arrest and seizure of the Inquisition archives, set fire to the documents and they perished in the flames.

The History of the Mexican Inquisition, published in 1905, is the final treatise in Medina's national series of South American Inquisitions. It is a major work, perhaps his finest on this general theme.

The tribunal in Mexico was established simultaneously with that of Lima. Both institutions ran a parallel course and, in the words of Medina, gave rise "to misery, passions, conflicts and deeply rooted hatreds." In this history, Medina fortifying the authenticity of his treatment by copious citations from the original sources is more outspoken and sharper in his delineations.

We shall make no attempt to reproduce the subject matter of this work. After reviewing his earlier treatises, especially that of Lima, the story in essence, if not in actual detailed fact, is a manifold-told tale. We shall limit ourselves to some of Medina's utterances that strike a personal chord.

In some of these statements, Medina offered judgment on men and events in the passing scenes. He was saddened by the revelations of immorality among the clergy and continuous quarreling between the bishops and the officials of the tribunal. He painfully recited the series of autos-da-fé, vividly describing the tortures, the lashings, and the burning of human beings — some Protestants and many Jews — at the stake. He referred to the "autos," in general, as fiestas, as grandiose theatrical affairs, and one —"el auto grande"— the most spectacular of all, was deliberately arranged in 1649 for the grand coup of large fortunes that would fall to the Inquisition through the confiscation of the immense fortunes of the Portuguese Judaizers.

Among "Los ultimos quemados," the last to be burned, was the first martyr to die for the independence of Nueva España, Don Guillem Lombardo. The appearance of an aurora borealis threw the people into panic, such was the primitive condition of the Inquisition-ruled masses virtually on the eve of the French Revolution. The Inquisition fought desperately at the side of the state to keep the people in darkness and to prevent free ideas from penetrating the Spanish dominion.

When the sounds of the French Revolution echoed in Mexico, the Inquisition instituted intensive persecution of Frenchmen and lovers of freedom. Among the victims were two Frenchmen whose last days in jail belong to the epics of human heroism. Both took their own lives. The struggle between the passion for freedom and revolution against the decadent powers of the

Inquisition could have but one ending. The last two chapters are appropriately entitled "El Santo Officio y la Revolución" and "Extinción del Santo Officio." The triumph of independence spelled the extinction of the Holy Office.

Reviewing in his mind's eye the Inquisition in all its phases, Medina concluded his Introduction with these bitter words: "The reader no less than I must have felt more than once moved to take off his clothes for fear of soiling them . . . ."

Medina's last and final work on the Inquisition, in two volumes, chronologically should have been the first of the series. As indicated in the title, *La primitiva inquisición americana (1493–1569); estudio histórico*, this work treats of the early period from Columbus' second voyage to the Americas to the time when Philip II established the Holy Office in Lima and Mexico. During this period, the bishops acted as "inquisidores ordinarios" as distinguished from the apostolic Inquisition set up by the Spanish king. With the establishment of the Holy Office, the authority of the bishops in matters of faith was peremptorily withdrawn.

Medina had already treated this unsavory chapter of human cruelty and religious fanaticism as a prologue to each of his other volumes. Nevertheless he regarded this work as perhaps the most important historic contribution of all his writings on the American Inquisition. In this estimate he was thinking not so much of the first volume which is descriptive but of the second volume which consists wholly of documents and is so entitled: *Documentos.* The work of gathering, sifting and editing those rare and widely scattered documents consumed more time and effort, he said, than all his other works on the American Inquisition. Despite many difficulties and a curious accident by the printer which drove him to despair and almost made him abandon the project, he succeeded triumphantly in bringing these precious documents to light.

Medina's superlative regard for these literary remains, which are among the earliest documents of American history, expressed first and foremost the enthusiasm of America's most renowned and devoted bibliographer par excellence. It also expressed the self-vindication of the historian. These documents were the personal armor of defense against the attacks that were directed against him by contemporary reactionaries who charged him with prejudice and historic falsification.

The evils of the national past were a burden upon his soul and, as he said repeatedly, a leaden weight upon the national character. Only by laying bare the dark forces that corrupted the national heritage could the people be saved. He had indeed hoped to write also a history of the educational systems in these countries and to lighten the gloom and darkness by an account of the universities and their enlightened leaders, but little time was left him for this undertaking outside of Chile.

Medina remained defiant to the end. "Many a time," he said, "as we take pen in hand we feel like the surgeon who probes with his knife into the vital organs of a dead body in order to discover what caused the body to die." This is the key to an understanding of Medina's probing into the secrets of the Inquisition. It was to ferret out the secret of what makes a nation live or decay. Having discovered the cause, he laid it bare through his writings and constructed an appalling monument of human folly and degradation for his people to behold, to take warning, to renounce an evil heredity and through education to seek self-liberation in freedom of thought and conscience.

RELIGIOUS STUDIES

Judaism among the Great Religions of the Modern World

JUDAISM is the religion professed by a small people, the Jewish people, who numbered no more than sixteen million souls at the zenith of their numerical growth before World War II, and are now reduced to about ten or eleven million through the maniacal fury of a clique which set out to destroy the religion and the people, root and branch. They numbered less than a million in the days of their nationhood, when according to tradition, David composed Psalms and Solomon wrote epigrams and parables of wisdom; and probably not more than four to five million when their political fate as a nation was sealed in the year 70 and they set out upon their historic career as a global people with a religion and a Bible to live by and to defend, if need be, even unto death. At the height of the Middle Ages, during the thirteenth century, when Judaism had reached its full rabbinic development and was exerting a great influence upon the emerging European civilization, the Jewish population in Europe did not much exceed one million people.

This people, one of the smallest and oldest historic nations — now scattered over the globe — out of the depth of its own experience, attained to a lofty and unique vision of God, man, and the universe, and translated that vision into a program of living. That vision and that way of life constitute the philosophy and the precepts of Judaism.

The relationship between the people and the religion is unique in Judaism; for the religion is inconceivable without a continuous, living Jewish people. By the normal process of religious conversion Judaism can absorb and assimilate indi-

Reprinted from *The Great Religions of the Modern World* (ed. Edward J. Jurji), Princeton University Press, 1947.

viduals and even nations within its fold, and it has indeed done so. But were the Jews of the world to disappear, their religion would inevitably disappear with them. Other peoples who had no historic connection with the Jewish past could under such circumstances become heir to the universal teachings of Judaism; but the precepts, ceremonials, and observances in which these principles are incorporated and which make up the body of Judaism would have no relevancy for those whose ancestors did not "go out of the land of Egypt," and who were not born to the tradition that their fathers stood at the foot of Sinai and that they and their descendants were forever to be a kingdom of priests and a holy nation.

The indissoluble bond between the people and religion is a basic part of Judaism. Judaism was not given full grown to the Jewish people as was Christianity to the pagan nations. To its adherents, the Jewish religion in essence is not the distillation of the tears and sorrows of others, freely given them by an act of divine grace or acquired through the mysteries of faith. Slowly and painfully over the course of many centuries it was beaten out of the historic experiences of the nation, illumined by the vision of its prophets and sages. The prophets of Israel, profound mystics, who envisaged God the Infinite, who perceived that His Spirit filled the universe, and who spoke in His Name with the warmth, intimacy, and conviction of personal revelation, were not detached individualists or universalists. They were essentially national heroes of the Jewish religious genius. The problems, sins, failures, and sorrows of their people were the starting-point of their spiritual brooding. However universal and far-reaching the resulting prophetic vision may have been, its light was focused upon Israel and, through Israel, its rays were diffused round the world.

Secondary only to the people was the relationship of the land to the religion during the early stages of its development. In the Abraham covenant, the promise of the land follows closely upon the choice of Abraham's descendants as "a blessing to all the families of the earth." The possession of the Promised Land was not merely a national goal; it was not only the vehicle of a divine covenant and an instrument by which God's pleasure or displeasure with the people was manifested; it was the medium for a system of agricultural and land legislation which gave meaning to the ethical character of the religion. Rooted in the land are the biblical laws for relief from the curse of poverty, precepts to prevent land concentration in the hands of the few, provisions for a program of social justice. Even after the forcible separation of the Jewish people from their land, the skies and the soil of Palestine, the rain and the dew, the trees and the fruit of the Holy Land have continued to be mirrored in the prayers and festive days of the Jewish religion to this day.

Judaism therefore appears under two aspects: the universal and the national. As a system of religious thought it is transcendent and universal. As a religious cult, it is characterized by historic associations and even geographic coloring. Its ethical principles embrace all mankind; its religious discipline binds only its adherents. Through its own votaries in the Graeco-Roman world and later more effectively through its daughter religions, Christianity and Islam, it won the pagan world over to the Hebrew God of justice, mercy, and holiness. But even when the world was the prize at stake, Judaism would not surrender its distinctive historic ties. It could not abandon its religious system of law, rite, and ceremony any more than it could compromise with its conception of pure monotheism.

It may well be said that Judaism views theology through the eyes of history in contrast to Christianity, for instance, in which theology is primary and history is secondary. Basing itself on the record of the Pentateuch, the Prophets, and the oral tradition, Judaism beheld the gradual and manifold manifestation of God's Being and His active will revealed variously in its history, in the forces of nature, in prophetic utterances, and in a program of divinely inspired legislation. In the drama thus unfolded historically, the Jewish people was the chief instrument of the

divine revelation. Having revealed Himself through the instrumentality of Israel He was called the God of Israel, as formerly
He was called the God of Abraham, Isaac, and Jacob. But the
God of Israel was the Father of mankind, the Creator of the
universe, the Source of all life and the Ruler of all His creatures.
He was clothed in Holiness. His chief raiments were Justice,
Love, Truth, and Mercy. These attributes of God were manifested in the historic experiences of the people and were revealed
in their divine light to His prophets. They were channeled into
human life as an activating force for conduct through the Law,
written and oral. The Law, therefore, has an exalted place in
Judaism. No distinction divides so-called ceremonial or ritual
laws from ethical precepts, as both drew their sanction from the
living God. However detailed any part of the Law may be, it
speaks the language of the universal God. "Blessed art Thou,
O Lord our God, King of the universe" is the introductory in-
vocation to the performance of all religious precepts in Judaism.

In this conception, Israel is the custodian of a religion the
essence of which belongs to the world. It lays no claim to a
monopoly or the exclusive possession of God's truth. Rather
does it proclaim itself to be the God-appointed trustee of religion
in the interest of all mankind. This is the meaning which Judaism
gave to the verse: "And ye shall be unto Me a kingdom of priests
and a holy nation." As the priests served their people in the
Temple of God, so must Israel serve mankind in the kingdom
of God on earth. As the priests, serving in the Temple, observed
a priestly code to fit them for their special functions, so must
the Jews observe a special code, the Torah, written and oral,
to fit, or sanctify themselves for their world ministration.

The attitude of Judaism toward other religions is therefore
unique and distinctive, following therein too an historic pattern.
The stern religious discipline of the Law, which grew out of the
very history of Israel, was requisite for this priestly people, but
not for the general redemption of mankind. Indeed, according

to rabbinic tradition, God made a covenant with the human race which long preceded the covenant with Israel, and in that early covenant was laid the basis for a universal faith of mankind. The foundations, or principles, of this early universal religion were described as the "Laws of the children of Noah." These religious "Laws," or ethical principles, were elementary in character but not different in kind from the advanced religious-ethical principles which Israel was destined to develop under prophetic tutelage. They were the embryonic stage in the evolution of that religion which Judaism envisaged as the ultimate faith of mankind. Undoubtedly, the rabbis reconstructed imaginatively the "Laws of the children of Noah" with an eye to paganism. Their purpose was to construct a program to lead the nations away from the glaring moral and religious delinquencies of paganism. The nations were therefore bidden to abandon idolatry and blasphemy. Incest, murder, theft, cruelty to animals, as practiced in the eating of limbs torn from living animals, are the negative precepts of the moral law. The covenant to administer justice is the seventh and final commandment of the universal faith. On these minimal conditions, so the rabbis taught, the moral order of the world could be sustained and human well-being maintained. But it was the function of the priestly people to lead the nations to nobler heights of moral and religious perfection. How was this to be accomplished? Judaism never developed a religious army of missionaries. The driving impulse of an exclusive gospel, which would be the sole key to salvation, was utterly lacking. For salvation was open to all who honored even the minimum standards of the universal faith. The formal conversion to Judaism of the nations of the world was not part of the divine program. Rather was it the function of the priestly people by its life and its work to establish moral and religious standards which would of their own attractive powers draw the nations to the road of moral perfection and closer communion with God.

This ideal relationship between Israel and the nations, between Judaism and other faiths was not an isolated concept
limited to one period in the evolution of Judaism. It pervades
the entire course of Jewish history. In glowing and poetic
metaphor, the prophets pictured the fulfillment of the vision
"in the end of days." The rabbis, in turn, gave voice to this
hope in homily and legend. Through prayer, chant, and song,
the Synagogue kept this faith and hope active in the hearts of
the people from generation to generation down to our own days.

In the Jewish dream for the future of humanity, Christianity
and Islam play a divine role. Notwithstanding the inhospitable
spiritual atmosphere of the Middle Ages, Judaism, although
oppressed by its own daughter religions, recognized its spiritual
kinship with them. It regarded these dynamic conquering faiths
as carriers of divine truth to the nations of the world. Without
deviating from its uncompromising monotheism and its consequent opposition to the trinitarian conception of God, the
divine nature of Christ, the worship accorded to saints and
images, and other Christological features of the Church, Judaism
freely acknowledged the divine mission of Christianity, and
equally that of Islam, whose theism was pure and unblemished.
According to Jewish teaching, they were unconsciously — but
by God's design — Israel's apostles to the heathen nations. They
were the active agents spreading the basic truths which God
revealed to Israel, in forms which were more readily assimilable
to the nations because of their pagan background. The very
elements in Christianity which separated it from the mother
religion — the conception of God in human form, the priest as
an intermediary between God and man, the profusion of images
with supernatural attributes, the worship of saints, the dogma
of mysteries or sacraments, were interpreted as pedagogical
means for drawing pagan multitudes to the true God who
revealed Himself to Israel as the One God, the Creator of the
universe, the Father who created man in His image, who

inspired him to a life of holiness, through compassion, love and justice. Precisely during the period of medieval scholasticism, when Christian dogma was being crystallized in rigid concepts, Jewish philosophers interpreted sympathetically, as means to an end, Christian teachings which were unacceptable to them but which were effective psychologically in bringing about the mass conversion of heathen nations to Christianity. This enlightened attitude impressed itself also on Jewish canon law.

With the rise of Christianity and Islam, therefore, Judaism, in its own view, was not superseded. It remained more than ever "a light to the nations." Unwillingly, Christianity and Islam were profoundly influenced for good by the continued existence of Judaism. Christianity in its expansion from a Jerusalem sect to a world religion absorbed foreign pagan elements which needed purification. Judaism preserved the vision of God in its purest Hebraic form. Furthermore, the greater the expansion of a religion and the greater its secular power, the greater becomes the temptation toward worldliness, toward more power and wealth, and finally to the use of force in the defense of its institutions. Thus, inevitably, the worldly success of a religion, be it the Church or Mosque or Synagogue, is bound to carry with it dangerous germs of spiritual decay. Because Judaism during the past two thousand years has been dissociated from worldly power, it has carried a moral admonition of great historic import for the religions of mankind. Its defiance of worldly power, its loyalty to the God of Israel, its sacrificial devotion to religious truth, could not help but excite the imagination of mystics and daring religious spirits in their independent search for God in their own conscience and in the words of the Hebrew Scriptures. Above all, the defiant existence of Judaism as a protesting, or a Protestant religion, was a challenge for freedom of conscience, the most prized possession of free men throughout the world.

Viewed from an historic perspective, therefore, it can be seen that the ideal role which Israel cast for itself in the human drama that was mirrored in its own soul was reflected realistically in the course of human events. Whatever new interpretation Jewish religious thinkers may give to individual biblical and rabbinical concepts and however they may view the entire development and evolution of the Jewish religion as a result of critical historical methods, there is fair unanimity among all schools of Jewish thought as to the broad aspects of the historic role of Judaism in the religious evolution of mankind. That Judaism is still in the vanguard of the march of the human spirit, that the world must yet rise to the cosmic ethical concept of God upheld by Judaism, that the ancient faith contains within itself the seed of unlimited development that may prove as great a blessing to mankind in the future as in the past is the conviction which inspires its adherents today as in years gone by.

II

Because the source of the Jewish religion is to be found not in abstract dogma but in the historic experiences and insights of the Jewish people, its outlook upon the world of nations and other faiths is warmly realistic. By the same token, the ideational contents of the Jewish religion — its vision of God, and the ritual through which its relation to Him is expressed; its teachings of justice and holiness; its ideals of love and brotherhood which will pave the way to the happier world of the future — are to be explained introspectively in terms of historic experience, not by the artifices of prefabricated theology.

It is necessary to bear this in mind if one is to resolve the seeming paradox presented by Judaism in its theological aspects. On the one hand, every aspect of Jewish religious life is charged with the consciousness of God from the prayer at dawn to the prayer when the eyes close in sleep. Every detail of life is related through Jewish law to its divine origin and sanction. Through prayer, precept, and religious discipline, God's immanence is impressed upon the Jewish consciousness in multitudinous ways even in the prose of daily living. In the spiritual beauty of the Sabbath and the holidays, in the study of the Torah and in mystic prayer, the religiously sensitive person may soar to heights of religious ecstasy. The Talmud like the Pentateuch is not only a book of law but also a fountain of religious thought and inspiration. Such a religion is manifestly rich in the essence of theology; and yet it is singularly lacking in formal theology, in the systematic presentation of its theological principles. Some writers have indeed sought to read formal philosophy and theology into the thoughts of the biblical prophets. But such anachronism can hardly be taken seriously. In the main, modern writers on Jewish theology wonder at the surprising dearth of Jewish books on theology. Viewed in the light of historic perspective, however, the reason for the paucity is not far to seek. The rigid formalism of thought which the very term suggests is alien to Judaism. The Jewish people did not learn to know God through either syllogism or dogma. They happened upon God. As a sensitive child who awakens to the mysteries and wonders of nature, so were the early spirits in Israel in their awareness of God. Their God-perception was the result of intuition rather than reason and it unfolded as a psychological process.

With the race as with the child, there comes a period of self-consciousness. Growth and experience gradually widen the horizon of understanding and cause deeper penetration into the mysteries which are at first felt with childlike intuition. Thus stage by stage the vision of God expanded as the historic horizon of Israel widened. The tribal deity of its early history became the God of the nations. He became One and there was none other. In turn, Israel, conscious of the burden of its own religious genius, was committed to a fateful destiny as "a kingdom of priests and a holy nation." As God revealed His purposes through the extraordinary experiences of the nation and its prophets, His attributes became manifest to them. He was seen to be the Creator of the universe, the Father of man, the universal Ruler and Judge. He revealed Himself merciful, long-suffering, and compassionate, but also under the aspects of truth and justice, so that nations as well as individuals are held accountable by these standards. This was natural theology.

To the ancient Hebrew, then, the knowledge of God was not a matter of transmitted knowledge to be classified or codified, but a growing awareness of His Being through growth and experience, a spiritual sensitivity which eluded definition. To know God in the biblical sense did not mean intellectual perception or cognition, but a soul-stirring emotional reaction due to the impact of His will on the human being. The knowledge of God thus understood and thus acquired obviously does not fall into the convenient metaphysical categories so dear to the heart of a theologian.

Israel's feeling toward nature and man was part of its God-perception, a mystic, intuitive awareness. Thus as the nation through its prophets became increasingly God-conscious, the world itself was spiritualized, for it was filled with His presence. Its forces were visibly the instrument of His will. As man was led to probe deeper into his soul, he discovered within himself the image of God in whose form he was created. He discovered that he was born noble and free, with the power to emulate God Himself through the practice of holiness. At an early stage in their history, a divine law was given to the people through the medium of Moses, the greatest of all prophets, to guide them in the paths of social righteousness and personal holiness.

A series of prophets, seers, and sages, unparalleled in the history of any other nation, followed one upon another. National life took on dramatic, tragic aspects. The nation prospered, sinned, repented. God-conscious prophets stirred the

166

souls of their people with searing tongue and flaming eloquence. Conquering nations trampled over the little country. Exile followed and then religious regeneration. The process continued during the Second Commonwealth and thereafter in the lands of the Diaspora. Every age, every new experience was transmuted into deeper religious values. One can thus witness the rise of angelology, the stirring of Messianic hope, the dawn of the belief in the hereafter. There was no pause in the process of growth and development as Judaism passed from the prophetic to the rabbinic period, from Palestine to the Diaspora. Nor was there any disposition within Judaism itself to halt the free and manifold expression of the God-consciousness in the storm-tossed souls of the people during their historic transitions and forced migrations. Only when Judaism was challenged by a sectarian revolt from within or when it was forced by conflict with other religions or civilizations to clarify its own religious conceptions did Jewish teachers formulate their position on the specific issues under challenge.

Mountains of theology have been reared on Bible foundations but it would be difficult to point to any avowed formulations of a metaphysical doctrine in the Bible, save "Hear, O Israel, the Lord our God, the Lord is One," which indeed has become the cornerstone of Jewish metaphysics. This proclamation of monotheism, originally an affirmation directed against polytheism, remained to challenge the dualism of the Persians and stands to this day a protest against trinitarianism or any conception which beclouds the pure prophetic vision of God as the One and Only Being. Simultaneously with the rise of Christianity there are to be found in Judaism some traces of creedal doctrines as recorded in an early Mishna. These affirm the Jewish belief in resurrection, in divine revelation of the written and oral Law, and in the guiding control of Providence; and their creedal nature is indicated through the denial of a share in the world to come to those who negate these beliefs. Obviously, those were lingering issues of the old controversies between the Pharisees and the Sadducees. Strangely enough, early Christianity and the New Testament, which produced such grave political and social strains between the new sect and the mother religion, were not sufficiently provocative on the intellectual plane to force the rabbis to formulate a creed in opposition to the new tenets of faith.

Talmudic literature is replete with discussions and opinions on theological themes and doctrines. Flashes of thought and brilliant comments illumine a wide range of subjects that come under the heading of theology: God, His Kingdom, the Election of Israel, Revelation, Prophecy, the Law, Holiness, Sin, Forgiveness, the Messianic hope. But nowhere in the Talmud and its cognate literature was any attempt made to reduce these thoughts to a formal system, the prevailing feeling being, as it would seem, that "the true health of a religion is to have a theology without being aware of it." The characteristic talmudic teaching concerning God, like that of the Bible, is derived from experiencing God. It is of necessity direct, simple, personal. Formalism is alien to its essentially intuitive, emotional, mystical nature.

It was under Moslem influence and later in opposition to Christian scholasticism that Judaism was led to systematize its own views according to an established pattern which would readily reveal its points of agreement and disagreement in relation to the dominant rival faiths. Beginning with the ninth century there was a continuous development of philosophic-theologic literature within Judaism till Spinoza broke out of the bounds of religion into the area of pure philosophic speculation. Within these centuries lies the period of classic Jewish philosophy which, like contemporary Moslem thought and later Christian scholasticism, was primarily theological in content. It was a period of stirring theological ferment within Judaism. The basic beliefs of religion were subjected to rigorous critical analysis and opposing views and tenets were held by many writers. Parallel to the rational theology of the philosophic schools there was a deep undercurrent of mystic speculation which found its Bible in the Zohar (a mystical commentary on the Pentateuch) and its ultimate development and locale in the Holy Land in Safed during the sixteenth century. As the mystics eschewed transparency of thought, "systematic" theology must be sought in the writings of the rationalist schools.

These were the problems which agitated the minds of the Jewish thinkers during that classic period: what were the proofs of the existence of God? What is the nature of His Being and what are His attributes? In what sense is the Infinite one when there can be no plurality? Wherein lay the act of Creation: was it *creatio ex nihilo* or did matter coexist eternally with the Creator? Are miracles reconcilable with the laws which God implanted in nature? Has God withdrawn from the universe He created or does Providence still control the world? Is Providence general or collective only or does it reach out to the individual?

Most of these problems were basically philosophic questions and they were resolved according to the established thought patterns of Aristotelianism or Neoplatonism. But, as can be seen, they were also intermingled with theological issues which were rooted in the Hebraic thought of the Bible and the Talmud. Thus the Jewish philosophers struggled with the problem of divine revelation which was complicated by the anthropomorphic passages in the Bible. What were the means of divine communication with man? Wherein was the revelation on Sinai unique and how did it determine the role of Israel among the nations? In particular, they stressed the prophetic primacy of Moses, the father and greatest of all prophets. Hence the problem: what is prophecy and what are the criteria for gradations in prophecy?

With Moses' prophetic primacy was bound up the Law of

Moses — the Pentateuch — or, more comprehensively, the Torah. The word of God, revealed through Moses, was divine and immutable. A number of philosophic-theologic problems followed in its wake. Is retribution, or reward and punishment, of this earth or also in the hereafter? What is the hereafter and what is the nature of the divine retribution deferred to the hereafter? Reward and punishment implied free will. How then was this to be reconciled with God's omniscience? Was resurrection of this world or in the world to come? When is the longed-for Messiah to come? How is the true Messiah to be known? Is he mundane or supernatural?

It is readily apparent that the problems, though related to Hebrew thought and Scriptures, did not flow naturally and spontaneously out of the current of Jewish religious consciousness. Many of the terms of reference belong to another realm of thought, the world of Greek thought which was resurrected by Islamic and Jewish thinkers and subsequently opened up by them to Christian scholastics as well. Most of the problems and some of the solutions too were common to all three religions. Even those peculiar to Judaism alone were formulated in reaction to the postulates of the other faiths to which Judaism was opposed.

Out of this literature there developed characteristic theological attitudes and tenets in Judaism rather than an authoritative system of Jewish theology. The latter was precluded; for without an authoritarian Synagogue or Synod, the writings of no author carried authority beyond the force of their own logic. More important fundamentally, the sovereignty of reason, or the duty to think, was not only sanctioned but was regarded as a divine mandate in Jewish religious thinking. When there exists such wide latitude of mental freedom, regimentation of thought is impossible.

But regimentation of thought, or dogma, was part of the mental equipment of the age. Ineffectual attempts were therefore made also by some Jewish philosophers to formulate a series of cardinal beliefs in Judaism to which in their opinion every Jew had to subscribe or "have no share in the world to come." The nearest approach to an almost universally accepted creed in Judaism was that projected by the famous Jewish philosopher, Moses ben Maimon, or Maimonides, in the latter part of the twelfth century, as an appendix to his commentary on the Mishna of Sanhedrin. It consists of the following thirteen articles of faith: (1) belief in the existence of God; (2) in His unity; (3) in His incorporeality; (4) in the eternity of God; (5) belief that worship is due to Him alone; (6) belief in prophecy; (7) belief that Moses was the greatest of all prophets; (8) that the Torah (the written and oral Law) was revealed to Moses on Sinai; (9) that it is immutable; (10) that God is omniscient; (11) belief in reward and punishment in this world and in life hereafter; (12) belief in the coming of the Messiah; (13) in resurrection of the dead. This creed was later formulated as a credo, every article commencing, "I believe." It was also versified, set to music, and admitted to the prayer book. It allegedly inspired a Christian poet to exclaim: "Behold, the Jews sing philosophy and chant theology."

The Synagogue, however, admitted these articles of belief into the prayer book not because they were the creed. Rather may it be said that they became the creed because they crystallized beliefs already held by the people. But though the Synagogue for this reason sympathetically assimilated their contents in the prayers, it was not as dogma but as religious themes that they found such ready acceptance.

Judaism never furnished fertile soil for a dogmatic interpretation of the articles of faith. The concept that there is saving power in holding to a doctrine as dogma is foreign to Judaism. "Thou shalt believe" is a precept unknown in the Jewish religion. At most a dogma in Judaism is to be defined as a fundamental doctrine essential to the nature of Judaism.

The attack upon the creedal character of the thirteen principles of faith came from many quarters. Some argued against any kind of differentiation among religious principles and precepts. According to them all the religious precepts, which traditionally numbered six hundred and thirteen, were equally sacred. Others preferred making their own selection in the garden of faith. Critical philosophers expanded or reduced the number of essential principles according to their own more or less arbitrary reasoning, till Moses Mendelssohn toward the end of the eighteenth century, at the dawn of modern Jewish history, made the startling declaration that Judaism was a religion without dogma; in other words, it was a social religion with law as the primary cohesive principle.

Most penetrating of all was the criticism directed at the very heart of Maimonides' formulation by one of the keenest and most original Jewish philosophers of the Middle Ages, Hasdai Crescas, who has been characterized as a forerunner of Spinoza. Of keen analytical mind, he pointed out that Maimonides tended to confuse important doctrine with cardinal dogma. The former are more than thirteen in number, actually sixteen according to Crescas. Of dogmas Judaism knows only seven, he claimed. But far more important was Crescas' difference from Maimonides in the fundamental approach to religion. To Maimonides, religion, in essence, was metaphysics. Its truths were the fruit of the intellect. To Crescas, religion flowed from the heart. Without impugning the sovereign right of reason, he argued that piety was not the product of speculation but the child of love. Goodness was an emotional quality not an intellectual abstraction. The indispensable essentials of religion therefore could not be cast into metaphysical propositions. Thus Crescas sought to direct the trend of Jewish thought away from the artificial circle into which it had been drawn by the centripetal influences of medieval Moslem thinking into the original orbit of the intuitive, emotional religion of prophetic-rabbinic Judaism.

In this general attitude, Crescas did not stand alone. He had both predecessors and successors. But no substitute formula ever succeeded in obtaining universal assent. Maimonides' credo was not removed from the prayer book nor from Jewish religious consciousness. It remained a noble affirmation of basic fundamental truths which Judaism upholds in contrast to Christianity and Islam. But at no time did it exercise the curb of dogmatism. Within the general compass of a universe created by a personal God and a moral law to rule the children of man whom He created in His image, the human mind was free to explore the mysteries of religion and to follow the explorations of the soul in its search for the Infinite. Throughout the ages, therefore, it has been possible for Judaism to adapt itself theologically to the changing currents of religious thought and mystic movements whether these influences came from without or were impelled from within by the dynamics of Jewish history.

The Italian Renaissance was reflected not alone in Hebrew works on rhetoric like the *Nofet Zufim* but in the religious emotionalism of the younger Abravanel's *Dialogues of Love*. The shattering experience of the Spanish expulsion in 1492 inspired the most heroic figure of the period, Isaac Abravanel, to proclaim the near advent of Messianic salvation and to build his theology in a series of impressive works round this central theme. The Cabala which held sway for centuries and which ultimately found lodgment in the mystic movement known as *Hasidism*, or Saintliness, was in its earliest stages a reaction against rationalism which failed the people in the hour of despair, and in its later aspect was part of a social-religious revolution. In the nineteenth century there developed in some talmudic academic circles a significant religious tendency known as *Musar* (Ethical Discipline) which fostered classes for religious self-cultivation through ascetic and ethical practices, bearing in some aspects a faint resemblance to the Oxford movement.

In all these developments, the basic tenets of Maimonides' articles of faith were not consciously challenged or denied. Some of them were circumvented, or by-passed, as other religious concepts forced their way to the center of Jewish consciousness. A fundamental change and departure was inaugurated with the rise of the Reform movement in Judaism. A product of nineteenth century rationalism, its attitude to religion is that of the advanced critical-historical school. It has disavowed the belief in resurrection and the traditional view of divine revelation, and has otherwise interpreted freely Jewish doctrines that in the opinion of its votaries were not in accord with modern thought. Although this apparent break with a long tradition reaches to the very roots of Judaism and has naturally aroused violent opposition and heated controversy, its leading exponents have always maintained that their position was in harmony with the genius of the Jewish religion and its evolutionary process. Even in the ranks of Conservative Judaism, often called traditional or historical Judaism, there is such wide difference of opinion on basic theological tenets that it has not been possible in fifty years to formulate a theology acceptable even to this school alone. Indeed out of its ranks there has recently emerged a new movement, Reconstructionism, which, from a theological viewpoint, in its concepts of God, revelation, Providence, and every other basic religious idea, holds the most advanced revolutionary position in Judaism. Orthodox Judaism maintains the strictly traditional viewpoint, while in Palestine there has been a marked revival of cabalistic mysticism.

Despite these wide divergences of thought, there has been no schism, no attempt at forced reconciliation, and a broad unity of faith has been maintained by the thread of historic continuity and by the fact that these various modes of religion basically express the religious consciousness of one people, the people with whom the life of Judaism is coexistent. Thus it was in the days of the Pharisees and the Sadducees, in the opposing schools of Shammai and Hillel, in the differences among the academies of Palestine and Babylon, in the varying attitudes of mystics and rationalists, in the conflicts at certain periods between the Karaites (who disavowed the Oral Law) and the rest of the Jewish people, in the conflict between the *Hasidim*, the sect of mystic saints, and the traditional Talmudists, in the internal conflicts with the Enlightened Modernists, the *Maskilim* in the nineteenth century ghettos of Eastern Europe, and in the present day divisions of Orthodox, Conservative, and Reform Judaism. Only when a religious group cut itself off from the body of catholic Israel or set itself up in place of historic Israel, was it disowned and regarded outside the pale of Judaism.

From the foregoing it is clear that Judaism is infinitely rich in religious values and responsive to the varied moods of individual souls. The selection by various thinkers of what constitutes the fundamental doctrines of Judaism makes it evident too that these doctrines do not negate one another. Far from it. The selection has been primarily a question of emphasis. With every fresh wave of thought that would dominate a generation, a shifting of emphasis in religious values would cause some doctrines to recede to the background and others to assert their primacy.

III

Among the doctrines that held a relatively fixed position in the center of Jewish consciousness was the belief in the coming of the Messiah. This doctrine reaches deep into the roots of the Jewish past and extends far into the future, for it is tied up with Israel's vision of the ultimate establishment of the kingdom of God on earth. As may be expected from its ancient and complicated history, the Messianic ideal is not a clear-cut dry catechismic formula. It voices the varied contradictory moods of a religiously sensitive people, the yearning and aspirations of a religious community that has plumbed the depths of despair and soared to the heights of hope and joy. It is rich in poetic sentiment, lore and legend; it is imbued with the pathos of suffering, and exultant in the faith of the final triumph of Israel, humanity and the God of Zion.

Although the New Testament concept of the Christ was patterned verbally and figuratively upon the older prophecies of the Hebrew prophets, the consequent deductions of Judaism and Christianity are totally at variance and irreconcilable. The differences are not merely of tense but of consequence. Because the advent of the Messiah is to inaugurate the triumph of God's kingdom on earth, his coming according to Judaism is of necessity an event of the future, not of the past, with its record of wars, violence, greed and evil. The eyes of the Jewish community were always upon "the end of days." They could not possibly have endured their trials and ordeals if they had not been buoyed up by an unfaltering faith that a new order of peace and justice will prevail "in the end of days" under the rulership of God and His anointed.

That the Messiah was to be a descendant of the house of David not only seemed vouched for by Scripture but it also responded to the mood of a nation that identified the purpose of its very existence with being the carrier of the divine promise to mankind, and that envisioned itself in the vanguard of the universal procession to God in Zion. That the Messiah was to be without claim to deification was never questioned at any stage in the complicated development of the Jewish Messianic idea. The nature of the Messiah was differently conceived at various stages in the evolution of the ideal. For unlike the Messianic phenomenon in Christianity which was a startling and completely new revelation to the great masses who were won over to the new faith — literally a *fait accompli* — in Judaism the Messianic idea was throughout the centuries in a process of flux, following the ebb and flow of national experience and responding to the spiritual needs of the nation as it passed from one crisis to another. In the prophetic vision of Isaiah when the house of David still occupied the throne in Judaea the Messiah was idealized as a future scion of the royal house, a wise, just, and good king upon whom rested "the spirit of the Law, the spirit of wisdom and understanding, the spirit of knowledge and of the fear of the Lord." In his reign, surpassing peace and justice would prevail even among animals of prey. "They shall not hunt nor destroy in all My holy mountains; for the earth shall be full of the knowledge of the Lord, as the waters cover the sea." Not the personality of the King Messiah was stressed but the era of human brotherhood and peace which would be inaugurated in his reign. In the famous peace-prophecy of Isaiah and Micah all mention of the Messiah is omitted and the rule of God alone fills the framework of that Messianic picture "in the end of days." As political doom and exile darkened the horizon, the brooding spirits of prophet and psalmist depicted the Messiah as a conqueror over the hosts of evil who must be vanquished before lasting peace can come to Israel and man-kind. When the nation groaned under the trampling tyranny of Rome, the longed-for Messiah was lifted into the realm of the miraculous and was seen through the dim light of apocalyptic vision.

From that stage the ideal soars into the realm of mystery. The Messianic age is preceded by violent physical and moral struggles, the birth-throes of the Messianic era. Elijah, the harbinger of glad tidings, returns from Heaven to bring inner peace to the heart of the people and to effect reconciliation with God. It becomes more and more difficult to follow the course of the Messiah to come. But certain characteristics stand out boldly: the reunion of Israel in the Holy Land, victory over all hostile powers ranged against God, and an era of supreme happiness, peace, and good will among all men.

Needless to say, those ideals did not always float aloft

purely as visions of dreamers and apocalyptic visionaries. Claimants to the messiahship rose and fell. Bar Kokba, "the son of the star" who waged war with superhuman powers against the hosts of Emperor Hadrian, was acknowledged as the Messiah even by the immortal Rabbi Akiba. The soil of Jewish history is strewn with fallen Messiahs. In bitter disillusionment, some stray rabbinic voices could be heard despairing of a personal Messiah but still believing in the Messianic age, when God Himself would redeem Israel and be acknowledged by all men as sovereign ruler of the world.

Cutting through the fog of mysticism, Maimonides in his twelfth article of faith dealing with the belief in the coming of the Messiah uttered the following conviction: the Messiah will issue from the house of David. He will excel all rulers in history in the exercise of justice and peace . . . Notwithstanding the majesty and wisdom of the Messiah, he must be regarded as a mortal being and one who restored the Davidic dynasty. He will die and leave a son as his successor, who will in turn die and leave the throne to his heir. Nor will there be any material change in the system of nature and human life; accordingly Isaiah's picture of the living together of lamb and wolf cannot be taken literally . . . . We are only to believe in the coming of Elijah as a messenger of peace and the forerunner of the Messiah, and also in the great decisive battle with the hosts of heathendom embodied in Gog and Magog, through whose defeat the dominion of the Messiah will be permanently established . . . . The Messianic kingdom itself is to bring the Jewish nation its political independence, but not the subjection of the heathen nations. The Messianic era will not be merely one of material prosperity and sensual pleasure, but of general affluence and peace, enabling the Jewish people to devote their lives without care or anxiety to the study of the Torah and universal wisdom, so that by their teachings they may lead all mankind to the knowledge of God and make them also share in the bliss of the world to come.

Noble as was this teaching of Maimonides, its very clarity detracted from the force of its popular appeal. The strength of the Messianic ideal in Judaism lies in the mystic power of its vision to respond to many moods. Its moral texture is a blend of many hues. When the nation found itself chained and tortured in the web of cruel circumstance the vision of the Messiah to come held forth the promise of liberation. To individual sensitive souls, wearied and frustrated by pitiless struggle with the crushing forces of this material world, it was the rainbow at the end of the road. Above all, to the collective Jewish people carrying the message of God, human brotherhood, universal peace and justice as their historic destiny, but meeting with affliction, persecution, and frustration, the vision of the Messiah was a mystic light under which their suffering was suffused with a halo of glory. The Messiah was the symbol of national redemption. The restoration of Israel's nationhood in Palestine was to be not only a moral vindication of Israel through a political medium. It was to be a vindication of the reign of God in Zion whose light was to illumine the darkest crevices of the earth and whose influence was to unite all the nations in universal brotherhood under the Fatherhood of God.

Such a vision was necessarily compounded of many elements: prophecy, history, poetry, legend, apocalyptic hopes. It drew vitality not from the intellect but from the soul. It flourished not in the topsoil of the mind but in the deep, moist earth of mystic faith. It did not grow bare and upright as a poplar, but as a tree with "sinuous trunk, boughs exquisitely wreathed." At times, the personal Messiah was apotheosized as the collective personality of Israel, "the suffering people." Often his symbolic personality silently receded to the background and in his place stood forth the ideal of the Messianic age with God as the Judge and Ruler. Such a vision filled the soul of the prophets of old. It inspired medieval Jewish saints who gloried in martyrdom. It is this matured vision which upholds and in turn is upheld by countless modern Jews who no longer look for the

Messiah in human form but look forward all the more eagerly to the more natural redemption associated with the Messianic era. Whatever form the Messianic ideal assumes, however, it is in any event an embryo in the womb of time.

Although the state of the world is far from the Messianic goal, it is a hopeful sign that two corollaries of the Jewish Messianic ideal have impressed themselves upon the advanced religious thinking of our age. They have far-reaching implications for the role which religion is destined to play in the future of organized society. One concerns human nature, and the other is the concept of this world as the theater of the religious drama of mankind. Judaism never wavered in its espousal of these ideals and it may well take heart as this influence is making itself increasingly manifest in the religious conscience of our time.

The Jewish Messianic idea whether idealized in a millennial era or incarnated in a human personality implies the concept of human perfectibility. According to Jewish teaching, man must perfect his own nature to prepare the way for the Messiah. For the function of the Messiah is not to redeem a race which is incapable of redeeming itself. On the contrary, he is the symbol and the triumph of man's self-redemption. The Messiah is the climax of man's ascent to moral perfection. He is the denouement in the human drama of history.

IV

There were fleeting periods in the early centuries of the common era when the story of the fall of Adam cast the shadow of original sin upon Jewish thought. In later cabalistic doctrine, this concept was reflected obliquely in the theory of ultimate human redemption through the restoration of the original soul of Adam. But, on the whole, Judaism did not allow the spell of original sin, this unhappy concept of human nature, permanently to affect its outlook. That man, born in the divine image, was capable through his own endowments to reach heights of infinite self-development remained a basic concept of the Jewish religion. Those who accepted the biblical narrative literally and the philosophers who treated it allegorically met on common ground in this regard. Neither party tolerated the idea of original sin. They both viewed the biblical episode in the Garden of Eden as depicting a passing phase in the hopeful development of the human race. Not only was man endowed with divine possibilities, but he was assigned a supreme role in the completion of the work of creation. The cultivation of nature, the harnessing of natural forces, the building of civilization, and above all the fulfillment of man's moral potentialities were incumbent upon man, and within his grasp to achieve. Viewed in this light, every advance in science, in government, in the organization of social justice helps to complete the program of creation and brings nearer the advent of the Messiah. The organization of the society of nations for the assurance of international peace, the recognition of the right of all peace-loving nations to share in the natural resources with which God has dotted the world, the safeguarding of the individual in religious and political freedom and equal economic opportunity — the translation of these ideas into actuality will, in the language of Judaism, hasten the footsteps of the Messiah.

As this faith in man, born pure as a child of God, is the antithesis of original sin, so is the cosmic optimism of Judaism in contrast to the other-worldliness which has dominated Christian thought throughout the centuries. At the heart of Judaism is the vision of God's kingdom on earth. Not in the world to come but on this earth in the hearts of living men and nations is the divine kingdom of justice and righteousness to be established. When religion views life as fleeting, the world transitory, and salvation is referred to life beyond the grave, man is deprived of the great religious incentive to struggle with the social forces of evil and to establish on earth a moral order of justice and truth. Jewish thinkers too were at times profoundly affected by this mood and their reactions left an indelible mark upon Judaism. Indeed, no religion can wholly escape the dilemma raised by such an influence. But the religious genius of Judaism, cast in the robust mold of the Hebrew Bible, successfully averted the paralyzing influence of the ascetic's surrender of this world.

From the opening chapter in Genesis, through the thunderous pages of the Prophets, the agonizing experiences of the Psalmists, and the calm wisdom of the sage literature; in the contemplation of the rabbis, matured in the academies of Palestine and Babylon, and throughout a long history of courageous martyrdom, the Jewish religious outlook upon the world has been one of energizing optimism. "God saw all that He had made and behold, it was very good," is not only the summation of the biblical narrative of creation; it is the consistent viewpoint of Judaism in many of its historic manifestations. In varied forms, the conviction appears and reappears in Jewish literature that a world created by God must necessarily partake of the nature of the Creator. Not even evil, suffering, and sin are shut out of this consideration; for they too serve toward a moral end. They are a goad to man's upward struggle toward moral perfection. Far from shunning this world, Jewish teaching made it the central stage of the human drama conceived by God.

In the Hebrew Bible — Pentateuch, Prophets, and Hagiographa — the notion of a hereafter, in so far as it exists at all, is a vague, dim vision without any power of motivation. Human life is bounded by earth, sky and sea, which are the handiwork of God and are moved by His will. Within this framework, amidst the powers of nature through thunder and lightning, rain and drought, and in the still small voice of conscience God speaks to the heart of man. The physical powers of nature are harnessed to the moral laws of religion. The divine commandments given to man are reinforced by the operations of the laws of nature. Divine retribution, reward and punishment, blessings and curses are visible in the physical manifestations of rain and drought, fertility and sterility, riches and poverty, freedom and bondage, peace and war. Man's religious hopes and fears, his joys and sorrows before God, his dreams and visions of the future were centered in the world of nature and in his social relations with man and society. "To walk before God in the land of the living" expressed the highest yearning of the religious soul.

The earthly concentration of religious hopes and aspirations did not exclude the belief in a shadowy existence after death in the nether world (Hebrew, *she'ol*). This was a universal belief in the entire ancient world; and the Hebrew shared it with the Babylonians and Egyptians. But neither lawgiver nor prophet was much concerned with the shadowy world after death. The goal of their task was to elevate the life of individuals and nations for this world to the end that "the earth shall be full of the knowledge of the Lord as the waters cover the sea."

Maturity and experience cut deeply into the moral optimism of the Bible. After the Jewish people experienced exile, restoration, and finally subjection and bitter persecution, the pious Saints, predecessors of the Pharisees, many of whom cheerfully gave their lives for their religion, had to look beyond this world for the vindication of God's justice. Belief in a future world and in a life hereafter where justice is meted out for good and evil deeds committed in this world then assumed overwhelming importance. It was one of the great issues which the Pharisees maintained against the Sadducees and on which they scored the final triumph indicated in the dictum of the Mishna that he who denies the belief in resurrection of the dead "shall have no share in the world to come" (Sanh. 10.1). The New Testament in this instance not only followed but intensified the Pharisaic teaching, so that in the Christian tradition the fate of the individual soul in the future world became the prime consideration; the social fabric of society was of secondary importance;

and renunciation of the world was the ideal of the holy man. Ascetism, monasticism, celibacy, and the denial of the flesh are only a few of the most significant signs of the surrender of this world in favor of the world to come.

Judaism emphatically rejected this attitude of the renunciation of society and the world. Judaism embraced two worlds, this world and the world to come. The nature of the hereafter, the character of its subdivisions of Paradise and Hell, the timing of the resurrection of the dead, the state of the soul in immortality — all these formed subjects of intense speculation and theorizing among the Jewish philosophers and mystics. The relative importance attached to the two spheres varied with the mood of the individual and the generation. But at no time did Judaism surrender its profound concern with the affairs of men and nations in this world. For it is in the hearts of men and in the lives of nations that the kingdom of God is to be established on earth. The Messianic kingdom will not rest on supernatural foundations in a supernatural world but on a moral order of justice, peace, brotherhood, and truth. It required heroic courage for a people generally disowned by the world to retain such faith in the future of mankind. But Judaism never wavered in its belief in the ultimate triumph of God's will on earth. As crucified humanity in our time struggles to lift the clouds of war and turns yearningly to the distant horizon for the dawn of lasting peace, the Synagogue prays more fervently than ever:

We therefore hope in Thee, O Lord our God, that we may speedily behold the glory of Thy might . . . when the world will be perfected under the kingdom of the Almighty, and all the children of flesh will call upon Thy name, when Thou wilt turn unto Thyself all the wicked of the earth. Let all the inhabitants of the world perceive and know that unto Thee every knee must bow, every tongue must swear. Before Thee, O Lord our God, let them bow and fall; and unto Thy glorious name let them give honor; let them all accept the yoke of Thy kingdom, and do Thou reign over them speedily, and for ever and ever.

To keep before the world and the Jewish people in particular the vision of the kingdom of God on earth and to prepare the Jewish people for moral leadership in the Messianic era, Judaism does not place reliance wholly on emotional inspiration. Prophetic utterances, moral exhortations, picturesque homilies, and parables were incorporated in the prayers and the daily speech of the people. They stirred thought currents and set the pattern of religious idealism. But to carry out the lofty purposes of the kingdom, a special vehicle, unique and distinctive of the Jewish religion, was created. This vehicle is a social organism, the Torah, the Law of Judaism. It served the double purpose of advancing the progress of the kingdom and saving the kingdom for this world. Torah, or Law, in Judaism was both an institution and a faith. It is a theological concept and a legal constitution. Both notions are complementary and interrelated. The Torah is the constitution of a people whose ideal of government is the kingdom of God.

V

A proper understanding of the term Torah is the indispensable key to a comprehension of Judaism. The fatal misconstruction of the nature of Judaism so prevalent in the writings of non-Jewish historians and theologians is due in great measure to a failure to grasp the subtle connotations of this profoundly spiritual concept. Torah, which literally means a teaching, is used in so many senses and in so many gradations that one may easily be led to confuse the part for the whole, the word for the spirit, the literary content for the poetic soul itself. For Torah denotes variously the Pentateuch, the whole of Scripture, the revealed Word, written and oral, wisdom in its most elevated and spiritual sense, and also the entire content of religious thought and feeling as it is expressed in the literature and experience of the ages. Still more loftily, the rabbis describe the Torah as the premundane plan which existed, as it were, in the mind of God in accordance with which He called the world into being and by which it is governed.

With love and poetic flight of imagination, the rabbis mystically personified the Torah and invested it with romantic, supranatural character. The Torah was the heavenly bride wedded to Israel at the revelation on Sinai. Nature interrupted its course, the angels refrained from chanting the song of glory, "Holy, Holy, Holy," as heaven and earth witnessed the union of Israel and the Torah. The Torah came down from heaven endowed with humility, righteousness, and uprightness. In her are to be found "peace, strength, life, bliss, happiness, joy, and freedom."

Changing the mood of poetic metaphor, the rabbis exalted the Torah as the manifestation to mankind of God's will. "Whosoever labors in the Torah for its own sake, merits many things . . . he is called friend, beloved, a lover of God, a lover of mankind; it clothes him in meekness and reverence, and fits him to become righteous, pious, and upright; it keeps him far from sin, brings him toward the side of virtue, and gives him sovereignty and dominion and discerning judgment. To him the secrets of the Torah are revealed; he becomes a never failing fountain, he grows modest and long suffering, forgives insults, and is exalted above all things."

This description of Torah is barely suggestive of the riches of thought and the joyous love which filled the Jewish consciousness of Torah. But it may at least serve as a background for that aspect of Torah with which we are immediately concerned: Torah as the Law of Judaism. To enter into the spirit of the Law, to appreciate its mystic hold upon the Jewish mind for thousands of years, to see it in its ultimate relation to the kingdom of God, it must be viewed not merely as jurisprudence, dogma, or canon law but as the crystallization in human terms and social forms of an ideal drawn from the fountain of mystic faith on the heights of theology.

At the core of Torah are the laws of the Pentateuch. This was the base on which was reared the structure of Jewish law in all its branches. Like the laws of the Pentateuch which cover not only the duties of man toward God but also toward man and society, the system of rabbinic law that evolved out of the basic law of the Bible embraces all possible human relationships, personal, social, national, and international. Many of the laws are prohibitive: Thou shalt not. The greater number are affirmative commandments: Thou shalt. The positive laws, or commandments, regulate the personal life of the individual, his property, his social conduct; they define his duties toward the state and the cult and his ethical obligations. There is no aspect of the life of a nation or a country which is overlooked. The farm, the flocks, the home, the wages of the worker, the very garments of a man are subjects of legislation in the Pentateuch and correspondingly in the more comprehensive and mature development of rabbinic law.

In Jewish doctrine these laws are looked upon not as ordinary legislative enactments. They are divine decrees; they are the laws of God's kingdom. As the rabbis put it: God said, "You have received my kingdom in love, receive now my decrees." Because they are divine in nature, the potentiality of these laws is infinite. There is no limit to their study or comprehension. Transcendent wisdom, truth, and justice are hidden in the Law, and it is the supreme duty of the faithful to immerse himself in its study day and night. In its ultimate and perfect development the Torah could be regarded as the law or constitution of the kingdom of God on earth.

Translated into modern terms, the Torah is a system of law which was applied by divinely inspired teachers to the conditions under which the Jewish people were living. As the conditions changed from time to time, some of the laws became obsolete and others had to be modified. But these laws embodied indestructible principles of justice and truth which can give rise to ever new legal concepts and social institutions as mankind is striving toward a new and better world. This was the spirit of the aphorisms of the famed Rabbi Simeon, son of Gamaliel: "The world rests on three pillars: truth, justice, and peace." The *potential* values and ideals still to be derived from the Law constitute the dynamic element in the Law, or Torah.

The laws of Judaism fall naturally into several categories. There are those which relate to the cult and the ritual. They are interspersed in the Five Books of Moses and considerably elaborated in the talmudic and later rabbinic literature. They were intended primarily for the adherents of the Jewish religion. Their function is disciplinary, to train the priest-people through a special regimen of life for their historic role of moral-religious leadership. The other laws touching the general life of the people socially, politically and economically, and constituting general Jewish jurisprudence, are also based on the Pentateuch but by their very nature kept closer pace with the inherent evolution of Jewish life and the changes imposed from without by the peculiar political fate of the Jewish people. Both branches of Jewish law influenced the historical development of Western civilization. It is a matter of great moment as to what extent the *potential* ideals imbedded in the entire Law of Judaism, or Torah, will be permitted to develop and to influence the future course of civilization.

As previously indicated, Judaism makes no distinction between the sanctity of religious law, so-called, and the general law covering human relationships. All law is sacred in Judaism. The laws of mine and thine, the laws safeguarding honest weights and measures, profits and wages, the laws protecting the weak, the underprivileged, the stranger in the land, have the same degree of sanctity as the laws regulating the duties between man and God. In a society that recognizes the rulership of God there is no phase of human life whether of the individual or the group which is outside the sphere of religion. All the infinite threads of human life are woven into one harmonious pattern. The laws which Judaism has in the past developed in theory and in practice are like a blurred mirror which reflects the ideal Torah, the hoped-for pattern of society in the golden age of the Messianic era. The laws of the Torah are to the ideal Torah what the mechanism of a clock is to the eternity of time.

The Torah is reflected in the institutions of Judaism: the Synagogue and its auxiliaries, the Sabbath, the Festivals and Holy Days and the laws of daily religious living. In their growth and development is manifested the ever widening horizon of the Torah and the social vision which permeates the religion of Judaism. This vision is held steadfastly in view not only in the laws of man's relationship with his fellow man, but also in those touching man's approach to God in prayer and worship.

Worship as it was practiced in the Temple of old through animal sacrifices at the hands of priests and Levites vanished completely with the destruction of the Temple and the fall of Jerusalem and the Jewish state in the year 70 CE. The Synagogue replaced the Temple, and prayer took the place of sacrifices. Child of the Babylonian exile and mother of the Church and the Mosque, the Synagogue was from its very origin and throughout its long history a socializing and democratizing institution. Its character is indicated by the various names under which it was designated in Hebrew: the House of Prayer, the House of Study, and the House of Assembly. Whether the Synagogue had its origin, as some scholars think, in early Palestine prayer-meetings dating back to the days of the First Temple or whether, as others hold, it was organized originally as a meeting-house for social purposes during the days of the Babylonian exile and gradually incorporated the other features, it is clear that when the Synagogue emerged into the full light of history, whether in Palestine or in the Diaspora, before and after the destruction of the Second Temple, it had the three features of prayer, study of Torah, and public assembly, each reacting upon the others.

Prayer is the most intensely personal expression of the human soul. But just as in the Psalms, so in the general prayers of the Synagogue, the individual worshiper immerses his individuality in the collective soul of Israel. No mediator is permitted to stand between the worshiper and Him to whom worship is directed. But granting some exceptions of prayers of an individual character, the chief prayers are designed for the individual as a member of a human brotherhood, or the household of Israel.

As the Jew bows in prayer before the Lord God, King of the universe, and pours out his heart before "the God of our Fathers, the God of Abraham, Isaac, and Jacob" he no longer stands before his Maker as a naked soul but as a social personality with hallowed memories. The contents of the prayers are cast in the collective plural. The worshiper in the Synagogue prays not for himself alone but for the common welfare. Petition, in general, is but a small part of the Synagogue prayers. Adoration, praise, and thanksgiving form the major theme of the Hebrew prayers and all living creatures are invoked to raise their voice in songs and hymns of glory. Although prayers may be recited in the home and when "thou walkest by the way" it is believed that they find greater merit when uttered in unison with other worshipers. Some themes, such as the *Kaddish*, the exalted prayer for the coming of the kingdom of God, are to be recited only when there is a quorum of at least ten male worshipers assembled. Through these and other subtle psychological suggestions, the Synagogue utilized the mystic power of prayer to foster the feeling of social responsibility and community conscience.

Of immense social consequence was the incorporation of study as a function of the Synagogue and as an integral part of the religious service itself. The Synagogue made of the Torah "an inheritance of the congregation of Jacob." What

Ezra began so brilliantly, the Synagogue carried on. Ezra inaugurated a momentous spiritual revolution by bringing the Torah to the people. The Synagogue housed the Torah and made it the spiritual possession of the nation. Knowledge of the Torah made the people free from priestly domination. No priestly tyranny was possible as long as the Law was the subject of popular study and understanding. Furthermore, the diffusion of the Torah among the masses paved the way for the success of the revolutionary Pharisees whose innovations were fought so obstinately by the entrenched priesthood and aristocracy. The Church Father Jerome left eloquent testimony of the role of the later Synagogue of his time in fostering devotion to learning among the Jewish populace.

Without interruption, for two thousand years, the Synagogue continued to be a storehouse of learning as well as a fountain of prayer. Piety rooted in ignorance was discountenanced. One of the most popular aphorisms of the Ethics of the Fathers reads: "A boor cannot be God-fearing nor an ignoramus a saint." This attitude of the Synagogue, this program of spreading knowledge and cultivating learning as an act of piety, encouraged religious independence and discouraged many of the antisocial evils to which religion is liable under the excesses of religious emotionalism. It invested Jewish personality with an intellectual cast and a high social conscience which reflected the vision and ideals of the Torah.

The Synagogue was not only a place of prayer and study. It was the locale in which all public life was centered. For fifteen hundred years, from the early Middle Ages to the dawn of the modern era, the democratizing influence of the Synagogue radiated in all directions, political, social and philanthropic. Here political meetings were held during the long centuries that preceded Jewish emancipation when Jewish communities were self-contained miniature republics. In the councils of these communes which met on synagogue premises, democratic principles were pursued in the name and under the sanction of the Torah. Justice was administered by rabbinical courts in the synagogue precincts. An aggrieved person could demand a hearing and if necessary interrupt the synagogue service till he was assured that his cause would be heard. The Synagogue preached and practiced charity. It tended to the needs of the poor and dependent. It housed the stranger and wayfarer in its auxiliary buildings. It fostered a wide range of philanthropic institutions. Two centuries before the dawn of Christianity, the Synagogue taught, in the words of Simon the Just, that benevolence and worship were the pillars upon which human society rested. How fitting and characteristic therefore was the following selection from the Mishna which was incorporated in the prayer book and recited by the worshipers as a prologue to the morning devotions: "These are the things the fruits of which a man enjoys in this world, while the stock remains for him for the world to come: namely, honoring father and mother, the practice of charity, timely attendance at the house of study morning and evening, hospitality to wayfarers, visiting the sick, dowering the bride, attending the dead to the grave, devotion in prayer, and making peace between man and his fellow; but the study of the Law is equal to them all."

With the transition to secularism that is so characteristic of the modern era the Synagogue no longer holds sway to the same degree. The institutions which it created — philanthropic, social, and educational — are no longer housed within synagogue precincts nor can they be said to be under its direct control. But their moral relation to the Synagogue is unbroken. They draw their life and light from its moral sanction and social vision. The prime motivating force within these institutions emanates consciously and subconsciously from the traditional ethical teachings of the Synagogue.

VI

Of all the institutions with which the Jewish religion enriched the spiritual life of mankind, the Sabbath is pre-eminent. It commences traditionally with the setting of the sun on Friday and concludes with the appearance of the stars the following evening. Notwithstanding its primitive Babylonian origin, the Sabbath is a true creation of the Jewish religious genius. Judaism endowed the Sabbath richly with the poetry of custom and ceremony and deepened the spiritual significance of the day through song, prayer and precept. At no time was the Jewish Sabbath merely a day of bodily rest. As a covenant between man and the Creator, its purpose was to release man from labor and worldly cares for the sake of moral cultivation and a deeper understanding of his own spiritual personality. Thus the Sabbath not only suffused Jewish life with light and rejoicing, but it also exerted a far-reaching and beneficent influence on human civilization itself.

The Sabbath holds a place of central importance in the Torah: that is to say, Torah as identified with the written and oral law of Judaism, and Torah as the ultimate idealized law of the kingdom of God. Its centrality in the Pentateuch is of course indicated by its inclusion in the Decalogue: "Remember the Sabbath day to keep it holy." Its deep religious symbolism is in full consonance with the high place it occupies. For it is not merely a day for the cessation of work. It is a testimony of the Creator and creation itself: "Wherefore the Lord blessed the Sabbath day and hallowed it." Its holiness extends even to the slave in the household and the stranger, who are thereby endowed by the Sabbath with a dignity akin to that of the freeman and the native. This note is stressed in Deuteronomy where the socializing, emancipating influence of the Sabbath is emphasized: "And thou shalt remember that thou wast a servant in the land of Egypt and the Lord thy God brought thee out thence . . . therefore the Lord thy God commanded thee to keep the Sabbath."

The vagueness of the wide-sweeping prohibition "Thou shalt not do any manner of work" opened wide the door of religious controversy. Its meaning was heatedly debated among the Sadducees and Pharisees, and it remained a subject of sectarian contention throughout the ages as illustrated by the sect of the Karaites who have survived to this day. The Pharisees undertook to define the meaning of "work" and, using the analogy of the work done for the tabernacle, divided it into thirty-nine categories, such as sowing, reaping, spinning, weaving, kneading, writing, and analogous forms of labor. Against the background of Sadducean teaching, this was a liberal interpretation on the part of the Pharisees who consistently sought to free religion from the chains of literalism while retaining the essence of the Law under precise definition. The victorious rabbis safeguarded their conception of the Sabbath through numerous precepts which they derived from biblical interpretations and legal inventiveness. These constitute a considerable portion of the written and the oral Torah. Two large tractates of the Talmud were devoted to the Sabbath and its laws.

The elaborate framework of the Sabbath which the Pharisees thus constructed, however, did not meet with favor in antinomian circles among whom are to be counted the writers of the Synoptic Gospels; so that the Jewish Sabbath has been a target of sarcasm and irony as well as a cause for complete and utter misunderstanding. Instead of a "gift of heaven," partisan theologians pictured it as a burdensome day of repression, gloom, and sorrow. Because the prohibition of work was defined in such minute legal detail, those who were strangers to the inner warmth and spiritual beauty of the Sabbath conceived of it in negative terms as a legalistic instrument of repression — a grave injustice to one of the noblest creations of the religious spirit.

To the exilic prophet (Isa. 56.58) the Sabbath is coupled

with justice and righteousness. It is a bond of union between His people and the alien that hath joined himself to the Lord. It is an everlasting memorial, a covenant, and a delight. From a Pharisee, who was one of the younger contemporaries of the Apostles, the Sabbath evoked these words: "Through the love with which Thou, O Lord our God, lovest Thy people Israel, and the mercy which Thou hast shown to the children of Thy covenant, Thou hast given unto us in love this great and holy seventh day." The same sentiment is echoed in song, prayer, and hymn composed over many centuries by Hebrew poets in many parts of the world. In the synagogue, the congregation ushers in the Sabbath by chanting:

"Come, my beloved, to meet the Sabbath bride . . . . Though last in creation, yet it was first in the design Divine . . . . Awake! awake! Thy light is come, arise and shine forth! Awake! awake! Chant a hymn, for the glory of the Lord is revealed upon thee . . . ."

At home the Sabbath is introduced at sundown with the kindling of lights; the children are blessed with biblical blessings; the wife is praised with the recital of the classic chapter of Proverbs (31.10–31); and the Sabbath is welcomed with the ministering angels of peace:

> Peace be with you, ministering angels,
> Angels of the Most High,
> Coming from the King who rules o'er kings,
> The Holy One, blessed be He . . . .
> Bless me in peace, ministering angels,
> Angels of the Most High,
> Coming from the King who rules o'er kings,
> The Holy One, blessed be He.

Every feature of the Sabbath is lighted with hope and joy, even the very meal with its special food and delicacies and the table songs touching God's love, the banishment of worldly cares, the soothing of all sorrows. The Sabbath brings a new soul in its wake; such was the popular belief. Those who probed more deeply sensed in the Sabbath a foretaste, or symbol, of the Messianic bliss of universal peace and brotherhood.

Like the Sabbath, the festivals of Judaism tended further to spiritualize human life and blended nature and history in a divine pattern. Seasonal festivals associated with nature's manifestations of spring, summer, and fall took on new meaning as they were correlated with dramatic historic events in the life of Israel. Primitive celebrations were thus raised to the level of Holy Days impregnated with deep religious aspiration. Some of the earlier stages in the religious evolution of the festivals are delineated in the Bible record. But much of the poetry and the spiritualizing effect of the holidays was developed later in the talmudic and medieval periods. As the Church from the very beginning cut itself loose from historic Israel, it remained indifferent to the spiritual content of the holidays which were so intimately associated with the history of the Jewish people. It is true that the Church retained some of the holidays by name in the Christian calendar. But the names took on a new and strange meaning that had little or no relevancy to their original character. The biblical holidays remained the spiritual treasures of Judaism and it was through the Jewish people and its literature that their influence radiated throughout the world.

First in time and season is the spring festival of Passover. From its earliest beginnings to this day, the holiday was surrounded with picturesque ceremonies, and observances which grew out of historic memories and stirred the religious imagination. Many of the customs are traceable to pastoral and agricultural celebrations of spring. But even in the earliest Bible records, they are associated with the springtime of Israel's nationhood and the religious epic depicting the triumph of freedom through a covenant between God and man.

The Passover observances celebrated in our time are among

196

the oldest religious symbols consciously preserved in the memory of man. Feast of Unleavened Bread is the Bible designation for the Passover holiday. To this day, the eating of unleavened bread to the exclusion of that which contains any form of leaven is one of the conspicuous features of the Passover celebration. Over the great span of time, the *mazzah*, or unleavened bread, has stood for one symbol: the hasty flight of Israel from Egypt — the redemption wrought by God in leading Israel out of bondage into freedom; more pointedly, human freedom under the covenant of God. More than a thousand years later, when the Jews lost their freedom to the Romans, they expressed their undying hope by designating Passover "the Season of our Liberation."

In the days of the Temple, the paschal lamb, slaughtered in every household on the fourteenth day of Nisan, inaugurated the festival in the evening, when it was eaten with great ceremony amidst song and psalmody. Among the small dwindling sect of Samaritans in Palestine, the sacrifice of the lamb is still practiced, so that their Passover celebration annually attracts many curious, interested onlookers. In Jewish observance, however, the paschal lamb sacrifice was abandoned with the destruction of the Temple and the consequent abolition of all animal sacrifices. But with the disappearance of the sacrifice, the name of Passover which formerly had been attached to the sacrifice came to designate the holiday itself. The transference of the name was not an arbitrary act; the meaning of the symbol itself had grown and expanded. In the Bible the paschal sacrifice and the sprinkling of the blood commemorated the act of God who caused the angel of death to "pass over" the homes of the Israelites. What was more fitting than to attach the name Passover to the holiday itself which perennially commemorated the far greater and continuous miracle of Jewish survival since the dark ages that followed the burning of the Temple and the destruction of the Jewish state?

In ancient days, the inauguration of the holiday celebration

197

centered round the family hearth when the paschal lamb was eaten amidst symbolic accompaniments. To this day, the most distinctive feature of the Passover celebration is the family ceremony — the Seder ritual — which is enacted on Passover eve around the dinner table with the festive candle lights, the sanctification wine, and the ornamental platter containing the symbolic food items: three *mazzot*, bitter herbs, parsley, other symbols, and the shank bone as a reminder of the paschal lamb. The Seder ceremony is a pageant: partly drama, partly ritual. Legend and history are woven into its composition. There are dialectic discussions for the learned, fun and humor for the children. The youngest child is encouraged to ask the four set questions concerning the nature of the ritual, whereupon the head of the family, the chief celebrant, commences to narrate: "Once upon a time we were slaves unto Pharaoh in Egypt; and the Lord our God brought us forth from there with a mighty hand and outstretched arm." The recital of the story, loosely woven together from Bible passages and later rabbinic compositions, is complemented by the chanting of psalms. The festive food is served, grace is said, and the service is concluded with chants, psalms, and songs. Throughout the ceremony, questions are encouraged, the symbolic objects are pointed to and explained, so that the Seder ceremony may aptly be described as a demonstration of spiritual pedagogy.

The education conveyed through the Passover holiday had enduring effect upon the soul of the Jewish people. Redemption, freedom, undying hope for the future of mankind became deeply ingrained ideals commanding Jewish allegiance. Jewish sages came to speak mystically of a millennial Passover that will complete the historic Passover of the past. In the days to come, the promise of Passover will be fulfilled in the national redemption of the land of Israel and in an era of universal brotherhood, justice, and peace that will embrace all His creatures. This universal spirit was painted with poetic fantasy in Jewish legend in the scene at the crossing of the Red Sea. On the day of the drowning of the Egyptians, the angels in heaven wished to sing the song of glory to God as is their wont. But God silenced them. "My creatures are drowning in the waters; would ye sing before me on such a day?" The Passover pageant in the Seder ritual opens with the prologue: "Let all who are hungry enter and eat with us; let all who are in need come and celebrate the Passover." This may well be the call of Passover to all the nations and faiths of mankind. It is the everlasting cry for freedom, unity, and brotherhood. This too is symbolized in the midst of the Seder service when the door is dramatically opened for Elijah, the invisible, to enter, Elijah the prophet of glad tidings, the harbinger of the Messiah.

The complement to Passover is the succeeding holiday, known as the Feast of Weeks, or Festival of the First Fruits. This holiday was the subject of protracted controversy between the revolutionary Pharisees and the die-hard Sadducees. While the controversy ostensibly centered around the day from which the count of seven weeks is to be made (Lev. 33.15), there is little doubt that a strong contributory factor in the agitation was the fundamental change which had been wrought not long before in the very nature of the holiday itself.

In the Bible, the Feast of Weeks was wholly an agricultural festival with little or no historic association. It marked the completion of the wheat harvest, the beginning of which was signalized during Passover by an offering in the Temple of a sheaf of barley, the *Omer*. On the Feast of Weeks, which was seven weeks after Passover, the harvest was completed and the farmer this time brought to the Temple some of the first ripened fruits and two loaves of wheat flour from the new crop. This was on the fiftieth day after the *Omer* was offered in the Temple. There was much rejoicing connected with the celebration and always the social-ethical motif was emphasized that rejoicing before the Lord meant that the means to share in the joy must be given to all, without regard to class or station.

Under the influence of Pharisaic teaching, and especially

after the destruction of the Temple, the concept of the Feast of Weeks was completely transformed. It became the Festival of the Giving of the Law, a holiday commemorating the Revelation of God on Sinai and the giving of the Ten Commandments. This interpretation was readily harmonized with the Bible account of the Theophany and may indeed have followed an age of long oral tradition. The Festivals of Passover and Weeks were linked in spiritual union to proclaim a new truth: freedom from bondage is not an end in itself but a means to spiritual emancipation. Thus rabbinic Judaism converted an agricultural feast into a spiritual harvest. A Palestine festival became a universal symbol. To this day, the holiday is the occasion of Israel's perennial dedication to the Torah, God's covenant with mankind. The Book of Ruth with its setting in a wheat harvest scene is read on this festival — an idyl of love and loyalty which transcends the bounds of country and nation, presaging the birth of David, the ancestor of the Messiah.

The Feast of Tabernacles, "the Season of our Rejoicing," completed the biblical cycle of holidays, or pilgrimages. This was the major harvest festival in autumn at the close of the ingathering season when the people flocked to the Temple in Jerusalem to give thanks and to rejoice before the Lord. Rustic booths, or tabernacles, were set up for seven days and from them the holiday derived its name. The harvest festival was given spiritual connotation in the Bible by associating these pilgrimage booths with God's care of the children of Israel who also dwelt in booths as He guided and protected them during the forty years in the wilderness. Public processions with "the fruits of the goodly trees," palm branches, myrtle twigs, and willows of the brook gave festive color to the general celebration. Great solemnity was attached to a special procession from the silver pool at the foot of the Temple Mount to the altar in the Temple. Great was the joy at this ceremony of water-drawing for the libation which was offered on the altar in symbolic prayer for the hoped-for autumn rains. Always a note of spiritual aspiration permeated the ceremonies; the libation of water was accompanied by the chant: "With joy shall ye draw water out of the wells of salvation."

Nature's profusion was paralleled at the altar by numerous sacrifices, seventy bullocks in all, which led the rabbis later to offer this significant interpretation: that the Jewish people offered those seventy sacrifices on the altar of God in behalf of the seventy nations which comprised all the peoples of the world. The universal idealism suggested in this rabbinic thought evidently harmonized with an old tradition of the later prophets. For it was Zechariah who prophesied that the day would come when the nations would go up to Jerusalem from year to year to worship God and to keep the Feast of Tabernacles.

When the Temple was destroyed and the people were uprooted from the land, the Feast of Tabernacles, like the other holidays, had to be adjusted to the new conditions. The ceremonials of the sacrificial cult could no longer be observed; the festive features of the harvest holiday lost much of their significance as the people were forcibly detached from the beloved land in ever increasing measure. All the more did the holiday take on symbolic spiritual characteristics in the new orientation of Judaism under the aegis of the rabbis whose religious genius proved them worthy successors of the biblical prophets.

The booth is now the central symbol of the holiday. This is an improvised frail structure like a rustic cabin. It has no roof but a thatched covering of leafy branches and twigs, sufficient as a protection against the sun while allowing the stars to shine through at night. It is customary to decorate the interior with fruits and vegetables as a reminder of the harvest in Palestine. In these booths the faithful are supposed to eat their meals during the seven days of the festival and also to sleep therein. It is a religious duty for every family to have its own booth but as this is not practical nowadays, especially in urban communities, the booth is usally set up near the synagogue premises to which the congregation repair for a brief repast after the regular morning and evening service in the synagogue.

Ethical religious symbolism guides the detailed rules laid down for this quaint construction: the frailty of life, the shelter of God's wings, Messianic hope, the stars of faith that pierce through the darkness that besets the life of individuals and nations. Likewise "the goodly fruit"— the *Etrog*, or citron — and the *Lulab*, consisting of the palm branches, the myrtle twigs, and the willows of the brook which were featured so prominently in the biblical observances of the festival are endowed with mystical thoughts and are retained as a biblical precept and a remembrance of Palestine. They are blessed in the home; and in the synagogue, as in the Temple of old, they are waved in concert in all directions, and carried in procession around the altar, symbolizing God's presence in all points of the world's compass. Mysticism and joyousness were blended in the spirit of this festival, and this mood reached a climax on the seventh day known as *Hoshana Rabbah* when the refrain *Hoshana* or *Hosanna* was the recurrent theme in the processional service. A similar mood of solemn prayer when the soul is uplifted with joy and exultation in the Law is continued on the day following, the Eighth Day of Solemn Assembly. In the communities outside of Palestine, where an extra day is traditionally added to the holiday, the ninth day is known and celebrated exuberantly as the Day of Rejoicing in the Law.

The festivals of Judaism are thus history reincarnated and theology in action. This theology is a dramatic living history, not abstract dogma. The voice of God which speaks in the rhythm of nature, the poetry of the stars and skies in Palestine, the music of its hills and valleys — these living themes of Israel's prophets and psalmists — are captured in the picturesque symbolism of the festivals. And as with the prophets and ancient bards, they inspire visions of universal truth and holiness. Nature is blended with moral philosophy and theology is scented with the fragrance of earth and soil, fitting it for habitation in the heart of man.

VII

In contrast to the luxuriant associations of the festival cycle is the chaste atmosphere surrounding the holy days of New Year and the Day of Atonement. On those days, Judaism stands at the highest peak of religious vision. The kingdom of God is clearly visible on the horizon. It is seen peopled with all races of mankind. It is filled with righteousness, holiness, justice, and goodness. To cause the Kingdom to descend upon the earth, to cause it to penetrate the individual soul and also to make it coextensive with the whole world is the object of prolonged prayer, penitence, and fasting during those holy days.

In the Pentateuch the first day of Tishri, which is the New Year Day, is called simply the Day of the Blowing of the Trumpet. What occasioned the trumpet blowing is not indicated in the Bible. But the Pharisees and the early rabbis filled the gap with deep religious thought. According to their tradition, the first day of the seventh month (Tishri) was the day of creation, the day when time began. It was truly the New Year Day. The blasts of the *Shofar* in three groupings proclaimed three divine manifestations: God the King of the world; God the Judge who on New Year passes in review the actions and designs of men and nations for reward or punishment; God the Ruler of history Who once revealed Himself to Israel on Sinai through the shout of the trumpet and Who will again blow the trumpet on Judgment Day to gather all men and nations under the rule of the Messiah.

This threefold theme is developed in many prayers. They are intoned in chants which are among the oldest music in Jewish tradition and create a feeling of profound solemnity. The combined effect is designed to make man feel vividly the majesty of God; to stir within him the feeling of repentance and a resolve to put himself in harmony with the Judge on high; and as an Israelite to prepare himself for God's ultimate redemption of mankind with Israel leading the nations to the God of Zion.

It is characteristic of Judaism that the day of judgment is not deferred to the hereafter but is effective at the beginning of every year in this living world. It may also be regarded as significant that the Jewish New Year is made to coincide with the autumn season when nature is about to be denuded and to enter the decline of winter. It is then that the trumpet blasts blow to proclaim the God of life and the coming of the day when His rule will bring hope, light, and redemption to all who walk in darkness, bowed down and stricken.

The New Year Day marks but the beginning of the ten penitential days which are considered a special time of grace "to seek the Lord while He may be found." The culmination is reached on the tenth day of Tishri, the Day of Atonement, the Day of the Lord, great and fearsome. On New Year Day, according to a poetic rabbinic conception, the actions and thoughts of every living being pass before the Divine Judge and are recorded for judgment in the Book of Life. On the Day of Atonement, after man has been led to the path of penitence, the judgment is rendered; the fate of men and nations is decreed; and the verdict is "sealed." Atonement rather than judgment is the dominant note of the holy day, for the contrite heart has repented and sin is mercifully forgiven. Thus it becomes a day of salvation; a day of moral regeneration; or as the rabbis expressed it: "On the Day of Atonement, I will create you a new creation."

The growth of this religious concept from the time of the Bible through the pharisaic-talmudic period into the days of rabbinic Judaism reflects the widening horizon of the Torah vision vouchsafed the priestly people. In the Pentateuch the theme of human sin and atonement by divine grace is delineated in clear, bold outline. The Day of Atonement is a day for the affliction of the soul when all the people are bidden to fast — from sundown to sundown — and the high priest offers solemn atonement sacrifice: for himself and his household, for the priests, and for all Israel. The priest, the altar, and the sacrifices were the media through which atonement reached the nation, and the eyes and the hearts of the people were upon the high priest throughout the solemn day. Even when the entire system of priest, Temple, and animal offerings ceased to exist after 70 CE, the ancient Atonement service was reproduced in the form of a dramatic recital in the Synagogue liturgy of the day. Nevertheless a revolutionary advance in religious conception came about inevitably with the vanishing of the sacrificial cult. The mediation of the priest between God and man was gone forever. Mortal man appears before God on the Day of Atonement to confess his sins, to repent with contrite heart, and to receive divine forgiveness without the benefit of priest, altar, and sacrifice. Said Rabbi Akiba: "Happy are ye Israelites! Before whom do ye cleanse yourselves and who cleanses you from sin? Your Father in Heaven."

In the rabbinic conception, confession must precede repentance. According to Maimonides, "Repentance means that the sinner gives up the sin, removing it from his mind, and determining in his heart not to repeat the evil action again." Confession furthermore must be expressed in words. Even an offense committed against a human being is not expiated by mere restitution but must be accomplished by confession to the injured person; how much the more when the offense is against God. But the spoken confession is addressed to Him alone. It must be accomplished with a feeling of shame. "To him who commits a transgression and afterwards is ashamed of it, all his sins are forgiven."

Prominent in the liturgy of the Atonement Day, therefore, is the rite of confession. It is a recurrent feature of the service from sundown to sundown. It is recited with moving lips but inaudibly by the individual and repeated with the congregation in unison. The sins cited in the confession are intended to cover every possible transgression to which the human being is liable, but significantly enough ritual sins are almost entirely omitted. The stress is wholly on ethical sins.

The Day of Atonement cannot, however, even with repentance and confession, absolve violations committed against a fellow man. Restitution and reconciliation are necessary concomitants of moral regeneration. On this subject, rabbinic judgment is emphatic: "Matters between thee and God are forgiven; matters between thee and thy fellow man are not forgiven till thou hast appeased thy neighbor."

To bring into bold relief the ethical demands of atonement, the architects of the Synagogue liturgy selected the immortal utterance of the exilic prophet as the prophetic reading for the Atonement Day.

Cry aloud, spare not,
Lift up thy voice like a trumpet,
And declare unto My people their transgression,
And to the house of Jacob their sins . . . .
Is not this the fast that I have chosen?
To loose the fetters of wickedness,
To undo the bands of the yoke,
To let the oppressed go free,
And that ye break every yoke?
Is it not to deal thy bread to the hungry,
And that thou bring the poor that are cast out to thy house?
When thou seest the naked, that thou cover him,
And that thou hide not thyself from thine own flesh?
Then shall thy light break forth as the morning,
And thy healing shall spring forth speedily.

As the Day of Atonement nears the climax in the hour of twilight, the call to repentance reaching out to distant heathen nations is echoed ringingly in the synagogue from the book of Jonah. Great and universal is the power of human repentance from whatever source. "It ascends to the very throne of God," say the rabbis. With mounting intensity the theme of the Atonement Day is developed in hopeful prayer and majestic chants as the sun sets and the last rays come over the tree tops till the service is finally concluded with the fervent proclamation of God's Unity and Sovereignty, and the seven-fold rallying cry, "The Lord He is God." With dramatic fitness, the fast is concluded with the blowing of the notes of the ancient trumpet blast.

The philosophic and ethical principles of the Jewish religion which are thus poetically portrayed in the institutions of Judaism — in the Sabbath, the holidays and holy days — are developed and expounded in the rabbinic literature. Each of these forms the theme of one or more tractates of the Mishna and the Talmud where the laws and principles pertaining to the subject are fully elaborated. While the Talmud deals primarily with the laws prescribed for the observance of these religious institutions, its pages are illuminated with ethical comments and brilliant interpretations that bring to light the eternal religious values embodied in these observances. These mystic aspects of religion are especially elucidated with flashes of wit and wisdom in the Midrash, a quaint literature that is supplementary to the Talmud and is mostly contemporaneous with it. It consists of loose collections of homilies, legends, ethical discourses, parables, and pithy sayings. The Talmud and the Midrash are thus mutually complementary. They are two faces of the one medal.

Even so minor a holiday as Purim is treated in a special tractate of the Talmud and a corresponding homiletic Midrash based on the Scroll of Esther. This festive day, the fourteenth of Adar, a month before Passover, commemorating the deliverance of the Jews from the plot of Haman is celebrated as a day of popular rejoicing with plays and games, the exchange of gifts, and the giving of bounties to the poor. Underneath the merry-making, however, is the sober realization that Haman's plotting never ceases and that deliverance from such designs and persecutions is both a saddening and inspiring feature of Jewish history.

On the other hand, Hanukkah, the eight day Festival of Dedication, or as Josephus called it, the Festival of Lights, commencing on the twenty-fifth day of Kislev (*ca.* December) and commemorating the victory of Judas Maccabeus over the hosts of Syrians as narrated in the books of the Maccabees, is glossed over in rabbinic literature; the military victory is ignored; and the triumph of war is replaced by an imaginative tale of a small cruse of pure Temple oil that burned miraculously for eight days during the rededication of the Temple, whence arose the custom to kindle lights for the eight days of Hanukkah. Modern historians have been at pains to explain this apparently studied rebuff to the great heroes of the Maccabean revolt who saved Judaism by their marvelous exploits on the battlefield. But the rabbis left little doubt as to their religious motivation. For they turned to the book of Zechariah to furnish the prophetic commentary, the Haftarah, on the Sabbath of Hanukkah: "Not by might, nor by power, but by My spirit, saith the Lord of hosts."

The distinctiveness of the Jewish religion is not confined to its sacred calendar or its religious-historic institutions. The nature of Judaism is equally revealed in the daily religious practices, in the ethical studies prescribed for everyday living, in the laws of social justice, and in the emulation of holiness which is the heart of the Jewish religious system. Rabbinic law is coextensive with life itself. Talmudic law, known under the name of *Halakah*, draws its inspiration as well as its etymological origin from the phrase "to walk in the ways of God."

Every phase of life and every human relationship is treated from this standpoint in Judaism, both in its sacred literature and in the detailed system of law and practice.

Only a fleeting view of the duties that circumscribe the life of the religious Jew can be conveyed within the compass of this essay. Jewish piety begins and concludes the day with prayer. "I accept upon myself the fulfillment of the commandment: 'Thou shalt love thy neighbor as thyself,' " is a preliminary to the morning devotions. And the last words recited before the eyes close in sleep are:

> I place my soul within His palm,
> Before I sleep as when I awake,
> And though my body I forsake,
> Rest in the Lord in fearless calm.

On the threshold of the Jewish home, in an encased bit of parchment known as the *Mezuzah*, is inscribed Israel's creed of faith, "Hear, O Israel, the Lord our God, the Lord is One"; also the following verses: "And thou shalt love thy God with all thy heart, with all thy soul and with all thy might." Whatever possible talismanic association the *Mezuzah* may have had, Maimonides voiced its true meaning in Judaism: "Every time one enters or leaves the house, he meets the name of God inscribed on the door post, recalling to him His love and thereby teaching him that there is nothing true and enduring but the recognition of the Creator. Then he will walk in the paths of uprightness."

Within the home, the feeling of spiritual dedication is accentuated through many precepts and religious practices. Food is treated as a symbol of God's providence. Therefore, to express gratitude to God, the recital of blessings is punctiliously prescribed before and after partaking of food. It is a popular Jewish concept that the table where food is eaten partakes of the sanctity of the altar of ancient days. The laws separating "clean" and "unclean" beasts, fowl and fish, permitting the one and forbidding the other species to be eaten, are the foundation of the elaborate dietary laws which under talmudic and rabbinic development became one of the most distinguishing marks of personal and home life in traditional Judaism. The rationalist view that those laws were devised as hygienic measures cannot be maintained seriously. In the Bible, they are clearly part of the code of holiness: "I am the Lord your God, who have set you apart from the peoples. Ye shall therefore separate between the clean beast and the unclean, and between the unclean fowl and the clean . . . . And ye shall be holy unto Me; for I the Lord your God am holy, and have set you apart from the peoples that ye should be Mine." The ideal of "separation" for the sake of holiness was immeasurably strengthened under the influence of the Pharisees in their heroic struggle to preserve Judaism against the attacks of Hellenism and the antinomianism of the Christian sects of the times. To the talmudic sages, therefore, the sole purpose of these laws which separated the Jews was moral purification and voluntary submission to the will of "our Father in Heaven." They were part of the moral discipline of a priestly people whose eyes were upon the kingdom of God. Morally and physically the need for this spiritual discipline was accentuated during the Middle Ages both as a protest and as a shield of protection. Such was undoubtedly the concept of the rabbinic jurists and moralists; and the Jewish home of today where these laws are still observed bears testimony to this Jewish concept of the ages.

The distinctiveness of Judaism, however, is not to be sought solely in the visible and mystical symbols of religion but even more so in the laws governing the moral and ethical conduct of the individual and those regulating the economic, social, and political relations in organized society. This conception of the function of religion takes on special significance in these days when the eyes and hearts of the nations are set upon creating a

new world in which peace shall be secured through justice. The
Hebrew Bible, or Torah, is not a testament, old or new. The
Torah fundamentally signifies Law, the law as the will of God,
the law that is to prepare individuals, nations, and society for
the rule of God. Unlike the New Testament, the Hebrew Bible
is not primarily concerned with the salvation of the individual
soul in the hereafter but treats men and nations as units of
a society that acknowledges God as king. Its laws are the
crystallization of a lofty conception of God, man, and the universe. Hence they are not limited to the national boundaries of
one people alone, but extend to other nations and to relations
between nations in war and in peace. Basic to these laws is the
concept of the fatherhood of God and the brotherhood of man
and their corollaries touching the dignity of man and the inalienable quality of his rights under a universal law of justice
and righteousness. The Mosaic law consequently is a program
of life and a code of law. It was actually the constitution of the
Jewish State in Palestine under the Second Commonwealth.
Fifteen hundred years later, in a totally different environment,
it was recognized in a limited degree as basic law in the Puritan
commonwealths set up in colonial America. Having in mind
the universal principles underlying the laws of the Bible, Philo,
the Hellenistic-Jewish philosopher at the beginning of the
Common Era, declared: "As God Himself pervadeth all
the universe, so hath our law passed through the world."

VIII

From the historic viewpoint, the Mosaic law was only one
step in the evolution of the Torah. This also accords somewhat
obliquely with the fixed tradition that prophecy succeeded the
Mosaic revelation, which in turn was followed by the teachings
of the Pharisees and the interpretation of the later rabbis, the
fathers of rabbinic Judaism. Thus interpreted, the laws of the

Torah are the distillation of a growing, expanding vision of the interrelations of God, man, and society. It is the vision back of the law which is greater than the law itself, and this vision has constituted the religious genius of the Jewish people throughout the ages. It is a living, continuous function which makes itself manifest in the harmonious development of the Jewish spirit over a period of three thousand years. As in the Bible, so in the Talmud, Jewish law was expanded to embrace the totality of human life under those aspects which society then assumed: religion, ethics, morality; and also the government of society: civil, political, and ecclesiastical.

By liberal interpretation of the biblical law and by new legislative enactments, the rabbis implemented the social and democratic ideals inherent in the Bible. Law was sovereign and universal. Equal justice for all was its paramount aim. The dignity of the human being was not left as a theme for moral preachment but was safeguarded by laws protecting the inherent rights of the individual and the minority. The rights of property were recognized but subordinated to the interests of society. Labor was protected and commerce was regulated. Slavery was not abolished but substantially humanized through laws guaranteeing even the heathen slaves fundamental human rights, which if violated resulted in emancipation. The status of women and children during minority was revolutionized. The laws regulating marriage, dower rights, and divorce were liberalized to protect the wife and mother from the handicaps of the older codes.

Nor did the living law cease with the close of the Talmud at the end of the fifth century. On the contrary, the post-talmudic rabbis — the Geonim who later succeeded the talmudic rabbis in Babylon and were acknowledged as spiritual heads of world Judaism as well as the European rabbis from the tenth century onward — continued to develop new principles of law and created moral institutions in order to make the biblical-talmudic law keep pace with life. Political and social conditions in the Middle Ages were not as favorable toward a natural evolution of the Jewish system of life as they had been in Palestine and Babylon, respectively, in earlier epochs. The implementation of Jewish ideals and principles of justice was greatly hampered by arbitrary governmental restrictions and the hostility of the populace and the Church. Nevertheless, throughout the Middle Ages, when the Jewish communities were generally granted a measure of autonomy, the rabbis heroically applied their own standards of law amidst all the complicated relations of the feudal order, aiming consistently to emulate the eternal pattern of a society formed "on truth, justice and peace."

The rise of national states in European countries from the thirteenth to the end of the fifteenth century caused a drastic reversal of the status of the Jews and Judaism. It was precisely in the centuries of the Renaissance and of the exploration of new world frontiers to which the Jews had contributed so heavily that they experienced the misfortunes of wholesale expulsions or segregation into ghettos. This turn in the historic fortunes of the Jewish people brought about temporarily at least a spiritual metamorphosis. The people that had so richly given of its spirit to the world experienced the bitterness of worldly disillusionment. The need for solace and inner compensation gave a strong impetus to the intensive cultivation of the Cabala and the sway of mystic forces in Judaism. Were it not for the moral restraints and the discipline of Jewish religious law, and in particular the robust intellectual vigor with which talmudic studies disciplined the Jewish mind, Judaism might have fallen into the pitfall of antinomianism and the extravagances of unrestrained mystic orgies. As it was, a forced abortive Messianism in the seventeenth century caused much havoc, but the impetuous current of mysticism was finally restrained and channeled within the bounds of Judaism. Nevertheless, the growth and expansion of Jewish law was retarded. After a dynamic course of thousands of years, the law of Judaism became relatively static during the dark ghetto days of the seventeenth and eighteenth centuries. Within the ghetto the old-time exponents of talmudic erudition clashed with the new movement of mystic saintliness (*Hasidism*). Between the ghetto and the outer world, all lines of vital communication were disrupted.

Out of this state of isolation Judaism was forcibly brought back to the center of the world's arena by the political and spiritual storm of the French Revolution and its sequels in the nineteenth century. The physical and mental walls of the ghetto were broken down in all West-European countries. Judaism as a religion was compelled overnight to meet the challenge of history, science, and philosophy with which Christianity had had to contend, none too successfully, over the course of several centuries while Judaism was living a sheltered existence in the ghetto. In the meantime, political surgery was applied to prune off vital limbs from the Jewish "tree of life." For political emancipation which conferred citizenship upon the Jews necessarily involved on their part the surrender of the so-called mundane laws of a civil, political, constitutional character which in the Jewish conception emanated from the will of God. They were the means for implementing the ideals of social justice, righteousness, and holiness in human society. Indeed, it was these laws which were directly related to the vision of the kingdom of God. But their exercise would be inconsistent with citizenship and the law of the land. This was in great measure true even in reactionary Russia with its unhappy Pale of Settlement. As a result of this dilemma, a process of spiritual self-curtailment was set in motion. Judaism as an over-all program of living gave way to a more limited regimen of piety, spiritual devotion, worship, ritual law, and ceremonialism. The Torah as a law governing the totality of life became more of a theological concept than a living reality.

But this revolutionary course in reverse was not destined to stop midstream. Too many diverse currents, political, cultural, spiritual, had been set in motion. The sudden transition from the medieval ghetto to the modern city produced a feeling of giddiness rather than stability. The lure of Western culture proved intoxicating to the descendants of those who had once been its masters and teachers, but from which they had been rudely separated by the European disciples. The advent of historical criticism, the application of critical methods to the study of ancient texts, the skeptical attitude toward tradition, the effects of which were so disturbing to the established Christian religions, proved even more revolutionary in their effects on Judaism.

Added to this was the confusion brought about by the interplay of political aims upon religious ideals. In the hearts of the emancipated children of the ghetto there burned a passion for political, social, and civic equality. To share in the cultural and civic life of their fellow citizens and to gain their esteem religiously and civically was a fervent goal, especially in Germany, strong enough to override in many quarters the biblical-talmudic aim to keep the Jewish people "separate" through precepts and commandments in order to make them a "kingdom of priests and a holy nation."

Out of this spiritual ferment, new religious parties arose, the most radical of which was that of Reform Judaism. This branch of Judaism, which developed principally in Germany and in the United States, represents a complete revision of the philosophy of Jewish history; a modernistic interpretation of religion according to the accepted historical, critical standards of comparative religion; and a break with tradition in its attitude to Jewish law in general and especially in relation to the binding authority of the Bible and the Talmud in matters ceremonial and ritual, which it categorically denies.

Accepting the basic principle that the Messianic ideal is to be the ultimate fulfillment of Judaism and the end-all of Jewish history, Reform Judaism accentuates the principle of the historic mission of Israel as the priest of humanity and the champion of God's truth; it is the historic function of the Jewish people to lead mankind through the ages until the kingdom of God is established on earth and the highest ideals of a united humanity are realized through the universal knowledge of God and the love of man. Identifying the Jewish nation with the suffering servant of the Lord, depicted in Deutero-Isaiah, Reform Judaism accepted the belief "that Israel, the suffering Messiah of the centuries, shall at the end of days become the triumphant Messiah of the nations."

These affirmations are, as we have seen, part of the religious consciousness of the Jews throughout the ages. What was novel and striking were the negative implications deduced from the concept of the Messianic ideal. Not only was the belief in the personal Messiah formally negated but the entire concept of Jewish history and the destiny of the Jewish people was reversed. The loss of their country and the dispersion of the Jews in exile was not divine retribution for the sins of the people. On the contrary, it was a blessing for it opened to the exiles the gateway to the world and the fulfillment of their Messianic mission. The restoration of the Jewish people to the Holy Land which was vouchsafed them in biblical prophecy and was cherished in the Messianic dream of the ages was decried as contrary to the philosophy of Reform Judaism and all allusions to such a hope were excised from the new liturgy. To stress the common bond with their countrymen, the vernacular was substituted for Hebrew as the chief language of prayer and the study of Hebrew was either eliminated or subordinated to a minor place in the religious curriculum. Whatever savored of social segregation or emphasized ritual distinctiveness, such as the dietary laws and numerous other observances, was opposed on doctrinal grounds and by the denial of supernatural authority to ceremonial law in the Bible and later sacred literature. The Torah thus lost its realistic meaning as the law of Judaism and retained only its symbolic significance as the divine vision which spurs man on to the ultimate goal of God's kingdom on earth.

Reform Judaism was not at any time a spiritual revolt against moral or religious abuse. It was a movement of so-called enlightenment and in its initial stages was supported by brilliant Jewish scholars whose works created a literary-historical renaissance in Jewish scholarship and gave rise to what has since been called the Science of Judaism. But these scholars, in the main, came to feel that Reform Judaism violated historic truth by its one-sided trend toward universalism and away from the national, Hebraic character of the Jewish people and its religion. From these ranks therefore grew another school of thought that laid stress on historical continuity and the evolutionary character of Judaism. Thus arose the historical or traditional branch of Judaism, known in America as Conservative Judaism. Sharing with all religious elements in Jewry the belief in the Messianic goal of Judaism, the conservative branch, in contrast to Reform Judaism, emphasizes the distinctive Hebraic contribution which the Jewish religion is destined to make to the world and the need for preserving the Jewish people as a separate and distinct element consecrated by divine commandments through ceremonies and ritual to be a unique nation — "a kingdom of priests and a holy nation." Hebrew is not only retained as the language of prayer, but is also highly valued as a national bond of union, as a vehicle in which the Jewish soul is revealed historically, and as an instrument for preserving the living Hebraic consciousness. Conservative Judaism does not seem committed to a literal interpretation of the Sinaitic revelation, but it does acknowledge the authority of the Bible and the Talmud and deals reverentially with the customs and ceremonies that developed during the later centuries. The Torah is revered as a program of living as well as an idealized concept of divine wisdom. Particular stress is laid on home ceremonies, the observance of the dietary laws, the Sabbath, and the holy days according to the traditional laws and customs. The hope for the restoration of Israel to the ancient soil is vividly retained as a divine promise and a living ideal. With its realization are bound up national salvation and the condition preceding Messianic fulfillment.

The principles of Conservative Judaism have not been so categorically formulated as those of Reform Judaism partly because of an instinctive historic reluctance on the part of many of its rabbinical leaders to multiply religious parties in Israel. The lines of demarcation between Conservative Judaism and Orthodoxy, whose adherents form the third and numerically the largest part of Jewry, are not sharply delineated. The chief theological distinction of Orthodox Judaism is its adherence to the principle of literal revelation and its denial of the principle of historic evolution as applied to the theory and practice of religion. It has been pointed out significantly that the appellation Orthodoxy as applied to Judaism is not only etymologically alien but is also theologically foreign to the historic character of Judaism which has always been hospitable to difference of thought within the bounds of the traditional faith. The term Orthodox was borrowed from the vocabulary of Christian theology to offset the equally foreign name of Reform.

The three religious parties, Orthodox, Conservative, and Reform, constitute what has been felicitously called catholic Judaism. Wide as are some of their differences in belief and practice they are not separatist sects but differing members of one religion. They are united not only by kinship and history and the bonds of a common destiny but also by a deep abiding faith in religious principles which they hold to be immortal and which they cherish for the happiness of humanity.

Common to them all is the belief that Israel has a divine and prophetic role to play in the concert of nations and in the progress of united humanity toward an era of universal justice and peace. The millennial vision abides eternally in the Torah and illumines the hope of all its children. The creative religious genius which has produced the world's greatest prophets and has given the greater part of mankind its religion and ethics still holds great promise for endless generations to come who will build the foundations of "a new heaven and a new earth." Whatever interpretations a religious party or individual may give to this Jewish Messianic faith, its essence is spiritually alive with optimistic faith in God and the future of mankind. Therein lies the strength and the unity of Judaism.

IX

Noble but futile attempts have been made to define in precise terms the future function of the Jewish people in the religious drama of mankind. There are those who see Israel's destiny to be the spiritual mediator between the East and the West. However, the hand of Providence is firm without drawing blueprints. Of certain things there is surety. If there is to be security and peace among nations, this teaching of Judaism must be taken to heart: that religion must deal with nations, not only with individuals; with international law and ethics, not merely with personal salvation and beliefs. A world hungering for peace must recognize the religious axiom of Jewish teaching that the foundation of peace is justice. The tragedy of war and crime vindicates the Jewish conception that the religion of love must also be a religion of law.

Judaism does not however merely seek vindication of its historic teachings. It looks to greater spiritual fruition in the future. The restoration of Jews to their ancestral home in our day and the rebuilding in Palestine of a national home for the genius of the Jewish people may usher in a new epoch of prophetic creation comparable to that of the Second Commonwealth that saved Judaism and ended by giving birth to a new world faith. Holding firmly to the past the seers of Israel fix their vision, like the prophets of old, upon the end of days when many peoples shall go up and say:

> Come ye and let us go up to the mountain of the Lord,
> To the house of the God of Jacob;
> And He will teach us of His ways,
> And we will walk in His paths.
> For out of Zion shall go forth the Law,
> And the word of the Lord from Jerusalem.

The Immortality of Man
A Jewish Viewpoint

I DEEM it a great honor to have been invited to deliver the annual lecture under the Garvin Foundation. It is only fair to state at the outset that it was with considerable diffidence that I accepted the invitation of the Trustees. The theme, "The Immortality of Man," is one which has challenged and baffled the greatest minds of all time. The men whom you have brought here in the past to discuss this fascinating theme are among the celebrated scientists, philosophers and theologians of our generation. One feels naturally humble to stand imaginatively in such company.

I am not a scientist, nor do I lay claim to be a philosopher. It is true that my training has conditioned me theologically, but my deepest interest is history. Such contributions to knowledge as I have been privileged to make have been confined to this terrestrial globe, this vale of tears, in which the human race runs its earthly course, and in which the visible span of mortal man is the measure from the cradle to the grave. My dilemma, therefore, reduced itself to this vital question. Can the historian from his perch in the observation tower of history catch a glimpse of the inward mystery of man, his striving for the unattainable, his search for the invisible, his reaching out for the infinite, his yearning for personal immortality? I was helped in reaching an affirmative decision by considerations both far and near.

There was before me the letter citing that remarkable provision in the last will and testament of M. T. Garvin. I gathered that Mr. Garvin, a merchant, was neither a philosopher nor

Delivered in the series of The M. T. Garvin Free Lectures on God and Immortality at The Church of Our Father, Lancaster, Pennsylvania, December 1, 1949.

theologian. Yet in the contemplation of death, his thoughts were not centered upon the prospect of earthly dissolution. His eyes were not fixed upon the transitory existence of man ending in death. His spirit soared far beyond the grave, and he was filled with a yearning to bring to his fellow men a vision which illumined his life, a vision of God and life eternal.

As I visualized the spiritual image of this man whom I did not know in the flesh, I seemed to recognize the man as a familiar and friendly character in history. I experienced a feeling akin to the excitement we feel when suddenly we meet an old acquaintance in a far-off land. I was particularly struck by his kinship to another person whom I never knew in life, the founder of the Dropsie College for Hebrew and Cognate Learning, with which, as you may know, I am intimately associated.

Moses Aaron Dropsie, like M. T. Garvin, was a man of broad vision and profound religious convictions. He held firmly to the belief that man was a cosmic creature who derived his significance from his conscious relationship to the God idea. Intuitively he perceived that in history, God's will is revealed and in God, man's divine image is mirrored. He, too, was neither a philospher nor theologian. A Philadelphia lawyer, engaged in mundane affairs, an historian in his leisure hours, a patron of the arts and letters, he knew the worldly side of the human being and shared his interests in full measure. But as he contemplated the end of his earthly existence, his deep concern was with the growing estrangement of his generation from the eternal values and visions of religion. He desired earnestly and enduringly to redirect the thoughts of men to a deeper knowledge and understanding of the sources of the Hebrew religion; to the exploration of the languages, cultures and civilizations out of which emerged the religions of Judaism, Christianity and Islam. For such knowledge generates faith and such understanding begets love: this was his credo. It was this faith and vision that led him to dedicate all his earthly possessions to the establishment of that unique college for the advancement on a high academic level of those profound studies that he quaintly styled Hebrew and cognate learning.

Such lives as these afford a glimpse into one phase of human immortality. Their faith assuredly was not buried in the silence of the grave. Are we not here tonight because M. T. Garvin willed it so? In a sense, my presence here this evening is directly attributable to the fact that Moses Aaron Dropsie and M. T. Garvin, who never met in life, shared like convictions about the world and the hereafter. The ancient rabbis rightly declared that the voices of the righteous speak with greater clarity and eloquence in death than in life. Multiply the example of these two men, magnify their aspirations on a worldwide scale and the objective historian, too, is compelled to weigh the meaning and significance of such testimony and to take into account the imperishable quality of their hopes and dreams for the future destiny of mankind.

What then can the historian contribute to our understanding of the immortality of the soul? It is not the province of the historian to explore the hereafter or to study the soul in its disembodied state. This has been the classic occupation of philosophers and theologians, who in turn owe much to the poets and the mystics. The historian's task is more modest but nevertheless valuable and clarifying. He can, in the first place, trace the growth and development in the hearts of men of the concepts of the soul and immortality. Set into such a frame, these ideas take on dimension and perspective. It becomes possible to observe the process by which these ideas implanted themselves in the human composition. One can then sift the ingredient elements out of which these ideals were fashioned. One can distinguish between the accretions of popular beliefs rooted in primitive superstition and the ideas that were born out of a lofty conception of religion. But the historian need not, must not stop there. It is his function and prerogative also to record the impact of these ideals on human personality and their influence on the moral evolution of society.

It is with this viewpoint in mind that we approach the subject of this evening's discussion, the immortality of man. We are, however, imposing a limitation on the scope of our discussion. We shall treat of the immortality of man as reflected in Hebrew thought and literature. This self-imposed limitation, we hope, will prove advantageous not only out of regard for economy of time, but principally for the sake of sharpness of focus.

The moment we begin to probe and analyze the concept of immortality, we become aware that we are dealing with an involved organic complex of thought and emotion. For many thousands of years, man has stood inquiringly at the portals of death, peering into the unknown and wondering about his exit with an uneasy feeling of fear and hope and resignation. Man has persistently refused to accept death as the end of the self within him. The belief in the survival of the soul, the spirit or the ego after death, has strangely fascinated and haunted the imagination of man from the earliest stages of personal and social consciousness to our own day. Were we to trace this idea indefinitely, our steps would lead us over a trail that extended into every crevice of the earth's surface throughout the eras of recorded time. We would also find that at every stage in human history, such beliefs were related through symbol, rite and ceremony to the general cult of the religion of that time and place.

For life and death, man and God are symmetrically conceived. As the concept of man's being flows directly out of one's conceptions of God, so are the ideals of life and death intertwined like light and shadow. Moreover, the degree in which the pall of death fastens itself upon the life and religion of a people, determines the light in which man looks upon his God. Preoccupation with the mystery of death led repeatedly to ancestor worship or actual worship of the dead. In time it became necessary to dispel the shades of the dead spirits to make way for the God of life. On the basis of the Hebrew historical record, one may indeed pose the question whether an intense vivid concern with one's personal immortality is an essential concomitant of a profound belief in God. It is the latter consideration which lends peculiar significance to the Jewish conception of immortality and its relation to the total concept of religion.

The Jewish and Christian conceptions of immortality run parallel over many centuries. At times, they seem basically identical both in the philosophic formulations of the intellectual elite and in the naive imagery of the pious masses. But there are also mutually illuminating divergences. These stem from many sources: historic influences; the doctrine of God and its impact on man as conceived in each religion; the relative valuation put upon the two spheres of this world and the future world. Not the least important is the effect of the time element: that is to say when, at what stage and in what form the idea of immortality was admitted into each of these religions.

Immortality through resurrection is the first affirmation of Christianity. That Jesus rose from the dead is the cornerstone on which the structure of historic Christianity has been reared. One might conceivably add to or subtract from the ethical or doctrinal teachings of Jesus found in the New Testament without necessarily destroying the unity or integrity of the Christian religion. But remove the dogma of the resurrection of Christ and what is left can no longer bear the name of Christianity.

To appreciate the full significance of this Christian affirmation, it must be recalled that neither resurrection nor immortality as a belief of soul experience was at that time either a new or startling doctrine in the villages of Galilee and in the streets of Jerusalem. On the contrary, these were the common beliefs of the Pharisees, the rank and file of the Jewish people. It was the ostensible manifestation of Jesus' bodily resurrection on this earth before the eyes of living witnesses as reported by his disciples — it was this assertion of fact rather than theory or

doctrine that constituted the startling revelation. As Doctor
Sperry stated in one of the Garvin lectures: "Whatever else the
disciples thought and knew about Jesus, they knew that he had
risen from the dead. The Christian religion was launched on
the world as a confident assurance of immortality. All the books
of the New Testament ring the changes on this conviction. . . .
There is no doubt that the appeal of Christianity rested from
the outset in no small part upon its absolute assurance in this
regard. Christ had risen from the dead. Believers in Christ
would rise with him. . . ." In Doctor Sperry's striking phrase:
"The issue was, as the lawyers have it, not justiciable."

It is the relevance of the message of resurrection to the personality of Jesus that sets this doctrine at the very center of Christian
theology. By a process of intellectual accommodation, liberal
Christians who cannot adhere to the literal interpretation of
Scripture have etherealized the concept of bodily resurrection
into soul immortality. But the assurance of life in the hereafter
is under no condition removed from its primacy in religious
belief. Again quoting Doctor Sperry: "A religion that is purely
this-worldly and confessedly indifferent to any next world, has
departed so far from the original that common decency in the
use of words might suggest the impropriety, if not the outright
falsehood of designating such a religion as 'Christian.' . . . The
man who thinks that Jesus, a Galilean carpenter who lived for
some thirty years, is now dead and gone forever save for what
is called his 'immortality in history' — and that this is to be the
fate of all the rest of us — can hardly be called a Christian in the
historic sense of the term."

Now Judaism has for the past two thousand years, both
prior to and since the proclamation of the Christian gospel,
adhered firmly to the belief in the immortality of man. Almost
contemporaneously with the New Testament, the rabbis sol-
emnly stated: "He who declares that the dead are not restored
to life," or as a later incorrect reading has it, "he who asserts

that the belief in the restoration of the dead is not warranted in Hebrew Scriptures will have no share in the future world." Such a person is classed with Epicureans and those who deny divine revelation, who also "will have no share in the world to come." Indeed, the hope for a future life was too vital to remain congealed solely as a doctrinal formula. It furnished an inspirational theme for prayer and was at an early date incorporated into the daily Jewish liturgy. From days dating centuries prior to the New Testament, to our own time, the pious worshipers in the Synagogue have recited thrice daily a Hebrew prayer, which in literal translation reads as follows: "Thou, O Lord, art mighty forever; Thou revivest the dead with great mercy; Thou causest the wind to blow and the rain to fall; Thou sustainest the living with lovingkindness; Thou upholdest the falling and healest the sick; Thou loosest the bound and keepest Thy faith with them that sleep in the dust. Who is like unto Thee, Lord of power; who resembleth Thee, O King, who causest death and givest life and causest salvation to flourish. Faithful art Thou to revive the dead. Blessed art Thou, O Lord, who revivest the dead." In all probability Jesus himself daily recited this prayer.

Those who are biblically conscious will recognize in the resurrection phrases echoes of I Sam. 2.6; Dan. 12.2. Allusions to other aspects of the prayer are to be found in Ps. 145.14 and 146.7. The Hebrew text is sufficiently flexible to enable modernists to read into the prayer solely spiritual immortality. Thus the pertinent passages are made to read: "Thou callest the dead to immortal life. . . . Faithful art Thou to grant eternal life to the departed. Blessed art Thou, O Lord, who callest the dead to life everlasting." In the prayer book of the Reform movement in Judaism the Hebrew text itself is emended to make it clear beyond doubt that the idea of resurrection has been abandoned in favor of the pure idea of the immortality of the soul.

However conceived, the immortality of man is therefore a

basic tenet of the Jewish religion. This belief was a vivid, dynamic element of the religious life; it engendered hope and faith; it sustained the people in their daily struggles and in their long career of religious suffering. As we shall soon see, it also created intellectual problems, then as now, with which Jewish philosophers and theologians struggled; and their solutions contributed much to scholastic thinking on this subject. But while this joint adventure of the two faiths in their common exploration of the hereafter is enlightening, their difference in perspective created striking, illuminating effects. The effects were produced by a difference in timing, a variance in historic origin and the circumstances surrounding the central theme of immortality.

Paradoxical as it may seem, the idea of immortality in Judaism was not homocentric in origin. It arose not to appease man but to vindicate God. The sphere of God's operations had to be extended in time beyond death, and in space beyond this earth, if His attributes of justice and truth were to be fully revealed. The ancient Hebrew prayer, which we cited earlier, in which God's power to revive the dead is so confidently asserted, is described by the ancient rabbis under the heading of *Geburot*, God's omnipotence. If proof were needed that this rabbinic designation was not an artificial device of abstract academicians, one need but read the exultant Song of Hannah. It is in this wondrous paean glorifying God's power and holiness that we first meet the theme: "The Lord killeth and maketh alive; He bringeth down to the grave and bringeth up."

Immortality in Judaism is therefore a doctrinal belief about God and man on a par with other aspects of the Deity. It does not derive its validity from a supernatural phenomenon connected with the life of any of its prophets. It is a religious perception rather than a divine revelation. Its truth was not proclaimed on the mystic background of a theophany. No external fact is claimed for its authenticity, and it is not in the Christian sense an article of faith. From the Hasmonean period

228

to the end of the Second Commonwealth, a period of over two centuries, the question of resurrection and immortality was debated between the Pharisees and the Sadducees. On this question, Jesus sided with the Pharisees. With the end of the Commonwealth in 70 CE, the Sadducean party disintegrated and the views of the Pharisees prevailed as the unchallenged doctrines of Judaism. Henceforth immortality was no longer a subject of party controversy. The voice of the Pharisees was the voice of Judaism. One may well say that as the flames consuming the Temple on Mount Zion leaped heavenward, faith in human immortality was for all time burned into the soul of Judaism.

The crucial point in this spiritual denouement is the fact that a thousand years intervened between the Mosaic era and the period when the belief in resurrection became established in the heart of pharisaic Judaism. We have thus a vista of a long stretch of time in which the religion of Israel did not invoke the vision of a future life as a religious motif. From Moses the Lawgiver, whom the Jews reverently regard as the greatest of all prophets, to Daniel the apocalyptic visionary, no prophet, no inspired seer, poet and psalmist scoured the heavens in search of the human soul. In the theophanies of Moses, Isaiah and Ezekiel, no semblance of man is visible. As the veil of divine mystery is lifted in the heavenly vision of Isaiah, he beholds the majesty of God upon His throne; he sees the seraphim as they call to one another: "Holy, holy, holy is the Lord of hosts; the whole earth is full of His glory." Ezekiel is more fantastic and extravagant in his colorful imagery. Angels, living creatures of symbolic representation, inhabit the divine spheres. But no saints, no human beings as souls or spiritual bodies mingle with the celestial hosts around the heavenly throne in any of these visions. What is still more significant and realistic is the well recognized fact that nowhere in the Hebrew Scriptures is the reward of virtue or the punishment of sin deferred to the hereafter in the disembodied state of the soul. And yet it was possible for such a religion to kindle in the hearts of men a vision of God clothed in holiness, justice and mercy; a God to be loved with all of one's heart, soul and might; a God to be worshiped and emulated through the practice of righteousness, holiness and lovingkindness.

Whatever the Hebrew prophets and teachers may have thought and felt about the destiny of the human being after death is covered over in silence. It would be fascinating in the extreme to know, for instance, Isaiah's personal thoughts about his own fate after death; what would happen ultimately to the being within him that "saw the Lord sitting upon a throne high and lifted up, and His train filled the Temple"; and that heard the voice of God say unto him: "Go and speak to this people." Would that soul die with the body? Alas, we find no answer to this poignant query even in the famous oracle in Isaiah, Ch. 26: "Thy dead shall live, thy [my] dead bodies shall arise. Awake and sing, ye that dwell in the dust. For Thy dew is as the dew of light. And the earth shall bring the shades to life." For this is a late apocalyptic oracle for the millennial future; and it is not the voice of Isaiah, the son of Amoz, who prophesied in the days of the kings of Judah. Not possessed of the art of the Witch of Endor, we must be resigned to mystifying silence on this issue not on the part of Isaiah alone, but all the prophets of Israel.

To be sure, there are numerous allusions throughout the Hebrew Bible assigning the continued life of the spirit beyond the grave to a vague subterranean region designated by the obscure Hebrew name She'ol. But these allusions, vague and contradictory as they often appear, are hardly to be taken as teachings of prophetic thought. This shadowy underworld in which the shades of the dead had their abode was not a new creation of the Hebrew religion; it was ancient folk belief. The She'ol was common Semitic property which they shared with other primitive peoples in providing room for the spirits of the dead. The belief in human survival being universal, every people created its own abode for the shades of the dead. For the Greeks it was Hades; She'ol was the Hebrew folk conception of such a habitat. In the Septuagint translation, the two names are equated. Like its Babylonian counterpart, it was a land of deep sadness:

> "A land of darkness and the shadow of death;
> A land of thick darkness, as darkness itself;
> A shadowy death-like land without any order,
> Where the light is as darkness."
>
> Job 10.21–22

This zone of gloom was pictured as "the house of meeting for all the living."

At times society appeared peaceful and democratic in the underworld:

> "There the wicked cease from raging,
> And the weary are at rest,
> There the prisoners are at ease together;
> They hear not the voice of the taskmaster,
> The small and great are there alike;
> And the servant is free from his master."
>
> Job 3.17–19

But there were also conflicting impressions. The distinctions of rank, the pomp of royalty persisted in the shadowy underground into which the king of Babylon was hurled in the vision of Isaiah. At times, equality seemed to reign in She'ol for all the inhabitants, the good and wicked alike. At other times, moral distinctions are sharply drawn.

To assemble all the highly charged, emotional descriptions of She'ol and to classify them under logical categories in accordance with their literal sense is to betray a lack of poetic imagination. To the poets and prophets of the Bible, the folk mythology

231

was as clay to the artist. They drew upon the imaginative world of popular belief for imagery and metaphor. The effects to be created varied with the mood of the prophet and the burden of his vision. At no time, however, was the land of the dead used for more than illustrative purposes or as a literary vehicle for the emphatic utterance of a prophetic truth. She'ol did not form the central theme of prophecy. The living and not the dead were the legitimate concern of prophets and prophecy.

In the ancient world, the great need was not to foster belief in the continuance of life after death nor to direct men's thoughts to their fate in the hereafter. The widespread cult of departed spirits and ancestor worship, the elaborate funeral rites and the ceremonial provisions deposited in the coffins of the dead, not to mention the cruel aberrations manifested in the death-rites in other parts of the world, show that the higher religious need was to liberate the living from the torpid hand of the dead. This was one of the leitmotifs in the early teachings of the Hebrew religion. Necromancy, the attempt to bring back the shades of the underground into the realm of human affairs, was condemned as an offense against the living God. It was essential for the religious growth of the race to suppress and to discourage the mingling of the dead with the inhabitants of the world. In view of popular beliefs it was impossible to completely shut off the dead from the religious horizon. But prophetic teaching aimed at least to effect complete separation of the two spheres of the living and the dead as far as possible.

She'ol was therefore characterized as the land of "no return." It was a region cut off from God as well as man:

> "For She'ol cannot praise Thee,
> Death cannot celebrate Thee,
> They that go down into the pit cannot hope for Thy truth.
> The living, the living, he shall praise Thee,
> As I do this day."

Isaiah 38.18–19

The Psalmist in the deep hours of the night, in a mood of dark despair facing, as he feared, the oncoming of death, counted himself already among the dead and cried out:

> "Thou hast laid me in the nethermost pit,
>   In dark places, in the deeps. . . .
>   I am shut up and I cannot come forth."
> . . . .
> "Shall the shades arise and give Thee thanks? Selah.
>   Shall Thy mercy be declared in the grave?
>   Or Thy faithfulness in the place of destruction?
>   Shall Thy wonders be known in the dark?
>   And Thy righteousness in the land of forgetfulness?"
>
> Psalms 88.7, 9, 11–13

In all of these utterances, the poet speaks the language of the people. The burden of his thought was not to portray the future life of the spirit. It was to discourage and to suppress the intrusion of the dead upon the living; to unshackle the popular mind from the bonds of death and to turn the hearts of the people to the living God.

Was there then a loftier vision of a future life among the Hebrew seers of old? The ancient rabbis in search of biblical support for their own advanced theological views resorted to artificial modes of exegesis to find an affirmative answer. A similar pattern was followed by Jesus to convince the Sadducees of the truth of resurrection (Mat. 22.31–33). "Have you not read," he said, "that which was spoken unto you by God, saying, I am the God of Abraham, and the God of Isaac, and the God of Jacob? God is not the God of the dead but of the living." This was a form of exegesis well established in the academies of the Pharisee teachers. Therefore we read: "And when the multitudes heard it, they were astonished at his teaching." The Sadducees were effectively silenced, if not convinced.

Modern Bible scholars, similarly in search for traces of immortality in the Hebrew Scriptures, fall back on occasional

233

passages, usually culled from post-exilic writers, which seem to light the way to immortality. A classical example is Psalm 16 — a psalm saturated with the tears of prayer and hope of countless generations:

> "Keep me, O God; for I have taken refuge in Thee. . . .
> I will bless the Lord, who hath given me counsel; . . .
> I have set the Lord always before me;
> Surely He is at my right hand, I shall not be moved.
> Therefore my heart is glad, and my glory rejoiceth;
> My flesh also dwelleth in safety;
> For Thou will not abandon my soul to She'ol;
> Neither wilt Thou suffer Thy godly one to see the pit.
> Thou makest me to know the path of life;
> In Thy presence is fulness of joy,
> In Thy right hand bliss for evermore."

This psalm and other impassioned utterances in similar vein are like fleeting flashes of lightning. They seem momentarily to illumine the horizon but they do not yield enduring light. The poetic language of prayer in time absorbs the sentiments of the heart and responds to the yearning of the soul. But the language in this instance, when viewed in its own context and historic setting, can hardly be construed as more than a doubtful and equivocal allusion to immortality.

Confronted by these doubts, some modern apologetes adopt the view that the Hebrew prophets and psalmists were vaguely and imperfectly straining for a vision of immortality which they did not consciously apprehend; they are described as feeling their way and fumbling in vagueness; they are pictured as feebly and ineffectively reaching out for a truth which was to be revealed later in God's own time. Such a viewpoint, it seems to me, is not only untrue to history but fails in its understanding of the revolutionary dynamics of Hebrew prophecy. The hallmark of Hebrew prophecy was daring vision; intensity of conviction; boldness of utterance; picturesque clarity of poetic conception.

"Thus saith the Lord" is the sharp, incisive opening of prophetic utterance. No hesitancy or doubt disturbed the soul of the inspired poet of the Song of Moses:

"Give ear, ye heavens, and I will speak;
And let the earth hear the words of my mouth.
My doctrine shall drop as the rain,
My speech shall distil as the dew;
As the small rain upon the tender grass,
And as the showers upon the herb,
For I will proclaim the name of the Lord;
Ascribe ye greatness unto our God."

It is this song that proclaims:

"I kill and make alive;
I have wounded, and I heal."

If there is doubt, the doubt is in us, not in the souls of the men who spoke in the name of God. If there appears to be equivocation in their words, it lies in our faulty understanding of the prophetic language and imagery.

There is a rabbinic saying which later Jewish philosophers frequently cited to explain away the anthropomorphisms in the Bible. *Dibrah Torah bilshon b'nai adam.* "The Torah speaks in the language of man." The Torah, which denotes divine revelation, must accommodate itself to the understanding of the common man. This is an interesting psychological approach to religion. Man cannot be suddenly uprooted from his habits of life and thought. Divine revelation of necessity relates itself to the psychological needs of the race in accordance with the stage of its spiritual development. Ideas and practices rooted in primitive social life must be neutralized or transformed by being infused with new meaning in order to make possible the advance of the human mind to a higher level of religious perception. This principle, which is in effect what we today call progressive revelation, was applied, for instance, in the twelfth and thirteenth centuries

235

by the great medieval philosopher Maimonides to rationalize the place of animal sacrifices in the Bible. The same principle in the view of the Jewish philosophers also carried the implication that over and above the simple literal meaning, there inheres in Scripture a hidden allegoric or philosophic meaning. Translated into modern terms, this is equivalent to saying that there are profound religious implications in the Mosaic-Prophetic writings which are not readily discernible to one who does not look beyond the literal text.

We, too, in seeking to evaluate the concept of immortality to be found in the Hebrew Scriptures must draw upon this principle: "The Torah speaks in the language of man." *Locuta est lex lingua hominum.* We must distinguish between the potential and the actual power and aim of the prophetic spirit. Potentially the immortality of man is implied in the kind of world portrayed in the Bible, a universe that is the handiwork of God whose supreme creation is man. But such consciousness could and necessarily would be long delayed. The first and primary task was to fit man to be a denizen in a God-created world; to teach him "to walk before God in the land of the living." This is the view that recommends itself to us.

I find it difficult to believe, for instance, that Moses, Amos, Hosea, and the long range of their successors, whose souls were wrapped up in the mystery of divine communion; they who beheld God in vision and in dream, who heard the voice of God in the stillness of the night and in the crashes of thunder and lightning; they whose vision extended to the end of time, should have succumbed to the paralyzing, popular belief in a twilight existence of their shadowy spirits in She'ol so soon to be cut off from God and the temple of His universe. It is inconceivable that the mind that painted the panorama of creation unfolded in Genesis, reaching its climax in the creation of man in the image of God, should warp and destroy the image after a mere span of mortal years.

236

The silence of early Hebrew prophecy on the subject of immortality cannot be construed either as negation or confusion. It was infinitely more important to reveal the might and holiness of God than the composition of the human soul. The revelation of the nature of God is primary. Man's self-revelation is secondary to the transcendence of God. Man ascends as his idea of God soars. It was, therefore, the function of Hebrew prophecy first to raise man to an ennobling conception of a living God whose attributes are justice, truth, mercy and holiness. To realize this end, a lofty conception of God was promulgated in which man and nature were shown to be the creations of the divine spirit, and a living people was charged with the responsibility of carrying this vision to the nations of the world.

This is the keynote struck by Hebrew prophecy: all of life is God-centered. Man and nature were formed to carry out His will and purpose. His Holiness fills the universe. He formed light and darkness. He created heaven and earth. He breathed the breath of life into the soul of man. He placed the forces of nature at the command of man, if man would but heed the commands of God. These commands lie in the practice of justice, righteousness, morality, and holiness. Man's abiding by these laws renders his life godly and secure. Virtue is promptly rewarded. Sin meets with quick retribution. The eyes, the hearts, the hopes and fears of man are focused upon life with God. There was no need to defer to the hereafter.

To declare God's will to the world, a people is chosen by Him to be a prophet and priest — His emissary — to the nations. Israel is that instrument through whose life experiences God reveals His being. He is revealed in the faith of Abraham, in the sacrifice of Isaac, in the spiritual wrestling of Jacob, in the triumph of freedom over bondage in Egypt, in Israel's self-dedication as a priestly people serving in the Kingdom of God. The Kingdom is everywhere; in life, in nature, in the heart of man. This was the vision and the faith in which the prophets

237

reared their people. They put before them a religion of life which by indirection at least ignored and spurned the shadowy underworld as a motivating religious force. As long as the here-after served as a breeding ground for the forces of fear and superstition, it could not form a plank on which to build the religion of the God of Israel.

As we look back upon the work of the early prophets, we stand in awe of their achievement. They transformed the world into a temple of the divine spirit and man into a child of God. Without the moral reserve of an other-world, they balanced the accounts of virtue and reward, evil and retribution in this world. Only a passionate love of God and faith in divine justice could hold the precarious scales in balance.

The time came, however, when this robust optimism could not stand up under the blows of personal misfortune and national adversity. Such was the crisis of the exile to Babylon in 586 BC. Loneliness and despair threatened to undermine the religious faith of the exiles. They felt abandoned by God, trapped on alien soil under foreign skies. A series of great prophets arose to meet the crisis: Jeremiah, Ezekiel, Isaiah (Deuter-Isaiah) and a group of inspired psalmists. They led the people heroically through the valley of suffering and sorrow. But they did not lead them to seek refuge in a heavenly retreat. Instead, they reinvigorated their faith and stirred their hearts with a new hope, the Messianic dream of the ages. The anointed of God would arise in time to redeem them. He would restore their people to the land of Israel and establish God's rule on earth. The triumph of divine justice was deferred to an indefinite future; and its fulfillment would be enacted on this earthly stage.

In vain are the wishful efforts of certain Bible scholars to read into some of the post-exilic writings pronouncements of human immortality. None of the suggested passages in the Prophets, Psalms or Job, when viewed in their context, bears out such interpretation. However, the period of the exile did effect

238

profound changes in the religious climate which proved favorable to the planting of the seed of immortality. History, prophecy and psalmody united to broaden the horizon and to deepen the religious consciousness of the exiles by the rivers of Babylon.

In exile, history completed the teachings of the Mosaic and early prophetic traditions. Idolatry with its gross conceptions of God and man was effectively uprooted from Jewish consciousness. In a far-off land, the people of Israel realized at last that their God was not limited to one land or to one nation. He was the Father of all the nations and His dominion extended over the whole universe. A deeper insight into the nature of God fostered a truer insight into the spiritual nature of man. With the new awareness of the divine element in the human being, there was awakened a mystic longing for communion with God. The Psalms of this period are filled with yearning for a vision of God.

"As the hart panteth after the water-brooks,
    So panteth my soul after Thee, O God.
    My soul thirsteth for God, for the living God."

                                                                Psalms 42.1–3

Or again:

"Whom have I in heaven but Thee,
    And there is none upon the earth that I desire but Thee.
    My flesh and heart faileth;
    But God is the strength of my heart and my portion forever."

                                                                Psalms 73.25–26

These and other striking utterances are not yet a declaration of immortality. For this denouement, other factors had still to be brought into play. But the psalmist linked man and God in a divine relationship which, carried to a conclusion, could not be severed by death. By its very nature, such relationship must prove imperishable. The exile enhanced human sensitiveness to the perplexities of sin and suffering which find intense expres-

sion in the post-exilic literature. A suffering nation longed for
the coming of the promised Messiah, and the prophets responded
with glowing fervor. For centuries the agony of the individual
soul was quieted in the hope of national redemption. But despite the valor and the faith of the prophetic spirit, the realization of the Messianic vision seemed to recede on the distant
horizon. The little colony that bravely returned to the mother
country with high and exalted hopes to lay the foundations of
the Second Commonwealth was doomed to disillusionment. An
intangible miracle far greater than that which was anxiously
anticipated was actually wrought by Ezra and Nehemiah. A
new spirit entered the soul of the Hebrew religion. It was the
spirit of Judaism, conceived in the Mosaic revelation, nurtured
in prophecy, ripened in wisdom, and now brought to maturity
by Ezra and Nehemiah and their successors: the Men of the
Great Synagogue, the Scribes and the Pharisees. Under the new
dispensation — if I may use this term in a rather loose sense —
we meet for the first time the declaration of the immortality of
man.

This new declaration, which was destined to have such momentous reverberations in the religious thought of mankind,
forced its way into Jewish consciousness through diverse channels.
There was the inner impulse to reconcile the justice of God with
the glaring injustice that prevailed in the world. The existing
social order did not fit into the framework of a divinely ordained
system. The more exalted and spiritual the idea of God, the
more pressing became the conflict in the soul of man. How
indeed was one who had learned to commune with God and to
love Him with personal tenderness to understand the apparent
defiance of His will, His majesty and power? For several centuries the Messianic hope seemed to offer shelter to the storm-
tossed soul of the Jewish people. But as the Perisan Empire fell
before the onslaught of Alexander the Great, blow upon blow
descended upon the little Jewish state from the Hellenistic
successors, from Egypt on the south and Syria on the north.

Strong was the faith of Israel's saints, the Hasidim, later the Essenes. When Antiochus Epiphanes sought to destroy the Jewish religion, old and young gave up their lives in martyrdom for the sake of God and His Torah. But the renegade Hellenists among the Jews prospered. Was not this mockery of divine justice? Lesser souls might have lost faith. Not so the elect of God. Their faith could not be shaken. God will not abandon His saints. All who live by His word will be faithfully rewarded. They who defy His will face doom and perdition. The scene and time for the dispensing of divine justice may be shrouded in mystery; but of a certainty it will be enacted after death and beyond the grave. This was the setting and these the circumstances in which Daniel proclaimed: "And many of them that sleep in the dust of the earth shall awake, some to everlasting life, and some to reproaches and everlasting abhorrence. And they that are wise shall shine as the brightness of the firmament; and they that turn the many to righteousness as the stars for ever and ever." Dan. 12.2, 3.

To this period belongs the striking passage we quoted earlier from Isaiah, Ch. 26:

"Thy dead shall live, thy [my] dead bodies shall arise —
Awake and sing, ye that dwell in the dust —
For Thy dew is as the dew of light,
And the earth shall bring the shades to life."

Because these passages are embodied in canonical Scriptures, it need not be assumed that these utterances carried authority when they were first enunciated. On the contrary, the books of the Apocrypha, which the Jews subsequently renounced, show that following the Book of Daniel there arose a considerable apocalyptic literature revealing a wide range of conflicting Jewish opinion and fantasy on the subject of resurrection and immortality. No attempt was ever made to reconcile these differences and they have persisted in Jewish thought and in Christianity as well to this day, as we shall see.

The conception that immortality would be attained through resurrection at the time of consummation presented no intellectual or ethical difficulty to generations that put their hope in the Messianic era. Indeed, the Messianic period created the occasion for the miracle of resurrection to be enacted. In part, the concept of resurrection may have reflected the influence of kindred Persian beliefs. The manner in which Judaism and Zoroastrianism affected each other is a debatable subject among historians into which we need not enter. But there was one stream of thought that undoubtedly diverted Jewish thinking from bodily resurrection into a purer concept of spiritual immortality. I refer chiefly to the philosophy of Plato and his concept of the soul, which deeply affected Alexandrian Jewry and thus influenced Palestinian Jews as well.

In facing the problems of God, man and the universe, the Greek mind was analytical, the Hebrew, intuitive. The Hellene reasoned through the faculties of the mind; the Hebrew perceived truth through soul intuition. The Greek was the logician who was precise in definition; the Jew was the poet, the prophet who spoke under divine compulsion. In the Bible, the soul of man is spoken of in metaphor as the "breath of God," the "breath of life," a "lamp of the Lord" filling the body with light. In Greek thought, the soul is analyzed and dissected in terms of philosophical speculation. In the syncretism of Hellenism and Hebraism, which reached its fullest development in Alexandria, the Greek mode of thought revolutionized the pattern of thinking among Hellenistic Jews and also affected Palestinian Jewry in the centuries immediately preceding the Christian era. One of the startling results was a change from the concept of immortality through resurrection to that of a purely spiritual immortality of the soul.

In the philosophy of Plato, the souls inhabit the heavens from the eternity of time. They are incorporeal and immortal. Only some of the souls descend into human bodies. The others continue unembodied in their heavenly abode. As to the manner in which souls are chosen for the unhappy descent into the human frame, Plato resorts to a picturesque metaphor. The souls are compared to pairs of winged horses and charioteers. When they are "perfect and fully winged they mount upward. When one has lost its wings, it is borne along until it gets hold of something solid, when it settles down, taking upon itself an earthly body."

Fascinating as the soaring of the unembodied souls to ever-mounting celestial heights may be, our present concern is with the less perfect souls that descend to our earthly bodies. The soul in the mortal frame reveals two aspects: the rational and irrational. Only the rational element in the soul is incorruptible and immortal. Death releases the immortal part of the soul which then wings its way upward whence it came. As the natural function of the wing is to soar upward, "so" says Plato, "each soul returns to the place whence it came."

It is not necessary for our purposes to follow a trail into the labyrinth of Platonic thought. For those who may be interested in pursuing the course of Platonic philosophy as it percolated through the mind of Philo into Jewish and Christian thought in later ages, I recommend the brilliant treatment of this fascinating subject by Professor Harry Wolfson in his two-volume work on Philo. For the moment, we are not yet concerned with Plato's impact on Philo, a contemporary of Jesus. All that we wish to bring out at this stage is the fact that side by side with the older conception in which body and soul are so intertwined that the soul can come to renewed life only through the revival of the body, we have here a new concept of the independence of the soul in utter freedom of the body. This general concept rather than any specific philosophy is the new element which began to manifest itself in Jewish thought.

Between Daniel and Philo, a period of two centuries intervened in which, on the one hand, Judaism was crystallized in the form which it assumed under the later rabbis of the Mishna and the Talmud; and, on the other hand, an unofficial, religiously turbulent and impetuous literature grew up now known as the Apocrypha and Pseudepigrapha. Although this literature was subsequently abandoned by the official exponents of Judaism, it is a rich and indispensable source of information for the development of the ideal of the immortality of man in Judaism as well as Christianity.

Any attempt to co-ordinate the religious views contained in this literature would be futile. On the subject of immortality they run the gamut from complete negation to capricious fantasy. It is this uncontrolled element that enhances the value of these writings. They are uncensored literature. They mirror faithfully the ideational battle of rival beliefs in their struggle for the control of man's heart and mind.

A few contrasting selections will suffice. The resurrection scene is thus described in IV Esdras (7.32–38):

> "And the earth shall restore those that sleep in her,
> And the dust those that are at rest therein,
> And the chambers shall restore the souls that were committed
> to them.
> And the Most High shall appear on the throne of judgment
> And compassion shall pass away,
> And longsuffering withdrawn;
> But judgment alone shall remain
> Truth shall stand
> And faithfulness triumph
> And recompense shall follow,
> And the reward be made manifest.
> Deeds of righteousness shall awake,
> And deeds of iniquity shall not sleep.
> And then shall the pit of torment appear
> And over against it the place of joy.
> The furnace of Gehenna shall be made manifest
> And over against it the Paradise of delight.

And then shall the Most High say to the nations that have been
    raised [from the dead]:
Look now and consider whom you have denied, whom you have
    not served, whose commands you have despised.
Gaze, now before [you]:
Here delight and rest,
There fire and torments."

Contrast this with the challenging words in the Wisdom of
Solomon (3.1–4):

"But the souls of the righteous are in the hand of God,
    And no torment shall touch them.
    In the eyes of fools they seemed to die. . . .
    But they are in peace,
    For though in the sight of men they be punished,
    Their hope is full of immortality."

In the Apocrypha, strains of Greek thought were often
blended with Hebraic elements. Thus the Platonic conception
of the pre-existence of souls finds clear expression in the Slavonic
book of Enoch (23.5): "all souls are prepared for eternity before
the foundation of the world." The same thought is echoed more
picturesquely in IV Esdras, "the souls of the righteous live like
birds in a cage guarded by angels until they are ready for earthly
descent." (IV Esdras 4.41; 7.32) On the other hand, we also
meet with a new and distinctive Hebraic note despairing of this
world and seeking moral refuge in an other-world hope. "Depart
from this vain world," God spoke to Abraham, "leave the body
and go to thy Lord among the good." (Testament of Abraham I)

A faithful Hebraic note is sounded in the Psalms of Solomon,
contrasting the fate of the sinner with the triumphant end of the
righteous (3.11–16):

"The sinner stumbleth and curseth his life,
    The day when he was begotten, and his mother's travail.
    He addeth sins to sins, while he liveth,

He falleth — verily grievous is his fall — and riseth no more
The destruction of the sinner is forever,
And he shall not be remembered when the righteous is visited.
This is the position of sinners forever.
But they that fear the Lord shall rise to life eternal,
And their life shall be in the light of the Lord, and shall come
to an end no more."

As we leave the Apocrypha and enter the portals of rabbinic Judaism, we find the rabbis strangely hospitable to all these contrasting viewpoints. Every phase of immortality, every shade of opinion to be found in the richly imaginative Apocrypha literature has its counterpart in the rabbinic writings. Only against the Sadducees, who denied resurrection and every other form of immortality, was the opposition strict and uncompromising. Such denial was denounced as heresy and, as we have seen, the person who adhered to it forfeited his share in the world to come.

The immortality of man as portrayed in resurrection was incorporated by the Pharisees into the law of Judaism, with every device of ingenious exegesis invoked to stamp the doctrine with the seal of biblical authority.

Having achieved this doctrinal acceptance, however, the rabbis gave free rein to the religious spirit to explore the mystic possibilities of the human soul. A daring parallel is drawn between the illumination of the soul and the Godhead. "As the world is filled with God, so is the body filled with the soul; as God sees but cannot be seen, so the soul sees but cannot be seen." (Ber. 10a.) Rabban Gamaliel put this thought before a heathen in another form: "Thou wishest to know where God dwells, who is as high as are the heavens above the earth: tell me where dwells thy soul which is so near." (Sanh. 39b.) Another rabbi offered the thought: "better is one hour of spiritual bliss in the world to come than all of life in this world." (Ab. 4.22) The purely spiritual life in the world to come is expressed by a notable Babylonian teacher: "In the future world there is neither eating nor drinking, no sensual pleasure or strife. The righteous sit at the table of God, feeding upon the splendor of His Majesty." (Ber. 17a.) A mystical ladder leading to immortality was set up as follows: cleanliness leads to purity; purity leads to godliness; godliness to humility; humility leads to saintliness; saintliness leads to the gift of the Holy Spirit and immortality.

It would be misleading on the basis of selected passages to construct a consistent rabbinic theology on immortality. Every stratum of thought and feeling on this mystifying and emotionally tangled subject is represented in rabbinical literature. Once the basic idea of resurrection and immortality was recognized, the imagination of mystics and rationalists was allowed free rein. Philosophic ideas and views bordering on superstition; ideas catering to primitive fears and ideals expressing the highest aspirations of the human spirit are voiced freely without discrimination or regimentation in the intellectually democratic society of Judaism. The native faculty of the Hebraic spirit, which experienced poetic delight in feeling its way to truth intuitively, almost in defiance of logical techniques, was still dominant in rabbinic thought. It was only with the rise of Jewish philosophy as a distinct discipline with a mission to reconcile faith and reason, revelation and philosophy, Judaism with the philosophies of Plato and Aristotle, that a revaluation of the problem of immortality became necessary from the double standpoint of religion and philosophy.

Jewish philosophy, in the main, dates from the tenth century onward through the late Middle Ages. By its very nature it was a combination of Hebraism and Hellenism. More precisely, it was the task of Jewish philosophers to interpret Hebraic truths in Greek philosophic concepts and to defend these truths by the scientific standards of pure reason as developed in Hellenistic philosophy. As applied to the issue of immortality, it involved a study of psychology of the soul, its nature, origin and composition, its fate and destiny, its relation to man and God. It was no longer possible vaguely to harness immortality to resurrection. For the immortality of the soul in a purely spiritual existence was a philosophically established thesis. What then was the rationale of resurrection? What was its purpose and function? Was it to be a mundane or supermundane, a transitory or enduring phenomenon? Thus the ethical and religious ideas of the Bible and the Talmud, noted for simplicity of language and warmth of poetic feeling, were forced unnaturally into metaphysical systems.

The biblical and rabbinical concept of the soul as created by God for man invited analysis and deepening of thought, but presented no philosophical difficulties. It was not difficult to prove either on the basis of Platonism or Aristotelianism that man had a soul; that the soul was neither material nor corporeal; that it had independent existence; that it was not a mere quality or accident of the body. The view that solved many difficulties was the assumption that the soul had a dual aspect: the one spiritual and pertaining to the intelligible world, and the other sensory, belonging to the lower material world of change and decay. From this it followed that the intelligible soul, if it did not allow itself to be corrupted through bodily contamination, would return to the celestial or intelligible world which is its true home.

It was the doctrine of resurrection that tested the temper and the ingenuity of Jewish philosophers. Its assumption of bodily reincarnation was not only inconsistent with philosophic theory, it seemed utterly superfluous. Yet this belief had struck deep roots in the religious consciousness of the people. It assumed the force of dogma. To discard it was to endanger the very foundations of popular faith. Jewish philsophers were therefore forced to accommodate this doctrine into their system with doubtful success.

Saadia (882–940), among the earliest Jewish philosophers during the Middle Ages, synchronized resurrection and immortality on a cosmic timetable. Resurrection will take place upon the coming of the Messiah. Until then, the soul remains in a spiritual state separated from the body upon death. At the close of the Messianic period, the present world will be destroyed, a new eternal world created, and the righteous who had experienced resurrection would be translated bodily to that world. This will be the period and the world of final judgment, when the dead of all the nations will come to life again (*Kitab al-Amanat*, Ch. 7).

Maimonides (1135–1204), the greatest Jewish philosopher of the Middle Ages, frankly avowed that resurrection was not susceptible to the proof of reason. It must be accepted on faith as a divine miracle with no speculative proof to support it. As if to ward off suspicion, he included the doctrine of resurrection in his thirteen articles of faith. But disbelief among his followers was widespread, and he was led later to compose a special treatise on resurrection. In this tractate, he propounded a unique theory that the miracle of resurrection would be enacted on this earth for a temporary period only, after which the reincarnated would die as ordinary mortals and their souls alone would continue in immortal existence. This strange affirmation of resurrection was clearly a concession to traditional belief, for it reduced the miracle itself to a meaningless divine whim. Little wonder that Maimonides studiously avoided the subject of resurrection in his great philosophic opus, *The Guide to the Perplexed*, and referred to it only casually in his Code of Jewish law. It is in the latter work and in his earlier commentary on the Mishna, both written for students of the law and for the guidance of his people, that he stated his view on the future of the soul, which I cite from the late Doctor Kohler's paraphrase:

"Not immortality but the power to win eternal life through the knowledge and the love of God is implanted in the human soul. If it has the ability to free itself from the bondage of the senses and by means of the knowledge of God to lift itself to the highest morality and the purest thinking, then it has attained divine bliss, true immortality, and it enters the realm of the eternal spirit together with the angels. If it sinks into the sensuousness of earthly existence, then it is cut off from eternal life; it suffers annihilation like the beast. In reality, this life eternal is not the future, but is already potentially present and invariably at hand in the spirit of man himself, with its constant striving toward the highest. When the rabbis speak of paradise and hell, describing vividly the delights of the one and the torments of the other, these are only metaphors for the agony of sin and the happiness of virtue. True piety serves neither from fear of punishment nor from desire for reward, as servants obey their master, but from pure love of God and truth. . . . Only children need bribes and threats to be trained to morality. Thus religion trains mankind. The people who cannot penetrate into the kernel need the shell, the external means of threats and promises."

Time runs out, though the theme is limitless. We have run a course of nearly three thousand years in the span of an hour. Conscious of my limitations, I turn to the *Ethics of the Fathers* (II, 15–16). Said Rabbi Tarfon: "The day is short, the work is great. . . . It is not incumbent on thee to complete the work, but thou art not free to evade it."

To summarize: we have traced the development of the immortality of man in Jewish thought from early Bible days to the dawn of the modern era. If our analysis is correct, the thought of immortality as we understand it today, emerged late and gradually into the consciousness of the Jewish people, first as an apocalyptic vision and then as a religious doctrine which, in its purest form, has remained to this day a cardinal belief in modern Judaism. Before this belief was consciously formulated, the establishment of the kingdom of God as a Messianic goal was deeply implanted in the heart of the Jewish people as an ideal to be realized on this earth in the society of men and nations. Judaism has retained this vision as a divine hope and a millennial goal for mankind.

The belief in the immortality of man became an integral part of the faith of Israel as an outgrowth of an advanced conception of God, a realization of the spiritual nature of man and a response to the craving of the human heart with its deep-seated longing for an ethical view of life. Judaism, therefore, embraces both worlds in the bosom of its faith. For this world, the Torah is its guide. To the world beyond, it looks with trust and hope. Only the Cabalists dared scale its heights with the bold, daring imagination of profound mysticism. For the main body of Judaism, a Palestinian sage of the third century has spoken these noble words (Ber. 34b): "Concerning the Messianic future the prophets have spoken with clarity; but concerning the future state of the soul it said: 'Men have not heard nor perceived by the ear, neither hath the eye seen O God beside Thee, what Thou prepared for him that waiteth for Thee.' "

ADDRESSES ON CONTEMPORARY ISSUES

Relation of the Hebrew Scriptures
to American Institutions

THE focusing of the world's attention upon the adoption of the American Constitution one hundred and fifty years ago, makes it peculiarly timely to pass in review some of those influences, spiritual and political, which helped to govern the personal lives and public institutions of the American colonists during the earlier century and a half of colonial history. Neither the Declaration of Independence nor the Constitution of the United States is comprehensible without an appreciation of the emotional and mental attitudes of a people, engaged upon a great spiritual adventure of life and government. The compulsion of the spiritual appeal was not always a conscious power, nor was its force equally distributed among all the colonies; but its potency was real and abiding from the day that forty-one Pilgrim Fathers entered into a solemn covenant and signed the Mayflower Compact, until the thirteen colonies federated into the Union of the United States of America.

In all the annals of supreme daring and adventure with which the story of America's discovery and exploration abounds, the achievements of the intrepid Englishmen and their followers who settled upon this continent strike a distinctive and unique chord. Theirs is not the saga of man's conquest of nature alone. It is the deeper and more stirring revelation of man's self-conquest in the search of an ideal.

Gold and spices lured the Spaniards. Dreams of oriental riches and luxury spurred the Italian-Iberian explorers to face

Address delivered at the Jewish Theological Seminary of America, New York, May 26, 1938.

death and danger upon the uncharted oceans. Religion was but a secondary motive with the conquistadors. Soldiers of the Cross they may have flatteringly pictured themselves, as they forced Christianity upon the hapless Indians. But their religious visions were reserved for the heathen. They, themselves, felt no need of a self-regenerating religious experience. How vastly different was the fiber of the northern settlers who left their homes in England, or their voluntary exile in Holland, and fared across the sea to set up for themselves and their progeny free homes in a wilderness of primeval forests.

To be sure, they, too, were moved by hopes of material reward — and, above all, by an elemental land-hunger which craved satisfaction. Certainly the Crown and the capitalists who shared in those bold ventures expected to reap a harvest in the form of substantial dividends of expanded commerce and profit, if not in outright gold. But neither the chimeras of gold nor the realities of trade and commerce can possibly account for the Plymouth Colony or the Puritans of Massachusetts Bay, or the colonies of Rhode Island, Maryland and Pennsylvania. It was not the earlier buccaneers and free-booting adventurers of Elizabethan England that struck root in the soil of the wilderness. It was the hard-working, God-fearing Puritans whose lives were swayed by religious passion, whose souls were caught up in the Hebraic spirit of the Bible, determined to serve God in freedom and to worship Him in the light of their own conscience; it was they, who with a fortitude so characteristic of the People of the Book, overcame the pangs of hunger and loneliness, and defied the terrors of disease, death and massacre.

"It is never to be forgotten," said John Higginson, Puritan Minister in Salem, "that our New England is originally a plantation of religion and not a plantation of trade. If any man among us," he continued with a quaint mathematical formula, "makes religion as twelve and the world as thirteen, let such a man know that he hath neither the spirit of a true New England man nor yet of a sincere Christian." When he was a lad of thirteen, and was starting out with his family on the voyage to Salem in 1629, he heard his father exclaim as they caught the last sight of England, "We will not say, as the Separatists were wont to say at their leaving of England, Farewell, Babylon! Farewell, Rome! But we will say, Farewell, dear England! Farewell, the Church of God in England, and all the Christian friends there. We do not go from England as Separatists from the Church of England, though we cannot but separate from the corruptions in it. But we go to practice the positive part of Church reformation, and propagate the Gospel in America."

It would be difficult, indeed, to find in the royal chanceries a document to match in pathos and sublime religious idealism the address which the General Court of Massachusetts sent to King Charles II in December, 1660, in defense of their religious liberties:

> We could not live without the publicke worship of God. Wee were not permitted the use of publicke worship without such a yoake of subscription and conformity as wee could not consent unto without sinne. That wee might therefore enjoy divine worship without the humane mixtures, without offence either to God, man, or our owne conscience, wee, with leave, but not without teares, departed from our country, kindred, and fathers' houses unto this Pathmos. Ourselves, who came away in our strength, are, by reason of very long absence, many of us become grey-headed, and some of us stooping, for age.

It is customary from a political angle to distinguish between three colonial types: the royal, the proprietary, and the charter colonies. In the first two types, the colony was headed by a Governor and Council who were appointed by King or Proprietor, while the lower Assembly alone was elected by the people. On the other hand, the charter colonies, limited wholly to New England, were virtually autonomous republics, as the entire government was chosen by the people. Important as this distinction is, undoubtedly, its true significance can be best understood when related to the vital difference in the religious character of the respective colonies. Virginia, the premier royal colony, was of the established Anglican Church. So were most of the other royal colonies. New England was Puritan.

Now this is not the time nor the occasion to enter into an involved theological discussion of the bristling differences between the Conformist Church and the Sectarian Dissenters. What we are concerned with are their social and political influences upon American institutions and ideals. That these were important factors to the very eve of the Revolution, let the testimony of James Madison suffice. He, a communicant of the Anglican Church, wrote in 1774 to a college classmate in Philadelphia: "If the Church of England had been the established and general religion in all the northern colonies, as it has been among us here, and uninterrupted tranquility had prevailed throughout the continent, it is clear to me that slavery and subjection would have been gradually insinuated among us." It may be idle to speculate whether "if the colonists of Massachusetts had been Episcopalians, under the royal head of the English Church, there might have been no American Revolution." But it cannot be gainsaid that Puritanism was the crucible of the American conscience, and that in the fire of its religious soul was kindled the torch of liberty.

Now Puritanism was, in essence, the rebirth of the Hebrew spirit in the Christian conscience. It was the Hebrew religious genius come to life to wage battle for God and soul-freedom, once more to impress upon the world the sovereignty of God and the holiness of life. It was a crude, imperfect human medium in which the spiritual revelation took effect. The generation whose souls were scarred by tyranny and bigotry could but imperfectly perceive the new light. Freedom of conscience was for the elect alone. "The world belongs to the saints, and we are the saints," was a gibe which carried more conviction than humor in the Puritan age. Little did they understand their true inward kinship with the living Jewish people who were the world's ageless martyrs. Cromwell's sentiment, "Great is my sympathy with this poor people, whom God chose and to whom He gave His law" was unpopular with his followers, save with the most radical wing of Baptists. What an inspiring parallel the Pilgrim Fathers might have drawn between the fate which drove them to Plymouth in the new world, and that which led the Jewish community of saints a century earlier to gather in the Holy Land in the obscure town of Safed, there in relative freedom to set up a colony that would bend its life to the will of God and to commune with His spirit. What pitfalls the New England colonists could thus have averted in their crude application of biblical laws to their self-governing communities.

But such has ever been the devious, tortuous march of the human spirit. The supremely significant fact is that the early colonists felt the full impact of the God of Israel upon their lives — that their whole life was a covenant with Him. They walked in His way. And this New England way, steep and narrow at the start, ultimately broadened into the highway of religious liberty and political democracy. A declaration of the colonists of Salem reads like an echo of a prophetic portion of the Hebrew Scriptures: "We covenant with the Lord and one with another, and do bind ourselves in the presence of God, to walk together in all His ways, according as He is pleased to reveal Himself unto us in His blessed word of truth."

The Puritans may not have been unduly conscious of their kinship with the living Jewry, but in every fiber of their Puritan soul — in language, in thought, and in sentiment — they identified themselves with the Chosen People of the Book. They christened their offspring with the Hebrew names of the Bible, abandoning the saints who had formerly been favored.

They related the events of their life to Bible episodes. Of a certainty, divine history repeated itself, and theirs was the replica of Israel's early history. The heroes of the Old Testament were the models of heroism to be emulated. Tyrants were Pharaohs. Tyranny was Egyptian bondage. Revolutionary leaders were likened to Moses and Joshua.

The Hebrew language was the sacred tongue. Its cultivation was desired not merely as an ancient language comparable to Latin and Greek, but as the key that unlocked the secret of God's will. Basic as the knowledge of Hebrew was to the cause of the Protestant Reformation, as a whole, it held special fascination for the New England Puritans, whose courting of the Hebrew muse was part of a thorough renaissance of the Hebrew spirit. The amazing extent of the Hebrew studies in New England should be well-known through the publications of the American Jewish Historical Society. Strangely enough, this phase is almost wholly ignored even in specialized studies of colonial history in any of its aspects, religious, political or cultural. I cannot help but feel that thereby a subtle, spiritual influence is being overlooked. In their own intuitive way, the Puritans sensed more truly the bond between the genius of language and the integrity of its inner creations. How, otherwise, can one account for the prominence given to the discipline of the Hebrew language amidst all the perplexities and hardships of a pioneering era, when forests were to be cleared, virgin land to be subdued and plowed, huts and shelters to be erected and savages to be fought off.

Hebrew learning was brought to the New England shores on the Mayflower. Elder William Brewster was an ardent devotee of Hebrew, as the Hebrew inscription on his tombstone would indicate; and his library contained a small collection of what was probably the earliest Hebraica in North America. Governor Bradford, also of the Mayflower elect, was a notable linguist in his day, but Hebrew claimed his soul allegiance. An examination of the original manuscript of his "History of Plymouth Plantation," or its photographic reproduction, shows, in his own hand, pages of Hebrew roots and Bible quotations in the original. The list of New England Hebraists includes the most prominent names that figured in the annals of its early history: John Eliot, "apostle to the Indians"; John Cotton (1585–1662), allegedly a Hebrew conversationalist, whose devotion to Hebraic studies is extolled by his learned grandson, Cotton Mather of Magnolia fame; Richard Mather (1596–1669), one of the editors of the Bay Psalm Book; Henry Dunster, first president of Harvard College; his successor, Charles Chauncey, who perfected his studies under a Jewish teacher; Increase Mather, prolific author and likewise president of Harvard, notable for his literary defense of the Jews and Judaism; and shall we arbitrarily conclude the list with Cotton Mather at the close of the seventeenth century? Not, at least, without mentioning the irrepressible Judge Samuel Sewall, diarist and would-be poet who turned his muse to the hope of the speedy conversion of the Jews.

Needless to say, it is not the erudition of the select few that we wish to trace. Rather is it the impact of the Hebraic interest on the popular mind through these personalities that dominated the social and religious thinking of their age. Several curious citations, culled by the late George Kohut, may therefore be of interest. In the book, "Remarkable Providences" by Increase Mather, there is recorded the story of a deaf man who could not learn to speak and was finally advised to try the Hebrew tongue as an aid to speech, and "in a short time the dumb scholar became an excellent 'Hebrician.' " Very revealing is Cotton Mather's praise of the popular delight which Hebrew affords, and the facility with which it can be acquired. "Hence," he says, "we see even our English women, sometimes in a little while and with a little pain, grown as expert at it as the ladies whom the Church-Father Jerome praises in his works." "Nevertheless," he adds, "this tongue is as easily forgotten, but being once attained and therewith preserved and improved, good men will find, as our Mr. Chauncey did, that the conjunct of profit and pleasure of it were inexpressible, and that the talents wherewith it would furnish them to do so many services for the Church of God were such as to make them join with Luther in his protestation that he would not part with his knowledge of Hebrew for many thousand of pounds." It must be added that poor Michael Wigglesworth, the learned and pious diarist, was not so sanguine. No doubt he had good reason to complain of the "obstinate untowardness" of his students as he prayed God to move their spirit and incline their hearts to the study of the sacred tongue so dear to him.

Hebrew Bibles in the New England "wilderness" were not the prize possessions of the few. They were owned by many of the early settlers. The famous Dutch Hebraist, John Leusden, received at one time an order for fifty copies of the Hebrew Psalter for the use of Harvard College students. We may well believe that it afforded him pleasure to fill the unusual order. Indeed, the prominence given to Hebrew in the curricula of the early American colleges — into which we need not enter here — is in itself the most striking testimony of the importance attached to the language during the time that the ideals and institutions of the colonists were taking on crystallized form.

In this connection, it is well to bear in mind that what was impressive about New England Hebraism was not the peak of its scholastic attainment. For this was the classic period of Christian-Jewish scholarship in the Old World too. Originally a phase of humanism, the storehouse of Hebrew lore was turned into the very arsenal of the Protestant Reformation. Certainly the Christian Hebraists in England and Holland, Germany and France, far excelled our New England enthusiasts in profundity and originality. The distinctive element about Puritan Hebraism was its hold upon the popular imagination, which can only be described as a phase of the Hebrew spirit that inspired the movement in all its aspects.

No one has pointed out, as far as I know, the striking parallel between the reforms introduced by the Puritans in the Church and town government of the New England settlements, and the community organization of the Jewish *Kahal*. I am not referring to the imprint of biblical legislation upon both groups, of which more anon. I have reference solely to the important non-biblical features which the Puritan institutions and the *Kahal* had in common, both in outer form and inner principle. The resemblance is not superficial. It calls for interpretation.

I am not suggesting for a moment that the Puritans modeled their institutions after the pattern of the medieval *Kahal*, which was probably unknown to them in any of its details. All the more significant, however, is the implied kinship between them. In form and in substance — literally and figuratively — Puritanism and Judaism spoke the same spiritual language, albeit with different tone and accent.

The central institution of a New England community was the meeting-house, as the synagogue was in a Jewish settlement. The name at once invites attention. It is reminiscent of the Hebrew, *Bet ha-Keneset*, the equivalent of synagogue. The Puritan had an aversion to the designation of church for a house of worship, as a modern traditional Jew frowns upon temple as a substitution for synagogue, though for a different reason. The Puritan case is stated by Cotton Mather in that he "found no just ground in Scripture to apply such a trope as church to a house of public assembly."

It was the duty of every community to build a meeting-house in its midst, preferably on a hilltop, which was also the favorite location for a synagogue in the older centers. No sooner did the Pilgrim Fathers land at Plymouth, when they assigned "a timber fort, both strong and comely with flat roof and battlements" as a Lord's Day meeting-place. To this fort, they walked every Sabbath, three in a row, reverently but armed, each man equipped on Sunday morn with psalm book, shot and powder-horn. Carrying a gun on the Sabbath required religious justi-fication, in the Hebrew halakic sense. It was sanctioned on the ground of danger, of course. Therefore, it was forbidden to discharge the gun excepting on their two "greatest inconven-iences," an Indian or a wolf. This ruling held true for many years while the Puritans continued to go armed to meeting.

The most drastic reforms which Puritanism introduced in the church polity, when it broke away from the Anglican Episcopacy, lay in the decentralization of the Church, the abo-lition of the hierarchy, and the bridging of the gap between the minister and the laity. In all of these directions, Puritanism paralleled or unconsciously followed Jewish precedent. Every synagogue was an independent entity: formal ranking and grad-ing of the rabbinate was unknown; and the rabbi, like the Puri-tan elder — the order should properly be reversed — laid no claim to supernaturalism in any form. Learning, piety, inter-pretation of God's will as revealed in the Law — a source open to all — these were the essential qualifications for spiritual authority in Judaism as in the Puritan Churches. In both institutions, the religious head was chosen by the people.

The function of the elder was strikingly similar to that of the rabbi. He was the political as well as the religious adviser and guide to the civil magistracy. His authority was directly com-mensurate with the weight of his character, his learning and his ability. He had no official position in the town administra-tion, but he was consulted in all matters. His opinions carried authority only through "opening the rule of God's word" and fortifying his opinion by one or more "Scriptures," in other words, by a text. This was the adolescent equivalent of the mature rabbinic responsum. Even in the outward manifesta-tions of reverence which the rabbi and the elder received from their respective congregations, there was complete accord.

Thus, in many of the churches, "the members rose reverently when the parson, dressed in black skull-cup and Geneva cloak, entered the door; and they stood, in token of respect, until after he entered the pulpit and was seated." This is still a widely prevalent custom among Jews in the so-called old-fashioned congregations.

Returning to the interior of the meeting-house, we are again struck by many parallels. The white, bright daylight in place of the "dim religious light," the bareness and simplicity of the interior, the absence, on principle, of an organ or other musical instrument, are all analogous to synagogue features. There were striking differences, too, of course. There were aspects of physical austerity about the meeting-house that remind one of karaitic gloom. There was no lighting of the interior nor was it ever permitted to heat the meeting-house. Church attendance at services that lasted for the better part of the Sabbath day during the freezing winter season of Massachusetts weather was, indeed, a test of Puritan fortitude. The elders were forced to preach with their hands cased in woolen or fur mittens, while women were sufficiently pampered to be allowed to bring footstoves as an aid to comfort. At least, it afforded the Reverend Mr. Wigglesworth with a ready theme for a sermon on the text "Who Can Stand before His Cold." Alas, that he could not. For "by his own and people's sickness, three Sabbaths passed without public worship." However, by February twentieth, he preached again, this time on the text "He Sends forth His Word and Thaws Them." And believe it you may, a thaw set in the next day!

If time permitted, one could multiply numerous analogies and contrasts suggested by the "seating of the meeting," the call to prayer by drum, horn and shell, the interruptions of the services, and the contrasting social significance of the practice in Synagogue and Meeting-House. We should like to linger a little longer and watch that curious equivalent of a beadle, the tithingman, who was the colonial sleep-banisher in church. Equipped with a long staff, which had a heavy knob at one end, and at the other a long foxtail or a hare's foot, he strutted during meeting, waking the drowsy sleepers by rapping the masculine heads with the heavily knobbed end but using the furry end to tickle the Priscillas into gentle but startled wakefulness.

One resourceful preacher, scorning the tithingman's aid, resorted to a curious device which had rabbinic analogies. In the midst of his sermon, the Reverend Mr. Moody shouted "fire, fire" and when the blinking men, startled into wakefulness, called out "Where?" he roared back, "In hell, for sleeping sinners."

The attitude to education is the touchstone of the character of a nation or community. No single feature of the organized life of a New England settlement was so indicative of the bond that linked Puritanism to the spirit of Judaism, as the solicitude for the education of the young and the measures adopted toward that end. In 1670, the British commissioners of foreign plantations made a survey of conditions in the American colonies. On the subject of education, the governor of Connecticut reported, "One fourth part of the annual revenue of the Colony is laid out in maintaining free schools for the education of our children." Contrast this with the Virginia Governor's reply to the commissioners. "I thank God," Sir William Berkeley wrote, "that there are no free schools nor printing, and I hope we shall not have these hundred years; for learning has brought disobedience, and heresy, and sects into the world, and printing has divulged them, and libels against the best government. God keep us from both."

But for a slight change in phraseology, the statutes of Massachusetts might have been culled from the earlier *Takkanot* passed by a Spanish-Jewish synod in 1432. Thus one reads in the Preamble to the Act passed by the General Court of Massachusetts in 1642, "Forasmuch as the good education of children is of singular behoof and benefit to any commonwealth; and whereas many parents and masters are too indulgent and negligent of their duty in this kind...." More fully, the statute passed in 1671 reads: "It being one chief project of Satan to keep men from the knowledge of the Scriptures, as in former times keeping them in unknown tongues, so in these latter times, by persuading from the use of tongues, that so at least the true sense and meaning of the original might be clouded and corrupted with false glosses of deceivers; to the end that learning may not be buried in the graves of our forefathers, in church and commonwealth, the Lord assisting our endeavors; it is therefore ordered by this court and authority thereof, that every township within the jurisdiction, after the Lord hath increased them to the number of fifty householders, shall then forthwith appoint one within their towns to teach all such children as shall resort to him to write and read, whose wages shall be paid either by the parents or the masters of such children, or by the inhabitants in general, by way of supply, as the major part of those that order the prudentials of the town shall appoint: Provided that those which send their children be not oppressed by paying much more than they can have them taught for in other towns.

"And it is further ordered that where any town shall increase to the number of one hundred families or householders, they shall set up a grammar school, the master thereof being able to instruct youth so far as they may be fitted for the university; and if any town neglect the performance hereof above one year, then every such town shall pay five pounds per annum to the next such school, till they perform this order."

Let me now cite the language of the earlier enactment by the Jews of Castile in 1432. "This is the gate of the Lord, the righteous shall enter into it. The opening of our works and the beginning of our ordinances are to support those who occupy themselves with our Holy Law; for the teaching of God is the pillar on which the world rests, as our sages, may their memory be a blessing, expressed it: The world is based on three things: study, service and the practice of charity." . . . "As we behold that the hands of the learned in most places are benumbed, and that the scholars are but meagerly supported; and for this reason the students of the Talmud are diminishing while the pupils of the primary schools are decreasing because the poverty of the parents does not enable them to pay the fees of the teachers, and thereby the teachings of God are in danger of being forgotten in Israel, therefore, in order to restore the ancient glory, that there may again be found scholars versed in the law and that students may again abound in our communities, be it resolved that in the entire kingdom of both Castiles, the members of every community be obligated to take measures and raise contributions for a Talmud Torah Fund in the following manner." There follow then a series of excises and imposts, the proceeds of which were to be applied to the educational fund. Although the Jewish educational standards in the European centers were superior to those set up even in the most advanced colonies, it is clear that they both sprang from the same conscience and were distilled from the same source of reverence and idealism.

The common source from which both Jew and Puritan drew their inspiration was the Bible. It cannot be overemphasized that for the Puritan, as for the Jew, the Book revealed in an immediate personal sense the mind and the will of God. When the Reformation substituted the authority of the Bible in place of the Church, a great spiritual force was set in motion which reached its greatest intensity in the soul of the Puritan and those who came spiritually out of his loins. The Bible was, of course, venerated in all Christendom. No sincere Christian doubted the Book or questioned its infallibility. But to the Puritans, the impact of the Bible was overwhelming. It came upon them with all the power of prophetic revelation. The God who was thus revealed to them was a stern, dread sovereign, the King of Kings, whose overwhelming might ruled out the freedom of the human will. Thus had Calvin envisioned Him, and his vision cast a spell over most of the colonial ancestors. Verily, "a living coal from the altar of Calvin touched their lips."

The Old Testament was restored to a high place in the Christian conscience. For in the Hebrew Scriptures were clearly revealed the mind and the will of the Supreme Being, for the rule and government of human beings. It was the Old Testament that contained "the statutes, laws, and ordinances of God" and the Puritans who came to these shores to set up a civilization free from the corruptions of the old world, needed, above all, a divine statute-book.

At the very threshold of the Bible, however, the fall of Adam cast an hypnotic spell over them which almost paralyzed their souls with the crushing weight of original sin. Out of this grew the terrifying belief in the eternal damnation of mankind "to grievous torments in soul and body without intermission in hell-fire forever"— save for the elect few who were preordained for divine redemption by the unaccountable judgment of God. Thus the "Confession of Faith" continues, "The rest of mankind God was pleased — according to the unsearchable counsel of His own will, whereby He extendeth or withholdeth mercy as He pleaseth for the glory of His sovereign power over His creatures — to pass by and to ordain them to dishonor and wrath for their sin, to the praise of His glorious justice." For non-elect infants the slender comfort was held out that they would be assigned "the easiest room in hell."

Little wonder that a pall was cast over the Puritan mind which gave such tragic tone to his heroic fatalism. Present-day apologetes of Puritanism, who ascribe the gloom of its theology to the austerity of the Old Testament God, fail to see that it was the principle of the redemptive sacrifice in New Testament theology that distorted the fall of Adam into the blighting curse that doomed mankind.

While theology played a great part in coloring the thoughts and the emotional life of the period, a greater interest inheres historically in the Puritan attitude toward the Law and its influence upon the political and social institutions which are the foundation of American civilization. In no other Christian communion was there such intense, literal, wholehearted acceptance of the biblical laws. Antinomianism was a fiercely contested heresy in Massachusetts. Law, divinely revealed in the Hebrew Scriptures, was the cornerstone of public government and private life. It was accepted as an axiom that true government rested on the foundations of divine religion: that the magistrates were entrusted with the task of re-enacting and enforcing the laws and statutes which were of God. The set purpose and goal of the Puritans was to re-establish on the American continent the Biblical Commonwealth of the Hebrews. This was inaugurated not as a social experiment, but as a divine call. In 1635, the Reverend John Cotton drew up for the use of the General Court a law-code based on "Moses, his judicials" and this became the groundwork of legislation in the Bay Colony for many years.

There were numerous regulations concerning land, laws relating to Indians, and detailed laws governing slavery and other forms of servitude in which the Bible influence is particularly marked. We have alluded to the statutes providing for public education. The field of religion and morals covered a variety of subjects ranging from the notorious laws of witchcraft to babbling women and scolds. Blasphemy was a heinous crime in all the colonies, and was punishable in Massachusetts by the "pillory, by whipping, boring through the tongue with a red-hot iron, or setting upon the gallows with a rope upon the neck."

The Sabbath laws were made the subject of renewed and

constant legislation. All servile labor and all passing from place to place, save for necessity, mercy or attendance upon worship, were prohibited with severe penalties. Constables and tithing-men were to arrest all Sabbath breakers. Noisy offenders were put into a public "cage." The most innocent pleasures were strictly forbidden. Children playing on the streets, youths and maidens strolling in the fields, were "things tending much to the dishonor of God, the reproach of religion and the prophanation of the holy Sabbath."

Needless to say, these punishments are not traceable to the Bible, but to the medieval barbarism of the English and the continental codes of law. The interpretations of the Sabbath laws seem to harp back to outmoded conceptions of sects disowned by Judaism. What a gulf separated the *Oneg Shabbat* from the Puritan Sabbath! Having broken with tradition, the Puritans in a sense resembled the Karaites and fell into their errors of literalism and asceticism. How much they could have learned at the feet of a Pharisaic rabbi!

So strange are the ways of history that man's stumbling-blocks often become the stepping-stones to larger visions of truth. Not of the breadth of mind, but of the narrowness of spirit was the soul of America fashioned in those early days. It was the ardor and not the mellowness of religious convictions that drove the colonists to stake their life and happiness upon the great spiritual adventure of America. To create a new order of society, a commonwealth in which God is King and the revealed Word is the law of the land, called forth an intensity of passion which alone can revolutionize the soul.

Not democracy, but theocracy was their ideal. Thus we are told that Winthrop "expostulated about the unwarrantableness and unsafeness of referring matters of counsel or judicature to the body of the people, *quia* the best part is always the least and of that best part the wiser part is always the lesser." This sentiment was emphatically repeated by John Cotton. "Democracy," he said, "I do not conceive that ever God did ordeyne as a fitt government for church or commonwealth. If the people be governors, who shall be governed?"

Social equality was still the exclusive dream of the fanatical and disturbing Quakers. Class distinctions had the full sanction of the Puritan mind. Sumptuous dress was forbidden to the common people only. In Harvard and Yale Colleges the names of the students were arranged according to social standing. The change to the alphabetic order was introduced only a few years before the social creed of the Declaration of Independence proclaimed that "all men are created equal." Indeed, human equality was fundamentally irreconcilable with the theology of the saints and the elect. Freedom of conscience, which was to be defended with one's very life, was for one's own salvation and for those who shared the same creed. Religious liberty for a community of saints was compatible with ruthless persecution of heretics of the type of Roger Williams, Anne Hutchinson, and the tribe of Quakers. When Roger Williams thundered, "The armies of Truth like the armies of the Apocalypse, must have no sword, helmet, breastplate, shield or horse, but what is spiritual and of a heavenly nature," he was speaking as the prophet of a new era, but in Massachusetts, he was a heretic and a disturber of the peace.

But again we are faced with one of those paradoxes which the history of errant humanity takes delight in springing upon the surprised spectator. A slight mistake in Columbus' geography made him the discoverer of America. Out of the pent-up passions of the divided colonists, torn with religious strife and dissension, was born the glorious vision of human freedom. The more intolerant the individual group, the more determined were its adherents to defend their convictions with their very life.

Under this tension, the exigencies of their common life forced upon them religious peace. That this peace was not a patched up truce, that out of the mixed emotions engendered by religious differences there were evolved concepts of liberty and universal freedom which have tended to liberate mankind, was due to the inherent grandeur of the Bible and its profound influence upon the American genius.

In the evolution of the American ideals, religious liberty was primary, political freedom was an afterthought. Not till they were driven to despair by the bungling, stupid tactics of Parliament on the very brink of the Revolution, did the American ancestors break with the mother country. But from the day that the Pilgrims set foot on Plymouth Rock, the principle of religious independence was established. It was to keep religious freedom inviolate that civil liberties had to be safeguarded. Lord Acton expressed this thought succinctly: "The idea that religious liberty is the generating principle of civil, and that civil liberty is the necessary condition of religious, was a discovery reserved for the seventeenth century. That great political idea . . . has been the soul of what is good and great in the progress of the last two hundred years."

The late Oscar S. Straus in his book entitled, *The Origin of the Republican Form of Government in the United States of America*, described fully and adequately the immediate influence of religious leadership and Old Testament teaching upon the course of the American Revolution. From the vast sermonic literature of the period he traced the profound influence exerted by the religious leaders in creating moral sentiment for the Revolution, and showed how they based themselves, principally, on the hatred of tyranny, so forcibly taught in the Hebrew Scriptures. The citation from Jonathan Mayhew, the father of civil and religious liberty in Massachusetts and in America, will suffice here: "God gave Israel a king (for absolute monarchy) in His anger, because they had not sense and virtue enough to like a free commonwealth, and to have Himself for their king — where the spirit of the Lord is, there is liberty,— and if any miserable people on the continent or isles of Europe be driven in their extremity to seek a safe retreat from slavery in some far distant clime — O let them find one in America."

Again and again we meet in legislative assemblies and in popular treatises, the Prophet Samuel's graphic portrayal of the evils of monarchy, and Gideon's noble renunciation of rulership. Our attention is also called to the seal for the United States which was drawn up by Franklin, Adams and Jefferson, portraying "Pharaoh sitting in an open chariot, a crown on his head and a sword in his hand, passing through the dividing waters of the Red Seas in pursuit of the Israelites; with rays from a pillar of fire beaming on Moses, who is represented as standing on the shore, his hand extending over the sea, causing it to overwhelm Pharaoh, and underneath the motto, 'Rebellion to tyrants is obedience to God.'"

It is not necessary in the present company to dwell further on this aspect of the subject. But in the year which marks the one hundred and fiftieth anniversary of the adoption of the Constitution of the United States, it is well to call to mind the enormous influence which the Bible exerted upon the parent body that formulated the great Charter. The Continental Congress leaned heavily on the sanctions of the Bible and religion. It was the main strength of the Congress as its legislative authority was deplorably weak. The precepts of the Bible were recognized as sound political maxims. The Congressional proclamations and other state papers are filled with biblical phrases. They invoked the name of "God," "Lord of Hosts," "Almighty God," "Nature's God," "God and the Constitution."

One of the first acts of Congress under the Articles of Confederation was to recommend the printing of an American Bible. On October 26, 1780, a resolution was adopted, "That it be recommended to such of the states who may think it convenient for them that they take proper measures to procure one or more new and correct editions of the Old and New Testament to be printed and such states regulate their printers by law so as to secure effectually the said books from being misprinted."

That the name of God was omitted from the Constitution

274

gave offense to several religious bodies. It was one of the elements that delayed its adoption by some of the states. The omission was fervently defended by ardent religious leaders. Had they been familiar with the Hebrew exegetes of the Bible, they would have drawn upon the explanation offered by them for the same omission in the Book of Esther — that God is revealed in history as well as through the Word. Verily, the spirit of God is revealed in the ideals of liberty, justice and equality, which have their noblest expression in the Constitution of the United States of America.

May we conclude with this thought. We have seen the working of the Hebrew spirit through the Bible upon American institutions during the critical formative period of our early history. The ideals upon which this civilization rests are being challenged today. Strange, menacing forces have been let loose in the world. The fate of mankind hangs in the balance. All the values that the American genius has created — religious liberty, political freedom, the inalienable right of human beings to live their own life in peace — are threatened.

In this critical hour, America is more than ever the hope of the world. Our country must not fail humanity in its direst need. It must remain true to the ideals which in the wisdom of God it was privileged to bring into the world. But we too are bewildered amidst the baffling problems, economic, political and social, that assail us. We need to renew our strength in the fount of eternal wisdom.

As Jews, an emphatic obligation rests upon us. We were a feeble, small community in the early days of the colonies. We have grown to be an important community of four million souls. We have established great centers of Jewish learning and Hebrew scholarship in this country. As heirs of the prophetic heritage, as lineal descendants of the Bible heroes who were the inspiration of American ideals and institutions, it is our inescapable duty to lead in the interpretation of the hopes, the ideals and the social message of the prophetic voice.

Doctor Adler and the Dropsie College

WHEN Judah the Prince, author of the Mishna died, a disciple announced his death in the following language: "Angels and mortals wrestled for the ark of the covenant; the angels prevailed: the ark of the covenant has been removed from our midst." Hidden almost in the picturesque language of the parable is this noble thought of the sage: the truly great human spirit is like a cosmic force. When the earthly career of that spirit is ended, its force is not spent. It continues as a transcendent power — in more naïve language, as an angelic force — influencing the thought of later generations.

Since we were last assembled in these halls a year ago on Founder's Day, our ark of the covenant was taken from us. Cyrus Adler is no longer in our midst. The angels prevailed. With them is the ark of the covenant. With us, however, is his living spirit.

In these halls, in these classrooms, his life is a continuing abiding influence. The shadow of his physical presence is still upon this platform which his distinguished presence graced for thirty years. We can almost see the beaming smile, the twinkle in the blue eyes, as they swept over these annual audiences. We can hear the earnest, pleading voice. We are still warmed by the mellowness of his wise utterances, strengthened by the faith which he exhibited amidst the rising moral deluge which he saw coming upon the world. From this platform he delivered public utterances that revealed a panoramic vision of the contemporary scene, a broad understanding of world events, an accurate and unerring appraisal of scholarly values and intel-

Address delivered at the Dropsie College, Founder's Day, June 2, 1940.

lectual trends. Who amidst these surroundings and associations can believe that the life-force of Doctor Adler is spent now that the ark of the covenant has been taken from us?

Doctor Adler was an Olympian figure on the contemporary scene. American Jewry had not seen his like before. Generations may pass before another figure of like stature may once again arise to guide and lead his people. Born in a small town in Arkansas in 1863, when the unity of the American nation was being forged by the fire and blood of the Civil War, the heroic energy of that conflict, it would seem, was poured into his life. No American loved his country more fervently or expounded more faithfully the principles and the ideas of the American way of life. In speech and in thought, in outer bearing as well as in the more subtle habits of mind, he was the embodiment of American culture at its best.

All the zeal and the pride of that American spirit he brought to his Hebrew heritage. There was not the slightest trace of the apologete in his self-appraisal as an American or as a Jew. He was proud of his Jewish birthright. He gloried in the Jewish tradition of religion and ethics. A man of profound faith, he drew inspiration from the Bible, the Talmud, and the vast storehouse of rabbinic literature. I venture to believe that it was this essential unity and harmony of spirit that was the secret source of much of his strength and creative energy.

However one may explain or trace the inner recesses of his mental and spiritual powers, there stands before us an enduring historic figure. To this simple fact, we in this College bear eager testimony, we who were privileged to work at his side, who caught intimate glimpses of his crystal-clear mind, and who understood him with the insight which the love of a master begets in his disciples. No single individual on the American continent touched the life of his fellow-Jews at so many angles and left the impress of his personality so indelibly upon the whole of American Jewry as Cyrus Adler. The record of his

277

achievements spans fully half a century. As a young man in his thirty-first year he revealed the faith which was to sustain him all his life. I consider that statement one of the most eloquent utterances of the credo of a Jew to be found in English literature. It bears the title עברי אנכי "I am an Hebrew." I repeat it verbatim:

"I will continue to hold my banner aloft. I find myself born — ay, born — into a people and a religion. The preservation of my people must be for a purpose, for God does nothing without a purpose. His reasons are unfathomable to me, but on my own reason I place little dependence; test it where I will it fails me. The simple, the ultimate in every direction is sealed to me. It is as difficult to understand matter as mind. The courses of the planets are no harder to explain than the growth of a blade of grass. Therefore am I willing to remain a link in the great chain. What has been preserved for four thousand years was not saved that I should overthrow it. My people have survived the prehistoric paganism, the Babylonian polytheism, the aesthetic Hellenism, the sagacious Romanism, at once the blandishments and persecutions of the Church; and it will survive the modern dilettantism and the current materialism, holding aloft the traditional Jewish ideals inflexibly until the world shall become capable of recognizing their worth."

This passionate faith of the young man, expressed exuberantly in the glowing enthusiasm of early manhood, became the driving force of his career. It led him to abandon the congenial surroundings of the capital in Washington and a brilliant future in the Smithsonian Institution in order to dedicate himself unreservedly to the service of his people. The immediate cause for the great decision of his life was the establishment and organization of the Dropsie College.

What this College, founded by the munificence of Moses Aaron Dropsie and formulated by the genius of Cyrus Adler, has come to mean in the field of Jewish scholarship, what the

278

accomplishments of its faculty and alumni have been to secure for this institution a position of dignity and respect in the general academic world, and how the influence of this College under the leadership of Doctor Adler has spread far beyond the borders of this country, these constitute the principal theme to which we wish to address ourselves this evening. It may not be amiss, however, at this stage to point out that American Jewry, and the Philadelphia community in particular, owe a profound debt of gratitude to this College. It was the Dropsie College that made possible the full release of Doctor Adler's boundless energy and creative powers in the service of his people. It was this institution too that brought back to Philadelphia one of its most distinguished citizens. This city became his home. He grew to be an important factor in its civic life, and in such institutions as the Board of Education, and the Free Library of Philadelphia, of which he was President. He was a member of the Council and Vice-President of the American Philosophical Society. He came to be looked upon as father of the local Jewish community — "grandfather" he would jocularly retort in the latter years.

Above all, the College became the nerve center from which there radiated intellectual and spiritual currents throughout the Jewish world. In this building great projects were planned and executed. Here under Doctor Adler's chairmanship and Professor Margolis' editorship the Bible translation of the Jewish Publication Society was carried out by the most distinguished and diversified assemblage of Jewish scholars in America. Here too the Jewish Classics Series was inaugurated. Only three weeks ago from this platform, at the annual meeting of the Jewish Publication Society, Doctor Adler's co-workers described with deep feeling his role in making possible the Bible translation as well as the Jewish Classics Series, his pioneering work in procuring for America the first monotype Hebrew Press, his fruitful and farsighted leadership in the program of the Publica-

279

tion Committee. Indeed, much of the work of the American Jewish Committee, the Joint Distribution Committee and the Jewish Welfare Board, in all of which he was a founder and guiding spirit, was carried on from the same office almost to the last days when his life ebbed away. The College was host to the American Jewish Historical Society, the American Oriental Society and to many celebrated scholars of international renown who lectured in these halls.

We marshal these facts to remind a grateful Jewry of the part which this College played in the career of Doctor Adler. As we recall the ark of the covenant which has been raised to its celestial home, let us also remember the terrestrial house which was its earthly abode. It is this institution which embodies his living spirit. As in the past, Doctor Adler and the Dropsie College were inseparable, so in the future the spirit of its first President will live in the College and will guide and inspire its work.

One may well marvel at the act of Providence that led to the selection of Doctor Adler as the person to carry out the trust of Moses Aaron Dropsie. Mr. Dropsie had a great vision. He had the courage and the munificence to place his fortune back of that vision. We have been told that he was moved to this act by a profound religious intuition. But it was still only a dream in the mind of Mr. Dropsie. It required the remarkable talents that Doctor Adler possessed for clear thinking and practical idealism to interpret the dream and to give it reality. This task Doctor Adler performed as no other man in his generation could. He was in perfect accord with the Founder's purpose, and the College became the medium in which he expressed his own ideals and deepest convictions.

The story of the early days of the College — how it was organized, when it was chartered, how it came to have its present name, which was not required or suggested in the will of the founder — I shall not repeat. Doctor Adler has on various occasions told the story. He also gave us a sketch of the early Governors of the College and described their first meeting in Washington in the office of Oscar S. Straus, then Secretary of Commerce and Labor, adding quaintly that it was "possibly the only College that ever had the first initial step toward its organization taken in the office of a member of the President's Cabinet." If you have not heard Doctor Adler's account or wish to refresh your memory, you may obtain a copy of these addresses which have been reprinted. I may also refer you to two earlier addresses contained in more permanent form in the volume of *Lectures, Selected Papers, Addresses* by Cyrus Adler, published by his colleagues and friends on the occasion of his seventieth birthday. What I feel will be most helpful at this juncture in the affairs of the College will be to review the underlying principles and purposes of this College: the philosophy upon which the Faculty, from the beginning to this day, have based their instruction and researches, and the results which were thus obtained in literary scientific output and in the training of a new generation of scholars.

There exists a strange misconception in the minds of the laity that Jewish literature is wholly theological or religious in nature and, as a natural corollary, that in this age of specialization, it is exclusively the domain of the rabbi and theologian. This is an old error. More than a century ago, Leopold Zunz, father of *Jüdische Wissenschaft*, valiantly set out to combat this erroneous conception. The source of the popular notion can be readily traced. It arises partly from the undoubted fact that Jewish civilization is religious at the core. In part, however, it is due to a curious misunderstanding of the title rabbi, which in time came to have only a euphonious meaning. The word rabbi prefixed to a Hebrew name does not indicate that the person so designated was the holder of a rabbinical title or post. It is equivalent to our Mister, or Master, which also does not bear the original meaning of lordship. Thus, for example,

Abraham or Moses ibn Ezra or Solomon ibn Gabirol, or the host of Hebrew scientists, literary men and poets who never aspired to rabbinic honors were ignorantly included, by non-Jewish scholars especially, among the medieval rabbis, and their works were classed as rabbinic literature. To obviate this error, Zunz coined the term *Jüdische Wissenschaft*, the science of Judaism, and pleaded for the emancipation of Jewish literature from the shackles of prejudice and theological bias. He pleaded with passionate eloquence for the inclusion of Jewish literature among the humanities studied in the European universities. Needless to say, his plea went unheeded. No great help was to come from German academicians. Of infinitely greater importance was the effect of this great passion upon the lifework of Zunz, the vivifying spirit it infused in the lives of the rising generation of Jewish scholars and the miraculous transformation it wrought in the *Zeitgeist* of the whole Western Jewry.

Zunz was not only the father but the prophet of the science of Judaism. His vision was sheer inspiration. He was almost a child when he was touched by the divine fire. Abandoned in youth by the little band of friends — Gans, Moser and Heine — who supposedly had shared his enthusiasm for the renaissance of the Jews and Judaism, he cried out, "What alone survives and is imperishable in the midst of the deluge is the science of Judaism; it continues to live, even though for centuries no finger has been raised on its behalf. I confess that next to my submission to the justice of God, my hope and support consist in the cultivation of this science. These storms and experiences shall not so influence me as to bring me into collision with myself."

Before the advent of *Jüdische Wissenschaft*, Gans, the later apostate, coldly analyzed the Jewish dilemma of his time. "Enthusiasm for religion, together with the solidity of ancient institutions, has vanished, but no new enthusiasm has come to light, and no new state of affairs has established itself. We have not gone beyond that negative enlightenment, which consists in despising and condemning things as they are, without troubling to infuse a new spirit." But long before the sun was to set upon Zunz's life, Heinrich Graetz described the miracle of resurrection wrought by the science of Judaism. "It is no fantastic idea," he wrote in his immortal history. "A nation actually did arise from the darkness of the tomb, the only example in the annals of man."

What is this miracle-working science of Judaism? It has no mystic or esoteric element in its composition. It means simply the application of scientific method to the study of the Jewish past. It consists in research, delving into original sources, publishing dust-laden, forgotten manuscripts, and reconstructing the memories and thoughts, the experiences and lives of your own ancestors. More perhaps than other branches of study, the science of Judaism is exacting in the demands it makes upon its votaries for strict discipline, integrity of mind, the training and blending of intellect and imagination. The startling element in this science has been the magnificent results obtained. New vistas of Jewish history were opened up. A rich undreamt of literature came to life. The people that had allegedly been buried under the debris, so-called, of the Talmud and the Cabala was revealed as a torch-bearer of light in the dark ages. In the heart of this people, it now appeared, East and West were linked in fruitful union: and the Jew, embracing both, interpreted one to the other. The Jew, furthermore, appeared in the new perspective as an integral factor of unique importance in the national evolution of Western Europe. It became evident that he had played a vital part in the break-up of feudalism, in the building up of the national economy of the emerging new states, in the stimulation of independent religious thinking, and in the preservation of the sciences and philosophy for the day when the great universities were to arise. Most important of all, the new knowledge gave heart to a wavering generation. It restored their faith in Judaism and therefore in themselves.

"That is the science of Judaism," said Graetz, "a vivid realization of its great history, and its peculiar doctrines. This effort of memory is not merely an amusing game, a pleasant pastime, the satisfaction of a desire for knowledge akin to curiosity, but an irresistible impulse of self-examination. It arouses the dormant strength in the breast of the inquirer, and inspires him with self-confidence to act in the future as in the past."

The faith which inspired the founders of *Jüdische Wissenschaft* is the basic philosophy of the work of the Dropsie College. This College is dedicated to the principles of the science of Judaism. It aims through independent research and the training of young scholars to add to the sum total of the knowledge of Judaism and to a fuller understanding of the history and literature of the Jewish people. The scope of our studies is imperfectly revealed in the departmentalized language of a college register: Bible, Rabbinics, Cognate Languages and History. The range of the studies actually pursued in the Biblical Department covers not only the Bible and all its versions but also the science of philology and Hebrew grammar. Great stress is placed upon the classic Bible commentators in Hebrew and Arabic. The Apocrypha and the writings of the Church Fathers are studied in the twilight zone between the Biblical and Rabbinical Departments. Under the heading of Rabbinics are included not only the Talmud, the various tannaitic compilations and the later medieval literature, but also a most intensive and detailed study of the Second Commonwealth, which involves a comparative study of the New Testament, Josephus and Philo. Jewish philosophy and medieval Hebrew poetry are still a desideratum. The fascinating subject of the rise of sects in Judaism from the days of the Second Commonwealth down to the period of Hasidism are studied in this Department from the social-legal standpoint. The Department of Cognate Languages offers instruction not only in Syriac, Ethiopic and classical Arabic from the elementary to the advanced grades, but also in Judaeo-Arabic. I stress Judaeo-Arabic because it is the medium in which the greatest works of Jewish philosophy, ethics and science were written. It was the linguistic vehicle of Saadia, Judah ha-Levi and Maimonides. It was the language of the Jews in the golden age in Spain. As far as I know, the Dropsie College is the only institution in this country that is equipped to teach Judaeo-Arabic and offers full instruction in this subject. A comprehensive field of study is covered under the nomenclature of Egyptology. It embraces various Egyptian languages, including Coptic, the study of Hieroglyphic and Hieratic texts, the literature of the ancient Egyptians, the Greek papyri and the whole field of Ptolemaic civilization, so important for Jewish history and literature. In the Department of Jewish History, we have limited ourselves in the past to a period of only twenty-five hundred years. By the very nature of the subject we overlap all the other Departments. We lay greatest stress upon the study of original source-material, whether it leads us to the reading of Hebrew historical texts, rabbinic responsa, papal bulls and conciliar decrees, or archive material.

A survey of the publications and researches conducted by the faculty and the alumni reveals the wide scope of the studies which are fostered here. I shall limit myself principally to the theses printed under the imprimatur of the College. With rare exceptions, they are universally recognized as meeting the most rigorous standards of scholarship. In their respective fields they are original contributions to knowledge. As a collection of scientific studies they will bear comparison with the best of similar publications by other universities.

We cannot enumerate them all, nor do we wish to single out a select number, but perhaps we may attempt a rough summary under general headings. They include the publication of manuscripts; studies in the Bible; Hebrew and Arabic commentaries by Rabbanites and Karaites; grammatical treatises; aspects of Greek versions of the Bible; investigations in the Halaka, the standard Halaka of rabbinic tradition as well as the rival sectarian Halakot. Chronology and folklore, Cabala and philosophy are represented in the series. Full-sized biographies of Moses Hayyim Luzzatto, Jacob Emden, and now Solomon Judah Rappaport have come to life. Community studies based on manuscript sources, social studies drawn from responsa literature, an authoritative account of the relation of the Church to the Jews collated from the original papal bulls issued by the Popes at the height of their power in Christendom are among the historic series.

In Jewish tradition, moreover, we recognize that Torah or learning has a twofold aspect. There is the Torah *shebiktab* and the Torah *shebe'al peh*, the written and the oral word. The two are interdependent. In the estimate of any vital postgraduate institution, it is important to know where and how the alumni function in their chosen fields.

We may well let the record speak for itself. To begin at home, most of our own Faculty are equally alumni of the College. The University of Pennsylvania is indebted to the College for its Professor of Semitics. The Gratz College is staffed almost entirely with our alumni. We are represented in the Jewish Theological Seminary through two graduates, besides the Curator of its Museum. The President of the Yeshiva College is our first alumnus; and that institution has also drawn upon our College for several of its professors. Our survey will lead us to the Baltimore Hebrew College, headed and staffed by our alumni, to Johns Hopkins University where we are worthily represented in the research work of the Semitics Department, to the Westminster Choir College of Princeton, to the University of Iowa, to the Junior College in San Francisco, the Brooklyn City College of New York, and lastly to the Hebrew

University on Mount Scopus. Its archaeologist and Director of the new Museum, the Dean of the Hebrew University Extension Department in Tel-Aviv, the President of the Hebrew Authors Association and several other literary figures there comprise our Palestine Alumni Association. We have given the Synagogue Council of America its Director of the Statistical Bureau. Perhaps the best index of the catholicity of our institution is the fact that two of our graduates are editors of such diverse organs as the Jewish Publication Society and the *Jewish Daily Forward.*

Through *The Jewish Quarterly Review,* the name of the College is carried into every part of the world where there exists a university or educational center interested in our field of studies. Founded fifty years ago in England by Israel Abrahams and Claude G. Montefiore, it has been the official publication of the Dropsie College since it was taken over by Doctor Adler thirty years ago. An organ of higher Jewish learning, its columns are open to all scholars. The list of its literary contributors reads like a roster of the most noted scholars of our generation. Today it has the distinction — a very sad distinction — of being the only non-Hebrew quarterly devoted to the science of Judaism. Its confreres have fallen victims to the plague of Nazism and Fascism or have been war casualties. The duty has devolved upon Professor Zeitlin and me to continue the *Quarterly* in the name of the College and in the spirit of Doctor Adler. For the generous support that we have received from friends of Jewish learning throughout the country and for the assurance of hearty co-operation proffered by the scholarly fraternity, we here express our heartfelt appreciation.

Not only does the scope of our studies span the whole field of the science of Judaism; equally important in the relationship is the viewpoint of the College. This may be described succinctly. In method, the objective is strictly scientific. In purpose, the College is dedicated to the advancement of the knowledge of Judaism. This twofold objective makes clear the importance that is attached to our institution wherever the love of Jewish learning prevails. It also explains the distinctive character of our student body. For its modest size, it is incomparably the most cosmopolitan student group to be found on any campus.

From the day that the College opened its doors to this day, students have been drawn to this institution from foreign lands and from every part of this country. Obviously the College has filled a deep-felt want. It has no theological bias. It is neither orthodox, conservative nor reform. No religious demands are made upon the students. All qualified persons who fulfill the requirements of admission are welcomed either as special or regular students regardless of race, sex, creed or color. This is indicated clearly by the number and caliber of our non-Jewish students. Trained men, holding, in some instances, high academic positions, having previously studied in the most notable Semitics departments of American and European universities, they have sought out this institution in order to increase their knowledge of the Bible, the Talmud, Jewish history, and the languages that serve as aids to these studies. In seeking out Jewish teachers and interpreters of these subjects they have followed the best traditions of Judaeo-Christian scholarship.

It is, however, understood by all — and there can be no equivocation in this position — that this College is not merely an Oriental institute or a detached Semitics department. It is a Jewish institute, devoted to Jewish learning. It was created as an instrumentality to advance and interpret Jewish knowledge so that the culture and the latent spiritual powers that inhere in our history and in our literature may play their part in the upward struggle of the human spirit for light and truth.

How often has Doctor Adler raised his voice for the saving power of Jewish knowledge. How earnestly he pleaded for the cause of this College and all that it symbolizes as a means of strengthening the moral and intellectual defenses of our people against the forces of reaction and anarchy. Alas that he stands no longer at our side. Perhaps "the Lord gave His beloved sleep" that his soul might be spared the ravages and the cruelty of the dark days that lie ahead. To the College and to all of us who leaned upon his strength, his loss is irreparable. But dare we falter? The passing of a great leader creates a void — a sense of bewilderment, numbness and doubt. But is there any doubt where the path of duty lies? We have a citadel to defend. A fearful process of intellectual blackout threatens to engulf the world. Like every other people that has a precious heritage to defend, we must look to our spiritual and intellectual defenses.

We would be derelict in our duty to the Jewish people and to the world of free thought if we failed in courage at this crucial hour. A great trust has been reposed in the Faculty. A grave responsibility rests upon the Governors of the College. Unitedly, I hope, we shall go forward with the high courage that the hour demands, with faith in the spiritual resources of the Jewish people — the rest we leave to God.

Americans All

I HAVE come from Philadelphia upon the invitation of your Patriotic Foundation to participate with you in the solemn dedication of the George Washington · Robert Morris · Haym Salomon Monument on this day dedicated to the Bill of Rights.

I bring you greetings from the city in which these three immortals were united in the fellowship of service to their country — the city which cherishes their memory as part of the heritage of American independence. In turn, I promise you that I shall proclaim to my fellow-citizens at home that you in Chicago have enshrined in bronze and granite the spirit of the Liberty Bell; that you have immortalized in sculptured form the chimes that pealed forth the words of the Hebrew lawgiver, "And ye shall proclaim freedom throughout the land unto all the inhabitants thereof."

In a more personal manner, I also bring you the greetings and the benedictions of the historic Congregation Mikveh Israel in Philadelphia, of which I have the honor to be rabbi. This is the congregation where Haym Salomon worshiped the God of his Fathers. In its synagogue, he chanted the ancient Hebrew prayers. There he read the words of Scripture and learned the lesson of sacrifice and devotion. There the great patriot drew the inspiration to battle for freedom and to give up all so that his country might triumph in the desperate fight for liberty and independence.

This congregation, which last year celebrated its 200th

Address delivered at the Dedication of the George Washington · Robert Morris · Haym Salomon Monument on Bill of Rights Day, Chicago, December 15, 1941.

anniversary, has a proud history and a long roll of honor. During the Revolutionary War, the President of the congregation was an aide-de-camp of George Washington. Among the membership of this Jewish congregation are included men high in the military and diplomatic service of our country — also historians, jurists, poets, educators, artists, as well as founders of colleges, libraries and museums. But highest of all, we honor the memory of that modest, self-effacing patriot, Haym Salomon, who freely gave of his fortune and his very life to hold up the hands of Washington and Morris and to support all lovers of liberty in their struggle for freedom. We are happy to see him represented in this monument, at the side of men who turned to him repeatedly in the darkest hours of our country's need and were unfailingly met by him with high courage and vital material aid.

This monument, I take it, was planned as an act of patriotism in the days of peace. Now that war has come upon us, it takes on new meaning. It stands forth as a beacon light. It calls upon all Americans not only for sacrifice, courage and patriotic devotion, but even more so, it is an inspiration for a deeper understanding of the American way of life, which we are now arming to defend with all our might.

For this monument was not designed merely for the glorification of its heroes. George Washington is too deeply engraved in the hearts of his countrymen to require external symbolization. No monument can add to his glory. Robert Morris' brilliant contribution to the success of the Revolution is indelibly inscribed in the historic annals of our country's early struggles. Haym Salomon toiled, sacrificed, lived and died in the very shadow of anonymity. Pride and vainglory were alien to his nature. He would have shrunk from worldly acclaim.

The true purpose of this monument is to bring out in the enduring features of bronze and granite the story of America's genius, the epic of the American nation.

These three men standing on one pedestal symbolize the

greatness of America and reveal the secret of its moral strength. Each of these men was great in character, strong in faith, valiant in the battle for freedom. No one will for a moment suggest that these men were equal in greatness of conception or in the role which they played in the historic destiny of America. There was only one George Washington in the history of America; his place is unique in the annals of history, and he will always be first in the hearts of his countrymen. But Washington would have been the first to acknowledge — and he did — that without the material aid represented by Morris and Salomon and the self-denial and sacrifices of the American civilian population represented by these men, he, Washington, could not have kept his soldiers in the field. In the struggle upon which we are engaged today, victory will come to our armed forces if we, the un-uniformed civilian population, will emulate the undaunted spirit, the high morale, the courage in sacrifice and self-denial which is so nobly exemplified by Morris and Salomon.

But your monument typifies more than this truth alone. As I gaze upon Haym Salomon in the light of his background, as an immigrant lad who came to this country to seek happiness and religious freedom, as I think back upon the deeply rooted passion for freedom which he derived from his Jewish religious heritage, I am reminded of an ancient Hebrew legend. This legend states that when God was about to create man from the dust of the earth, he gathered the precious dust from all parts of the earth, the East and the West, the North and the South, so that no country may at some future time say, "Of us alone did God create the human race."

The same American conception of human brotherhood is revealed in eloquent form by this monument. Our nation is one: North and South, East and West. All elements of the world's population, from every point of the earth's compass, have entered into the making of the American people. Indeed, no day is more fitting for the utterance of this truth than this day dedicated to the Bill of Rights. What the Ten Commandments proclaimed on Sinai, what the Sermon on the Mount has meant to Christian civilization, the Bill of Rights has expressed in terms of human rights for the society of men and the democratic way of life.

Let us then gather inspiration from this day and scene and meet the challenge of our day with high faith and courage, fighting side by side, not as white and colored, not as natives and immigrants, nor as Jews, Catholics and Protestants, but as Americans all — under one flag, united in the faith of American brotherhood — with love of God and country in our hearts, determined to roll back the savage forces that have risen against us — determined to fight to the end till the coming of the day when victory and true peace shall bless our people, and all freedom-loving nations throughout the world shall resume the agelong march of human progress with none to make them afraid.

A Millennial Sage and Our Times

SIX days ago, May 18, 1942, marked the thousandth anniversary of the death of one of the great figures in the history of human thought. A thousand years ago, Western civilization had not yet emerged from the womb of time. Philosophy, science, law and the lighter graces then held sway in the lands of the Orient in the fabled cities of the Arabian Nights. To those cities in Babylon by the banks of the Tigris and the Euphrates we are being transported as we turn to our theme, "Saadia Gaon, The Millennial Sage and Our Times."

The very name Saadia is redolent of the Oriental background. Gaon, or Excellency, was the title conferred upon him as head of the famed academy in Sura near Bagdad. It was the highest distinction possible in Jewish life in the tenth century. The story of his life, which literally had to be pieced together from tattered shreds of papyri found in Egypt in our time, is a fascinating one. But pray do not expect from me a biographical sketch of Saadia this evening. Suffice it to point out the countries whose civilization and culture his mind reflected.

He was born and grew to manhood in Fayyum, Egypt, the land of the Pharaohs and the pyramids, the country that nurtured Moses the prophet and lawgiver and Philo the philosopher of Hebraic and Hellenic wisdom. Something of the brooding spirit of that ancient land must have filled his soul. But like his ancestors of old, Palestine lured him to its sacred soil, and we find him a pilgrim or a temporary sojourner in the Holy Land. Palestine was then stirring with new life and hope. A century and a half before the advent of the first Crusade, Palestine Jewry was experiencing the upsurge of renewed

Address delivered at the Dropsie College, Founder's Day, May 24, 1942.

294

spiritual vitality. For half a millennium, the Jewish community of Palestine, crushed by Roman tyranny and seared by the flaming jealousy of the daughter religion, had endured the humiliation of playing a secondary role to the more prosperous community of Babylon. When Zion fell, Babylon lifted up its scepter. But now the Holy Land, under vigorous religious leadership, was about to lay claim to spiritual supremacy in Israel. Ardent lovers of Zion hoped that soon the Law would again go forth from Zion and the word of God from Jerusalem.

It cannot be said that Saadia shared this enthusiasm. He was no Zionist in the accepted sense of the word. He left Palestine and wandered eastward through the cities of Syria to the land of the Geonim. He cast his lot with the Babylonian academies. He became their redoubtable ally in fighting off the challenge of the Palestinian authorities. No doubt, he feared that the Palestine adventure might lead to a rift in the ranks of Israel. Was not the breach of Karaism — a sect hardly a century and a half old but one that for a time seriously endangered the entire structure of Judaism — a clear enough danger signal? Such reasoning, to be sure, must have motivated Saadia, the champion of Babylonian Judaism. And he received his reward dramatically several years later, after the victory, when he, a foreigner and without aristocratic lineage, was called to the gaonate of Sura and he became indeed the spiritual head of Israel throughout the world.

Nevertheless, I cannot wholly escape the impression that the mood of Palestine in that creative period of its history exerted a dynamic influence upon him. In the new atmosphere of enterprise and daring which he imbibed there, he was emboldened to dream even greater dreams of a new philosophy of Judaism that would answer the eternal questions of all seekers of truth, whether these be Mohammedans, Christians or Jews. However and wheresoever we may seek his motivation, this was the objective of his *magnum opus, Philosophic Ideas and Religious*

Beliefs, and this was the achievement which places Saadia among the immortals of the human race. Such is the man whose thousandth anniversary we call to mind in these halls of the Dropsie College in the city of Philadelphia — a scholar, a philosopher, a Jew out of the lands of Egypt, Palestine, Babylon, who strove mightily for the unity of his people and even more ardently for harmony in the heart of man as he grapples eternally with the mysteries of God and Creation, Man and his search for immortality.

A thousand years in Thy sight are but as yesterday when it is past and as a watch in the night — so said the Psalmist. To this truth, my theme tonight is both a testimony and a commentary. For here, in this College, Saadia came to life after a thousand years. The first full-size biography of Saadia Gaon in any language was written by the late Henry Malter, Professor of Rabbinics in this College, and was published by the Jewish Publication Society of America in this city. Henry Malter also devoted a great part of his scholarly life to the preparation of the first and only scientific edition of Saadia's philosophic classic. He rightly regarded this as his greatest contribution to Jewish learning. Unfortunately, Malter died before he could arrange for its publication. More than a decade has passed and the work is still in manuscript form somewhere in Palestine.

I make this declaration both as an indictment and a confession. Should this work perish or be lost — and there is reason to fear such an eventuality — it would represent a major loss to Jewish scholarship and to the history of philosophic literature. Is it too much to hope that, moved by the associations of a thousand years, a Maecenas may arise among us in this millennial year and enable us to reclaim and to bring to the light of day this master work? Those of us who have some knowledge of Malter's treatise can testify that this would be not merely a new edition of an ancient classic. It could be more aptly described as a resurrection.

The entire program of this College may, in a sense, be described as a projection of Saadia's genius. He was literally the creator or the father of the science of Hebrew and cognate learning in all the branches that are taught in this institution. His was the first complete philosophic system of the Jewish religion. More broadly conceived, it may be said to have marked a new epoch in the history of the philosophy of religion. This year, we established a Department of Jewish Philosophy. The major part of Saadia's work was written in Arabic, which was the spoken language of the Jews in Moslem countries. In that language were written the great Jewish classics of philosophy and ethics during the golden age in Spain. It is recognized in scholarly circles that our Department of Cognate Languages is second to none in the instruction offered in Arabic and that in the special field of Judaeo-Arabic our institution is without a peer anywhere in America. Saadia was a pioneer in the legal, or halakic, aspects of Judaism. This subject falls within the Rabbinical Department. One of the students majoring in Rabbinics is at work upon a thesis entitled "The Halakic Contributions of Saadia Gaon." Saadia enriched Jewish liturgy with original compositions of hymns and prayers. This subject is now being taught at the College by one of the visiting professors who is the world's leading authority in this field of study. Egyptology affords a rich background for the civilization of the country in which Saadia was born and in which he had his being. All these aspects of Saadia's life and works are interwoven and interpreted in their historical trends in the Department of History.

As yet, we made no reference to Saadia's epoch-making translation of the Bible into Arabic. Historic Bible translations have in a strange way proved to be dynamic forces in the evolution of the human mind. They mark the culmination of the revolutionary spirit of an age or they are compelling harbingers of a new world outlook for generations to come. The Septuagint in ancient times forced into the mold of Hellenism a fusion of Greek and Hebraic thought and made possible the rise of Christianity. The Vulgate is synonymous with Catholicism. John Huss' translation was a symbol of revolt for which he was burned at the stake. You have but to think of Luther's translation and the dynamics of Protestantism, or the King James' version and the culmination of the Elizabethan age. In modern times, Moses Mendelssohn's German translation of the Bible opened the new literary and scientific activities of modern Jewry. Saadia's translation of the Scriptures into Arabic ushered in a new era in the history of civilization. It heralded the coming of the golden age in Spain; it directed Jews into the historic role of intermediators between the Orient and the Occident; it led to a brilliant era in which Jewish scholars richly contributed to Mohammedan and Christian civilizations original works in all the fields of science as well as philosophy and ethics. You may take for granted that in our Bible Department Saadia's translation of the Scriptures, his available commentaries and his numerous exegetical works are fundamental studies.

The far-off millennial sage is therefore very much at home in these halls and classrooms. Reverently we hail his thousandth anniversary. To be sure, we hope that we will be excused for not following the example of the Spinoza enthusiasts who gave their hero a testimonial banquet on his three hundredth birthday. Rather have the editors of *The Jewish Quarterly Review* — the scientific journal of this College — extended an invitation to scholars and lovers of Saadia to greet the sage in the columns of the *Quarterly* in his own spirit and in his own image. For this purpose, they announced that the October issue of the *Quarterly* will be devoted wholly to Saadiana studies, and we have every reason to feel that it will be indeed a gala number.

But Saadia does not belong to the scholarly fraternity alone. He was essentially a democrat, a man of the people, who fought their battles and suffered for justice and truth. Furthermore, although he lived wholly among his own people, the intellectual horizon of his vision melted into the infinite. Like every true genius, his home was among the crags and mountain peaks of the spirit, at which height artificial barriers vanish from sight and the world blends in a pattern of unity and harmony which can only be described as divine. Even when Saadia cultivated the vineyard of his people — and to this task he devoted his life — it was always with the thought and the hope that all the world would share in the fruit. Thus he broke with precedent when in rendering the Bible into Arabic he transcribed it not in the customary Hebrew alphabet but in the Arabic script in order that the whole Mohammedan world might thus be brought closer to the original source of revealed religion. His major works were written for all the world to read, Christians as well as Mohammedans and Jews. This was his destiny — this was his historic role — profoundly to affect the current of medieval thought as it flowed from Bagdad to Cordova and from the capital of the Spanish caliphate to the cities of Western Christendom.

This son of the tenth century — call him a medievalist, if you please — has profound significance for our times. He was more than a scholar, more than an exegete, more than a philologist and a philosopher. You cannot under such divided nomenclature collect the precious distillation of genius any more than you can retain the fragrance of a rose by dissecting it under a microscope.

Saadia the man was greater than his collected writings. To him, scholars were not merely schoolmen. They stood in the line of prophetic succession. This was good rabbinic doctrine: the scholars of every generation are the successors of the prophets. Their writings are not only the outpourings of individual minds. Collectively, they constitute the culture of their generation — and what is culture but the self-revelation of a people in literature? In the rabbinic conception, scholars stand guard over the soul of a nation. In times of stress, they man the watch in the tower. Their eyes are trained to scan the distant horizons. They are illumined with an inner light which is fed by knowledge and devotion. They sound the alarm when danger threatens. They lead the fight when moral poison threatens the vitals of a nation's existence. They build morale. They feed national faith.

We must hold this picture of a scholar before us if we are to understand the mainsprings of Saadia's inner life. He was a scholar-prophet. His mind soared in the clouds; his heart lived with his people. He was a rationalist with a touch of the mystic. His learning was dynamic, purposeful, passionate. He was equally militant in defense of reason or faith, religion or philosophy. He was a knight militant for truth, whether its source was human or divine.

His was a fighting faith. All his life he was engaged in combat for religion, philosophy and justice. Personal recriminations were inevitable in the course of the conflict; but rarely, if ever, was the fight originally joined on a personal issue. The pen was his sword but the battle was real; the risk was imprisonment or death. In Egypt, he was at swords with the Karaites, the sect that sought to undermine the basis of traditional religion. More painful must have been his protracted duel with Ben Meir, the head of the Palestine academy, on the issue whether Palestine or Babylon should have spiritual supremacy. On a question of simple justice to a litigant he dared throw down the gauntlet to the Exilarch, the Jewish prince of the Exile, a descendant of house of David. But however big these struggles and issues loomed in his own day, his greatest and most significant victory for all time was in the realm of the mind as he grappled with the eternal searchings of the human heart in man's unending struggle to comprehend the Infinite and the truths that flow therefrom. This triumph of the spirit is crystallized in his greatest work, written toward the end of his life, *Philosophic Ideas and Religious Beliefs*. Historians are accustomed to regard this work as a break in the continuity of his life. They point out that it was written during a time when the Gaon had been thrown from his high estate, when he was forced to live in seclusion, disowned by the authorities, deposed from his high office — a thoroughly humiliated and defeated man. Malter, the biographer, writes admiringly "that it was not the work of a recluse brooding in despair over a shattered career and seeking to drown his grief in literary occupation, but that of a great and highsouled thinker who, having gone through a trying experience, and having realized that from the very beginning it was a lost cause, dismisses the whole matter from his mind, and with serene superiority turns his attention to what was the real aim of his life, the elaboration of a system of Jewish thought."

This certainly seems a fair statement of fact. And yet it appears to me that this supreme effort of the mastermind is the outgrowth and the sequence of the manifold struggles in which all his life was spent. Far from spelling disillusionment with the world or indifference to the struggles that agitate the lives of men, it represents a deeper, intuitive understanding that the sordidness of man, his quarrels, wars, lust for power, bigotry and hatred are the externalized soul aches of a race suffering from spiritual frustration. Compassion and love for his fellowmen of all races and creeds flowed from his heart as he penned these words in introducing his theme: "My heart grieved for mankind and my soul was moved on account of our own people Israel, as I saw in our times many of those who adhere to their faith entertain impure beliefs and unclear ideas, while those who deny the faith boast of their unbelief and triumphantly deride the men of truth, albeit they are themselves in error. I saw men sunk, as it were, in a sea of doubt and overwhelmed by the waves of confusion, and there was no diver to bring them up from the depths and no swimmer to come to their rescue. But as God has granted unto me some knowledge by which I can be useful to them, and endowed me with some ability which I might employ for their benefit, I felt that to help them was my duty and guiding them aright a moral obligation."

As his life is about to come to a close, the scholar-prophet realizes that man's supreme and final battles are to be fought out in his own soul. He is confident of the ultimate outcome for "man is the axis of the world and its foundation." Both reason and faith dictate to Saadia that human happiness is at the heart of creation. No one possessing such a philosophy can despair of man or the world. But man can fulfill his destiny only if he is conscious of his cosmic significance. To this high plane Saadia painfully seeks to lift us as he urges us to follow his steep, philosophic trail to an understanding of the Creator and his creation, free will and immortality.

We are removed by a thousand years from the days of Saadia. The scene has shifted. Bagdad no longer holds the center of the stage. The entire tenth century has receded into the obscure background of that period in history. But Saadia the scholar-prophet has strangely come to life. He stands as a "watch in the night"; even as the Psalmist said: A thousand years in Thy sight are but as yesterday when it is past, and as a watch in the night.

The American people and the United Nations are locked in a desperate life-and-death struggle to protect the ideals and the freedoms that we hold dearer than life. All the resources of this vast country are being mobilized in the titanic struggle with an intensity and concentration unprecedented in this free land of one-time rugged individualism. Our manpower, our natural wealth, the limitless industrial capacity of this country, the scientific and inventive genius of America — all are being welded into an engine of war that shall forever destroy war. Every nerve is increasingly strained for the war effort, for the stakes are colossal. At such a time, it is good to look back a thousand years and behold the figure of the scholar-prophet, standing watch in the night.

There he stands in the hazy mist of forgotten time. The brilliant, colorful world of which he was part is crumbled in the dust. The kings and caliphs, the potentates and their satellites are shadowy ghosts who no longer evoke love or hate, who no longer inspire terror or yield protection. But Saadia, whose heart "grieved for mankind" because he "saw men sunk in a sea of doubt and overwhelmed by the waves of confusion" and who dived into that perilous sea to rescue them from their fate, is prophetically alive. He speaks with a commanding voice to the conscience of the world today as he did to the hearts of his contemporaries. A nation has a soul as well as a soil to protect. Man is a cosmic being. He was endowed by God with reason, with freedom, with infinite possibilities for good and for happiness. Discord, strife, hatred, war are exterior manifestations of an inner disorder of the soul which can only be righted by a revivified consciousness of the moral realities that undergird the world. This vision is eternally true — vitally true in war and even more dynamic a force in the making of peace. For as a Christian divine expressed it: "He who hath not meditated upon God, the human soul and the *summum bonum* may possibly make a thriving earthworm but will most indubitably make a sorry patriot and a sorry statesman."

What will be the face of the world a thousand years hence? He would be a bold prophet and a daring visionary to portray that millennial day. At best we can see only a little way ahead. We are moving rapidly into a hidden unpredictable future. The world will pass our generation by with far greater speed and momentum than that with which we traveled over the lap of the last thousand years. Man will need all the faith he can muster to sustain him. In such a world, there will be no room for brigands and tyrants. Dictators will molder in the dust, execrated, if not forgotten.

Will any of our contemporaries be remembered and honored a thousand years hence? Each of us may nominate his own candidate. But I venture to believe that however crowded the galaxy of immortals may be in that day, Saadia, the scholar-prophet, will be counted among them.

303

The Destiny of American Jewry

IN EVERY period of Jewish history, rabbinical ordination was regarded as a solemn covenant of faith. The teachers who bestowed ordination, the disciples who received it, were mutually aware that they engaged in a rite through which they carried the will of God into the life of the nation. In times of crisis, when Judaism was threatened by the brutal violence of the heathen or was faced with sectarian dissension which endangered the soul of the people and the integrity of its faith, the ordination of rabbis became the signal and the symbol of Jewish survival.

It was thus in the days of Hadrian, the arch enemy of the Jewish religion. Reasoning that the only way to encompass the fall of the Jewish people was to extirpate their religion, he closed the Palestine academies and decreed the death penalty for all who would engage in the rite of ordination. If we are here today, happy in the rabbinic consecration of these graduates of the Jewish Institute of Religion, it is because that ancient challenge, like every succeeding threat of emperor, tyrant and dictator, was met with heroic resolute determination by the rabbis and the Jewish people. The aged Rabbi Judah b. Babba was riddled with Roman arrows like a sieve, but not until he placed his hands in ordination upon the heads of his faithful disciples.

The institution of ordination in the mystic sense vanished with the dispersion of the people and the decentralization of religious authority. But rabbinic authority endured and rab-

Address delivered at the Commencement Exercises of the Jewish Institute of Religion, New York, January 28, 1945.

binical leadership carried the Jewish people through every crisis.

After the collapse of European Jewry through expulsions and massacres in the fourteenth and fifteenth centuries, an inspired teacher in Palestine, Rabbi Jacob Berab, sought to restore the ancient rite of ordination, to recreate the Sanhedrin and thus to pave the way for an autonomous spiritual life in Palestine, which would herald the coming of the Messiah. That dream shared the fate of many other Messianic visions. It was unfulfilled but never died. God willing, it may come to life in our time in a free democratic Jewish Palestine. Until that day comes, the transmission of the title rabbi from master to disciple, from a theological faculty to its students, is the accepted and only mode of preserving religious authority and spiritual leadership in Israel. What we are witnessing then today is a solemn rite, an act of consecration fraught with incalculable consequences for the future well-being of the congregation of Israel.

"Congregation of Israel" is a fitting name to denote the Jewish people in the light of our theme. I am not one inclined to indulge in the favorite exercise of defining the nature of the Jewish people. Are we a race, a people, a nation, a church, a secular or religious entity? We are all of these and more. A living organism does not dissect itself. It acts. It does not wait upon a definition in order to breathe, to live, to create. You will look in vain in the prodigious writings of Maimonides, in all the commentaries of Rashi or in any of the writings of the Jewish classicists for a morbid self-analysis of their Jewish personalities. But one feature is writ large over the face of Jewish history. The Jewish people is cast in the mold of its spiritual leaders. It is in the thoughts and writings of the rabbis, in the literary works of the scholars and the poets, in the ethical and philosophical systems of its thinkers that the soul of the Jewish people is mirrored. In the poems of Ibn Gabirol, the Ibn Ezras, Judah ha-Levi and numerous other Hebrew poets, the names of the wealthy patrons are preserved and many a philanthropist of their time is held up to praise or scorn. But never, never did the Jewish people look to its men of wealth and social position for spiritual guidance or the road to salvation.

Many are the men of wealth and political influence who are gratefully remembered in the annals of Jewish history as saviors of their people. They are the men who poured out their wealth in support of Jewish academies, who generously sustained scholars and their disciples, who supplied their communities with books and tools of scholarship. They are the men who used their high position in the courts of princes and emperors to defend their people against the threat of evil decrees and court machinations. But invariably they were men under the sway of religion who bowed before the spiritual authority of the great rabbis who voiced the conscience and the immortal hope of their people. Only in the darkest days of spiritual decadence did ghetto life fall under the shadow of oligarchical rule. The decline of the rabbinate gave rise to secularist rule in Jewish community life. It brought in its wake, as we know only too well, intellectual confusion, divided counsel, and spiritual inertia. If we are to be redeemed from this thraldom, a spiritual revolution in community leadership must be effected. Scholars, rabbis and kindred forces in Jewry must regain a position of spiritual ascendancy in the councils of Judaism. Theirs, and theirs alone, is the power to release the creative impulses in Jewry and to lead their people into the dawn of a new and happier life.

*

This is a challenge to the American Jewish laity of all classes, but especially to those laymen who are loudest in their protestations that we are wholly a religious sect. Sheer consistency on their part demands that in all matters of Jewish policy involving principles and ideals of Judaism or growing out of religious philosophy that they, as good religionists, defer to the views of those who have a right to speak in the name of religion — not the lawyers, merchants and industrialists, not the dwindling collection of minority rabbis whom history is passing by because they lost contact with the living impulse of their people, but the great body of Jewish scholars, teachers, and rabbis who embody the living traditions of their faith and who are endowed with the learning, the traditional wisdom and philosophy of Judasim which are the sole criteria for authority recognized in the Jewish religion.

Greater still, however, is the challenge to the rabbinate. Rabbinical authority is not one of mere ecclesiasticism. There is no religious hierarchy in Judaism. A rabbinical diploma, or *Semikah,* is requisite for the exercise of routine rabbinical functions; but it cannot of itself confer the high power of spiritual leadership. For this high prerogative, there are additional requisites: character, vision, inspiration, courage. There are obvious graces of character and personality with which the rabbi must be innately endowed. But above all, he must enter upon his calling with a profound sense of personal consecration. He must be filled with exalted faith in Israel and its spiritual destiny; and he must personally feel a deep sense of historic responsibility in the line of succession to the sages, saints and martyrs who sanctified the name of God and glorified the role of rabbi and teacher in Israel.

If there is to be a shifting of leadership in American Jewish life, it will not be brought about by the mechanics of class substitution. The rise of lay leadership in Jewish life was not always accomplished by the process of usurpation. In great measure, it was the weakness, if not the bankruptcy of inept rabbinical trusteeship that led to lay receivership. Nor can anyone contemplate Jewish community life without the strong participation of zealous and devoted laymen. What we envisage is a restoration of the proper balance between lay strength and spiritual force. The ascendancy of religious leadership in American Jewry, if it is to come, must be achieved not through a weakening of lay interest but through the dynamics of a spiritual revolution within the scholarly and rabbinical world itself.

This then is the charge which I want to leave with you, graduates of the Jewish Institute of Religion. An historic challenge confronts you. As you leave these halls of learning to assume the reponsibilities of your calling, serve your congregations well. Imbue them with all the faith that is in you. But keep your vision high. Not the parish but the whole world is your domain. You must live not only in the physical world of today, but in the spiritual realm of Israel's dreams and aspirations. Render allegiance to your congregation and to the general community in which you live; but remember always that as a rabbi, you are a symbol of the indwelling of the divine spirit in human destiny. Above all, in you the immortal hope of Israel's eternal faith must never be crushed by the grief and despair of the hour. These are the requisites of your divine calling. These are the requisites of spiritual leadership in American Jewry at this critical hour of world history.

For American Jewry is on the eve of a great destiny. As America is the hope of the world, so in far more tragic accents the eyes of world Jewry are upon us, their American brethren. Thus far our response to their appeal has been one of philanthropy, public demonstration and political assistance. We have raised millions for relief. We have cried out in agony at the unspeakable torture which the common enemy inflicted upon our people, and we helped to awaken the public conscience. We have used our rights as American citizens to plead the cause of Jewish Palestine and gained the sympathy of our government and the American people and their promised aid in the attainment of the Zionist ideal. The physical and spiritual resources of American Jewry will be drawn upon in more intensive measure when the war is won and the work of reconstruction will begin. But American Jewry is summoned to world Jewish leadership in a far more compelling historic and philosophic setting.

*

There is rhythm and movement in Jewish history. The rhythm beats regularly like a pulse. It throbs almost with the regularity of a law of nature, as one center of Judaism recedes and another emerges on the panorama of world history.

Palestine was the land of our national birth. From the days of Joshua to the era of Nebuchadnezzar, Palestine was the center of a rich Hebrew culture. Prophecy and song, poetry and wisdom literature had their birth there. The scene shifted in 586 BCE when the Jewish population was forcibly transported by the Babylonian conqueror to the valley of the Tigris and the Euphrates. For a brief period, the voice of prophecy and psalmody resounded by the rivers of Babylon. Then the pall of silence fell upon Babylonian Jewry. Judaea, rising from the ruins, was being rebuilt by the handful of intrepid settlers who returned from exile. For six hundred more years Palestine was again the land of the Hebrew genius. Prophets gave way to lawgivers, psalmists vied with composers of gnomic wisdom. The written word was expanded and expounded by the oral teaching. Prophets were succeeded by scribes; and these, in turn, by Tannaim, the rabbis who continued in unbroken succession till Rabbi Judah the Prince, the composer of the Mishna, early in the third century.

During these many centuries, the bulk of the Jewish population lived peacefully and prosperously in Babylonia. They engaged in commerce, owned landed estates, held high offices in government service and were even accorded limited sovereignty through the Exilarch. Undoubtedly the land was dotted with Jewish schools and academies. But — and this is the strangely recurring phenomenon I want to point to — during this long period, Babylonian Jewry, loyal, numerous, rich and prosperous, was culturally sterile. Not a single work, not a single page or line has come down to us from Babylonian Jewry during the half millennium preceding the compilation of the Mishna in Palestine about the year 200 C.E.

But the shadow of impending events was darkening the skies of Palestine. Only another century and the Roman Empire would adopt a new revolutionary religion which would use the power of the state to suppress the mother religion Judaism. The struggle was destined to be most desperate in the mother country, with the result that Jewish cultural life would cease to exist in its native land. But miracle of miracles, a century or two before this catastrophe was to befall the Jews of Palestine, Babylonian Jewry which had lain dormant for over half a millennium suddenly burst forth into active creative life. As Palestine receded in the background, Babylonia emerged with the creation of the Talmud, the systematizing work of the Saboraim and the far-reaching activities of the Geonim. Then, for almost a thousand years, the spiritual leaders of Babylonian Judaism held sway over the Jewish religion and were accorded hegemony over world Jewry.

But the creative genius of Babylonian Jewry was destined to fade at the turn of the first millennium. Meanwhile, Jews in great number had settled in Italy and Spain for a thousand years. In Egypt and some of the North African communities, the Jewish settlements were lost in antiquity. Again the same phenomenon appears. For the first eight centuries of the Common Era there is no sign of creative literary activity in any of these countries. But a hundred or more years before the vanishing of Babylon as the center of the Jewish world, there is a marked stirring of the creative impulse in all of these countries. Talmudic commentaries appear in North Africa and philosophical works in Egypt; literary works sprout in Italy and a rich and varied literature heralds the golden age of the Jews in Spain. The centers of Judaism move westward and as the sun sets on Babylon, a pillar of light rises in Spain which now appears as the center of the stage for five hundred years.

With the edict of expulsion, Spanish Judaism came to a violent end in 1492. Again the same beat marks the rhythm of the shifting of the centers of Judaism. A century or more before the Spanish catastrophe, great academies arose in Poland. Jewish settlements in that country date back to the 10th century. Flourishing communities receive the attention of the Polish kings in the 12th and 13th centuries. But it was not before the 14th and 15th centuries that great rabbinical personalities transformed Poland into a world Jewish center of learning and authority. As Spanish Judaism neared the end, Poland — and Turkey too — succeeded to Jewish leadership.

The same rhythm manifests itself as Poland yields its place to Lithuania and as Eastern Europe, subjected to the dissolving influence of Western culture paves the way for the great centers of *Jüdische Wissenschaft* in Germany and the countries under its influence. The rhythm is uniform. Before one great center of Judaism is destroyed, a mysterious protective genius fashions a new home for the immortal Jewish spirit.

*

Viewed thus on the broad panorama of Jewish history, can there be any doubt as to the spiritual destiny of American Jewry as the next great center of world Judaism? In the brief span of a few years, we have witnessed the greatest calamity that has befallen the Jewish people in two thousand years. Thousands of Jewish communities were wiped out and millions of innocent lives were subjected to cruel torture and death. On the entire European continent, not one academy, seminary or yeshivah — not a single library, museum or other cultural institution was allowed to stand. And here we have grown, great in numbers,

great in resources, and above all great in the possession of freedom and in the dignity of citizenship in the greatest democracy
on earth.

Little could the early Jewish settlers in the colonial period
or the Jewish patriots who fought in the War of Independence
realize the ultimate world significance of the Judaism which
they planted on this American continent. Nor was there a
deeper appreciation of the destiny of American Judaism among
the tens and hundreds of thousands that came to this country
with increasing tempo in the 19th and 20th centuries. Only
now in the great tragedy that has befallen the world and the
Jews can we trace the outline drawn by the invisible hand that
fashioned the destiny of our great community. What the enemy
destroyed over there we rebuild tenfold here. The agony and
grief of our martyred brethren will not crush our faith but steel
our determination to build a greater, richer and nobler Judaism
in this land.

A flaming fire burns over the graves of our tortured martyrs.
The bodies may be dead in the sodden earth but their souls
hover over the soil saturated with their holy blood. Their souls
will find no peace till their spirits find new life in the hearts
of their living brethren. Even now one can hear these invisible
spirits move in two columns. One is being wafted over the hills
of Palestine in the dreams and hopes of the builders of Zion.
Another column is advancing upon us in America to vivify and
vitalize the greatest Jewry in the history of the Diaspora.

A great era lies before us. We are indeed on the eve of a
mighty Jewish destiny. The rhythm of Jewish history is beating
with irresistible force. Graduates of the Jewish Institute of
Religion — rabbis in Israel — you are entering upon a stirring
era which will demand all the strength of your Jewish faith.
Meet it with courage, vision, imagination, and you will be
worthy of spiritual leadership in this dynamic period of American
Judaism.

312

Universities: Guardians of Democracy

IT IS a great privilege to be part of this Convocation, to share with the graduates the high mood of this hour, and to be able from now on to look upon this venerable university with the affection and pride of an honorary alumnus.

These are soul-stirring days for the college youth and heart-searching days and nights for those entrusted with the destinies of our colleges and universities. To students, war is more than a terrifying experience; it is more than a gamble with life; it is a challenge and a threat to all the ideals that make life precious and meaningful. The greatest hazards in war are not life and limb but soul and spirit. Fill the heart of a brave American with an ideal to which his soul is committed, and no sacrifice will be too great for him to bear. A poet who witnessed a pilot come crashing down in a plane on fire exclaimed, "There goes a flaming meteor." This, it seems to me, is an inspired description not only of an aviator, but of every soldier or sailor on land, in the air, or in a typhoon at sea, who makes the supreme sacrifice when the sacrifice is illumined by the hero's faith in the cause for which he gives his life. They are all flaming meteors, stars of a night, lighting the horizon around us with a mystic light and a divine fire.

All accounts agree — whether they are drawn from the letters and the diaries of the boys themselves or from the reports of their chaplains and the writings of correspondents on the battlefield — that underneath the swagger and the fatalistic veneer on ships, in barracks and fox-holes, there is elemental

Address delivered at the Convocation of the University of Pennsylvania, March 6, 1945. Reprinted from *Crozer Quarterly*, Vol. XXII, 1945.

hunger for spiritual assurance on the issues of life. Americans crave for something spiritually deeper and richer than the urge for personal salvation of the medieval warrior. They are concerned not only with their own well-being, whether on earth or in heaven, but far more so with the world in which they and those they love will live. Surrounded by destruction and death, filled with the cries of agony and suffering, they ask in wonder and in bewilderment whether these are indeed the death throes of a dying civilization or the birth pangs of a new world dedicated to justice among nations, righteousness within the nations, and enduring peace for all groups within the fabric of society. Called upon to give their lives in the name of democracy, the definition of democracy looms big in their thinking. They probe deeply into its meaning. Is it another mirage, perhaps a new Moloch demanding myriads of human sacrifices, or is it the gateway to freedom, to justice, and to peace? In their quest, some turn earnestly to their chaplains, others commit their thoughts to writing. Countless numbers turn nostalgically to their alma maters, the colleges and universities to which they look for vision and reinforcement in the hour of supreme crisis. It is the recognition of this moral bond between students and their alma mater which impels me to speak on the theme: Universities: Guardians of Democracy.

When the history of this war is finally written after the peace and an analysis made of the basic institutions that contributed to victory, a grateful nation, it is hoped, will applaud the heroic role played by our colleges and universities. For the present, no one removed from the academic life and its responsibilities seems to realize fully the dilemma which confronted our institutions of higher learning, and the miraculous manner in which they turned weakness to strength and became a bulwark of national defense. Faced on the one hand by the depletion of students as a result of the Selective Service Act and confronted by the superstitious prejudice which supposed realists feel toward the alleged visionaries and dreamers of the cloistered life, many of the colleges of the country faced extinction through bankruptcy or, what in the long run might have been worse, absorption by the armed forces. That neither of these alternatives came to pass, that the classroom, the laboratory, and the campus were co-ordinated into a scientific and intellectual arsenal of democracy without utter destruction of humanistic values is a tribute to the devotion of the teaching and research staffs of our institutions of higher learning and in particular to the statesmanship and resourcefulness of the college presidents and their executive aides.

But it is not the war effectiveness of universities which would entitle them to the high rank of guardians of democracy. I recall a pertinent incident in Palestinian history about two thousand years ago. In that little Jewish commonwealth, universal compulsory education for boys was introduced in that early period. A commission of educators was sent on a tour of inspection. Whenever they entered a city, they called upon the chief magistrate to introduce them to the guardians of the city. Invariably the police officials, the judges, or the heads of the military garrison were summoned. But the commissioners shook their heads sadly. "These are not the guardians of your city," they exclaimed, "they are symbols of disorder in your midst. Bring before us your teachers. They are the guardians of your city."

Universities are guardians of democracy because they are essentially instruments of civilization, and because their native spiritual climate is democracy. By nature, they are tools of peace, not of war, and the riches which they create are democratically distributed to all who seek knowledge and truth. Great as has been their contribution to this war of destruction, their long history is contiguous with the growth of civilization. For of wisdom hath it not been said, "Her ways are ways of peace." So it may be confidently premised that in the immediate future, too, the universities will come into their own as builders of civilization, guardians of democracy.

Already countless projects are engaging the best minds of our academic institutions, and there will be many more as the days of peace draw near. These projects will range over the whole realm of human thought and inventiveness. Indeed, I do not know of any era when a government has drawn so heavily upon the learning and the specialized knowledge of the scholars of the country as in our time, both in the prosecution of war and in the planning for the peace and the new world order after the war. But quite apart from individual projects and publicly sponsored designs that will be fostered by men drawn from academic ranks, the universities of the country collectively will bear great responsibility for national education in the broadest sense. Theirs will be the task of public enlightenment to prepare the nation for the new role which America must play in the concert of nations. Theirs will be the duty to inculcate a deep sense of social responsibility where it is most needed in order to relieve tensions and prejudices which threaten the well-being of the American people. Above all, theirs will be the privileged role through education to deepen the concept of democracy in the national conscience, so that American civilization may indeed become the hope of the world as it was envisaged in the dream of the fathers.

For basic to the life of American civilization is the belief in democracy. But what is the popular concept of democracy? It was not necessary to poll the country before the war to prove that the national understanding of this concept was vague and shallow and confused. A metropolitan newspaper revealed to a startled world how widely prevalent was ignorance of the facts of American history. To me it was far more appalling to note the general ignorance of and apathy to the concept of democracy, which, after all, is the driving force which gives meaning to American history and civilization. The war has remedied this situation in part. One cannot long continue to suffer and make sacrifices for a cause without intuitively grasping at its meaning. I have seen, as you no doubt have, impromptu reflections on democracy written by young soldiers on the battlefield that are startling in their grasp and maturity. But this new acquisition is not altogether general, and the tuition fee has been far too costly in blood and tears. In the future it will be our responsibility as educators to plough deep the seeds of democracy as part of our national faith.

For democracy is a faith. It is not mere governmental machinery. Representative government is the agency through which this faith is best expressed, but one must not confuse the instrument with the ideal. Democracy is the assertion of a faith in man and his place in the universe which grows out of a belief in God, the Creator. Genetically at any rate, this has been the American credo of democratic faith. Man is primary; government is secondary. The perfect society is more important to the realization of the democratic ideal than perfect government. That our democratic way of life is incomplete, that it has deep, blighting imperfections no lover of democracy will deny, but the cure of the ills of democracy is more democracy. If we may for the moment borrow religious terminology, democracy can be either a faith by which we live or a heresy which leads man to perdition. The history of democracy is rich in illustrative examples.

The first and noblest expression of the democratic faith is the biblical narrative of creation. "And God created man in his own image . . . the Lord formed man of the dust of the ground, and breathed into his nostrils the breath of life, and man became a living soul." This is the text and inspiration of all true democracy. As a child of God, man is endowed with dignity; his soul is a spark of divinity; he is born free, equal in his rights before man and God. To focus the lesson of racial equality more sharply, an early Hebrew legend adds this embel-

317

lishment. The precious bit of earth from which God formed man was gathered from the north and the south, the east and the west, so that no country might at some future time say: "Of us alone did God create the human race."

Mosaic laws, prophetic exhortations, sage proverbs crystallized this democratic passion in the hearts of the Hebrew people. With all the fervor and rich imagery of the New Testament, this gospel was carried by the early apostles into the larger world beyond the borders of Galilee and Judaea. For a time it appeared that the essence of democracy might be distilled as the political social doctrine of the Judaeo-Christian world. But the momentous alliance between church and empire proved fateful. Imperial interests and traditions frustrated the social idealism of the new religion. The church became part of the feudal order. Aiming for spiritual supremacy, it compromised with the brute force of the Roman-Teutonic world. It became entangled as an integral part of a social order which spelled tyranny, oppression, and serfdom for the masses.

As a result, when at last in eighteenth century France the human spirit was driven to rebellion against tyranny, the rebels directed their attacks against the citadels of religion no less than against the castles of the hated nobles. The battle cry of the French Revolution, "Liberty, Equality, Fraternity," was not the shout of religion. It was not because man was endowed with Godlike attributes that he was declared a sovereign being, free and equal. The Revolution was in essence a rebellion of man against God. For God was to be deposed as Lord of the universe. Man in the nakedness of his animalic existence proclaimed that he was the ruler of the universe. Henceforth he was to be master of his own destiny without resort to a supernatural being. By the powers of brain and brawn alone he would conquer the world and make it his domain.

How high the hopes, how steep the fall caused by this, shall we call it, heretical democracy! We of our generation who have twice witnessed the world in flames and ruins are living witnesses of the ravaging effects of this social heresy. We are the long-range victims of man's self-deception and conceit under the mask of democracy.

For man did not long stay at the helm of the universe. How could he? Without God as Father, man was but an animal, high in the stage of evolution, it is true, but an animal, nevertheless, whose survival was determined by the laws of the jungle. Morals were removed from the trend of history, ethics became irrelevant in the conduct of sovereign nations, and the laws of biology were substituted as norms in the struggle of national survival. It was right for nations to break treaties, to deceive, to betray, to rob, to murder, if greater power could be attained thereby, for is this not the law of the jungle?

It is a straight, precipitate line of descent from God to man to beast to the machine age and to the abstract state as the controlling power of human destiny. There is no retreat from this course of doom save by one gateway, the path which leads to the highway of American democracy.

American democracy differs from the European form in essence, in the source of its inspiration, and in the course of its development. With us, democracy was not a rebellion but a faith to live by. It was not the creature but the creator of political and social revolution. It inspired the Declaration of Independence, it lived in the hearts of the rebels of '76, it fostered the Constitution, it molded and shaped the Bill of Rights, it charted the course of the republic from Washington to Roosevelt. But its essence is not political theory but spiritual perception. It is rooted in the conviction that moral purpose lies at the heart of the universe. It is founded on the principle that man is not just another animal but bears the divine image in his soul. Because of man's Godlike attributes, the Declaration of Independence makes bold to declare that man "is endowed by his Creator with certain unalienable rights." It is the faith of

319

American democracy that man has the capacity and the high prerogative to complete the plan which God designed, the building of the ideal society in which poverty, ignorance, hatred, and exploitation shall no longer curse the human race, but truth, justice, love, and mercy shall set man free.

In this faith America was nurtured. It was the spirit which impelled the Pilgrim Fathers and the Puritans to embark upon the high adventure to build on this continent a replica of biblical civilization — the New Canaan or the Promised Land, they called it. As with all prophetic inspiration, the vision far exceeded the realization. Great is the structure of American civilization reared on these foundations. But incomparably greater is the challenge and hope of the future.

The challenge becomes daily more compelling as the end of the war becomes faintly visible over the bloodstained horizon. Three Titans met at Yalta to decide the fate of the world. Great was the distance they covered since the days of Teheran. Steep will be the road from Dumbarton Oaks to San Francisco and then onward. Vast stretches of mind and ideals are still to be explored. Not the statesmen alone but all the United Nations need a compass by which safely to traverse uncharted areas. That compass, that star is the faith of democracy. To bring down that star from its dreamy heights to the grasp of toiling men and women throughout the world is the greatest privilege of all time. It will be the high prerogative of the scholars, scientists, philosophers, and teachers who man our universities, the guardians of democracy.

The Future of Torah in America

IT IS a happy augury of the times that the inauguration of a
new President of the Hebrew Union College is initiated with
a symposium on "The Future of Torah in America." It reveals a
new awareness in the camps of Israel of the emptiness of modern
life in which religion has been relegated to a minor place and
the Torah, which is the heart of the Jewish religion, has been
deserted by the laity and neglected, alas all too frequently, in
the ranks of the rabbinate. A future for Torah in America, if
resolved upon in positive terms by American Israel, will go a
long way not only to strengthen the religious fiber of American
Jewry; it will have a curative, healing influence upon the widespread, spiritual malady of our times.

The need for filling our lives with greater spiritual content
is not limited to modern Jewry. There is spiritual hunger
abroad in the world and sickness has affected the soul of man.
Civilization is starved spiritually at the roots and the result has
been mass, moral stultification. The problems that plague society
on all levels — personal, national and international — economic antagonisms, political conflicts, social strife, are being
increasingly recognized as manifestations of spiritual frustration
and moral desensitization. As part of the modern world we
share its guilt and failure commensurate with our numbers and
minority status. Our suffering, however, the retribution visited
upon our people through the moral, religious bankruptcy of
Western civilization, is appalling on any scale of measurement.

As the first victims to fall prey to the evil whims that blow

Address delivered at a Symposium on the occasion of the installation of
Doctor Nelson Glueck as President of the Hebrew Union College, Cincinnati,
March 12, 1948.

upon nations, as a people of prophetic heritage gifted with religious perception, we must be the first to realize that the hope of the world rests not on might or on materialism, but on the redemptive power of the spirit. If history imposes obligations upon faiths and nations, ours is the duty in this desperate hour of human history to seek inspiration where our fathers found it, in the fount of Torah, and to render ourselves fit by faith, fortitude and moral courage to lead, as our ancestors did, in the moral regeneration of society. The whole world is threatened. Not in the underground hide-outs of thugs and bandits, but in the proud laboratories of our universities and in the brains of our foremost scientists, statesmen and military leaders, are the seeds of death and destruction being sown for the slaughter of humankind. We who first proclaimed the Kingdom of God on earth, great is our shame, deep is our humiliation for the children of men.

It is in fitting accord with our traditions that when a religious teacher in Israel is elevated to an eminent post of leadership and spiritual responsibility, that we scan the moral horizon of our age and define anew the religious wants and qualifications of our people in the moral climate of the current generation. I take it that this is the design of those who arranged our symposium as a prologue to the solemn service when the *Keter Torah*, the crown of the Torah, will be transferred to the new incumbent who will preside over this sanctuary of Jewish religious learning.

What then is Torah? It is a coat of many colors, a spiritual garb of infinite variety. Torah is the embodiment of Jewish thought and vision; the repository of Israel's historic experiences; the vehicle of its communion with the Infinite; the medium of divine speech and human love; the authoritarian voice: Thou Shalt, Thou Shalt Not; the alternating currents of divine, thunderous wrath and the warmth of Messianic hopes and dreams for Israel and mankind. Torah is the distillation of the soul of Israel into the written word of its classic literature,

322

in the institutions in which it has taken shelter. But the Torah in the ideal cannot be chained to the written word nor contained wholly in the institutions designed for human beings. It is the indwelling of the divine spirit in living souls as expressed in the genius of Israel.

What of the future of Torah in America? As I have defined it, Torah is the quintessence of Judaism. There can be no Judaism worthy of the name without Torah. A Torah-less Judaism would be pulseless, nerveless: a corpse, without life or potency.

But what of Torah in the more limited sense as the literary content of Jewish thought and feeling, the classic literature of Judaism, the Bible, Mishna, Talmud, Rabbinics, philosophy, ethics, mysticism, poetry, history and the other writings? They are the tangible habitation that houses the spirit as the body is the shrine of the soul. Body and soul are not interchangeable, but neither can they be divorced in the life of man. Unless the literature of Torah is illumined by the living spirit, it is a body without a soul. Conversely, the ideal Torah is elusive and transcendent unless we seek it in the corporeal forms into which its spirit is poured.

Judaism cannot experience the vivifying spirit of Torah in its ideal conception unless it draws inspiration deep from the wisdom and holiness which are distilled in the written Torah of the ages. The future of Torah in America cannot be conjugated in the subjunctive mood. It is an imperative. There must be a future for Torah in America if our Judaism is to retain the distinctiveness of its moral, religious perceptions, if indeed it is to regain the power to influence the future course of civilization.

Those who question the feasibility of a future for Torah in America base their skepticism on two counts: climate and language. The sacred, traditional literature which denotes Torah in the literal sense and its indwelling spirit, which is an emanation of Torah in its ideal conception, belongs to a climate, geographical and mental, in which, superficially at least, the

American of today does not seem to be at home. The literature is ancient, old as the cedars of Lebanon and oriental in its imagery, quaint in the cast of thought. The Talmud is a labyrinth of thought without the majestic sweep and grandeur of the Bible. Later rabbinic literature, including the classic works of philosophy, ethics, mysticism, reveal clearly their medieval religious climate. Many of the laws of the Torah are Palestine-centered geographically, and their universal application seems questionable to the modern man. The laws governing society — civil jurisprudence in particular — which kept the Jewish community intact in the Diaspora for almost two thousand years, and which is so great a part of the body and spirit of Torah — the laws, for example, contained in the tractates *Baba Kamma, Baba Mezia* and *Baba Batra* — seem antiquated, outmoded, and no longer applicable in the climate of modern living. The suggestion was even seriously propounded that American civil law be substituted as a subject of instruction in Jewish religious education in place of the more antiquated Jewish law, as if an *ersatz* Torah could be made psychologically effective or religiously defensible!

A deeper understanding of the continuity of history and the processes of religious evolution, interpreted with poetic imagination, without which neither history nor religion is intelligible, tends to dissipate the climatic clouds of doubt and confusion. Torah is the creation of the central soul of our people. It will elude the cold logic of the rationalist as it must escape the snare of the literalist. Of course it is fatal to Torah to choke it with the prose hand of narrow literalism. The essence of the living Torah, its very pulse, is to be found in its flexibility, in the rhythm between the law as it is and the ideal which it incorporates. To be sure, the Torah is a system of law applicable to certain temporal conditions continually subject to change. But basic to the concept of Torah is the assumption that its laws embody indestructible principles of justice and truth which can give rise to ever new legal concepts and social institutions as mankind strives towards a new and better world. The dynamic element of Torah lies in the potential values and ideals still to be derived from the Law.

That many of the concrete laws are bound to be anachronistic and therefore dispensable, may well be conceded. The degree of their dispensability will vary with the mood of the individual and with the varying schools of thought within Judaism. But it matters greatly to all of us that the potential ideals imbedded in the Torah be permitted to develop in America through our identification with it in intense study and contemplation and, in a free Jewish State, through the embodiment of its principles in the institutions that will arise in the new Judaea. It is not too much to hope that through such a development, the Torah of Judaism may once more influence the future course of civilization. For, as I stated elsewhere, the laws which Judaism has in the past developed in theory and in practice are like a blurred mirror which reflects the ideal, hoped-for pattern of society in the golden age of the Messianic era. The laws of the Torah are to the ideal Torah what the mechanism of a clock is to the eternity of time.

Moral climate alone, then, affords no reason to doubt the possibility of a creative future for Torah in America. More formidable are the obstacles of language and the endless toil and devotion which mastery of its vast literature entails. To cite but one branch alone, the Talmud. The average student finds the acquisition of even a superficial reading knowledge of the Talmud in the original a challenging task. But to be and to stay at home in the Talmud entails a lifelong process of study which in modern times seems to be reserved for the specialist alone. And yet a Talmud-less Torah is a truncated, misshapen caricature of the Jewish tree of life. The program of Torah study looms formidable indeed when it is borne in mind that the entire Babylonian Talmud from the days of Rab and Samuel to Rab Ashi and Rabina is the product of but three hundred years of Jewish life on the banks of the Tigris and the Euphrates. Are we to assume that American Jewry of the future will produce a comprehensive and intensive system of education comprising the whole of Torah from the Bible to our own time, and that a generation of devoted students will be drawn to this program, sufficient in number and in zeal to act as a leaven in the development of a Torah-conscious American Jewry? Or perchance if such a development should seem remote and utopian, are we to prepare for the day when the house of Israel in this country will live spiritually, as in prefabricated houses, in English translations?

This is not a new problem in Jewish history. Other generations have faced it. During the Second Jewish Commonwealth, in Judaea itself, a transition had to be effected from Hebrew to Aramaic. Aramaic in turn had to yield to Arabic in some of the most important outposts of Jewish culture in the Middle Ages. Subsequently, Judaeo-Arabic was rechanneled into the main stream of Hebrew literature. The vernacular languages of the European countries did not become the vehicles of Torah until modern times, but even in the Middle Ages they were the dialects of the Jewish people in daily life, penetrating religious usage at home and in the Synagogue.

If we seek historic parallels, however, it would appear that the problem of Torah in American Judaism is closest in affinity of spirit to that which confronted Hellenistic or Alexandrian Judaism. Alexandrian Judaism is held in disrepute in some Jewish circles. It is held up as the classic example of cultural and religious assimilation, and its subsequent disappearance is pointed to as the inevitable fate of any Jewry that will follow its pattern of accommodating Jewish life and religious thinking to the mode and to the language of the prevalent culture and philosophy of the non-Jewish environment.

That Jewish culture should be cast in Hebraic mold; that

326

the historic function of the Hebrew language should be retained as a bond of union among the scattered communities of Israel; that Hebrew is the natural, historic and pure language of Torah, and a mystic bond between God and Israel — very few will doubt in an age that witnessed the resurrection of Hebrew as the living tongue of a people born to new life and hope in Eretz Yisrael. The cause of Hebraism in relation to American Judaism, however, should not be bolstered by a shallow reading of history, and the deprecation, if not the renunciation, of one of the most potent creative communities in Jewish history, whose influence was world-wide, even if it was not directly funneled to the world through recognizable Jewish channels.

If Alexandrian Jewry declined in numbers, and all but disappeared in the days of the ascendancy of Christianity, in the Roman Empire, so did Palestinian Jewry for similar reasons. In the three centuries from the translation of the Pentateuch into Greek to the days of Philo, the Jewish population of Alexandria wrote a unique chapter in the history of religion and philosophic thought. Alone among all the varied nationalities that came under the influence of Hellenism, to quote Doctor Wolfson, it "produced out of its midst a school of philosophers who consciously and deliberately and systematically set about remaking Greek philosophy according to the pattern of a belief and tradition of an entirely different (Jewish) origin."

Far from losing its spiritual identity in Hellenism, Alexandrian Judaism refashioned Greek philosophy in the image of its own Torah. A culture which gave rise to the Septuagint, contributed to the religious literature of the Apocrypha, inspired original philosophic writings, and under the wider scope of Hellenism included the monumental works of Josephus, is a rich heritage and a noble chapter in the Torah of Judaism.

Nevertheless, Alexandrian Judaism cannot serve as a model for the future of Torah in America. Granted that the intellectual milieu in which we live bears striking resemblance to the

327

Hellenistic cultural world of that ancient Jewish community, the differences are still greater. It would take us too far afield to develop the contrasting social, political and religious attitudes of the two eras. Suffice it to single out but one differentiating historic element. Alexandrian Judaism reached the end of its creative period at the time of the destruction of the Jewish State in Judaea. We stand on the threshold of the rebirth of Jewish nationhood in Palestine. The latter fact alone will be far-reaching in determining the Hebraic character of living Judaism.

At the very dawn of the new movement toward Zion the revival of Hebrew was its spiritual concomitant. Amidst the babel of polyglot languages which they brought with them, the pilgrim settlers in Palestine found in the Hebrew tongue not only the medium of common speech, but the soul of Israel re-united. Hebrew has grown in potency not only in Palestine but in every other center where Jews are concentrated in large numbers. The revival of Hebrew in our time is a symbol which holds forth the promise of spiritual resurrection. No segment of Jewry can isolate or immunize itself to this Hebraic influence, least of all American Jewry, the hope and strength of world Judaism in the Diaspora.

Viewed from this perspective it is clear that Torah in America must be strongly Hebraic in tone and content. This does not mean that it is feasible or desirable for Jewish learning to be exclusively Hebraic under the civilization in which we live. The Torah speaks to the heart of Israel; but its message must be carried to the world. We may well hail as historic witnesses the Jewries of medieval Spain and Italy. A great Jewish literature which derives its nurture and inspiration from the Hebrew source may also be created in other friendly languages. We too may find translations useful and even indispensable for the transmission of Jewish thought to the world and to large masses of Jews, who, even as in Spain, may remain Hebraically un-lettered. But for original creative power, Torah must live in its native medium. It must strike deep into the original sources of Judaism. Above all, the channels of communication with the overflowing Hebrew spirit of the new Israel must be kept open.

Will American Jewry meet the requirements to assure a future for Torah in America? There are hopeful signs. On the lower elementary level there is a growing awareness of the need of intensifying Jewish education. The drive for increased enrollment is giving way to the more urgent need of improving the content and quality of the existing educational programs. Hours of instruction are being increased in all systems from the Sunday School to the weekly Talmud Torah. Most significant is the startling development of Hebraically conducted summer school camps and the all-day Jewish School.

Whereas Sunday School registration throughout the country declined two percent in 1947, and weekday schools showed an increase of about that figure, all-day schools increased by more than twenty percent, according to the tabulation of the American Association for Jewish Education. There are fifty-eight all-day schools functioning in New York City, with an enrollment approximately of twelve thousand pupils. Despite the widespread resistance on the part of communal leaders, who fear parochialism, the movement for all-day schools is gaining momentum in many parts of the country. These schools grew out of the grass-roots of American Jewish life. Whatever their shortcomings in theory or practice, they are the soil in which the seeds of Torah are planted.

On the higher level too, there are signs that point hopefully to the future of Torah. The development of Yeshibot on a scale hitherto unknown in America, is one of the signposts. The increase in the number of teachers' training schools — the use of Hebrew as the language of instruction — the introduction of Departments of Hebrew in undergraduate colleges, and in some public high schools — the serious study that is given to the goals and objectives of Jewish education, these are distinct landmarks. The higher institutions of Jewish learning have played an important part in this development. At the Dropsie College we established a postgraduate School for Jewish Education, in which emphasis is laid not only on curriculum, texts and techniques, but upon the development of an American philosophy of Jewish education, that is, a broad theory of education which shall integrate the principle of Torah with the fundamentals of democratic society.

Jewish scholarship has struck firm root in American soil. America is now a world center of Jewish learning. The weekly newspaper published in Hebrew is not merely an agency for the dissemination of news. It is a literary venture in the renaissance of Hebrew. American themes have inspired the Hebrew muse of American Jewish poets. The pendulum has swung far from Alexandrian Judaism, when instead of pouring Hebrew wine into Greek vessels, Greek poems, comedies and tragedies are being set to the cadence of the Hebrew language by a Jewish poet in our own New England.

A renaissance of Jewish culture in America, a creative future for Torah, is within the power of our age to attain. Will American Jewish leadership rise to the glory of that vision? Only if the rabbis and educators, scholars and heads of the institutions of higher learning have the zeal to inspire and the courage to lead.

Our lay leaders are displaying heroic courage in shouldering enormous responsibilities for the physical sustenance and the rehabilitation of our brethren in Europe and in Palestine. They are setting precedents of philanthropy and human engineering that reflect the wisdom and compassion of the Jewish heart. But that leadership has not developed the keen sensitivity and sacrificial devotion for Torah which are so essential for the rebirth of a creative spirit in American Judaism. The fulfillment of the destiny of American Judaism will be retarded, if not thwarted, until there be a spiritual revolution in the attitude of the leaders of American Jewry toward Jewish learning and cultural institutions.

The term, "the Golden Age of the Jews in Spain," used so glibly was more than a gilded phrase. Literally great riches of gold were poured out for institutions of learning inspired by the love of Torah, by devotion to God and by overflowing faith in the abundance of Israel's spiritual riches. Until the day when this attitude becomes the dominant mood and conviction of American Jewish leadership it behooves our spiritual leaders to guard, to cherish and to nurture this ideal in our midst.

Above all, the guardianship of the ideal of Torah must be assumed by those who are charged with the direction of our institutions of learning. They must be zealous guardians, zealous in carrying out their charge with integrity, ever watchful against the intrusion of popular idols into the sanctuary of learning. They must have the courage to resist the lure of popular appeal, especially that most insinuating appeal to the craven fears induced by anti-Semitism. A people grows spiritually through the strength of moral conviction, not by flight to protective covering. It is high time that we utter the stern warning: Jewish life is in danger of being debauched by the pandering of professionals to the fears and to the weakness of American Jewry. Good will and amity among faiths and peoples are ardently desired by all God-loving people. But like the bluebird of happiness they are rarely attainable through frantic pursuit. Our institutions of learning are the most effective carriers of good will only by indirection: by training rabbis, scholars and teachers steeped in the knowledge of Judaism; still more, by fostering research and investigation which are the bases of all subsequent philosophic and historic structures of Jewish life; by the publication of learned works in religion, history and literature. In the entire range of Jewish writings, no single great work of thought or spirit was ever inspired by the motive to please or appease.

331

A noble future for Torah in America is visible on the horizon. It is foreshadowed by the wings of history. In its realization lies the destiny of American Judaism. As Babylon carried the torch for Palestine; as Spain together with France and Germany lifted the torch that fell from the grasp of the gaonate leadership in Babylon; as Poland forged to the front when other Jewries fell back; as Judaism came to life in the Ottoman Empire and in Palestine after the debacle in Eastern Europe until Poland and Lithuania became flourishing centers for Torah and mysticism; as Germany assumed leadership in the nineteenth century by breathing new life into modern Judaism through *Jüdische Wissenschaft*, so it is American Jewry which is now sternly cast in the role of spiritual leadership in the Jewish world. We cannot falter, we dare not fail; America will lift high the flaming torch of Torah.

332

American Jewry and a Jewish Renaissance

IN THE course of this evening I have been made to feel that my topic as originally announced, "The Apocrypha: The Jewish Version and Its Place in a Jewish Renaissance," sounds forbidding and formidable. Some faint-hearted persons, I am afraid, have actually been discouraged from coming to this meeting by fear of a lack of understanding of what is going to transpire. To compensate for this imposing approach, I shall speak quite informally, and as simply as possible, of this very important project which was undertaken by the Dropsie College, and I shall point out its bearing on the larger aspects of the future of Jewish culture in America, which I believe is destined to experience a veritable renaissance.

When the Dropsie College first announced its project with regard to the Apocrypha and the Pseudepigrapha the news created quite a sensation. Inquiries came from many sources. After I explained the project, I was usually confronted with the question: "How do you spell *Pseudepigrapha* and *Apocrypha*, and what do they mean?" Well, I shall assume that the members of the Judaeans are better informed. Nevertheless, a general description of the nature of the Apocrypha may be quite in order.

Jewish apocryphal literature comprises about thirty-five scriptural books similar to the Bible. As the Bible is a literature and not merely a compilation of books, so the Apocrypha represents a considerable literature of varied character covering several centuries. The books of the Bible cannot be placed in

Address delivered at the Spring Meeting of the Judaeans, New York, April 23, 1950.

one category, nor can the Apocrypha. While the biblical literature covers a period of over a thousand years, the Apocrypha
embraces approximately three hundred years. In theme, too,
the Apocrypha is as varied as the contents of the Bible. There
are books of a legal character similar to the Pentateuch. Others
are of a prophetic nature. Still others are comparable to the
Psalms or books of Wisdom. And again there are books of
historical import, such as the First and the Second Book of
Maccabees, which may be compared with the historical books
of the Bible, though they are more limited in scope, dealing
with one great and moving historic period.

The beginning of this literature can be traced to the fourth
century before the Common Era, not so long after the period of
Ezra and Nehemiah; it extended into the first century of the
Christian era. It was a period of deep religious turmoil, an
era of religious revolution. Old ideas were discarded; new ideas
were born. Ancient traditions were given new meaning. The
religion of the Jewish people was virtually recast into the form
by which Judaism was to be known through the centuries. In
the process of religious transformation, many sects arose and
died. Christianity had its birth during this period as a Jewish
sect, the child of many complex religious ideas in Judaism, before
it emerged as a world religion. The apocryphal literature is
the literary medium in which these tempestuous religious
currents are channeled.

The creators of this literature were men of prophetic cast.
Some were close to the spirit of what we might call today
Traditional Judaism. Others dared to deviate from the
paths of the ancients. Some were inspired mystics, who saw
divine visions, wandering spirits who scaled the heavens in
search of God. There were those who stood tremblingly before
the vision of a theophany. Others were lost in visions of man's
fate in Heaven and Hell. For many were those who were moved
and stirred by the tragic experiences of the Jewish people during

334

those centuries to seek escape into another sphere and to create a conception of an other-world in order to justify God and His justice. It is among this group of religious visionaries that the concept of immortality was born.

The rise of this doctrine, it may be pointed out, throws much light on the character of the apocryphal period. Nowhere in the Hebrew Scriptures proper is there clear reference to the immortality of the soul, except for a single phrase in the Book of Daniel, which really belongs to the apocryphal period. Nor did the concept of human immortality wait for the dawn of Christianity. The immortality of the soul was an accepted doctrine in Judaism several centuries before the rise of Christianity. It is in the apocryphal literature that we may trace the rise and development of this momentous doctrine.

What then was the reason for the birth and expression of that religious faith in immortality precisely during this period? For a thousand years Judaism, without promising or denying immortality, had built up a great system of religious belief and social justice without depending upon an other-world compensation: that is, without depending upon the promise of life in a future world to repay mortal man for the sorrows and the tragedies of this world. But the time came historically and spiritually when the power of faith in God and in this world was not sufficient to sustain the heroic beliefs of the Jews. For disillusionment followed in the wake of the glowing visions of the latter prophets in the dismal history that succeeded the period of Ezra and Nehemiah. Public life presented glaring contradictions to the teachings of prophet and scribe. Injustice, wickedness and corruption in high places wounded the religious sensibilities of the pious in Judaea before the rise of the Hasmoneans. The wars of the Hasmoneans, the martyrdom which preceded the insurrection and the strife of the combat itself — all these forces stirred up a storm in the souls of a sensitive people. Nothing less than the promise of life in another celestial

335

world where the wicked would be punished and the righteous rewarded could assuage the storm and stress within the Jewish soul. The evolution of this cardinal dogma of Judaism comes to light in various books of the apocryphal literature.

I have selected this accepted Jewish doctrine out of the maze of religious ideas to be found in the Apocrypha in order to illustrate more cogently the central problem which relates to the entire literature. Why were all these books banned from the scriptural canon and doomed to oblivion by the Jewish religious authorities of that day? Clearly the criterion of religious acceptability was not one of style or literary excellence. The considerations which had weight with the Pharisee teachers were primarily of a theological and doctrinal nature. Only those books which were inspired by the Holy Spirit were regarded as sacred. To guard against the intrusion of foreign or heretical doctrine, furthermore, another complementary ruling was officially declared: namely, that the Holy Spirit ceased to manifest itself with the demise of the latter prophets, Haggai, Zachariah and Malachi. Thus the Pharisees closed and sealed the sacred record: What is contained herein is holy, what is not included is secular, profane or heretical.

Consequently, a strange and fateful development followed. Not only were questionable or heretical books eliminated from Scripture, but likewise all other works of a scriptural nature that indicated a late origin. Books claiming an ancient, pseudo-authorship were subjected to careful scrutiny and sometimes accepted into the canon, as in the case of Daniel, while books like Enoch were excluded. To render the sacred scriptural boundaries more secure, special measures were taken to ban from circulation "the books outside the canon." A later ruling forbade the reading of these books as religious heresy, and declared that he who violated the ban would not have "a share in the world to come"— a very grave threat, which indicated the strong feeling of the Jewish religious leaders.

But the course of ideas is strange and devious. Officially, Judaism disowned its own literature created from the period of the close of the Bible until roughly New Testament times. But these books, though banned, could no more be destroyed and completely eliminated from Jewish consciousness than a ban of excommunication would affect modern literature today.

The ban was least effective in the large Greek-speaking Jewish communities outside of Palestine, in Egypt and other Hellenistic countries, where Hebrew and Aramaic literature of the Jews was current in Greek translation. In the official Bible translation, known as the Septuagint, many of the apocryphal books were included, while others originally composed in Greek or translated from the Hebrew or Aramaic were preserved independently as individual books.

When the new Christian sect arose and began to formulate its own religious ideas, it was naturally more hospitable to novel and radical ideas than Judaism, which had a crystallized theology. The new sect readily accepted whatever religious literature was afloat, not only the Hebrew Bible proper but all the so-called books "outside the canon," which in defiance of the official ban had survived in Greek translation. This process was the more natural as it was the Septuagint which served the new Christians as the sacred Bible, and many books of the Apocrypha were included in the Septuagint. Thus it was, thanks to the Church, that the Apocrypha was made safe for the world and was preserved to this day.

Now two observations are to be made regarding the consequences on the one hand of the renunciation of the Apocrypha by Judaism, and on the other hand of its admission into the bosom of Christianity. One, while the Apocrypha books were eliminated from the sacred Hebrew Scriptures, many of their ideas floated along in the stream of Judaism proper, so that one may find their expression in the rabbinical writings in the Mishna, in the Talmud, and especially in the midrashic litera-

337

ture. But as the books were cut off from Jewish literature, the relationship of those works to the midrashic current of thought was lost, and there was a consequent lack of complete understanding of the genesis and the full implication of those ideas within Jewish literature.

Much more important was the other aspect: namely, that the books became part of the Church literature, part of the very fiber of Christianity. It is a source of many important Christological ideas. The New Testament, for instance, with its concept of the son of God, with its stress on the other world, and even with some of its pacifist ideas, is completely unintelligible without an intimate knowledge and understanding of the Apocrypha. It is no exaggeration to say that without the Apocrypha, Christianity could not have developed in its present form.

The Church then, drawing much of its nature from the Apocrypha, and falling heir to the literature when the Synagogue renounced it, transformed these essentially Jewish writings into a form of Christian thought. This was accomplished in two ways: through interpretation and interpolation. As the Christian Fathers, moving away from the Jewish milieu, lost their understanding of intimate Jewish thought, they lost the true significance of the spiritual currents in the Apocrypha, and poured their own Christological notions and ideals into the interpretation of that literature. These Christological interpretations were supplemented by interpolations. This of course was a well-known method and was accepted as legitimate throughout medieval times. Just as in Josephus, for instance, the striking passage about Jesus was deliberately inserted by a pious soul who felt that such a passage ought to belong there, so in the same manner Christological ideas and passages were put into the apocryphal literature which had no place there.

This, then, is the story of the Apocrypha. Originally it was an outpouring of the Jewish spirit, the creation of deeply spiritual and literary personalities in Palestine and the Diaspora. By a religious fiat it was divorced from the Jewish people. The Church took possession of it; it breathed its own spirit into the literature, so that today the entire apocryphal series appears frequently under strictly Christian denominational authority and auspices.

The time has come when this literature ought to be reclaimed for the Jewish people. This was our resolve at the Dropsie College. The apocryphal books are our literature. They are part of the spiritual essence of our people. The considerations that were operative in the year 300 BCE are no longer applicable in our time. We need not fear the rise of new sects as a result of those ancient Jewish writings. On the contrary, by studying these books in the milieu in which they were created, and in the spirit of those times, and by reinterpreting this literature as only those scholars can who are intensely informed and filled with the spirit of Judaism and with the knowledge of Jewish life during those difficult years, the way is open for Jewish scholarship not only to enrich Judaism, but to make a spiritual contribution to the entire literary world. Jewish scholars would thus offer poetic compensation to the Church for having given shelter to these orphaned works during the two millennia when they were abandoned by the mother Synagogue.

It was with these thoughts in mind that about a year and a half ago we issued an invitation to various Jewish scholars from theological seminaries and general universities to join the faculty of the Dropsie College in creating a new edition of the entire apocryphal Jewish literature, including the Pseudepigrapha, re-editing the text of the most ancient available versions, translating it anew into the English of our time, and through scholarly introductions and critical studies to make clear, from a Jewish standpoint, the thoughts and religious ideals of the authors of this literature and their proper relationship to Judaism and to Christianity.

339

I am glad to say that the scholars we invited to join in this enterprise responded with zealous spirit, and many are devoting themselves with love to the task. I have the honor to be the Chairman of the Editorial Board. Our Professor of Rabbinics, Doctor Solomon Zeitlin, is our valiant Editor-in-Chief.

Now it is significant that this project should be undertaken at this time, at this critical juncture in Jewish and in world history so soon after the great centers of Jewish learning in the world were destroyed — and after we witnessed, to our shame, the burning of Jewish works in Germany and the uprooting of Jewish ideas in all places under Nazi influence.

Under any given circumstances, an enterprise of this character would be memorable. But when etched against the background of our time it takes on symbolic significance, and not merely because of the size and the cost of this project, which we estimate to require ten years and to fill at least thirty volumes at a considerable cost in funds. The true significance lies in the fact that it is an American undertaking by an institution of higher Jewish learning. In no other country could this task be accomplished, not even in Israel with its Hebrew medium of speech. For inaccessibility to a world forum is, unfortunately, one of the drawbacks inherent in the language of a numerically small people, however noble the language may be. Creating a new Hebrew edition of the Apocrypha would be a great service to Judaism, but not to the non-Hebraic world.

It is significant that the institution that has undertaken this task is of the character of the Dropsie College. We have a number of distinguished centers of learning in our country. There is the Jewish Theological Seminary of America right here in New York City; the Hebrew Union College of Cincinnati, which is now united with the Jewish Institute of Religion in this city; there is also the Yeshibat Rabbi Isaac Elchanan. In a sense all of these institutions are American transplantations of European models. The Yeshibah, of course, is a transplantation from Eastern Europe. The various theological schools are adaptations of the seminaries that originated in Europe, especially in Germany.

Dropsie College is unique in that it is an indigenously American institution growing out of American concepts and ideals. I do not know how many of you know, for instance, the fact that Moses Aaron Dropsie, the founder of the College which bears his name, was an American, born in this country in the city of Philadelphia, of a mixed marriage — a Jewish father and a Christian mother, who had a premarital agreement not to predetermine the religion of their children, and that young Dropsie at the age of fifteen became a Jew of his own volition and insistence. But it is not this fact alone which prompts me to describe the Dropsie College as an indigenously American institution. I have in mind a more penetrating factor which strikes deep into the very nature of the College.

Very early in the eighties of the last century, Mr. Dropsie came to the realization that America would some day become the center of the Jews of the world. He set his thoughts boldly into writing, stating his conviction that it was a matter of *noblesse oblige* on the part of American Jews to build in this country a center of learning that should be second to none in the history of the Jews of the world, not even excluding the great academies of ancient Babylon or the golden age of the Jews in Spain. As an American he proudly asserted his conviction that this could be accomplished in America because we had the men, we had the wealth, and above all we had freedom. Therefore he determined that he would leave everything that he possessed at the time of his death for the establishment of a college which would be postgraduate in character, whose aim it would be to train scholars for research and original investigation in all branches of Jewish and Hebraic learning, in all branches of Semitic studies and disciplines surrounding the Hebrew civilization; and that the school was to be non-sectarian, with no distinction in the admission of students on the ground of race, creed or sex. This concept, I submit, was typically American.

I sometimes indulge in the pastime of imagining myself transported back to an early age in history. I do this often as I pore through the volumes of Graetz's *History of the Jews*. When I come upon a passage in Graetz where the historian showed rapture because a Jewish author living in Greece wrote a mathematical treatise which seemed to Graetz to be a striking expression of the Jewish scientific mentality, I wonder then how Graetz would have glowed if he had found a record of an institution of learning under Jewish auspices, with Jewish professors, to which students flocked from every part of the world — Jews, Christians and Moslems alike — seeking within that institution learning, knowledge, inspiration — what a drama Graetz would have made of that!

Now that drama is American. Only in this country could that type of institution grow and flourish. Therefore it seems to me doubly symbolical that this gift to the world, a new edition of the Apocrypha, should emanate from the Dropsie College. For this enterprise to recreate an important part of our ancient Jewish heritage, and to place it proudly before the world spells courage and vision on the part of American Jewish scholarship. That this inspiration should have its source in the Dropsie College seems both natural and dramatic. Call it, if you will, a part of the American drama, a segment of the saga of Judaism.

I am now ready to report to you on the progress of the enterprise to date. The first volume of Jewish Apocryphal Literature will appear on May 15, 1950. The initial volume will consist of The First Book of Maccabees, with a new translation by Doctor Sidney Tedesche and commentary, introduction and critical studies by Professor Solomon Zeitlin of the Dropsie College. It is sufficiently clear from what I have said, that while we consider this work itself a very important contribution, its real significance lies not merely in its own intrinsic merit, but in the fact that it is the first volume of a great series.

The second volume is in the press now. It is The Letter of Aristeas, edited and translated by Professor Moses Hadas of Columbia University, who is also Secretary of our Editorial Board. There are six books now being processed by different scholars, all of which, we hope, will be ready for the press within a year or two.

I had deliberately phrased the theme of this evening in a manner to point to the Apocrypha as a symbol: The Apocrypha and Its Place in a Jewish Renaissance in America. This to me is basic; for just as I indicated that it was significant that the thought of creating a Jewish rendition of the Apocrypha should emanate from an institution like the Dropsie College, so on a larger scale, it appears to me, that the entire concept of the creation of Jewish Apocryphal Literature and its reinterpretation as a Jewish contribution to the larger world, is peculiarly appropriate to the time in which we are living, and in its relation to the destiny of America.

Earlier in my remarks, I stressed the fact that this under·taking could arise only in America, in an Anglo-American civilization, and not out of Israel. I need hardly say that I did not imply any derogation of the scholars of Israel, or of the hope and the future that reside in Israel. Not at all. But in the light of the historic forces of our time, it seems to me of utmost importance that thinking Jews in our country should clarify for themselves the position of America in relation to the Jewish future, and that they should understand clearly the role of Jewish culture and higher learning in American Jewish destiny. We will be assailed in increasing measure by voices from Israel that will become forceful, vigorous, demanding; by voices coming out of Israel that will claim that the future of Judaism and the future of Jewish thought and creative spirit is centered entirely and exclusively in Israel. I do not hesitate to say that

343

it would be a most unhappy and unfortunate day if it were at all conceivable that all the Jews of the world would find their center exclusively in Israel, and the fate of Judaism would become coincidental with the state of Israel proper.

This statement perhaps calls for an explanation as to my attitude toward general Zionist philosophy. Of course I am not speaking as an anti-Zionist or as a non-Zionist. I have been a Zionist all my life. The hope for Israel is something so deeply integrated in my personality that I would lose my spiritual unity if I were divorced from hope and faith in Israel. Therefore, what I stated comes from a deep historic conviction: namely, that Judaism has two centers of gravity, and by its nature it must always for its true development have these two poles: one in Israel, and one in the *Golah*. As one analyzes the nature of Judaism, one finds that there are certain unique and characteristic creations of the Jewish spirit that were generated in Palestine, and only that land could nurture those ideals. On the other hand, there are other phases of the Jewish creative spirit which are totally absent in the literature and in the intellectual development that has come out of the land of Israel. For instance, I do not know of any great philosophic texts that came out of Palestine; nor can I think of any great code, similar to the Maimonidean Code, that was produced in Palestine. What did come out of the country was, of course, far more important: God-consciousness, prophecy, prayer, mysticism in all its aspects, poetic insights and esoteric poetry. These precious distillations of the spirit were never equalled outside the Land. Only Palestine could nurture that which we associate with Bible mysticism: the innate genius, the poetic conception of the Hebrew spirit. In a future renaissance of Judaism, Israel will voice once again that which is uniquely and innately expressive of the eternal Jewish spirit.

On the other hand, Judaism has not only national, mystic, poetic aspects, but also universal and intellectual manifestations, which will develop primarily in the *Golah*, and only in the *Golah*. By far the greater corpus of rabbinic and Hebrew literature is the monumental production of Diaspora Judaism. For the complete symmetry of Judaism, for the wholeness of its creation, it is therefore necessary to maintain this interconnection: a vigorous Jewry in the world without, a concentrated Hebraic Jewry in Israel proper. If this thesis is granted then it is perfectly obvious that American Jewry has a unique and important role to play from which it dare not shirk.

Look back upon the panoramic view of Jewish history and behold our American community of over five million Jews. What does this mean to you? Does it not mean that the time has come when American Jewry must take up the banner, even as every great Jewry did in former days? Is not the hand of God upon us? I am using the theological term very realistically. Is it not we who are now summoned in the roll call of Jewish destiny? What other sense would this great phenomenon of American Jewry make? Are we merely an accidental conglomeration of human beings who have been brought together without plan or design, by forces of blind historic impact, like sand that is scattered by the wind and shifted aimlessly from place to place?

Ponder upon this amazing phenomenon of American Jewry and you will suddenly be liberated from the fears that beset and bewitch so many among us. You will then not be fearful or apologetic about our people in America. I, for one, do not feel that it is necessary for us to engage in counter-anti-Semitic polemics to show the world how good we are or, on the other hand, that we are not as bad as they think we are. I am willing without any apologia to assert and to defend the proposition that we are an honorable folk; that we do our part fully; that our people have played an important role in America; that we have repaid America to the full for everything that America has given us in such rich abundance.

I am fully confident that the honor of our family life will stand up well against that of any other social group, measured by any standard. I believe that our sons and daughters who have been admitted to American colleges have done well by the opportunities afforded them. Our judges, lawyers, physicians, journalists, social workers, merchants, industrialists and philanthropists have, on the whole, made a very good record. But I sometimes lie awake at night and think and wonder: did it really require the extraordinary record of three thousand years of history, during which our community produced prophets, poets, singers, psalmists, men of wisdom, martyrs, philosophers, ethical teachers, so that three thousand years later, out of them might be born a generation that would lead simple, decent, good lives — but uninspired by any great vision of destiny, unresponsive to any overtones of their collective life?

There is a poetic concept in Jewish lore that on the Sabbath every person who observes the holiness of the day is granted an over-soul. Surely there must be such an over-soul in the national being of a people. Faith in the over-soul of the Jewish people is that which alone can justify and validate our existence as a collective entity. This is a thread that makes our Jewish existence rational. We are children of destiny. We have been brought to this country of freedom and opportunity, and we have been vouchsafed riches, influence and power, not merely to accumulate personal fortunes; nor even solely to help sustain our people in other lands with the surpluses that we have accumulated. American Jews have a higher role to play in the drama of Jewish history. How shall we determine that role? As Jews always did: through their religion and their writings. Look at Jewish literature; read its poetry; study its philosophy, its ethical writings. These have been the instruments through which Jews made their contributions to civilization. These have been the means through which they promoted their own spiritual development and enriched the nations of the world. By these

346

high standards American Judaism is now to be counted, weighed and measured.

What will be the verdict of history? We need not be apologetic about the past nor fearful of the future. We are a young community in America. Our history as a community of over a million souls is not older than half a century. In this short period, we have done much, but our accomplishments must be interpreted only as a promise for the future. And this future will be molded and recorded in the writings of our learned scholars; above all, in the original creations of thought and spirit which American Jewry will add to the content of Judaism and the religion of mankind.

Viewed in this light, the Jewish version of the Apocrypha by the Dropsie College is more than a literary enterprise. It is symbolic in its implication of a cultural renaissance in American Judaism.

A Bridge of Understanding

IT IS my privilege to extend greetings to you, and to welcome you to these annual proceedings.

What I am about to say to you is described on the program under the heading of REMARKS. The heavy artillery — the addresses — are reserved for the honorary speakers, our very honored guests of this evening.

While marching in the formal procession a few minutes ago, a quick calculation flashed through my mind. I suddenly realized that this was the tenth year I have been presiding at these exercises, and the thirty-seventh or thirty-eighth year I have been sitting on this tribunal, this very august platform which is graced by these many eminent scholars.

If the mere cumulative repetition of a ceremony on such a statistical scale would be habit-forming, these exercises ought to have been by this time a matter of routine for me. And yet I confess to a sense of heightened excitement and a strange feeling of spiritual compulsion which is always with me when I stand before you at these annual functions.

I experience an inward challenge on these occasions to link you, the audience, in an inner unity with the erudite men seated on this platform. In figurative language, I feel impelled to build a spiritual bridge extending from this platform right into the heart of the audience; to bring into closer proximity the men of abstract thought with those who represent the world of action.

Unfortunately, there is no awareness among the general laity of the importance of this spiritual bridge. All too often we find

Address delivered at the Dropsie College, Founder's Day, May 28, 1951.

that there exists a yawning gulf between the men who represent pure learning and the more worldly folk who constitute the earthy substance of community life. This dichotomy between academic humans and plain mortals is a detriment to society and a hazard to culture, especially Jewish culture which suffers from greater isolation.

Society and scholarship are intertwined. They are mutually dependent upon each other, the one for its gracious living and the other for the release of its creative impulses. Scholars, for all their intellectual aloofness, are essentially human. They cannot live in a social vacuum. They require the sympathy and understanding of their fellows, and the sanction and the social valuation by the larger community of the things scholars hold dear.

The community, on the other hand, grows in grace by the success of scholarly progress. I am not thinking of physical science which provides us with the gadgets of our mechanized age, nor of the more grim aspects of that science, which has been geared to the machinery of war. I am alluding to pure learning in the traditional sense: the study of the classics, the ideals of the philosophers, the graciousness of the humanities. Without these graces of the spirit, society is an inchoate mass, despite the brittle glamor of its outward trappings.

The studies we pursue at this College in all branches of the Bible, Talmud, History, Literature and Philosophy; our immersion in the great civilizations that preceded our time; the wide range of our Semitic studies that throw light upon our civilization — all lend grace and meaning to the struggles of the human spirit.

These thoughts strike one with particular force when one contemplates the state of the Jewish community in America. The last few decades have witnessed a profound revolution in the character of American Jewry. Our community has risen to great estate. Numerically, America embraces the largest Jewish

349

community of all time. But far more important as an index of character is the vast amount of energy which has been generated within our social fabric. We have stored up an enormous fund of altruism. Our large scale philanthropies are no longer measured by millions of dollars but by hundreds of millions. We have applied the principles and methods of human engineering to the solution of Jewish problems on an unpredictable scale of vision, sacrifice and manpower.

And yet we are often haunted by a feeling of discontent and inadequacy. Our communal achievements are stupendous. They fill us with pride but they do not yield that deep spiritual satisfaction for which our hearts crave. Even when our emotions are deeply stirred, our spirits do not soar to high flights. Our souls are rarely kindled with the flame of holiness, for much of the inwardness has gone out of Jewish life.

There can be no substitute for the qualities that distinguished Jewish character: piety, love of learning, scholarship, the knowledge and love of Torah. For a community to attain true greatness, intense activism is not enough. To achieve grace and harmony of soul, American Jewry must recapture the lost art of *Torah lishmah*, learning for its own sake. It was the glorification of learning and contemplation, which found its highest expression in Judaism, that gave soul depth to Jewish existence.

To rekindle this faith on the American scene, to raise generations of scholars, Jews and Christians, who shall live by this faith, and to restore to our people a renewed sense of inner dignity and nobility through the regenerating power of Torah and contemplation, is the purpose, the basic philosophy of the Dropsie College.

This in essence is the message which I seek to communicate on these annual occasions which are taking on increasingly the nature of intellectual, spiritual pilgrimages. This is the meaning of the bridge we seek to build, the bridge of understanding and unity of purpose between the outer world and the scholarly world, symbolically represented in these halls this evening.

Under the spell of this mood, I feel with special poignancy the absence of a friend, a Governor of this College, who represented in many ways the type of individual whose ideal image we seek to portray. He is Isaac Gerstley, of blessed memory, known to most of you and beloved of many, who passed on to his eternal reward on April 2, 1951.

This is not the occasion for a memorial or a eulogy. If I nevertheless make this personal allusion, it is not only because of what Isaac Gerstley has meant to the Dropsie College but more so because of what his association with the College meant to him. I emphasize this aspect because to me it is a symbol of the spiritual bridge to which I alluded.

A man of distinguished and handsome presence, deliberate in judgment and scrupulously honorable in conduct, he was entrusted with many public responsibilities. He in turn gave of himself freely to every communal endeavor of a philanthropic nature. He served on the boards of many institutions, indeed so many that it would be pointless to catalogue them here. But over and above these many diversified interests was his attachment to the Dropsie College, which he had the spiritual insight to perceive was unique — standing high on the American scene, an intellectual citadel, a spiritual fortress. His devotion to the Dropsie College was deeply rooted. A layman, not a rabbi or scholar, he had the pride of a noble heritage. He was reared to love learning and to revere men of learning. The Dropsie College nurtured this faith within him. How vividly I recall that whenever he spoke of the reverence for learning — a phrase he often used with a touch of fervor — his luminous blue eyes sparkled with a brilliant light.

Would that our community could boast of more men like Isaac Gerstley. Would that others, too, would be inspired and

351

ennobled as he was by a love of learning and a zeal for spreading Jewish knowledge. This is uttered not only as a prayer but as an invitation to kindred souls everywhere to join with us in the Dropsie College as co-workers in the building of this noble structure, the highest academic center of Jewish learning in America. This would surely be the wish of Isaac Gerstley. And he would share with me, too, the feeling of thankfulness that a group of younger men have rallied round the College under the leadership of Justice Horace Stern to enable the College to carry out its high mission in the cultural destiny of American Jewry.

Let me now portray to you something of the work of the College and give you a glimpse of its essence and spirit. I assume that you are already acquainted with some of the basic principles governing our institution: negatively, that it is not a theological seminary; affirmatively, that it serves the cause of religion in a positive sense by training scholars and disciples of the Bible, the Talmud and other literatures of religion, by advancing original research and publications in these precious areas of the human spirit, and by contributing to the world through the contributions of its faculty and alumni, a deeper understanding of the sources out of which grew the great religions of the Western world. I shall resist the temptation of dwelling on the distinctive contributions that the College is making to American education through our establishment of the School of Education and more latterly the Institute for Israel and the Middle East, which has received acclaim in Washington and in Jerusalem.

I propose, rather, to relate to you some of the observations that have come to me during the past year concerning our alumni, our faculty and our students, which may collectively give you an image of what constitutes the spirit of the Dropsie College.

I had the privilege last summer to make an extensive trip in the company of my wife, through some of the European countries and Israel. This gave me the opportunity to observe some of our more distant alumni at close range. In Paris, we found one of our recent students serving as Professor of Rabbinics at the École Rabbinique. Another former student is Chief Rabbi of Luxemburg. Luxemburg was not included in our itinerary, but we had the pleasure of meeting the American Ambassador, who spoke of his work with warm appreciation.

It was in Israel that we had the heart-warming experience of a reunion with a group of alumni, who had grown in stature and distinction and were playing a vital role in the academic and intellectual life of Israel where learning is prized above material treasures. We met there individually and collectively: Doctor Yehudah Kaufman, well-known scholar and educator; Doctor Eliezer Sukenik, world-famous archaeologist and professor at the Hebrew University; Doctor Ben-Zion Netanyahu, chief editor of the great Hebrew Encyclopedia, three volumes of which have already appeared, with seventeen more to follow; Doctor Zev Vilnay, formerly a major in the Israeli army, a noted authority on the military topography of Palestine and the author of half a dozen works on the subject; and other alumni of the Dropsie College functioning in educational institutions throughout the country. Here we beheld a revelation of the world-wide influence of the Dropsie College. But above all, it was their love, their nostalgic feeling for the College and what it represented to them that warmed our hearts. It was a wonderful demonstration of the spirit that lives within these walls between masters and disciples, between the teachers of today and the teachers of the future.

Professor Zeitlin is now in Israel. He has recently lectured in London and also at Manchester University and he is in for a very challenging time in Israel where he will no doubt carry on the Battle of the Scrolls. We do not fear the outcome.

I had the pleasure of presenting to David Ben-Gurion, the Prime Minister of Israel, during his visit in Philadelphia, the two volumes of the Apocrypha, which the Dropsie College has recently published. It was a gratifying feeling to give books of such erudite nature to a prime minister who reads Greek and who, I am told, is almost as much at home in that language as he is in French or German.

Our Faculty have carried on investigations and researches in many fields. As to the Apocrypha Series, two or three additional volumes are scheduled to appear this fall. But to turn again to personalia, I want to greet Dr. Bonne of Israel who is here with us and who came from Israel as our visiting professor for this past year. While serving the Dropsie College, he was persuaded, almost forcibly co-opted, by the United Nations to serve as a member of its Economic and Social Commission. He made a lasting impression in this country and we wish him Godspeed on his return to Israel.

Another of our professors, Theodor Gaster, received a call from the University of Rome in Italy to teach Comparative Religion in that institution during the coming academic year, and we have accordingly granted him a year's leave of absence. In fact, we were threatened with a mild epidemic of professorial leaves of absence because of the many calls which foreign universities, with an eye to Fulbright grants, extended to various members of our Faculty. Reluctantly, we had to call a halt.

Our students submitted to an oral examination before the Faculty only two or three days ago. I wish some of you could have been invisibly present. Not that you would have witnessed a demonstration of dazzling brilliance. Some of the students were indeed brilliant; others not so. But I would have liked you to have seen the broad scope of their individual researches, which are far beyond the nature of the average Ph.D. thesis.

There is one student, for instance, and I will cite one only, who is engaged upon a thesis which requires a knowledge of mathematics, of ancient astronomy in the oriental world, and also of the Middle Ages in Europe, as well as a knowledge of

354

Arabic and Latin. His work, we believe, will be an important contribution to the history of mathematics and will illumine the role which the Jews played in the evolution of mathematics. But what struck me at the time when the student appeared before the Faculty was this conviction, that as far as I know there is no academic institution in America where this type of research could have been carried on with such integration and with such complete synthesis of a number of diverse fields of knowledge, all of which were harnessed to make possible an important cultural chapter in the history of humanity.

A number of our students have been drawn into the government service because of their knowledge of the languages of the Middle East. One student serves in the State Department; another is in the Defense Department. This is particularly interesting because quite independently of this development, the State Department has, during the past two years, assigned several of its officials to settle in Philadelphia for a year of study at the Dropsie College and elsewhere.

I have attempted in this informal recital of facts concerning students, alumni and faculty to give you a glimpse into the nature of this College and the spirit which inspires its work. I hope that I brought to you the realization that the Dropsie College is not merely just another institution of learning, not another seminary, not another oriental institute of a university department. It is a powerhouse of Jewish scholarship whose currents are radiated throughout the world. It generates creative personalities whose ideas and ideals become the dynamic forces of history. It is the unique creation of American Judaism. It should be the pride of all Jewry. All who come under its influence are warmed and ennobled thereby.

355

An Historian Views the Contemporary Jewish Scene

IT IS a pleasure for me to be with you this afternoon. This day marks a significant occasion in the lives of the young people who are being graduated this afternoon, and in the experiences of the Faculty and the Board of Trustees.

This occasion has also a wider significance for the Jewish people in America. With this realization, I have come to you, and in this spirit I shall address you.

It is fitting that I address you as the President of the Dropsie College. The Dropsie College is the senior and mother institution of the various teachers' colleges and institutions of higher Jewish learning, which you represent so honorably, and which are duplicated in other cities of the country. The Dropsie College is the senior both in years of service and, of course, in the extent and scope of its activities. We operate, if I may say so, in the stratosphere of Jewish learning — and you deal with the hearts of adolescent boys and girls.

We all realize that unless there is a broad base, the pinnacle is insecure. The corollary is equally true. Unless there are peaks to lure us to climb higher and higher, then the base must be flat, monotonous and uninspiring. Consequently, there is a mutual relationship and kinship of spirit between an institution such as you represent and the Dropsie College.

It is pleasant to look back upon the many personal relationships that link our respective institutions. Some of your graduates have continued their graduate studies at the Dropsie College. Among them are those who have since gained distinc-

Address delivered at the Commencement Exercises of the Hebrew Teachers College, Boston, June 15, 1952.

356

tion in scholarly work and educational careers. One of the members of your Faculty was a Research Fellow at the Dropsie College. We had the pleasure of having your Dean, Doctor Silberschlag, as visiting lecturer at one of our summer institutes.

But deeper than merely personal relationships is the spiritual bond of positive Jewish values. In your educational program, you represent the community in its entirety, the entity that we call *K'lal Yisrael*. We applaud the positive Jewish attitude that this College maintains. You stand for everything that is constructively, affirmatively Jewish, recognizing the artificiality of the many issues that so often separate the various segments of our community. In the Dropsie College School of Education, the first postgraduate institution in America dealing with Jewish education on the Ph.D. level, we are attempting to create a philosophy of education, indigenous to the American community, a philosophy which will formulate for American Jewry that sense of totality and unity which I believe is represented in your Faculty, in your student body and in the very soul of your institution.

It is for this reason that I attach such great significance to the fact that throughout our country there are arising institutions of the character which you represent. That you maintain high academic standards — certainly as high as any of your sister institutions — is widely recognized. But it is not merely the extent or the intensity of your curriculum through which you exert your greatest influence on other institutions. It is the spirit which inspires your curriculum and the high philosophy that is back of it, that has had far-reaching influence. Because institutions of your type are now growing up throughout the American Jewish community from the Atlantic to the Pacific, there is unusual significance in the ideals you represent and the work that you foster.

For what does this development of Hebrew colleges signify? It means that as we are approaching the tercentenary of the

357

Jewish settlement in America, there is a growing sense of maturity on the part of American Jews, a return to Jewish culture, an awakening to the fact that the great miracle of our time — second only to that which has happened in Israel — is the phenomenal rise of the American Jewish community, numbering five to six million persons. No community of like numbers, possessed of so high a degree of self-consciousness, dignity and moral influence, can be found in the annals of Jewish history during the past two thousand years.

It is this phenomenon that I want to treat with you from an historic standpoint. It is of the highest importance that we look upon the happenings of our time not merely as fragmentary, accidental occurrences brought about by external causes without inner Jewish relevance. Jewish fate has necessarily been affected by political, economic and other factors that have shaped international developments. But our history also possesses inner resources and spiritual forces which make possible a continuous character expressing itself in the various manifestations which Jewish life has assumed.

The Jewish people have been innately an historical people. And by this, I do not mean merely that we have survived the nations of antiquity. Far more significant is the fact that we are among the earliest nations to have exhibited a feeling and an inborn appreciation of historic events. If you study the history of history, you will find that modern historiographers usually accord the Greeks the distinction of having been the first people — certainly among the Western nations — to have created the art of history writing. This is a totally mistaken notion due partly to the fact that the historic writings of the Jews have had such dominant religious overtones that their actual values as histories have been overlooked. It is also partly due to the fact that modern historiography originated in Germany, which exhibited a hostile attitude towards all Jewish values.

Centuries before the famed Greek historians and for a long unbroken period thereafter, a remarkable series of historical books was produced in Palestine which are incorporated in the Bible from Joshua and Judges, through Samuel and Kings down to the close of the canon in the books of the Chronicles. These are more than narrative histories. They are interpretative histories, based on an older historic literature which is often cited by name. The historic art lived among the people even after divine prophecy supposedly ceased in Israel, as can be seen from the books of the Maccabees and other historical sections of the Apocrypha. Finally, historiography reached its climax with the monumental writings of Josephus, that great historian of antiquity.

This historic creativity was carried on at the same time that the Jewish people were giving birth to a new faith, a new philosophy and ethics that gave meaning and purpose to the life of mankind. But when the destruction of Jerusalem took place and with it the dispersion of the Jewish people and the loss of national independence, the very sense of historic perception vanished from the Jewish mentality, and it remained suspended for fifteen hundred years. During this long period, with the exception of the book of *Josippon*, not a single Hebrew book appeared that could come seriously under the category of history. And, moreover, this was not an uncreative period. Quite the contrary. This millennium and a half comprises the period of the Talmud, the geonic era and the most creative period of medieval Judaism noted for classic rabbinic literature, exegetical works, and philosophical and ethical writings. Within this brilliant creativity, one sense was lacking, the perception of history. Driven from pillar to post, unable to control their own destiny, lacking physical security and political stability, it would seem that the Jewish people lost their bearings in the world — they lost their historic sense!

Strange are the moods of the human spirit. Affliction

359

smiteth; it also healeth. What stirred the historic consciousness momentarily with the breath of life was the tragic expulsion of the Jews from Spain in 1492. It was the greatest calamity in Jewish history since the fateful dispersion in the year 70. The glory of Spanish Judaism was broken and its people scattered to the wind. Those who sought shelter in the mother country within the bosom of the church denied the God of Israel or kept His faith secretly at the risk of burning at the stake. Decades passed and the torture of the soul was harder to endure than bodily suffering. Had God really forsaken His people? Was there no meaning to Jewish history? Was the world right and the Jews in error? Was the majority not only brutally powerful, but also spiritually right?

These excruciating, agonizing doubts led thousands through the vale of despair to the font of baptism. Others were stirred to mysticism and Messianism. Under these circumstances, the muse of history came to life to guide and direct the faltering spirits upon the highway of Jewish destiny. Within one decade, three historical books were published in Italy about the middle of the sixteenth century: *Shebet Yehudah* (The Rod of Judah) by Solomon ibn Verga, *Emek ha-Bakah* (The Valley of Tears) by Joseph ha-Kohen, and in Portuguese, *Consolaçam as Tribulaçoens de Israel* (Consolation for the Tribulations of Israel) by Samuel Usque. Each of these writers turned to history for the key to the perplexities of the age.

The *Consolaçam*, in the form of a pastoral play, depicts through symbolical characters the drama of Jewish history, the many sorrows and tribulations, all of which were divinely foretold and, equally so, the happy events hidden in the womb of time which being also vouchsafed through the divine voice of prophecy were sure to come.

Joseph ha-Kohen reviewed the doleful experiences of the Jewish people throughout the centuries as divine retribution for the shortcomings, sins and misgivings of the many generations. The course of Jewish history was thus a passage through a vale of tears which will lead through the gates of penitence into the luminous highway of God's love.

It cannot be said that these historical books illumined the course of Jewish history or that they vitalized that generation with a new hope. They were at best a flickering light in the deep shadows of the ghetto. One other historical work of a far more advanced character made its appearance in Italy two or three decades later — *Meor Enayim* (The Light of the Eyes) by Azariah dei Rossi. But this light too soon died out. The two succeeding centuries were the most depressed years in the long exile. Denied their share in this world, the people sought shelter in the eerie magical world of the Cabala. In this dream world, there was no need for history; and the historic sense, so feebly revived, soon perished.

It was only after the French Revolution admitted Jews to citizenship and when, as a result of the liberating movements in Western Europe during the nineteenth century, the Jews began to strike root in the countries in which they were domiciled that the historic sense was reborn among them. Even amidst all the turbulence and persecutions in Romania and in Russia, and the anti-Semitic discriminations in Germany, the Jews did not lose their newly captured perspective of history. Modern men in a modern society, they were determined to resolve their problems in the light of their own history. This time, the awakening of the historic sense was genuine and enduring.

A series of great historic and scientific works ushered in a new era. The vital cord between history and the fate of a people was epitomized in the title of the first classic historic work of the new era, *Moreh Nebuke ha-Zeman* (The Guide to the Perplexed of the Age) by Nachman Krochmal, in Galicia. In Germany, Zunz, while reconstructing the rise of Hebrew poetry, the hymns and prayers of the ages, performed what may well be called the miracle of spiritual resurrection. In Graetz's

361

Geschichte der Juden, we behold the artist's recreation of the Jewish past in vivid, glowing colors; but greater than the artistic effect, is the prophetic quality of historic insight and integrity which inspires Graetz's work. To him, history was the touchstone of truth or falsity in all contemporary issues. It was the standard by which to judge the present and to plot the course of the future.

Most of us are the grandchildren, if not the children, of this nineteenth century Judaism. We are heirs to the riches and the spiritual diversity which the historian's art contributed to this epochal period. The startling and revolutionary events of the twentieth century have created new problems for the Jewish people. In consequence, we, too, are a deeply perplexed generation grappling with the manifold problems of spiritual survival. Our communities are weighted down with heavy burdens and ideological tensions. We are pioneering none too successfully with elementary Jewish education. We are still struggling with the difficulties of religious adjustments. Our programs of communal activities are imbalanced — often misshapen by group pressures — because we have not developed standards of evaluation that are derived from the spiritual experiences of the Jewish people. To develop such standards is the most crucial need of the hour.

We need the insights of the historian. We must recapture the art of historic perception which once distinguished the Jewish people. We must regain the intuitive judgment which is derived from conscious attunement and identification with our historic past.

In this spirit, let us review some aspects of the contemporary Jewish scene. I turn to education first because it is nearest to our hearts. Why is it that, by and large, Jewish education is subordinated in community planning to the needs of hospital expansion, homes for the aged, and other eleemosynary institutions? How is one to explain that higher Jewish education must go begging and pleading for a minimum of support to keep itself alive in this era of multi-million dollar chests of community funds? How does this attitude measure up with the sanctions and values of the long range of Jewish historic experience?

In every age, Jews gave expression to the goodness of their hearts through acts of loving-kindness. From time immemorial, Jews were trained by biblical precept and talmudic injunction to tend the sick, to feed the hungry, to shelter the orphan, and to protect the widow. Hostels for the wandering stranger, hospitals for the sick, homes for the aged were built by every important community on synagogue premises. These institutions were the normal features of the Jewish way of life. But no community in any of the great historic Jewish settlements of Babylon, Germany, Spain or Poland would base its claim to fame on these grounds.

The fame of Jewish communities rested on its scholars, the academies they founded, the disciples they raised, the books they composed, and the influence they wielded by their learning and wisdom. No program of social service, however vital and efficient, ranked in value with the academies of higher learning. In Jewish history, there was no *ersatz* for Torah.

It is in this historic light that we must view exultantly the growth of your College and the rise of Jewish institutions of learning in other parts of this country. You sustain the faith and the vision that inspires the work of the Dropsie College, the belief that America is destined to become the scene of a Jewish renaissance if only American Jewry will be true to its historic calling.

This College and its sister institutions are historic symbols. You are links in a great historic chain. As in former days, Spain succeeded Babylon, and Franco-Germany was followed by Poland and Lithuania, so now there is rising up under our eyes a potent American Jewry which is impulsively seeking avenues to express the Jewish genius that inheres within us. It is devoutly to be hoped that innate Jewish wisdom will prevail in our community councils; that our communal leaders will realize how vital our institutions of learning are for our spiritual survival as Jews. For let this warning be heeded. No Jewish community will survive in history or will be remembered a hundred or five hundred years hence, if it neglects and starves the institutions that are the reservoirs of its spiritual existence.

Closely related to Jewish culture and education is the moot question of Jewish public relations. The problems arising out of inter-cultural and ideological antagonism are not new to the Jewish people. We have dealt with this question for thousands of years, and by this time we surely should qualify as experts in the art and the mechanics of creating healthy public relations. How, then, do our elaborate agencies in this area appear in the light of Jewish history?

Long before the fall of Judaea to the Romans, the Jews had already experienced clashes with the religions of the conquering nations and with hostile civilizations. During the Hellenistic period, in particular, Judaism was derided and the Jews were mocked by the votaries of Hellenistic culture. The precepts of the Bible were ridiculed as crude and barbarous by the nations that adopted the ways of the Greeks. The disciples of the Hebrew prophets were compelled to defend their beliefs against the followers of the great Hellenes, Plato and Aristotle.

Particularly out of Egypt came bitter diatribes against the Jews and they had to defend themselves against the poison that we call anti-Semitism today. Every shaft in the venomous arsenal of anti-Semitism was poised against the Jews: slurs against their national origin, libels against their religion, attacks upon their honor and integrity, infamous attacks upon their loyalty to the state and their honorable relations toward their fellow-citizens. Who were the "public relations agents" then? Scholars, poets, philosophers. Some remained anonymous. Such were the translators of the Bible into Greek, the famed Septuagint, which revealed the Hebrew genius of the Bible to the outer world; such was the writer of the Letter of Aristeas, and the fervent narrator of Jewish martyrdom in III Maccabees. Those who are known by name are among the immortals: Philo and Josephus, among the Jewish Hellenistic writers; and among the early rabbis from the time of Rabban Gamliel after the destruction of the Jewish State to the time of Rabbi Judah the Prince, redactor of the Mishna, Judaism was ardently defended in Rome by a series of famous scholars, among whom the sainted martyr, Rabbi Akiba, was the most brilliant luminary.

How did these defenders of "Jewish public relations" function and what were their weapons? By boldly recording the truths of Judaism; by nailing down the falsehoods, the misrepresentations of their detractors; and by drawing upon the reserves of history, thus revealing the true character of the people and the faith they lived by. These battles of the mind and spirit were carried on in the arenas of scholarly debate and recorded writings.

The new edition of the Apocrypha which the Dropsie College is publishing is an illustrious example of scholarly achievement in the historic struggle for light. If I may interpolate, standing on this Boston platform, I would like to allude to the brilliant exposition of some phases of this battle in the revolutionary work of your townsman, Professor Harry Wolfson, on Philo. It is a pleasure in this connection, too, to remind you of the notable contribution of your own Doctor Silberschlag. He is performing an historic act of poetic justice in translating the ancient Greek classics into the language of Isaiah and Bialik, the language that links the Hebrew Commonwealth, the target of Hellenism, with the modern State of Israel.

It is by the great scholars of ancient times and by the scholars of our day that the fundamental philosophies which underlie intellectual and spiritual antagonisms can be solved, and only by them. The institutions of learning are the laboratories where weapons are forged with which to combat anti-Semitism to the

365

extent and to the degree to which anti-Semitism is open to ideological refutation.

I am fully aware that there is another phase of anti-Semitism of a lower variety, pandering to the baser instincts of greed, lust and hatred. I need not remind you that during the Middle Ages down to modern times our people had to contend with bloody attacks of this nature, and in consequence they developed standard methods of averting, as far as possible, such outbreaks. At the coronation of a king or pope, at the convening of an Ecumenical Church Council such as recently was held in Barcelona, at the sessions of national legislative assemblies — the Cortes in Spain, the Parlement in France — a Jewish commission to defend Jewish interests was sure to be present, openly or covertly. Lobbying is an ancient art. The commissioners — bankers, physicians, rabbis and courtiers — were fortified with gifts, with influence and with gold. They came to argue, to plead, and if need be to pay ransom in order to avert the threat of evil decrees.

Even in those dark ages, the Jewish communities realized that these measures were mere palliatives and that the invincibility of the Jew was of the mind and the spirit; that his almost superhuman strength and endurance were derived from the spiritual resources of his religion, his literature and history. Jewish schools flourished; the Yeshibah — the academy of higher Jewish learning — was looked upon as the normal fortress of the community. Learning was exalted not as an implement to a livelihood but as indispensable to life itself. Religion without learning to illumine its goal and purpose is dangerously close to mummery and superstition — a climate in which Judaism would languish and the Jew ultimately perish.

In all ages, scholars performed the double function of offense and defense in the struggle which was forced upon the Jewish people. They were the builders of morale within the camp; and they were the shock troops in the front lines of the battle for truth and human decency. A learned scientific essay by Zunz,

Die Namen der Juden, secured for the Jews in Germany the right to the use of so-called Christian names, or surnames, which had been denied them. An erudite work by Zechariah Frankel, *Die Eidesleistung der Juden in theologischer und historischer Beziehung*, brought about the liberation of the Jews from the humiliation of a special oath. The classic *Die Gottesdienstliche Vorträge der Juden* established the disputed right of the Jews to incorporate the sermon into the religious service. Not rights but right was the thesis laid down by the learned pioneers of Jewish public relations in the modern states; and on this broad base, the battle was fought and won — till the rise of Hitler and the recrudescence of medieval barbarism.

In America, the role of Jewish scholarship has not been understood. Aside from the training of rabbis, its resources have been but little utilized. In the earlier period of American history, there seemed to be no critical need of marshaling the forces of Jewish learning in defense of Jews or Judaism. Anti-Semitism of an ideological character was relatively unknown in the United States till recent times. The Declaration of Independence, the traditions of freedom and democracy generated a mystic faith and optimism about human relations in American society. We still cherish this faith dearly.

However, the climate has changed, unfortunately. The evil winds of Hitlerism, the threatening clouds blowing from Soviet Russia have cast a shadow over the skies of our country. Most unfortunate has been the effect upon the American Jewish community.

When Hitler crucified German Jewry and massacred millions of Jews in conquered countries, panic and terror struck the hearts of many Jews in America lest his evil spirit might penetrate our country too. In the hysteria that followed, Jewish communal leadership was bereft of historic perspective. Defense became one of the chief aims of organized community effort. Jewish education and higher learning, so vital for inner strength and

367

morale, were subordinated to the all-consuming demands of defense budgets.

Were this only a passing phase of a terrible era, its effect could now be written off the pages of history. But unfortunately the pattern has been set. Defense, a negative, repellent concept at best, is still the dominant mood of American Jewish leadership. I am not referring to the so-called local community relations councils. It is understandable that local difficulties and irritations may arise from time to time that call for wise counsel and treatment. Occasionally difficult situations of wider scope may require consultations and conferences on a larger scale. But it is an anomalous situation and a serious disfigurement of the Jewish position in American life when a network of institutions is spread over the country and millions of dollars are siphoned through them from community funds for "Defense." Defense against what? It would seem as if we were living in imminent danger in some benighted country, surrounded by myriad enemies and conspirators against whom we must always be on guard. But America is our home, the freest country in the world! Have we lost faith in the sanity, the justice, and the innate regard for the dignity and the rights of the human being on the part of the American people? That America has minority problems, that these lead to social stress and strain, that Utopia is still a distant goal, who will deny? But the glory of our country lies not in the attainment of perfection but in the capacity for perfectibility; in the proved determination of the American people progressively to effect relations of peace, equality and justice among the diverse elements of our population. Faith in America is inconsistent with craven fear of bigots and hate-mongers. Consciously to induce such fear in the Jewish community is to weaken American morale and to undermine Jewish self-confidence.

A reorientation of our attitudes towards community problems is called for and cannot be long deferred. We must recapture the vision of historic perspective. Jewish strength is of the spirit and is derived from the inner convictions of Jewish knowledge and historic experience. Our strength and our safety are with the creators of spiritual values — the institutions of learning, the writers, poets and scholars of our generation.

We are on the threshold of a great era. We have witnessed national tragedy in Europe, miraculous redemption in Israel, while American Jewry itself has risen greatly in numbers, influence and strength. These are momentous events of which heroic history is fashioned. But great history calls for vision and conviction, courage and faith.

If we are to meet the great challenge of this historic era, we must disown the kind of leadership that spreads fear and doubt in our midst. It is shocking to see how the fear complex is often being artificially stimulated, so that we may be "saved." There is no salvation in spreading despair and defeatism. They create a climate of disillusionment which breeds demoralization. Its influence upon the young may within a generation prove appalling.

A leadership that is inspired by faith, by enlightenment and Jewish knowledge will not play upon fear but upon the inexhaustible moral strength of the Jewish people. Such leadership will draw upon Jewish learning for guidance and wisdom. Anti-Semitism will be viewed in true historic perspective. Fighting this evil will no longer appear as the goal and end-all of Jewish existence. It will appear as only one phase of the millennial struggle of light against darkness, as only one fragment of the total Jewish endeavor. It will be recognized as an evil that has persisted for thousands of years; an evil, furthermore, which is deeply rooted in history, religion and mass psychology. If it is not likely to be eradicated in the near foreseeable future, it is to be fought as former generations, buttressed by faith and learning fought it, with positive moral convictions. Jews have fought anti-Semitism not merely to destroy an evil but to release a force that works toward a spiritual end: to make possible the good life, to release within the Jewish people the potential qualities that inhere in a prophetic people. This truth must be made clear once again. As of old, so now and always: the strength, the very heart and soul of the Jewish people are in its religion, its literature, its institutions of learning.

This is my charge to you, graduates of the Hebrew Teachers College. You represent the new generation of an heroic age in Jewish history. Your imagination has been stirred by your studies. Your hearts have been moved by events to which there is no parallel in two thousand years. It has been your happy lot to be born in this free country, to imbibe its principles and its traditions, to live under a system of government whose social philosophy is part of our own religious heritage.

I trust that you will face life courageously as befits Americans and Jews. Do not yield to prophecies of doom. You carry within your souls echoes of prophetic voices, the overtones of the Psalmist's songs, the prayers, chants and hopes of countless generations whose eyes were upon God. Cherish this noble heritage. Make it your strength and you will be invincible.